# The Text in the Community

# The Text in the Community

## Essays on Medieval Works, Manuscripts, Authors, and Readers

edited by

JILL MANN &
MAURA NOLAN

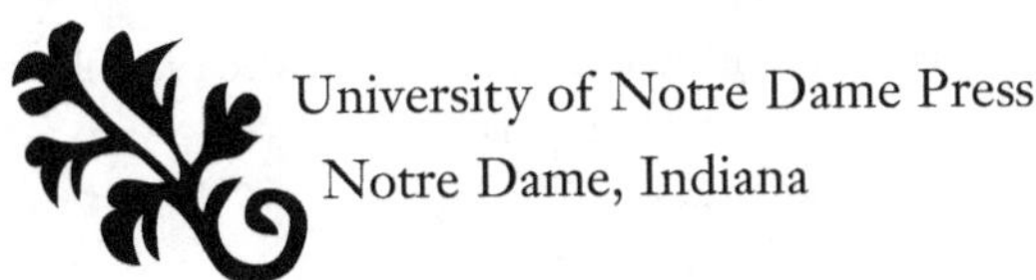

University of Notre Dame Press
Notre Dame, Indiana

Notre Dame, Indiana 46556
www.undpress.nd.edu


Designed by Jane Oslislo
Set in 9.9/13.8 Janson by Four Star Books

*Library of Congress Cataloging in-Publication Data*
The text in the community : essays on medieval works, manuscripts, authors, and readers / edited by Jill Mann and Maura Nolan.
p. cm.
Includes index.
ISBN 0-268-03495-8 (cloth : alk. paper)
ISBN 0-268-03496-6 (pbk. : alk. paper)
1. Literature, Medieval—History and criticism. 2. Manuscripts, Medieval—History. I. Mann, Jill. II. Nolan, Maura.
PN671.T38 2006
809'.02—dc22

2005035128

# contents

# list of illustrations

# list of contributors

MAUREEN BOULTON
University of Notre Dame

JESSICA BRANTLEY
Yale University

A. S. G. EDWARDS
University of Glamorgan

VINCENT GILLESPIE
University of Oxford

MICHAEL LAPIDGE
University of Notre Dame

JILL MANN
University of Notre Dame

MAURA NOLAN
University of California, Berkeley

ANDY ORCHARD
Centre for Medieval Studies, Toronto

DIANNE PHILLIPS
University of Notre Dame

# abbreviations list

| | |
|---|---|
| CCCM | Corpus Christianorum Continuatio Medievalis |
| *DLF*[2] | *Dictionnaire des lettres françaises: Le moyen âge*, ed. Geneviève Hasenohr and Michel Zink, 2nd ed. (Paris, 1992) |
| EETS e.s., o.s. | Early English Text Society extra series, original series |
| *IMEV* | *A New Index of Middle English Verse*, Julia Boffey and A. S. G. Edwards (London, 2005) |
| *IPMEP* | *Index of Printed Middle English Prose*, ed. R. E. Lewis, N. F. Blake, and A. S. G. Edwards (New York and London, 1985) |
| Jolliffe | P. S. Jolliffe, *A Check-list of Middle English Prose Writings of Spiritual Guidance* (Toronto, 1974) |
| *LALME* | *A Linguistic Atlas of Late Mediaeval England*, ed. Angus McIntosh, M. L. Samuels, and Michael Benskin, 4 vols. (Aberdeen, 1986) |
| *MED* | *Middle English Dictionary*, ed. H. Kurath, S. M. Kuhn, and R. E. Lewis (Ann Arbor, Mich., 1954–2001) |
| MGH | Monumenta Germaniae Historica |
| *MVC* | *Meditationes Vitae Christi* |
| *PL* | *Patrologia Latina* |
| *STC* | *A Short-title Catalogue of Books Printed 1475–1640*, 2nd. ed., begun by W. A. Jackson and F. S. Ferguson, completed by K. F. Pantzer, 3 vols. (London, 1976–91) |
| Walther, *Initia* | Hans Walther, *Initia carminum ac versuum medii aevi posterioris latinorum* (Göttingen, 1959); *Ergänzungen und Berichtigungen* (Göttingen, 1969); subsequent supplements in *Mittellateinisches Jahrbuch* |

# acknowledgments

Most of the essays in this volume were delivered as papers at an inaugural conference entitled "Medieval Manuscripts at Notre Dame," which took place at the University of Notre Dame from 13 September to 15 September 2001. Thanks go not only to our speakers and conference members, but also to Harriet Baldwin of the Center for Continuing Education, who helped to organize the event; to Christian Dupont for organizing the accompanying manuscript exhibition in the Hesburgh Library; to Sarah Weber for producing visual CD-ROMs; and to Gail Hinchion-Mancini for handling publicity. We are also grateful to our generous sponsors at the University of Notre Dame: the Office of the Provost, the Graduate School, the Institute for Scholarship in the Liberal Arts, the Medieval Institute, the Department of English, the Devers Program in Dante Studies, and the Center for Continuing Education. Finally, we should like to thank Matt Dowd for his meticulous and intelligent copyediting of this volume.

# Introduction

MAURA NOLAN

TEXTS DO NOT EXIST IN ISOLATION. EACH WRITTEN WORK IS embedded in a wide variety of contexts—literary, historical, geographical, social, political, religious—and derives its meaning in part from the intersection of those contexts in the reader's experience of the text. This volume understands that intersection as a "community": a social, sometimes affective grouping that both intentionally and unintentionally makes meaning. Communities appear in different guises in this volume—as Carthusian monks, Bridgettine nuns, or members of the laity; as writers, readers, scribes, students, or teachers; and even as the "community of texts" formed by borrowing and allusion. What makes them a community is that they share a common discourse (English, Latin, theology, for example) or set of practices (scribal, pedagogical, devotional) that shapes the various readings and misreadings of the texts produced and consumed by the group. Each of the essays in this volume considers texts in connection with communities—whether they be other texts and intertexts, scribes and illuminators, religious houses, women readers, or adolescent male students—as one way of re-embedding medieval writing in its multiple contexts.

Most of the essays pay special attention to medieval manuscripts as one of the material traces of such communities. In recent years there has been a renewed interest in manuscripts: their production, their decoration, their circulation, and their varying contents. Emerging in part out of a commitment by scholars to material culture and local contexts, this interest has revitalized our understanding of the way in which medieval literature was created and transmitted. It has also stimulated a fresh concern with the workaday texts of devotional and pedagogical literature, written by anonymous or hardly remembered authors. These are texts which may not seem groundbreaking when considered from the perspective of poetic or theological innovation, but which have much to teach us about the ways in which writing and reading functioned within specific medieval contexts. Such insights help to relate medieval literature to its conditions of production and dissemination, and to re-position such "canonical" authors as Chaucer and the *Beowulf*-poet within their historical and textual environments, contributing to a genuinely historical understanding of the complex networks of meaning in which they are embedded.

The conference at which most of the papers comprising this volume were read was conceived as a celebration of the inaugurations of Jill Mann and Michael Lapidge as Notre Dame Professors of English at the University of Notre Dame. The two papers by these scholars were delivered as inaugural addresses at the conference and illustrate the concerns of both scholars with the relationships between Latin and vernacular texts in the Old and Middle English traditions, as well as demonstrating their interest in the process of textual transmission from Latin school-text to vernacular poetry. Michael Lapidge examines the tradition of biblical paraphrase in late antiquity, in particular the poems of Juvencus, Caelius Sedulius, Avitus, and Arator, in order to show how these poets articulated the figural interpretation of biblical events. He shows how their works became the foundation-stone of the early medieval curriculum, particularly in Anglo-Saxon England, and then demonstrates that the figural interpretation of the Bible inculcated by study of these curriculum-authors has a clearly identifiable reflex in Old English biblical verse, notably in the Old English *Exodus*. The curriculum of late antique Christian-Latin biblical verse continued into the twelfth century and beyond, in works such as Peter Riga's *Aurora* (of which Notre Dame possesses two manuscripts), the *Tobias* of

Matthew of Vendôme, and other texts. Though manuscript glossing suggests that the tradition came to seem old-fashioned in the later Middle Ages in light of different methods of Bible study, its powerful influence on earlier English poetry has yet to be fully described. Lapidge points to a number of glaring lacunae in the scholarship on the Latin school-texts he describes, arguing that no discussion of vernacular literature can possibly proceed without a solid understanding of the medieval school curriculum, the basis and foundation of the learning that vernacular writers would have received, and on which they ultimately based their vernacular texts.

Pursuing her dual interest in Latin and Middle English literature, Jill Mann surveys the tradition of Latin school-texts and their relationship to Chaucer's and Langland's poetry. Taking its cue from two Notre Dame manuscripts, one containing the medieval Latin text known as the "moral" *Facetus*, and the other containing Alan of Lille's *Parabolae*, both of which were used as school-texts for those learning Latin, her essay surveys the body of writings used in this way throughout the Middle Ages, and how they were updated, added to, adapted, or "Christianized" by commentaries. Turning to the *Canterbury Tales*, Mann illustrates the many and varied ways in which school-texts such as the *Distichs of Cato* were deployed by Chaucer, making the crucial point that though proverbs may give the illusion of being experiential and oral, they were also textual and Latinate, "the stock-in-trade of 'clerkes'." This concern with the relationship of experiential and clerkly learning is carried through in her discussion of *Piers Plowman*, where she shows that episodes such as the debate between the Four Daughters of God and the Harrowing of Hell are infused with proverbs derived from school-texts. At critical moments, what seem like gestures toward experience reveal themselves to be forms of clerical commentary. Mann thus dissolves the seeming antinomy between experience and learning by showing how, for medieval writers, each epitomized and validated the other. The sustained and careful attention paid here to manuscripts and sources thus allows for a precise recalibration of our readings of Chaucer and Langland, and demonstrates again how essentially intertwined were Latin and vernacular texts and contexts in the later Middle Ages.

In the next essay, Andy Orchard uses the computer to uncover the interrelations between Old English writers and the texts they composed. From the earliest studies of Old English poetry, scholars have recognized similarities of diction between individual poems (notably, for example, between *Beowulf* and *Andreas*). Some similarities were originally explained in terms of verbal debts between poems, but from the middle of the twentieth century the emergence of oral-formulaic theory caused such similarities to be interpreted as manifestations of a formulaic word-hoard from which all poets drew, rather than as evidence for links between individual poems. Now, however, with the availability of machine-readable corpora of Old English verse and increasingly sophisticated concordance-packages, it is possible to analyze verbal links between Old English poems in a comprehensive and systematic way. Orchard identifies a number of distinctive links between Cynewulf's *Elene* and the Old English *Judith*, and shows how many of these links are shared uniquely by these poems among the surviving corpus of Old English verse; moreover, on significant occasions the links are shown to occur in exactly the same sequence in both poems. The most plausible explanation for these links is that the *Judith*-poet had Cynewulf's *Elene* specifically in mind and was influenced by the earlier poet's distinctive diction. The demonstration of such a relationship entails abandoning one conception of authorial communites—a group of bards drawing on a common oral tradition—in favour of another: a group of literate poets reading and imitating each other's work. It also raises the questions, in what manuscript-form Old English verse was read, and whether patterns of links between the four Old English poetic codices remain to be discovered—a process of discovery which will be greatly facilitated by the availability and accessibility of all four codices in electronic facsmile as well as machine-readable form.

A second stimulus for the conference was Notre Dame's purchase of an important Middle English manuscript from the Foyle collection, bought by the University on the occasion of the collection's dispersal at auction in London in 2000. Now University of Notre Dame, MS 67, this manuscript contains the texts of two devotional works, *A Mirror to Devout People* and *The Craft of Dying*.[1] Three essays are devoted to this manuscript and the texts it contains. Three different communities are important here: the Carthusian order to which the author of the *Mirror to Devout People* belonged, the Bridgettine house of nuns which was the work's most likely audience, and the aristocratic lay family for whom the manuscript itself was copied.

A. S. G. Edwards focusses on the last of these communities, which has left visible traces on the manuscript in the form of the imposing family coat of arms on its first folio. He locates the manuscript within the traditions of book ownership of the two families with which it is associated, the Chaworths and the Scropes, and details the activities of these families as collectors over the course of the fourteenth and fifteenth centuries, mapping an important picture of book ownership and transmission as they were commonly practiced by these two representative groups of owners. He shows the importance of regional piety and female readership in relation to the manuscript's intended audience. And, finally, Edwards suggests that Notre Dame 67 exemplifies both the strong identification between owners and texts that formed part of the practice of provincial book-collecting, and the emergence of gendered devotional texts in the fifteenth century.

In the two essays that follow, Vincent Gillespie and Jessica Brantley go back to the original contexts within which the *Mirror to Devout People* was produced, and consider the process of transmission that led from monastic production to lay consumption. Vincent Gillespie asks for whom the *Mirror* was most probably written. Questioning the assumption that Carthusian authors or scribes wrote directly for a lay audience (the notable exception that proves the rule being Nicholas Love's *Mirror of the Blessed Life of Jesus Christ*), he endorses the suggestion that the "gostely sustre" to whom the *Mirror to Devout People* is addressed was a nun in the Bridgettine house of Syon, across the river Thames from the Carthusian house of Sheen. He goes on to demonstrate the plural nature of the *Mirror*'s inscribed audiences (male as well as female, lay as well as religious), a plurality well suited to Syon, which included the Syon Brethren as well as the nuns whose spiritual needs they ministered to, and which had close contacts with the Carthusians of Sheen on the one hand and the lay aristocracy on the other. The close and frequent contacts between Syon and the lay community encourages Gillespie to suppose that Syon was the conduit by which texts of this kind flowed from Carthusian production into lay readership and ownership. Gillespie also draws attention to the fact that almost all of the sources on which the author of the *Mirror* drew are known to have been in the Syon library in the early fifteenth century. This essay shows how the analysis of a single manuscript such as Notre Dame 67 can illuminate our understanding of the complicated textual and religious culture of the post-Arundelian years. The contemporaneous foundation of Sheen and Syon (1415), Gillespie argues, was a "defining moment in the history of English religious writing." Notre Dame 67 is a classic example of the production and tight control of religious texts within this Carthusian context, with access to such texts restricted to a small circle of readers who were themselves part of the Sheen/Syon nexus, including a limited number of lay readers. His argument has important implications for further study of Carthusian textual production as well as religious writing in the fifteenth century more broadly.

In her discussion of the decoration of the Foyle manuscript, Jessica Brantley likewise focusses on the interface between Carthusian text and lay readership. Acknowledging that the manuscript was written for lay ownership, she nevertheless questions the sharp divide between monastic text and lay visual decoration. She considers the relationship between Carthusians and visual representation in a wider context, arguing that despite the order's explicitly antidecorative stance and extreme asceticism, by the fifteenth century various forms of visual decoration, representation, and embellishment (including lay coats of arms) formed part of Carthusian monasteries and books. Books in particular formed something of an exception to the asceticism of the order; she cites British Library, MS Additional 37049 as an example of a heavily decorated manuscript with evident Carthusian connections. Yet if one devotional tableau includes a figure of a tiny Carthusian monk in prayer, another, identical tableau includes a lay figure. In an analogous fashion, the coat of arms that represents the lay patrons of the Foyle manuscript embeds them as a material presence in the text.

In the concluding essays, Maureen Boulton and Dianne Phillips turn to other manuscripts held by Notre Dame, once again illustrating the fruitfulness of sustained attention to such documents for an understanding of the adaptations of texts to readers. Boulton's essay sets University of Notre Dame, MSS 34 and 51 into the context of the manuscript tradition of two very different texts (the *Roman de la Rose* and the *Chanson de Bertrand du Guesclin*) and provides a detailed codicological description of each one. Boulton shows that the pattern of expansions found in the *Chanson* in Notre Dame 51 can be related to the "process of rewriting history" after the end of the Hundred Years' War. This process of "rewriting" is also revealed, albeit in a very different way, in the glosses which appear in Notre Dame 34, a version of the *Roman de la Rose*; their philosophical character suggests that the commissioner of the text was a "serious, well-educated, and possibly misogynist reader." Both manuscripts are typical examples of the way that medieval texts were constantly "altered, adapted, and annotated to suit the needs and interests of different readers in different periods."

Dianne Phillips discusses a manuscript held by the Snite Museum of Art at Notre Dame, which contains a shorter Italian version (as yet unpublished) of the famous late medieval text of the *Meditations on the Life of Christ*, produced in Bologna ca. 1350 and extensively illuminated with forty-eight large miniatures in the shop of Alberto and Stefano Azzi. Phillips compares this cycle with illuminations in other manuscripts, and shows that the details of the images reflect the interests of a learned (but lay) male reader. In particular, she notes the striking emphasis the manuscript places on the figure of Joseph, arguing that the illuminator "masculinizes the domestic" as a way of appealing to the worldly Bolognese layman who probably commissioned the text. Like the *Mirror to Devout People*, the Snite manuscript reveals much about its intended audience and about the forms of piety that such an audience would be likely to embrace.

The papers in this volume are distinguished by a variety of approaches to the study of medieval texts and manuscripts and by the capacious time frame in which they are located, extending from the Anglo-Saxon period to the fifteenth century. Taken together, they constitute a demonstration of the ways in which the insights gained from careful attention to the multiple dimensions, material as well as verbal, of medieval texts can extend and complicate our notions of the literary tradition, medieval reading practices and audiences, and modes of composition.

## NOTE

1. The manuscript collection of the University of Notre Dame includes some sixty medieval manuscripts; those acquired before 1978 are catalogued in James A. Corbett, *Catalogue of the Medieval and Renaissance Manuscripts of the University of Notre Dame* (Notre Dame, Ind., 1978).

PLATE 1. Scrope/Chaworth coat of arms (University of Notre Dame, MS 67, f. 1r). Reproduced from the original held by the Department of Special Collections of the University Libraries of Notre Dame.

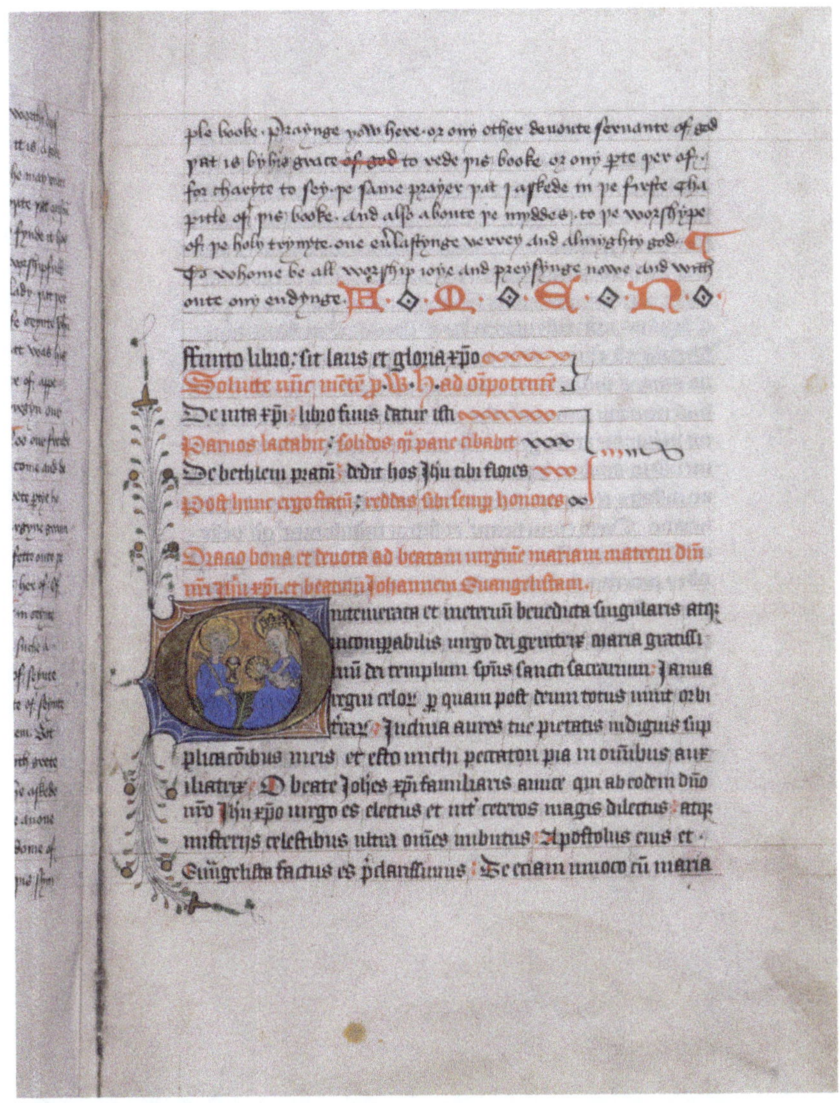

PLATE 2. Virgin and Child and St. John (University of Notre Dame, MS 67, f. 108r). Reproduced from the original held by the Department of Special Collections of the University Libraries of Notre Dame.

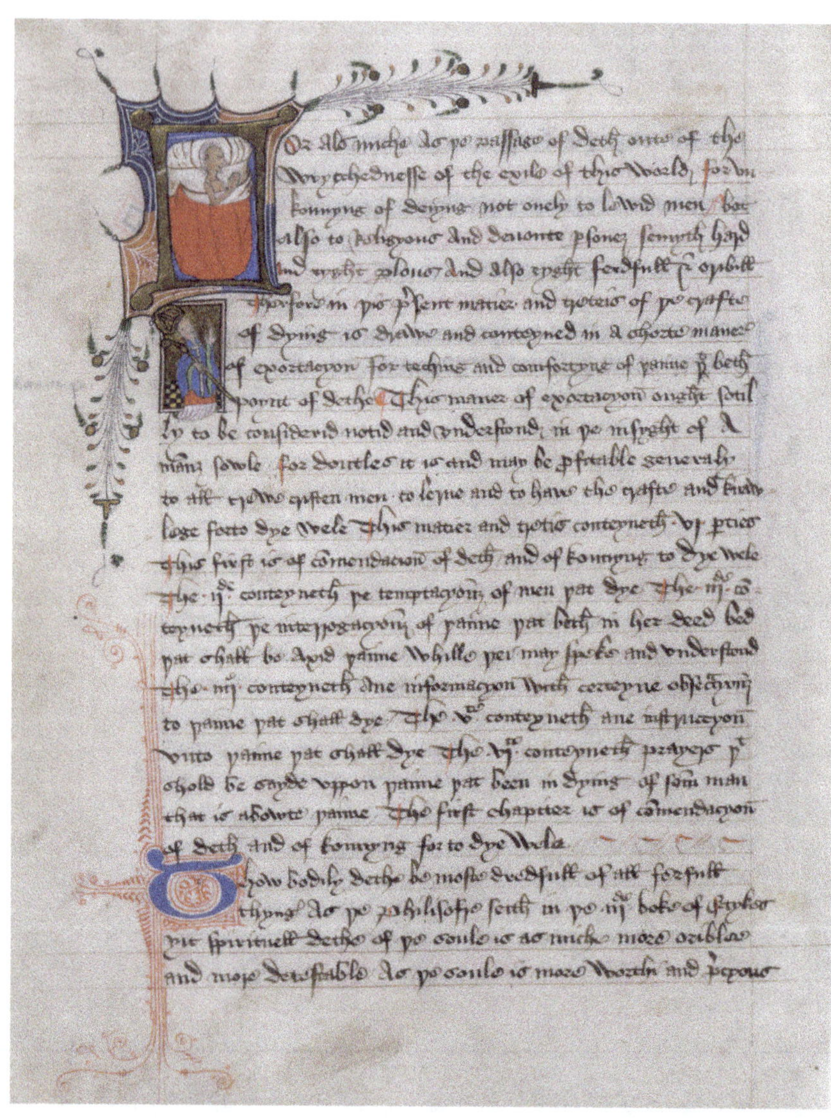

PLATE 3. Recumbent figure and bishop (University of Notre Dame, MS 67, f. 109v). Reproduced from the original held by the Department of Special Collections of the University Libraries of Notre Dame.

# Versifying the Bible in the Middle Ages

MICHAEL LAPIDGE

IT IS A TRUISM TO SAY THAT THE BIBLE WAS THE FUNDAMENTAL and defining text of Latin Christendom during the Middle Ages. Literacy during that period implied the ability to read Latin[1] and carried the implication that one had read or studied the Bible. Children were taught to read by memorizing the Psalms and the Wisdom books, and the mark of perfection in an oblate was that he could regurgitate the entire psalter, as is clear from numerous Lives of saints.[2] At a later stage of life, the monk's occupation consisted in meditation on the Bible through the agency of scriptural commentaries.[3] It is therefore surprising, perhaps, to learn that the curriculum of medieval schools consisted not in study of the Bible per se, nor in meditation on patristic commentary, but in the meticulous word-by-word parsing and interpretation of various poetic versions of the Bible (paraphrases, as they are often called).[4] In spite of the undoubted centrality of these poetic texts in medieval education, they remain curiously unstudied and virtually unknown.[5] In her inaugural lecture Jill Mann draws attention to the importance of the curriculum of late medieval school authors (below, chap. 2); I should like here to provide some background to that lecture by considering the four most important Christian-Latin poets of late antiquity (Juvencus, Sedulius, Avitus, and Arator) and the process by which their poems came to constitute the school curriculum of the early Middle Ages. I will try to offer some reflection on the effects that study of these curriculum poets might have had on those who read them in early Anglo-Saxon schools, and to illustrate this reflection by considering one notoriously difficult Old English poem (the *Exodus*) as the product of a vernacular poet trained in that curriculum. I want finally to trace the disintegration of this early medieval curriculum of biblical poets during the course of the eleventh and twelfth centuries, and their replacement from the thirteenth century onwards by a new biblical paraphrase—the *Aurora* by Peter of Rheims—and to speculate briefly on the effects that the study of texts such as the *Aurora* had on education in the late Middle Ages. In covering this span of over a thousand years, I shall be obliged to make more generalizations than I would normally prefer to do; but I shall try to provide enough detail to support at least some of my generalizations.

I begin with a poem entitled *Evangelia*, composed by the Spanish priest Juvencus (Gaius Vettius Aquilinus Juvencus),[6] who, to judge from his name, if nothing else, was a Roman aristocrat, and who, to judge from his poem, was well-read in classical Latin authors, especially Vergil.[7] His *Evangelia* consist of four books (some 3,200 lines in total), and follow closely the text of the gospels, drawing mostly on Matthew, but to a lesser extent on Luke and John. The final lines of the poem contain a dedication to the Emperor Constantine, and later authors (such as Jerome) assign the dedication to A.D. 329[8]—to a time, that is, some fifteen years after the so-called "Edict of Milan," when Constantine was resident at his new imperial capital in Constantinople (the new capital was dedicated on 11 May 330). After establishing the peace of the Church, Constantine had used his massive resources to effect Christian *renovatio* in major centres of the Roman empire, for example by endowing large numbers of lavish basilicas in Rome (the Lateran or S. Giovanni in Laterano, St. Peter's, S. Paolo fuori le mura, S. Croce in Gerusalemme, etc.)[9] and Constantinople (the church of the Apostolon, where Constantine was to be buried).[10] We also know from a letter—dated 332—of Constantine to Bishop Eusebius (quoted by Eusebius in his *Vita Constantini*) that Constantine commissioned fifty lavishly written bibles.[11] I would see the commissioning of Juvencus's *Evangelia* as part of this process of *renovatio*, the point being that, as new churches and new liturgical books were required, so too there was need for a "new" version of the gospels—a version cast in an elegant register of Latin rather than in the stumbling, colloquial prose "translationese" that is the Vetus Latina (recall that we are still fifty years or so before Jerome's revision of the Bible which resulted in the so-called "Vulgate").[12] It is possible, then, that Juvencus was working at Constantinople (and not in Spain, where he was born),[13] was a member of the imperial entourage that also included the Latin poet Publilius Optatianus Porphyrius,[14] and that the *Evangelia* were produced as part of Constantine's personal program of *renovatio*.

In any case, Juvencus produced in his *Euangelia* a hugely influential poem which was a pioneering effort in every respect: although there is a substantial corpus of elegant Latin prose dating from before the peace of the church and composed by highly articulate rhetors (Tertullian, Lactantius), there was no Christian-Latin poetry before Juvencus. He created, at a stroke, the diction of Christian-Latin poetry. Some sense of the register at which he was aiming can be gleaned from his version of the Lord's Prayer:

Sidereo genitor residens in uertice caeli,
nominis, oramus, ueneratio sanctificetur
in nobis, pater alte, tui: tranquillaque mundo
adueniat regnumque tuum lux alma reclaudat.
In caelo ut terris fiat tua clara uoluntas,
uitalisque hodie sancti substantia panis
proueniat nobis; tua mox largitio soluat
innumera indulgens erroris debita praui;
et nos haut aliter concedere foenora nostris.
Tetri saeua procul temptatio daemonis absit
eque malis tua nos in lucem dextera tollat.
(1:590–600)

O progenitor, residing in the sidereal summit of heaven, may the veneration of your name, lofty Father, be sanctified in us; may Your Kingdom come to the world and may kindly light enfold it in tranquillity. In heaven as on earth may Your will be manifest, and may the vital substance of Your holy bread sustain us today; may Your indulgent generosity forgive the countless debts of wicked error; and in the same way may we grant release from debts to ourselves. May the vicious temptation of the foul demon be far from us, and likewise let Your right hand raise us from evil into the realm of light.

For the most part, Juvencus adheres closely to the biblical text (which he was apparently following sometimes in Greek, sometimes in a Vetus Latina version); but even in as short a passage as this, several characteristic departures may be noticed. His entire poem, for example, is suffused with metaphors of light, and in this passage he has added to the biblical text the petitions that "kindly light" (*lux alma*) enfold God's kingdom, and that God's right hand raise us into "the realm of light."[15] Juvencus is undoubtedly master of the high style (note the zeugma in lines 3–4, the pentasyllabic cadence *sanctificetur* in the second line, which is itself a four-word hexameter, etc.).[16] But most important is the fact that he forged a diction which would be imitated and adopted by all subsequent Christian-Latin poets: not only the metaphoric of light (widely current phrases such as *Dominus lucis* derive from Juvencus), but also the appropriation from Vergil of epic terminology (the Vergilian use of the adjective *tonans*, the "thunderer," applied to describe the Christian God, derives from Juvencus) and the creation of neologisms to heighten the expression of crucial moments in Christian time, as in his lines describing Christ's baptism in the river Jordan:

Haec memorans uitreas penetrabat fluminis undas.
Surgenti manifesta Dei praesentia claret.
Scinditur auricolor caeli septemplicis aethra
corporeamque gerens speciem descendit ab alto
spiritus aeriam simulans ex nube columbam.
(1:354–58).

Recalling these words [of John the Baptist] he [Jesus] entered the glassy waters of the river [Jordan]. The manifest presence of God was made clear as he re-emerged. The golden-coloured ether of the seven-tiered heaven is rent, and the Holy Spirit, in corporeal form, descends from on high, resembling a heavenly dove [descending] from a cloud.

Here the sequence of end-stopped lines prepares us for the miraculous moment of the dove's heavenly descent, a moment which is pointed by the poet's creation of the adjective *auricolor* and the unprecedented application of *septemplex* to the multiple layering of the heavens.[17] Juvencus is a poet who has been neglected for too long—there is no English translation or commentary, and no scholarly edition has been undertaken since 1891—but it is mildly encouraging that a number of monographs, written at Regensburg under the direction of Klaus Thraede and published during the 1990s, have begun at last to draw scholarly attention to the original achievement of this pioneering poet.[18]

Certainly the Late Latin poets who followed Juvencus were aware of the importance of his achievement, and the imprint of his diction is found in all his successors, in none more so than in the *Carmen paschale* of Caelius Sedulius.[19] About Sedulius we know virtually nothing, save that he lived during the second quarter of the fifth century, was trained as a philosopher, and lived latterly in Greece, where he may have composed his poem.[20] The *Carmen paschale* consists of five books of roughly 500 lines each. The subject is the miracles performed by Christ in the New Testament, and these are related in detail in books 2–5; the first book prepares the reader for Christ's miraculous powers by treating the miracles that are recorded in the Old Testament. We may take as an example Sedulius's brief mention of the Crossing of the Red Sea:

> Peruia diuisi patuerunt caerula ponti
> in geminum reuoluta latus, nudataque tellus
> cognatis spoliatur aquis, ac turba pedestris
> intrat in absentis pelagi mare, perque profundum
> sicca peregrinas stupuerunt marmora plantas.
> Mutauit natura uiam, mediumque per aequor
> ingrediens populus rude iam baptisma gerebat,
> cui dux Christus erat, clamat nam lectio: multas
> uox Domini super extat aquas; uox denique uerbum est.
> (1:136–44)

The cerulean highways of the divided sea lay bare, rolled back on either side, and the sea-bed, thus exposed, is deprived of the waters to

> which it is naturally joined (*cognatis*); and the crowd enters on foot the sea of absent waters and amidst the deep the dry sands were astonished at the tread of unfamiliar footsteps. Nature changed its course, and advancing into the midst of the sea the people were carrying [the *figura* of] a simple baptism. Christ was their leader, as Scripture makes clear: for the voice of the Lord, which is the Word, was upon the waters.

Unlike Juvencus, who concerned himself solely with New Testament events, Sedulius attempted to understand these events in terms of Old Testament events, and to see in the Old Testament a prefiguring of the New, as here, where the Crossing of the Red Sea is a *figura* of baptism: the presence of Christ during the Crossing is stated explicitly and linked both to the passage at the beginning of Genesis where the spirit of God moved over the waters, and to Psalm 28 (29): 3, which reads "uox Domini super aquas."

A telling illustration of figural interpretation of New Testament events is provided by Sedulius's description of Christ's Palm Sunday procession, where Christ scorned transportation in a stately chariot and chose instead the humble conveyance of a donkey:

> Sed lento potius gestamine uilis aselli
> rectori suffecit honos, leuis ungula cuius
> ut tanto sessore decus mirabile portans
> nobilior sub fasce foret, non illius inpar,
> qui patulo Christum licet in praesepe iacentem
> agnouit tamen esse Deum.
>
> (4:297–302)

> But rather the slow conveyance of a lowly donkey was a sufficient distinction for the Lord, a donkey, whose gentle hoof, carrying the miraculous glory of so great a rider, would be more noble under this burden—not unlike that donkey who recognized Christ to be God, though He was lying in an open manger.

The prototype of the intelligent donkey is Balaam's ass, who in Numbers 22:23–31 was able to recognize the divine presence of the Lord's angel; and in his use of the word *agnouit* Sedulius was clearly alluding to Balaam's ass. But Sedulius extended the allusion to include the donkey who was present at the manger in Bethlehem at the time of Christ's birth.[21] However, the gospel narrative makes no mention of any donkey present on that occasion. In order to emphasize the figural associations of the Palm Sunday procession, Sedulius was prepared to go beyond the literal warrant of the scriptural text; and in doing so, he also went far beyond the precedent of Juvencus. His technique of figural interpretation set a model for subsequent Christian-Latin poets.

Juvencus created the diction of Christian-Latin biblical verse; Sedulius opened up the possibility of using it for figural and typological interpretation. Subsequent Late Latin poets followed these two models. A notable example is the early sixth-century bishop of Vienne, Alcimus Ecdicius Avitus (d. 518), whose epic poem *De spiritalis historiae gestis* includes five books based on Genesis and Exodus, concerning the Creation, the Temptation, the Fall, the Flood, and the Crossing of the Red Sea.[22] We have looked briefly at Sedulius's treatment of the Crossing of the Red Sea, and it will be helpful to set Avitus's treatment alongside that of his predecessor. At the beginning of book 5, Avitus states explicitly that "this story—the Crossing of the Red Sea—represented, more than anything, a pledge of things to come, and the nature of the salvation it promised surpassed in beauty the beauty of the narrative. The work's beauty was great enough at the level of the story it told, but greater still in the figurative sense."

> In quibus excellit longe praestantius illud,
> quod pelago gestum Rubro celeberrima perfert
> scriptorum series, in cuius pondere sacro
> causarum mage pignus erat pulchramque relatu
> pulchrior exuperat praemissae forma salutis,
> historiis quae magna satis maiorque figuris.
> (5:12–18)

Having stressed the figural significance of the Crossing of the Red Sea, Avitus turns later in book 5 to narrate the events of the Crossing itself, and the destruction of the Egyptian armies.[23] In violent and martial language reminiscent of Vergilian and Lucanian battle-scenes, the walls of water collapse upon the frightened soldiers:

> Hinc subitus crepitare fragor, tonat undique circum
> lympha ruens primumque illic conmittitur unda,
> qua monstrabat iter Phario sors ultima regi.
> Postquam clausa uia est fluctusque repellit euntem,
> paenitet intrati iam gurgitis et fuga serum
> molitur reditum: trepidae dant terga cohortes
> armaque proiciunt. Pontus fugientibus instat
> occurritque sequens: perit undique circumiectus
> decurrentis aquae laxatis murus habenis.
>
> (5:662–70)

> Then a sudden roar resounded, and the crashing water thunders all about, and the waters engage first at that point where ultimate fate was revealing a path to the Egyptian king. After the path was closed and the flood drove him back as he made to leave, he regrets that he had ever entered the gulf and attempts in his flight a tardy return. The terrified armies turn their backs and throw down their weapons. The sea presses upon the fleeing troops and hastens in pursuit. On all sides the wall of surrounding water collapses, its reins released.

It will be clear from this passage that, in amplifying the biblical narrative, Avitus went far beyond the warrant of scripture, which (rather blandly) states that "the sea returned . . . to the former place; and as the Egyptians were fleeing away, the waters came upon them" (Exod. 14:27); the vivid details of battle imagery—the terrified soldiers turning their backs in flight and casting down their weapons, the relentless pursuit of the waters—are drawn from the poet's imagination and his familiarity with earlier epic verse, notably, in this instance, Vergil (*dant terga: Aeneis* 12:463), Lucan (*sors ultima:* 5:692, 7:122, 7:444, etc.), and the *Ilias Latina* (*fugientibus instat:* 401–2).[24] And having risen to this battle-theme, Avitus goes on to describe the grisly deaths experienced by the Egyptian soldiers:

Ergo exaltatis pendens sustollitur undis
mox mergenda phalanx: lympharum monte leuata
pondere telorum premitur, fundoque tenaci
indutum reuehunt morientia corpora ferrum.
Pars exarmatis cum primum libera membris
implicuit nantes miseris conplexibus artus,
auxilio decepta perit pariterque tenentes
alterno sub fasce ruunt nexique necantur.
Ast alii, lassata diu dum brachia iactant,
incurrunt enses iaculisque natantibus haerent,
concolor et rubro miscetur sanguine pontus.
(5:683–93)

And so the enemy phalanx, on the very point of drowning, was lifted up and hung suspended on the rising waves. Because of the weight of their weapons, however, they sank into the rising mountain of water, and their dying bodies bore their iron clothing to the retentive sea-bed. Some freed themselves of their armaments first and then wrapped their swimming limbs around one another in wretched embraces until, cheated of rescue, they perished, for as they clasped each other for mutual support, they sank down and died with arms and legs intertwined. Still others, tossing their weary arms about for a long time, ran onto swords or hung upon floating lances, and the similarly coloured sea mingled with their red blood.

Exodus 14:28 simply says that the waters covered the chariots and cavalry of the Egyptians; there is no scriptural warrant for this vividly imagined scene: the soldiers clinging to each other in a final embrace as their heavy armour carries them to the sea-bed, others falling on their swords or grasping floating spears to provide the blood which enables Avitus in the final verse to engage in wordplay on the name of the Red Sea.[25] Yet in spite of the graphic martial imagery we should not forget the figural significance of the Crossing that for Avitus, as for Sedulius before him, unambiguously represents purification through baptism. Thus he concludes this episode with a pointed reminder that in the briny death of the Egyptians, "the guilt [of the world] is purged and washed away by baptism, and the waters bring forth the new progeny [which is Christ]" (5:706–8: "Cum purgata sacris deletur culpa fluentis / emittitque nouam parientis lympha lauacri / prolem").

The last of the Christian-Latin poets whom I wish to mention, Arator, developed even further the figural significance of the Red Sea Crossing. Of Arator himself we know nothing,[26] save that as a subdeacon in Rome he read his lengthy poem *Historia apostolica* (a metrical version of the Acts of the Apostles) on two successive days in 544, in the presence of Pope Vigilius in the Church of S. Pietro in Vincoli.[27] Of all the poems I have mentioned, Arator's is the most difficult, not only because of the extreme compression of its diction (some passages verge on the untranslatable), but because of the extreme complexity of its figural typology.[28] Arator's poem consists of two books (some 2,500 lines in total), the first being devoted to St. Peter,[29] the second to St. Paul. The poem consists of brief paraphrases of a biblical events,[30] giving the gist of the action, each of which is followed by twenty-five to a hundred lines of interpretation, in which the event itself may be referred to allusively, but is rarely spelled out. We may take as an example a passage from book 2 (lines 40–95), which treats St Paul's visit to Antioch and his preaching before the Jews (Acts 13:14–28). In his speech Paul referred briefly to the Israelites' forty years of enslavement in Egypt (Acts 13:17–18), and Arator uses this brief mention as a peg on which to hang some lengthy exegetical reflections on the Crossing of the Red Sea (which is not in fact mentioned in Acts):[31]

"nostis," ait, "patribus tellus Aegyptia nostris
qua posuit feritate iugum, crudelibus aruis
quos rapuit per signa Deus, quibus omnia cedens
mutauit natura uices cum uirga fugauit
terga maris fluctusque suis stetit exul ab oris
puluereo de calle placens pontique facultas
obsequio est subiecta pedum, redeunte profundo
naufragium factura reis, quae uertere iussa
per uarios sua iura modos his strauit arenas,
his cumulauit aquas; iustis uia, sontibus unda."

(2:43–52)

> "You know," he says, "with what harshness the Egyptian land placed a yoke upon our fathers, whom God through His miracles snatched away from the cruel fields, yielding everything to Whom, nature changed its course when the rod put to flight the ridge [lit. backs] of the sea and the flood stood still, banished from its banks, now proving favourable by reason of its dusty path; and the power of the ocean was made subordinate in obedience to feet, and, as the deep rolled back, it prepared to raise a shipwreck for the guilty; for, commanded in various ways to overturn its own statutes, it spread out the sands for these men [Israelites], and heaped up the waters for those [Egyptians]: a road for the righteous, a wave for the guilty."

In situating the Red Sea Crossing within the framework of natural law (*mutauit natura uices*), Arator reveals the first of many debts, verbal and doctrinal, to Sedulius; it is also probable that in referring to the *terga maris* (the ridge, or backs, of the sea), Arator is transferring the epithet used by Avitus to describe the sea's defeat of the Egyptians, who (as we saw) turned their backs and fled at the sea's advance (a similar transference may underlie Arator's wording of the sea's subservience to the Israelite pedestrians). In any case, Arator summarizes his verse paragraph with a blunt epigram: the path was opened for the just, and the waters for the guilty.

Arator then moves on to explore the figural significance of the Crossing:

> Consule signa maris, quae mystica dona susurrant
> temporibus uentura crucis, cum sanguine Iesus
> tinxit aquas laterisque uno de uulnere fluxit
> quod uitae tria dona daret. Rubor aequoris ille
> causa futura fuit: sic conditor abluit omnes,
> sic emit; hic pretii color est in gurgite ponti,
> apparentque uado miracula debita ligno.
>
> (2:89–95)

> Look at the signs of the sea, which whisper the mystical gifts to come in the time of the Cross, when Jesus tinged the waters with blood and from the one wound of his side flowed that which gave the three gifts of life. That redness of the water was an occasion which was to come:

thus the Creator washes all men, thus He redeems them. The colour of the ransom is here in the whirlpool of the ocean, and there appear in the deep miracles which belong to the tree [Cross].

We have seen that, of Arator's predecessors, Sedulius made explicit Christ's presence at the Red Sea Crossing and explained the event as a primitive (*rude*) baptism; and that Avitus, rising to the challenge of the name "Red" Sea, explained (rather improbably) that the Egyptian soldiers had fallen on their swords as the waters rushed down on them, hence that the waters became mingled with blood. Arator goes well beyond these somewhat elementary explanations. The miracle of the sea, in particular the mixture of blood and water, anticipates that of the Crucifixion, when one of the soldiers pierced Christ's side with a lance, and "immediately there came out blood and water" (John 19:34); the water and blood, in turn, represent baptism and the eucharist. What then are the *uitae tria dona*, the "three gifts of life"? The answer lies with Caelius Sedulius,[32] who in book 5 of his *Carmen paschale* had explained the significance of the perforation of Christ's side as follows:

Vulnere purpureus cruor et simul unda cucurrit.
Haec sunt quippe sacrae pro religionis honore:
corpus sanguis aqua tria uitae munera nostrae.
Fonte renascente, membris et sanguine Christi
uescimur atque ideo templum deitatis habemur.
(5:287–92)

And from the gaping wound ran down the purple blood and with it water. These things indeed represent the glory of our holy religion: the body, the blood, and the water are the three gifts of our life (*tria uitae munera nostrae*). Reborn in the font, we are fed with the body and blood of Christ, and thus we are reckoned to be the temple of His deity.

For Arator, in other words, the Crossing of the Red Sea is a significant event in salvation history precisely because it adumbrates at a stroke the crucifixion, baptism, and the eucharist.

I hope that these brief examples will give some notion of the complexity of Christian-Latin poetic diction. It was because of this complexity that these four poets—Juvencus, Sedulius, Avitus, and Arator—achieved immediate and immense popularity, and came to form a canon of texts for study by devout Christians with a taste for the higher registers of poetic expression.[33] That the canon had already emerged by the late sixth century is clear from a passage in the metrical *Vita S. Martini* of Venantius Fortunatus:[34]

> Primus enim docili distinguens ordine carmen
> maiestatis opus metri canit arte Iuuencus.
> Hinc quoque conspicui radiauit lingua Seduli . . .
> Sortes apostolicas quae gesta uocantur et actus
> facundo eloquio sulcauit uates Arator.
> Quod sacra explicuit serie genealogus olim,
> Alcimus egregio digessit acumine praesul.
>
> (1:14–25)

> First of all, setting out his poem in accessible form, Juvencus composes a work of majesty in metrical art. Thereafter, too, the tongue of the noteworthy Sedulius shines out. The poet Arator, with articulate eloquence, elaborates the fates and deeds of the apostles, which are called *gesta*. And that which the "genealogist" [Moses] once set out in holy sequence [i.e., the Pentateuch], Bishop Alcimus [Avitus] treated with outstanding subtlety.

Venantius Fortunatus composed these lines at Poitiers, in Gaul. But the process by which these four Christian-Latin poets emerged as an early medieval curriculum is attested not just in Gaul, but throughout Europe. There is no doubt that they were intensively studied in Anglo-Saxon England,[35] perhaps even before the Anglo-Saxons got there (the earliest surviving fragment of Arator is a paste-down from a manuscript in the Bodleian Library which palaeographers think may have been written in sub-Roman Britain, before the arrival of the Gregorian mission in 597).[36] In any event, it was the study of these four poets in Anglo-Saxon schools which defined the style of Anglo-Latin poetic diction. They are quoted *in extenso* by Aldhelm in his treatises on metre, and their verses and diction are recycled endlessly in his own hexameter verse, as Andy Orchard has shown.[37] Bede's introduction to Latin metre, the *De arte metrica,* draws all its examples of metrical technique from these poets, and the diction of his metrical *Vita metrica S. Cudbercti* bears the impress of their style.[38] Alcuin's poetry, too, is modelled on the diction of these poets, and he gives them pride of place among the books which were available in his master Ælberht's library at York when he was a student there:[39]

> Quid quoque Sedulius uel quid canit ipse Iuuencus
> Alcimus et Clemens, Prosper, Paulinus, Arator.
> (1:1650–51)

> [The library contained] that which Sedulius and Iuuencus sang, and what Alcimus [Avitus], and Prudentius, Prosper [of Aquitaine], Paulinus [of Nola] and Arator (sang).

In the later Anglo-Saxon period, Wulfstan of Winchester knew these poets by heart, as the diction of his hexameters reveals.[40] Dozens of Anglo-Saxon manuscripts of each of these poets survive, often encrusted with layer upon layer of glossing and annotation.[41] It is clear that, from the tenth century onwards, the poems were studied by way of commentaries, especially those of Remigius of Auxerre (d. 908),[42] who apparently composed commentaries on Sedulius and Juvencus, and arguably on Arator as well. (None of these Remigian commentaries have been published, so it is difficult to be precise about the extent of Remigius's contribution to the tradition.)[43] In some Anglo-Saxon manuscripts, interlinear and marginal glosses have simply been lifted from Remigius's commentaries.[44] Surviving booklists from Anglo-Saxon England give evidence of still more manuscripts—of the poems themselves and of Remigian commentaries—in various English libraries which by chance have not survived.[45] There can be no doubt, therefore, that study of Juvencus, Sedulius, Avitus, and Arator formed the core of the Anglo-Saxon school curriculum, at least down to the time of the Norman Conquest.

But for me the more interesting question is: what would have been the effect of studying these poets, day in day out, line by line and word by word, on the mental perception of a young Anglo-Saxon scholar? The question is impossible to answer fully; but it would seem reasonable to assume that the young scholar in question would end up being deeply aware of the possibilities of figural interpretation of biblical and historical events, and would understand biblical narrative in light of such awareness, instinctively seeing Old Testament events as *figurae* of those in the New Testament. Such a student would internalize figural interpretation, so to speak.

By way of testing this assumption, I should like briefly to consider one notoriously difficult Old English poem, that entitled *Exodus*.[46] This poem is preserved (incompletely) in a single manuscript, the so-called Junius Manuscript, written at an unknown centre some time in the later tenth century, say 960–990 (I accept Leslie Lockett's arguments for redating this important manuscript).[47] In spite of the tenth-century date of the manuscript, however, most Anglo-Saxonists are in agreement that the *Exodus* is among the earliest surviving Old English poems, and may have been composed in the first half of the eighth century.[48] As preserved, it consists of 590 lines. The poem is not a literal rendition of the biblical Exodus, nor does it treat the entire biblical book; rather, it treats a single episode, the Crossing of the Red Sea (as narrated in Exodus 14:21–31), with typological references back to Noah's flood and Abraham's sacrifice of Isaac, and forward to the Day of Judgement. As James Bright suggested a century ago,[49] and as Paul Remley has recently proven beyond doubt,[50] the biblical passages which form the basis of the Old English poem are precisely those which formed the readings for Holy Saturday liturgy in pre-Gregorian sacramentaries (Exod. 14:24–15:2). In the Holy Saturday liturgy, the narrative of the Crossing of the Red Sea prefigured the baptism of the catechumens which took place following the service. The choice of these readings by the author of the Old English *Exodus* indicates per se that the real subject of the poem is baptism, in all its figural and allegorical ramifications, although the poet never bluntly says as much. Certainly he intended his readers to contemplate the wider significance of the narrative, as he states (obliquely, however) in a passage which follows the destruction of the Egyptians:

Swa gyt werðeode on gewritum findað
doma gehwilcne, þara ðe him Drihten bebead
on þam siðfate soðum wordum.
Gif onlucan wile lifes wealhstod,

beorht in breostum, banhuses weard,
ginfæsten god Gastes cægon,
run bið gerecenod, ræd forð gæð.
(520–26)

Thus still the people find in writings each judgement, of those which the Lord enjoined on them on the journey, in true words. If life's interpreter [*lifes wealhstod* = the intellect, mind], bright in the breast, the body's guardian, wishes to unlock ample bounties with the keys of the Spirit, the secret will be explained, the counsel will go forth.

With this admonition from the poet in mind, we may turn to his description of the Crossing of the Red Sea itself. (Unfortunately the account is lacunose due to the loss of a folio from the manuscript; the account resumes with the Egyptians in mid-crossing, about to be drowned, as in Exodus 14:27–28.)

Folc was afæred, flodegsa becwom
gastas geomre, geafon deaðe hweop.
Wæron beorhhliðu blode bestemed,
holm heolfre spaw, hream wæs on yðum,
wæter wæpna ful, wælmist astah . . .
Laðe cyrmdon —lyft up geswearc—
fægnum stæfnum. Flod blod gewod.
(447–51, 462–63)

The Egyptian army was frightened; flood-terror befell the wretched souls; the sea threatened death. The cliffs were spattered with blood; the sea spewed gore; there was an uproar on the waves, the water full of weapons, a slaughter-mist rose up . . . The air above grew dark. The enemies cried out with doomed voices; blood pervaded the water.

The decisive detail here is that, as the Egyptians are destroyed, the waters of the Red Sea are mixed with blood. And if we follow the poet's exhortation to allow the intellect to unlock the meaning of the text, and recall that the entire poem is framed by lections from the baptismal liturgy of Holy Saturday, then we will recall that Sedulius described the Crossing as a "primitive baptism," and that Avitus and Arator more explicitly treated the mixing of blood and water at the Red Sea Crossing as a *figura* of baptism. To the poet of *Exodus*, trained in an Anglo-Saxon school, the figural meanings of the same event, as expounded in the curriculum poets, will have been inescapable and second-nature. It is these figural meanings which the reader's intellect must unlock, to paraphrase the poet's expression.

Surely, you might think, someone has already pointed out these parallels in the Late Latin poets. The answer is: yes and no. No one, I think, has ever attempted to read Old English verse in light of the school curriculum which all Old English poets must have studied; but in the late nineteenth century, one Gerhard Mürkens, in a doctoral dissertation produced at Bonn in 1891, argued that the sole source of the OE *Exodus* was none other than Avitus's poem (no mention was made of Arator, nor of any other Late Latin poet). Mürkens provided a long list of lines and half-lines which, he argued, were translated from Avitus. Twenty years later, however, Samuel Moore of Harvard, in a widely influential article published in 1912,[51] "demolished"—the word is that used by Peter Lucas,[52] the latest editor of *Exodus*—the arguments of Mürkens; and since then, Avitus has disappeared from scholarly discussion of the Old English *Exodus*. "Demolished," however, is not quite the right word. Moore pointed out a number of peccadilloes in Mürkens's Latin (while making a few himself); the gist of his argument is: why cite Avitus, when the features noted by Mürkens can be found in texts more easily accessible to the Old English poet? (He was apparently unaware of how widely texts like Avitus were read by Anglo-Saxons.) Thus, for the mixing of water with blood in the passage which I quoted (5:683–93), Moore argued that the *Exodus*-poet had lifted the idea from the *Beowulf*-poet's account of the haunted mere, in which the "water surged with gore" (1422: *flod blode weol*), as well as with sea-monsters.[53] (I could certainly be persuaded that the *Exodus*-poet had read *Beowulf*, and derived much of his diction from it, but I cannot think that the haunted mere was intended by the *Beowulf*-poet as a *figura* for baptism.) The other details common to Avitus and the *Exodus*, Moore argued, could more easily be found in "the very widely known *Antiquities* of Josephus."[54] But the *Antiquitates Iudaicae* of Josephus were not, unfortunately, as widely known as

Moore thought: even Archbishop Theodore, who had been trained in Greek schools in the Greek East, knew of the text, but quoted from it by way of a somewhat faulty memory, implying that even he did not have a copy of it with him at Canterbury.[55]

For over a century, Moore's "demolition" (which on inspection turns out to be more special pleading than demolition) has steered scholarship away from the obvious inspiration of the Old English *Exodus*, namely the curriculum of Christian-Latin poets which were studied in all Anglo-Saxon schools. Ever greater energy is expended on finding parallels either in Josephus's *Antiquitates*,[56] or in Origen's *Homilies on Exodus*.[57] But even assuming that there was knowledge of these texts in Anglo-Saxon England (and there is precious little evidence that there was), I doubt that sophisticated poets like the *Exodus*-poet took their inspiration from prose commentaries. We will see in a moment what happens to poetry when it is drawn from biblical commentary. The more obvious place to look for figural interpretation of Old Testament events is in the poets which every literate Anglo-Saxon author had studied in his schooldays. Anglo-Saxon poets did not have computer-assisted concordances to help them find patristic antecedents for the interpretation of biblical events, and it seems to me a falsification of their enterprise to assume that they searched for patristic sources in the same ways that modern scholars do. In short, I am arguing that we will better understand the ways in which Anglo-Saxon poets worked when we understand better the school curriculum in which they were trained.

By the time of the Norman Conquest, and the ensuing replacement of senior Anglo-Saxon abbots and bishops by Norman ecclesiastics, with concomitant changes in all aspects of ecclesiastical life, not least schooling, the early medieval curriculum had begun slowly to change. The slow process of change had been in train for two centuries. The ninth-century cathedral and monastic schools had initiated the study of the scientific quadrivium alongside the traditional trivium (as set out in the *De nuptiis Philologiae et Mercurii* of Martianus Capella), and philosophical texts, such as Boethius's *De consolatione Philosophiae* and Macrobius's commentary on the *Somnium Scipionis*, came more and more to occupy a place in the curriculum and to attract the scholarly attentions of commentators such as Remigius of Auxerre.[58] By the tenth and eleventh centuries, this nascent interest in philosophical texts led to the emergence of specialized study of logic, as (say) in the technical writings of Gerbert of Aurillac and Abbo of Fleury.[59] The development of this interest in philosophy culminated in the twelfth century in the scientific writings (for example) of Adelard of Bath and in the cosmology of the school of Chartres, as witnessed in the Chartrian writings of cosmologists such as William of Conches, Thierry of Chartres, and Gilbert of Poitiers.[60] The development of this "new science" is reflected, too, in the *prosimetra* of Bernard Silvestris (*Cosmographia*) and Alan of Lille (*De planctu Naturae*), and in cosmological poems on an epic scale such as the *Anticlaudianus* of Alan of Lille and the *Architrenius* of John of Hauville.[61] So different are these works from anything that had preceded them that modern scholars rightly speak of the "renaissance of the twelfth century."[62] The development of philosophical interests that these works represent was inevitably reflected in the curricula of the schools. From the late twelfth century onwards, and down to the fourteenth century and beyond, poems such as the *Anticlaudianus* and the *Architrenius* were studied intensively in cathedral schools, as the large numbers of surviving manuscripts clearly indicate. Such study was bound to have an effect on the curriculum of late antique Christian-Latin poets which I outlined earlier.

How quickly the change took place is difficult to say. Perhaps by the twelfth century, after five hundred years of study, the late antique poets were starting to seem stale. This much seems to be implied in the words of the twelfth-century poet who calls himself Sextus Amarcius, and who in his poetic *Sermones* speaks of the four late antique poets as follows:[63]

> Alchimus, Arator, Sedulius atque Iuuencus
> non bene tornatis apponunt regia uasis
> fercula: miror eos, non audeo uituperare.
> (*Serm.* 3:220–22)

> Alcimus [Avitus], Arator, Sedulius and Juvencus: they provide royal feasts in pots that are rough cast: I admire them, yes sir, I don't dare to castigate them.

Sextus's grudging admiration implies that the centuries-old curriculum was falling out of fashion. To judge from educators such as Conrad of Hirsau (d. ca. 1150), who compiled *accessus*, or introductions, to curriculum authors, poets such as Juvencus, Sedulius, and Arator were still holding their own alongside the works of Ovid, Lucan, and Vergil.[64] But the manuscripts tell a different story. Whereas large numbers of manuscripts of Juvencus, Sedulius, and Arator survive from the period before the eleventh century, only rare and isolated copies were made thereafter; and whereas pre-eleventh-century copies of these authors show extensive signs of classroom use (glossing and annotation), post-twelfth-century copies rarely if ever show such signs.

The late antique Christian-Latin poets may have disappeared from the curriculum, but the biblical interpretation which they had provided was still considered essential. In order to fill the void caused by their disappearance, new biblical poems, consisting in paraphrase and interpretation, rapidly came into being and took their place in the curriculum. One such poem was the *Tobias* of Matthew of Vendôme, a work of some 2,200 lines of elegiac couplets, which was completed ca. 1187. Matthew had studied at Tours with Bernardus Silvestris and subsequently taught logic at Paris; he is possibly best known for his *Ars uersificatoria*, a poetic treatise on the deployment of rhetorical tropes. His *Tobias* (a paraphrase which closely follows the text of the fourteen chapters of the biblical Tobit) is brimming with the new rhetoric, and it quickly assumed the status of a school-text (it is one of the *auctores octo* discussed by Jill Mann, below, 48–49, 52). This status is reflected in the fact that it survives in more than a hundred manuscripts, many of them densely glossed and annotated. But even more successful as a work of biblical paraphrase and interpretation was the *Aurora* of Peter Riga. Peter was born ca. 1140 in the vicinity of Rheims (possibly at a village called La Raye, latinized as "Riga"); with the exception of a period of study in Paris, he spent his life in Rheims, dying in 1209.[65] (In rubrics to the prose preface of his *Aurora* he states that his *biblioteca*, "bible," was composed *a magistro Petro Remense*, "by Master Peter of Rheims;" hence it seems more appropriate to call him Peter of Rheims.) Apparently taking Matthew's *Tobias* as his model, Peter's initial goal was simply to provide a metrical paraphrase—replete with allegorical interpretation and couched, like Matthew's poem, in elegiac couplets—of the Pentateuch, to which he added paraphrases of Joshua, Judges, Ruth, Kings, Maccabees, and part of the gospel story (up to the Sermon on the Mount). The work thus far may be described as Peter's first redaction. In two subsequent campaigns of composition, he produced versions of the books of Tobit, Daniel, Judith, and Esther (the text with these additions constitutes the second redaction), and to a third and final redaction he added versions (in rhyming hexameters this time) of Job, the Song of Songs, and the Acts of the Apostles.[66] (Later redactors, notably Aegidius—or Giles—of Paris, added and interpolated passages from other biblical books, but these do not concern us here.) The resulting poem was some fifteen thousand (14,958, precisely) lines in length. Some notion of Peter's poetic style can be gleaned from the following passage where he treats the chapters in Exodus describing the Crossing of the Red Sea:

> Ad maris ingressum succinctus curro, relinquens
> plurima, ne lector tedia longa trahat.
> Moysi uirga Rubrum tangit Mare, transit Hebreus,
> expirat Pharao cum legione sua:
> uirga crucem notat hic, baptismum sanguine Christi
> perfusum Rubri denotat unda Maris.
> Rex Pharao Sathanan, sua plebs peccata figurat,
> inque Mari Rubro perdit uterque suos.
> Regem cum populo uorat et sepelit Mare Rubrum:
> omnia delentur crimina fonte sacro.
> (*Exodus* 217–26)

> Girding up my loins, I hasten to [the Israelites'] entry into the sea, leaving out many things, so as not to cause boredom in my readers (!). The rod of Moses touches the Red Sea; the Israelite crosses; Pharaoh with his legion expires: the rod here signifies the Cross, the waters of the Red Sea denote baptism, suffused with the blood of Christ. The Pharaoh represents Satan, his people the sins: in the Red Sea each of them loses their followers. The Red Sea devours and buries the king with his people: all sins are deleted in the sacred font [of baptism].

Here the principal question is not, why would anyone write fifteen thousand lines of drivel like this, but why would anyone want to read it. Or, put differently, what would be the effect of studying such a poem in detail? Whereas in the Christian-Latin poets of the early medieval curriculum, figural meanings were implicit and multivalent, requiring to be teased out, here the allegory, crudely stated, is univalent: the pharaoh equals Satan, Moses's rod equals the Cross, the Egyptians equal sins, and so on. Peter has created not so much a poem as a biblical commentary in doggerel; and it is interesting to note that his version of Exodus is not a paraphrase of the biblical text, which he did not consult, but a versification of the *Expositio in Exodum* by Bruno of Asti (d. 1123).[67] The *Aurora* is what happens when a poet translates a biblical commentary into verse; and that—to revert for a moment—is why I do not think the *Exodus*-poet was following a commentary.

Whatever the quality of Peter's versification, his poem had a huge success in late medieval schools. Large numbers of manuscripts of the work survive. It was laid heavily under contribution by Johannes Balbus in his *Catholicon* (the most widely circulated Latin dictionary of the Middle Ages), by William Brito in his *Summa*, and by Ralph of Coggeshall in his *Distinctiones monasticae.* Gower quotes extensively from the *Aurora* in his *Vox clamantis*, and Chaucer refers to it in *The Book of the Duchess.*[68] Yet this popularity had apparently waned by the late fifteenth century, because the *Aurora* was never printed.

In fact the *editio princeps* of the *Aurora* was published in 1965 by Paul Beichner, then Dean of the Graduate School at the University of Notre Dame.[69] The edition, in two massive volumes, is a monument of editorial labor, and one of the finest editions to be printed by the University of Notre Dame Press. Although scholars have begun to question some aspects of Beichner's editorial work, especially the criteria by which he identified the successive stages of authorial redaction,[70] such criticism inevitably attends works of pioneering scholarship. Beichner was as well aware as anyone of how much work he had left undone. He based his edition on only nineteen of the roughly 400 surviving manuscripts which have so far been identified.[71] Two of the manuscripts which he used are at Notre Dame, and were acquired by the Library in the early 1950s for Beichner's use while he was preparing his edition.[72] Both date from the thirteenth century; both, I think, are French; both were elegantly written, with fine rubrication in red and blue ink, on carefully prepared, crisp white parchment. Neither manuscript shows the slightest sign of use, certainly not of use in a classroom: there are no annotations or glosses, no marks at all of the kind made by teachers and students, in either of them. If one wishes to learn how the

*Aurora* was studied, one will have to go elsewhere than Notre Dame (just where is not quite clear: indeed, a thorough census of *Aurora* manuscripts is very much a desideratum). The Notre Dame manuscripts suggest that the *Aurora* was a book that rich people or institutions wished to own, but was evidently not one that they wished to read. Of course I realize that two manuscripts out of 400 is not a very secure base on which to found judgements of this sort.[73] Clearly there is much work to be done.

This last statement is in effect the central theme of my lecture. Medieval education was grounded in the close study of a curriculum of Latin texts. This is an aspect fundamental to our understanding of medieval literature—whether in Latin or in the vernacular. Yet so little work on this subject has been (or is being) done: no edition for over a hundred years of Juvencus and Caelius Sedulius, and none for fifty years of Arator (of the poets I mentioned, only Avitus is being re-edited seriously); no philological commentary worthy of the name on any of them (excepting only the Latin commentaries on books 1 and 2 of Juvencus); no English translation of Juvencus or Sedulius; no scholarly edition of the commentaries on these poets by Remigius of Auxerre; and so on. There is work aplenty here for today's young scholars. If this inaugural lecture can inaugurate anything, I hope it will be an awareness that vernacular literature can only properly be understood within the wider context of Latin literature, and that the key to such understanding lies in scholarly awareness of the medieval school curriculum.

## NOTES

1. Herbert Grundmann, "Litteratus—Illiteratus: Der Wandel einer Bildungsnorm vom Altertum zum Mittelalter," *Archiv für Kulturgeschichte* 40 (1958): 1–65.

2. For Merovingian saints' lives, see P. Riché, "Le psautier, livre de lecture élémentaire d'après les Vies des saints mérovingiens," in *Études mérovingiens* (Paris, 1953), 253–56. Some examples from Insular Latin texts include: Stephen of Ripon, *Vita S. Wilfridi*, cap. 2 ("[Wilfrid] omnem psalmorum seriem memoraliter . . . didicit"); Hygeburg of Heidenheim, *Vita SS. Willibaldi et Wynnebaldi*, cap. 2 ("[Wilibald] protinus puer iste pudicus seu perfectus sacris litterarum studiis imbutus atque eruditus, sacras Dauitici carminis paginas sollerte mentis intentione peragrans"); the anonymous *Vita Alcuini*, cap. 2 ("postque memoriter lectionem recitatam

psalmorum"); Byrhtferth of Ramsey, *Vita S. Ecgwini* 1.8 ("didicit sollicite nectarea mella Dauitici carminis"); and Ieuan ap Sulien's comment on his father Sulien's schooling ("qui postquam primo nablam tener edidit infans"), in M. Lapidge, "The Welsh-Latin Poetry of Sulien's Family," *Studia Celtica* 8/9 (1973–74): 68–106, at 84.

3. The classic study of this process is by J. Leclercq, *The Love of Learning and the Desire of God: A Study of Monastic Culture*, trans. C. Misrahi, 3rd ed. (New York, 1982).

4. See esp. M. Roberts, *Biblical Epic and Rhetorical Paraphrase in Late Antiquity* (Liverpool, 1985), esp. 5–60 (the rhetorical tradition of paraphrase in antiquity), 61–106 (paraphrase as practised by Christian-Latin poets).

5. There are two useful surveys of the biblical verse of late antiquity: D. Kartschoke, *Bibeldichtung: Studien zur Geschichte der epischen Bibelparaphrase von Juvencus bis Otfrid von Weißenburg* (Munich, 1975), 30–123, and R. Herzog, *Die Bibelepik der lateinischen Spätantike* (Munich, 1975). See also Roberts, *Biblical Epic*, and J. McClure, "The Bible Epic and its Audience in Late Antiquity," *Papers of the Liverpool Latin Seminar* 3 (1981): 305–22.

6. *Gai Vetti Aquilini Iuvenci Evangeliorum Libri Quattuor*, ed. J. Huemer, Corpus Scriptorum Ecclesiasticorum Latinorum 24 (Vienna, 1891). The poem has never been translated. Access to the poem is facilitated by *Concordantia in Iuvenci Evangeliorum Libros*, ed. M. Wacht (Hildesheim, 1990). There are useful philological commentaries on the first two books by H. Kievits, *Ad Iuvenci Evangeliorum librum primum commentarius exegeticus* (Groningen, 1940), and J. de Wit, *Ad Iuvenci Evangeliorum librum secundum commentarius exegeticus* (Groningen, 1947). These two works are dissertations completed under the supervision of the great Latin scholar, P. J. Enk, and are rich in detailed analysis of Juvencus's poetic diction.

7. In addition to the commentaries cited in the previous note, there are a number of studies devoted to the poetic diction of Juvencus (and especially its debt to Vergil); see P. Flury, "Zur Dichtersprache des Juvencus," in *Lemmata: Donum natalicium W. Ehlers* (Munich, 1968), 38–47; M. Donnini, "Annotazione sulla tecnica parafrastica negli *Euangeliorum libri* di Giovenco," *Vichiana* 1 (1972): 231–49; idem, "Un aspetto della espressività di Giovenco: l'aggettivazione," *Vichiana* 2 (1973): 54–67; idem, "L'alliterazione e l'omeoteleuto in Giovenco," *Annali della Facoltà di lettere di Perugia* 12 (1974–75): 128–59; I. Opelt, "Die Szenerie bei Juvencus: Ein Kapitel historischer Geographie," *Vigiliae Christianae* 29 (1975): 191–207; A. Longpré, "Aspects de métrique et de prosodie chez Juvencus," *Phoenix* 29 (1975): 128–38; and C. Ratkowitsch, "Vergils Seesturm bei Iuvencus und Sedulius," *Jahrbuch für Antike und Christentum* 29 (1986): 40–58.

8. Jerome, *Chronicon* s.a. 329/330: *Eusebius Werke VII: Die Chronik des Hieronymus*, 2nd ed., ed. R. Helm (Berlin, 1984), 232.

9. L. Duchesne, *Le Liber Pontificalis: Texte, introduction et commentaire*, rev. ed., 3 vols. (Paris, 1981), 1:172–79; trans. R. Davis, *The Book of Pontiffs (Liber Pontificalis)*, 2nd ed. (Liverpool, 2000), 14–24.

10. See (briefly) R. Krautheimer, *Early Christian and Byzantine Architecture*, 4th ed., rev. S. Curcic (Harmondsworth, 1986), 69–70.

11. *Vita Constantini* 4:36, *Eusebius Werke I*, ed. I. A. Heikel (Leipzig, 1902), 131; for an English translation, see A. Cameron and S. G. Hall, trans., *Eusebius: Life of Constantine* (Oxford, 1999), 166, with discussion at 327.

12. See P. Burton, *The Old Latin Gospels: A Study of their Texts and Language* (Oxford, 2000).

13. The Spanish origin of Juvencus is endorsed, for example, by M. A. Norton, "The Prosopography of Juvencus," in *Leaders of Iberian Christianity*, ed. J. M. F. Maricq (Boston, 1962), 114–20.

14. The complex figure-poems of Porphyrius are known collectively as the *Panegyricus Constantini*, and are found in G. Polara, ed., *Publilii Optatiani Porfyrii Carmina*, 2 vols. (Turin, 1973); see the important discussion by T. D. Barnes, "Publilius Optatianus Porfyrius," *American Journal of Philology* 96 (1975): 173–86. It is interesting that Jerome in his *Chronicon* lists Porphyrius together with Juvencus: "Iuuencus presbyter natione Hispanus euangelia heroicis uersibus explicat. Porphyrius misso ad Constantinum insigni uolumine exilio liberatur" (Helm, *Die Chronik des Hieronymus*, 232). Some striking verbal parallels between Juvencus and Porphyrius are noted by Kievits, *Ad . . . librum primum commentarius exegeticus*, 139; such parallels imply that the poets were working in contact with each other.

15. See W. Röttger, *Studien zur Lichtmotivik bei Iuvencus*, Jahrbuch für Antike und Christentum: Ergänzungsband 24 (Münster, 1996), esp. 62–72.

16. See Kievits, *Ad . . . librum primum commentarius exegeticus*, 139–41.

17. For comment on the passage, see Kievits, *Ad . . . librum primum commentarius exegeticus*, 102–3, and R. Fichtner, *Taufe und Versuchung Jesu in den Evangeliorum libri quattuor des Bibeldichters Juvencus (1, 346–408)* (Stuttgart, 1994), 55–77.

18. See M. Flieger, *Interpretationen zum Bibeldichter Iuvencus: Gethsemane, Festnahme Jesu und Kaiphasprozeß (4, 478–565)* (Stuttgart, 1993); Fichtner, *Taufe und Versuchung Jesu*; Röttger, *Studien zur Lichtmotivik*; and A. Hilhorst, "The Cleansing of the Temple (John 2, 13–25) in Juvencus and Nonnus," in *Early Christian Poetry: A Collection of Essays*, ed. J. den Boeft and A. Hilhorst (Leiden, 1993), 61–76.

19. *Sedulii Opera Omnia*, ed. J. Huemer, Corpus Scriptorum Ecclesiasticorum Latinorum 10 (Vienna, 1885), 14–146. Access to the poem is facilitated by *Concordantia in Sedulium*, ed. M. Wacht (Hildesheim, 1992). Only excerpts of the poem have been translated, none well.

20. On Sedulius, see C. P. E. Springer, *The Gospel as Epic in Late Antiquity: The Paschale Carmen of Sedulius* (Leiden, 1988), as well as C. D. Small, "Rhetoric and Exegesis in Sedulius' *Carmen Paschale*," *Classica et Mediaevalia* 37 (1986): 223–44, and P. W. A. T. van den Laan, "Imitation créative dans le *Carmen paschale* de Sedulius," in *Early Christian Poetry*, ed. den Boeft and Hilhorst, 135–66.

21. See Springer, *Gospel as Epic*, 15.

22. *Alcimi Ecdicii Aviti Viennensis Episcopi Opera quae supersunt*, ed. R. Peiper, MGH, Auctores Antiquissimi 6 (Berlin, 1883), 199–294; for a translation, see *The Poems of Alcimus Ecdicius Avitus*, trans. G. W. Shea (Tempe, Ariz., 1997). A new edition, with facing page translation (French) and annotation, is in progress: *Avit de Vienne: Histoire spirituelle I (Chants I–III)*, ed. and trans. N. Hecquet-Noti, Sources chrétiennes 444 (Paris, 1999). Note, too, that there is a superb study of the Latinity of Avitus by H. Goelzer, *Le latin de saint Avit, évêque de Vienne* (Paris, 1909).

23. The episode is discussed by M. Roberts, "Rhetoric and Poetic Imitation in Avitus' Account of the Crossing of the Red Sea ('De spiritalis historiae gestis' 5. 371–702)," *Traditio* 39 (1983): 29–80.

24. The verbal debts cited here have been identified by recourse to *Poetria Nova*, an indispensable database of Latin poetry from its beginnings to the thirteenth century, issued on CD-ROM by SISMEL (Florence); cf. discussion by A. Arweiler, *Die Imitation antiker und spätantiker Literatur in der Dichtung "De spiritalis historiae gestis" des Alcimus Avitus: Mit einem Kommentar zu Avit. carm. 4, 429–540 und 5, 526–703* (Berlin, 1999), 290–91.

25. Cf. Arweiler, *Die Imitation*, 296–98.

26. See R. Anastasi, "Dati biografici su Aratore in Ennodio," *Miscellanea di studi di letteratura cristiana antica* 1 (1947): 145–52, and K. Thraede, "Arator," *Jahrbuch für Antike und Christentum* 4 (1961): 187–96.

27. *Aratoris subdiaconi de Actibus Apostolorum*, ed. A. P. McKinlay, Corpus Scriptorum Ecclesiasticorum Latinorum 72 (Vienna, 1951). There is a translation, not wholly reliable, by R. J. Schrader, J. L. Roberts and J. F. Makowski, *Arator's On the Acts of the Apostles (De Actibus Apostolorum)* (Atlanta, Ga., 1987).

28. This aspect of the poem is brilliantly analyzed by Richard Hillier, *Arator on the Acts of the Apostles: A Baptismal Commentary* (Oxford, 1993); for analysis of individual passages, see also J. Schwind, *Arator-Studien* (Göttingen, 1990), and idem, *Sprachliche und exegetische Beobachtungen zu Arator* (Mainz, 1995).

29. See P. A. Deproost, *L'apôtre Pierre dans un épopée du VIe siècle: L'Historia apostolica d'Arator* (Paris, 1990).

30. It has always been assumed that the prose paraphrases are the work of Arator himself; but it is striking that the earliest fragmentary manuscript of the poem (Oxford, Bodleian Library, e Mus. 66, on which see N. R. Ker, E. A. Lowe, and

A. P. McKinlay, "A New Fragment of Arator in the Bodleian," *Speculum* 19 (1944): 351–52) does not have the paraphrases. See also P. A. Deproost and J.-C. Haelewyck, "Le texte biblique des Actes et l'autenticité des sommaires en prose dans l'*Historia apostolica* d'Arator," in *Philologia Sacra: Biblische und patristische Studien für Hermann J. Frede und Walter Thiele*, ed. R. Gryson, 2 vols. (Freiburg, 1993), 2:583–604.

31. The passage is discussed at length by Hillier, *Arator on the Acts of the Apostles*, 151–79; my translation is based on that given by Hillier, at 152.

32. On Arator's debt to Caelius Sedulius, see N. Wright, "Arator's Use of Caelius Sedulius: A Re-examination," *Eranos* 87 (1989): 51–64.

33. On the formation of the canon, see G. Glauche, *Schullektüre im Mittelalter* (Munich, 1970), esp. 5–16.

34. *Venanti Honori Clementiani Fortunati presbyteri Italici Opera Poetica*, ed. F. Leo, MGH, Auctores Antiquissimi 4.2 (Berlin, 1881), 293–370, at 295–96; the passage is also quoted by Glauche, *Schullektüre*, 5–6.

35. See M. Lapidge, "The Study of Latin Texts in Late Anglo-Saxon England," in *Latin and the Vernacular Languages in Early Medieval Britain*, ed. N. P. Brooks (Leicester, 1984), 99–140, repr. in M. Lapidge, *Anglo-Latin Literature, 600–899* (London, 1996), 455–98.

36. See above, n. 30.

37. A. Orchard, *The Poetic Art of Aldhelm*, Cambridge Studies in Anglo-Saxon England 8 (Cambridge, 1994), esp. 161–62 (Juvencus), 163–66 (Sedulius), 166–70 (Arator), and 216–17 (Avitus).

38. Bede's *De arte metrica* is ed. C. B. Kendall, Corpus Christianorum, Series Latina 123A (Turnhout, 1975), 59–141; trans. C. B. Kendall, *Bede: The Art of Poetry and Rhetoric* (Saarbrucken, 1991). See also the *apparatus fontium* to W. Jaager, *Bedas metrische Vita sancti Cuthberti* (Leipzig, 1935).

39. *Alcuini (Albini) Carmina*, ed. E. Dümmler, MGH, Poetae Latini Aevi Carolini I (Berlin, 1881), 204; see also M. Lapidge, "Surviving Booklists from Anglo-Saxon England," in *Learning and Literature in Anglo-Saxon England*, ed. M. Lapidge and H. Gneuss (Cambridge, 1985), 33–89, at 45–49.

40. M. Lapidge, *The Cult of St Swithun* (Oxford, 2003), 342–43.

41. See H. Gneuss, *Handlist of Anglo-Saxon Manuscripts: A List of Manuscripts and Manuscript Fragments Written or Owned in England up to 1100* (Tempe, Ariz., 2002), *ad indicem* (149–84). The exception is Avitus, of whose poem *De spiritalis historiae gestis* no Anglo-Saxon manuscript survives. But there is no doubt that the work was known in England, as Alcuin's statement (quoted above) and Bede's verbal debts clearly demonstrate. See also below, n. 45.

42. For general orientation in Remigius and his numerous commentaries, see M. Manitius, *Geschichte der lateinischen Literatur des Mittelalters*, 3 vols. (Munich,

1911–31), 1:504–19, as well as C. Jeudy, "L'oeuvre de Remi d'Auxerre," in *L'école carolingienne d'Auxerre: de Murethach à Remi, 830–908*, ed. D. Iogna-Prat, C. Jeudy, and G. Lobrichon (Paris, 1991), 373–96, esp. 388–93, where evidence is presented for Remigius's composition of commentaries on the following school-texts: Arator, Boethius's *De consolatione Philosophiae*, the *Disticha Catonis*, Juvenal, Martianus Capella, Persius, Prudentius, Caelius Sedulius, *Carmen paschale*, and possibly the poems of Vergil.

43. Of the commentary on Sedulius, certainly by Remigius, some few excerpts are printed in Huemer, *Sedulii Opera Omnia*, 316–59. For Juvencus glosses plausibly derived from a commentary by Remigius, see H. McKee, *Juvencus: Text and Commentary* (Aberystwyth, 2000), 44–49. A commentary on Arator (which in my view is possibly by Remigius, though the editor does not at any point raise the question of authorship) is contained in A. P. Orbán, "Ein anonymer Aratorkommentar in Hs. London, Royal MS. 15. A. V," *Sacris Erudiri* 38 (1998–99): 317–51, and 40 (2001): 131–229.

44. See my discussion in "Study of Latin Texts," in *Anglo-Latin Literature, 600–899*, esp. 480–82, 486–94.

45. Lapidge, "Surviving Booklists." Note in particular the mention of a manuscript of Avitus in a list of books donated by Bishop Æthelwold to the monastery of Peterborough, ca. 970 (ibid., 54).

46. P. Lucas, ed., *Exodus*, rev. ed. (Exeter, 1994).

47. L. Lockett, "An Integrated Re-examination of the Dating of Oxford, Bodleian Library, Junius 11," *Anglo-Saxon England* 31 (2002): 141–73.

48. See discussion by R. D. Fulk, *A History of Old English Meter* (Philadelphia, 1992), 62–63.

49. J. W. Bright, "The Relation of the Caedmonian *Exodus* to the Liturgy," *Modern Language Notes* 27 (1912): 97–103.

50. P. G. Remley, *Old English Biblical Verse: Studies in Genesis, Exodus and Daniel*, Cambridge Studies in Anglo-Saxon England 16 (Cambridge, 1996), esp. 168–230.

51. S. Moore, "On the Sources of the Old-English *Exodus*," *Modern Philology* 9 (1911–12): 83–108.

52. Lucas, *Exodus*, 53.

53. Moore, "On the Sources," 16.

54. Ibid., 17.

55. See B. Bischoff and M. Lapidge, *Biblical Commentaries from the Canterbury School of Theodore and Hadrian*, Cambridge Studies in Anglo-Saxon England 10 (Cambridge, 1994), 216–17.

56. J. R. Hall, "The Old English *Exodus* and the *Antiquitates Judaicae*: More Parallels," *Archiv für das Studium der neueren Sprachen und Literaturen* 216 (1979): 341–44.

57. Lucas, *Exodus*, 57–58.

58. On these changes in the curriculum of Carolingian schools, see Glauche, *Schullektüre*, 39–61.

59. On Gerbert, see P. Riché, *Gerbert d'Aurillac, le pape de l'an mil* (Paris, 1987); on Abbo and the study of logic, see Abbo von Fleury, *De syllogismis hypotheticis*, ed. F. Schupp (Leiden, 1997).

60. For excellent orientation in the scientific and cosmological writings of the twelfth century, see *A History of Twelfth-Century Western Philosophy*, ed. P. Dronke (Cambridge, 1988), esp. 308–27 (William of Conches), 328–57 (Gilbert of Poitiers), and 358–85 (Thierry of Chartres). On Adelard, see C. Burnett, ed., *Adelard of Bath: An English Scientist and Arabist of the Early Twelfth Century* (London, 1987).

61. See W. Wetherbee, *Platonism and Poetry in the Twelfth Century: The Literary Influence of the School of Chartres* (Princeton, N.J., 1972).

62. The twelfth century witnessed a vast explosion of literature in many new forms and genres. The best introduction to this literature is P. Dronke, "Il secolo XII," in *Letteratura latina medievale (secoli VI–XV): un manuale*, ed. C. Leonardi (Florence, 2002), 231–302.

63. *Sextus Amarcius: Sermones*, ed. K. Manitius, MGH, Quellen zur Geistesgeschichte des Mittelalters 6 (Weimar, 1969), 136.

64. R. B. C. Huygens, ed., *Accessus ad Auctores, Bernard d'Utrecht, Conrad d'Hirsau: Dialogus super auctores; Edition critique* (Leiden, 1970), 88–90 (Sedulius), 91–92 (Juvencus), 96–97 (Arator).

65. Manitius, *Geschichte der lateinischen Literatur*, 3:820–31.

66. It has recently been shown that Peter also added a versification of the Book of Ezra to his enterprise; see G. Dinkova-Bruun, "The Story of Ezra: A Versification Added to Peter Riga's *Aurora*," in *Anglo-Latin and its Heritage*, ed. S. Eckard and G. R. Wieland, Publications of the Journal of Medieval Latin 4 (Turnhout, 2001), 163–88.

67. Bruno of Asti, *Expositio in Exodum*, *PL* 164, cols. 233–378; the passage in Bruno which was versified in the lines quoted above is found at cols. 264–66.

68. K. Young, "Chaucer and Peter Riga," *Speculum* 12 (1937): 299–303.

69. *Aurora: Petri Rigae Biblia Versificata; A Verse Commentary on the Bible*, ed. P. E. Beichner, 2 vols., Publications in Medieval Studies 19 (Notre Dame, Ind., 1965).

70. G. Antonelli, "Per il testo dell'*Aurora* di Pietro Riga," *Studi medievali*, 3rd ser., 32 (1991): 775–87.

71. Some 230 manuscripts are listed by F. Stegmüller, *Repertorium Biblicum Medii Aevi*, 11 vols. (Madrid, 1940–80), 4:380–382. Greti Dinkova-Bruun ("Story of Ezra," 163n.2) reports that she has identified "at least 400 manuscripts," but no printed account of her findings has yet been published.

72. See J. A. Corbett, *Catalogue of the Medieval and Renaissance Manuscripts of the University of Notre Dame* (Notre Dame, Ind., 1978), 48–50 (MS 5), 62–65 (MS 8).

73. Since delivering the inaugural lecture I have consulted some twenty manuscripts of the *Aurora* in British libraries (and have no intention whatsoever of consulting any more). These manuscripts broadly confirm the impression created by the Notre Dame manuscripts. The following contain virtually no glossing and no sign of classroom use: Cambridge, University Library, MS Ll. 5. 15; Cambridge, Trinity College, MSS B. 2. 23, B. 5. 21, B. 14. 2; Cambridge, Corpus Christi College, MSS 83, 397 part III, 520; London, British Library, MSS Additional 11883, Additional 31828, Arundel 226, Arundel 228, Harley 6578 (a very few glosses, but the parchment is supple and well-thumbed, indicating that the book was read), Royal 2. D. XXIII; Oxford, Bodleian Library, MSS Laud misc. 82, Laud misc. 242 (very sporadic glossing), Laud misc. 576 (sporadic marginal glosses), Rawlinson C. 132, Rawlinson C. 315 (sporadic glosses). Among the *Aurora* manuscripts which I consulted, only three show clear evidence of scholarly or classroom use: Cambridge, Corpus Christi College, MS 217 (the fact that the *Aurora* is accompanied by Matthew of Vendôme's *Tobias* and Alexander Nequam's *Corrogationes Promethei* marks the manuscript as a schoolbook); London, British Library, MS Sloane 1726 (margins ruled for glossing; and provided with extensive interpretative glosses); and Oxford, Bodleian Library, MS Rawlinson C. 51 (margins ruled for glossing, and heavily glossed throughout).

# "He Knew Nat Catoun"

## Medieval School-Texts and Middle English Literature

JILL MANN

MY TITLE IS—AS MOST READERS WILL KNOW—A QUOTATION from Chaucer's *Miller's Tale*. Introducing the elderly Oxford carpenter John and his beautiful young wife Alisoun, Chaucer comments on their disparity in age:

> He knew nat Catoun, for his wit was rude,
> That bad man sholde wedde his simylitude.
> (3227–28)[1]

By "Cato," Chaucer means the Latin proverb-collection known as the *Distichs of Cato* (*Disticha Catonis*), a work composed neither by Cato the Censor nor his great-grandson Cato of Utica, but the production of an anonymous author who probably lived in the third century A.D.[2] It is addressed by the author to his "dearest son," as is traditional in wisdom-literature (a term denoting works that impart moral instruction by means of proverbs or exemplary anecdotes). It begins with simple admonitory phrases ("pray to God"; "love your parents"), but the bulk of the work is made up of hexameter couplets, as the title implies. They teach elementary morality and homely wisdom: don't sleep too long, don't talk too much, love other people but don't neglect your own interests, don't believe your wife when she complains about the servants, don't trust flattery, and so on. This combination of simple Latin and simple morality earned the *Distichs of Cato* the first place in the elementary reading programme for students of Latin—a place which it held for over 1,400 years. After having memorized the psalter and basic liturgical texts (the Lord's Prayer, Ave Maria, Creed, and Ten Commandments), the young student would begin a course of secular reading with "Cato,"[3] not only construing but also memorizing the text so that it entered into his very bones. In saying that his Oxford carpenter did not know "Cato," therefore, Chaucer is saying that he had not reached even the bottom rung on the educational ladder, since "his wit was rude"; he is fated to be outsmarted and cuckolded by the clever young Oxford student Nicholas, who is his lodger, and who is as adept in sexual matters as he is in Latin learning.

In this instance, however, Chaucer's memory seems to have played him a trick. For the piece of proverbial advice that he is quoting does not come from "Cato" at all, but from another, very similar, but much later proverb-collection known in the Middle Ages as the *Facetus* (the word is an adjective meaning "courtly" or "urbane" or "polite," reflecting the work's aim of teaching good behaviour).[4] Like the *Distichs of Cato*, the *Facetus* consists of hexameter couplets, but in this case they are rhymed hexameters. It is around 250 lines long, but the number and order of the proverbial couplets varies considerably from manuscript to manuscript, as is natural in a work that lends itself so easily to abbreviation and expansion.[5] The date of the *Facetus* can be fixed only by circumstantial evidence, but it seems likely to have been composed in the twelfth century.[6] The opening of the work declares it to be a supplement to the *Distichs of Cato*, and it inculcates the same sort of basic morality: honour your parents (12); do as you would be done by (13); be careful whom you trust (23); don't talk too much (24). The couplet to which Chaucer is referring is apparently the following:[7]

> Duc tibi prole parem morumque vigore venustam,
> Si cum pace [*var.* pare] velis vitam deducere iustam.
>
> (*Facetus* 62)

> Take a wife who is your peer in birth and beautified by moral excellence if you want to lead a righteous life in peace.[8]

However, in addition to moral precepts of this sort, the *Facetus* also contains instruction in elementary good manners: don't laugh at people when they fall over (36); don't take a drink while you have food in your mouth (53); don't wipe your runny nose, eyes, or teeth with your table-napkin, or dry your wet hands on your clothes (56); don't put your elbows on the table (72); keep your legs covered with your robe (91); don't point (106); if you're sharing a bed with someone who is your social equal or superior, ask on which side of the bed he would prefer to sleep (74), and so on.

This "courtesy-book" element is taken one step further in another Latin text which is also called *Facetus*; the two texts are usually distinguished by their opening words, and referred to, respectively, as the *Facetus* "Cum nihil utilius" and the *Facetus* "Moribus et vita."[9] The *Facetus* "Moribus et vita" also seems to date from the twelfth century,[10] but it is written in elegiac verse rather than hexameters. It is largely devoted, not to moral wisdom, but to instructions on how to seduce girls—how to dress, how to speak and behave, how to choose a suitable girl, and how to make bold physical advances when one is lucky enough to find her alone, including the advice that the lover should ignore her refusals, however strenuous they are, since nice girls expect to be conquered by force (only prostitutes show no reluctance). If the carpenter of the *Miller's Tale* is ignorant of the *Facetus* "Cum nihil utilius," it seems that his lodger Nicholas is well versed in the techniques taught by the amatory *Facetus*.[11]

The *Facetus* "Cum nihil utilius" survives in numerous manuscripts, one of which is University of Notre Dame, MS 6.[12] The Notre Dame manuscript is clearly designed for use as a school-text: it is small in size (125 mm by 150 mm), and the written text occupies a single quire, originally of ten leaves (the last leaf has been cut away and only a stub remains). An outer bifolium, originally left blank on both sides, serves as guard leaves. A later hand has written the opening of St John's gospel on the recto and verso of the last leaf; on the verso, the text is so badly worn as to be virtually illegible.[13] In other words, the quire was intended to be used in an unbound state. Extra proverbs, not contained in the main body of the text, are crammed into the upper and lower margins, suggesting that more than one examplar was consulted and additional material added in. An interesting feature of the manuscript, which is probably to be accounted for by its use as a school-text, is that there are several changes of hand, which begin ten lines down on f. 6r. (By a happy coincidence, the first change occurs four lines after the couplet that Chaucer alludes to in the *Miller's Tale*; fig. 2.1 shows both.) There seems to be another such change at the second line on f. 7r, and yet another at the top of f. 7v (figs. 2.2–2.3). At least two of these hands have an awkward and unpractised air. It is interesting to speculate why so many scribes should be needed to copy so brief a text, and why the later hands copy such small portions of it. To me, it looks as if the first part of the manuscript was copied by a teacher, and the latter part by his pupils, who were learning to read, write, and behave like civilized human beings all at the same time.

This little manuscript of the *Facetus* offers a fascinating glimpse into the world of medieval school-texts. These are the texts that everyone (or at least every person educated in Latin) knew, the texts that were memorized, quoted, translated into the vernacular, adapted, parodied, and creatively transformed throughout the Middle Ages. Many texts of many different kinds were used in this way, but there is a recognizable and surprisingly consistent group of works that served as a sort of core curriculum. These core texts can be identified in various ways. In the first place, there is the evidence of the manuscripts themselves. In a classic article (so classic it was written in Latin), published in 1914, Marc Boas identified six texts which seem to travel together as a group in medieval manuscripts, and which were listed as school-texts in other sources.[14] These six texts are:

1. The *Distichs of Cato.*
2. A debate-poem known as the *Eclogue of Theodulus*, in which a male goatherd called Pseustis (Falsehood) argues with a shepherdess called Alithia (Truth) about the relative value of pagan and Christian myths.[15] For example, Pseustis summarises the myth of Saturn and the age of gold, and Alithia replies by referring to the garden of Eden and the fall of Adam. Deucalion's flood is matched by a reference to Noah; the attack of the giants on Olympus is matched by a reference to the tower of Babel. The usefulness of this poem as a school-text lies in its pairing of pagan and Christian myths,

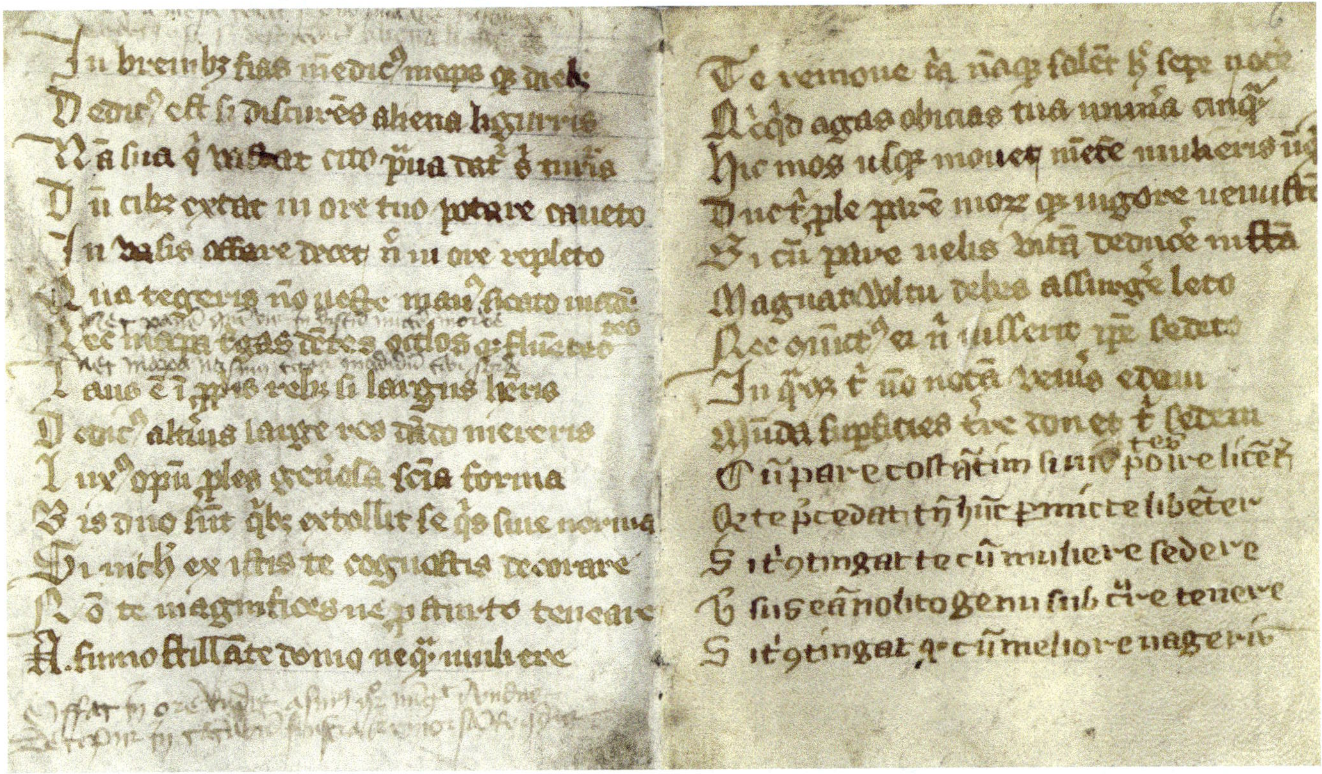

FIG. 2.1. University of Notre Dame, MS 6, ff. 5v–6r. Reproduced from the original held by the Department of Special Collections of the University Libraries of Notre Dame.

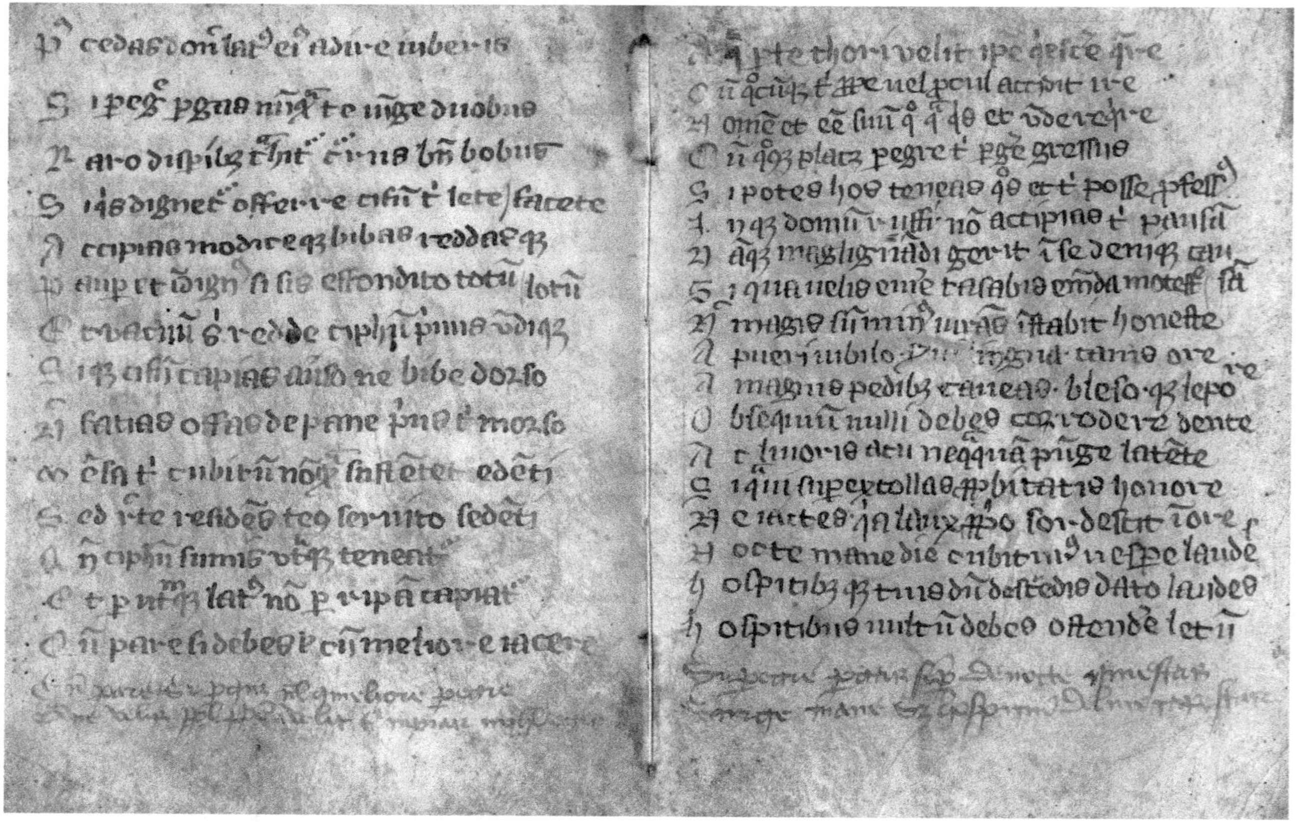

FIG. 2.2. University of Notre Dame, MS 6, ff. 6v–7r. Reproduced from the original held by the Department of Special Collections of the University Libraries of Notre Dame.

FIG. 2.3. University of Notre Dame, MS 6, ff. 7v–8r. Reproduced from the original held by the Department of Special Collections of the University Libraries of Notre Dame.

equipping young students with a double training in classical and Christian literature.

3. The fables of Avianus (fourth century?), which provide narrative interest alongside the same kind of proverbial wisdom as the *Distichs of Cato.*[16]
4. The elegies of the sixth-century poet Maximian[17]—a strange choice, it might be thought, since they are the musings of an old man on the erotic pleasures of his youth and his present impotence, but perhaps they were intended to hold the male student's interest.
5. The poem *On the Rape of Proserpina* by Claudian (writing at the turn of the fourth and fifth centuries).[18] Again, this is a slightly surprising choice, especially as the work is unfinished, but its brevity might have been an advantage in this context. Numerous manuscripts of the work are of a clearly "school-text" character—such as the one that bears the jotting "Willelmus Cayso est pravus puer."[19]
6. The *Achilleis* of Statius, (end of the first century A.D.), a minor epic that familarized the student with classical themes.[20]

Boas dubbed this group the *libri catoniani;* later scholars sometimes refer to it as the *liber Catonis* or the *liber catonianus,* a title which has misled some into thinking that the *liber Catonis* is a florilegium or anthology of excerpts. This is not the case; the texts are complete, but they are brought together to form a coherent and manageable reading programme for students of Latin. As evidence for the consistency of this grouping, Boas cited sixteen manuscripts. Rino Avesani objected that only eight of these manuscripts exactly fit Boas's model of the *liber Catonis;* in the others either one or more of the six texts is lacking, or other texts are interspersed with them. The order in which the texts appear also varies.[21] Avesani concluded that the picture is much richer and more varied than Boas allowed. Later scholarship has confirmed that the *liber Catonis* is not so much a fixed entity as a theme on which endless variations are played. For example, Elisabeth Pellegrin identified seven manuscripts in which "Cato" and the *Eclogue of Theodulus* are accompanied by Ovid's *Remedia amoris* (which may be seen as a replacement or equivalent for Maximian), and the *Tobias* of Matthew of Vendôme (which perhaps represents the replacement of classical epic with biblical narrative).[22] Similar manuscript groupings of texts with the *Distichs of Cato* at their core are described in the first volume of Tony Hunt's monumental work, *Teaching and Learning Latin in Thirteenth-Century England.*[23]

The numerous lists of school-texts contained in medieval outlines of educational programmes confirm that these school-text groupings were deliberately and purposefully created, rather than the result of happenstance. An early example is the *Ars lectoria* of an eleventh-century grammarian called Aimeric, which grades pagan authors as "gold" (Vergil, Ovid, Horace, etc.), "silver" (Plautus, Boethius, Donatus, etc.) and finally "tin" or "lead".[24] This last group consists of "Cato," the abridged version of the *Iliad* in Latin,[25] Maximian, Avianus, and "Aesop," which is at this date most likely to be the prose version of the fables of Phaedrus known as the *Romulus vulgaris.*[26] Conrad of Hirsau's *Dialogue on Authors*, written in the twelfth century, provides a similar list.[27] This work is cast in the form of a dialogue between a teacher and a rather cheeky student, who like many students imagines that his teacher has nothing to do when not actually engaged in instructing him. He begins "since I see that you have long been enjoying leisure and silence, which is of no value in eradicating my ignorance, I shall take the opportunity of rousing you to the fulfilment of your promise"—that is (as he goes on to explain), the promise of outlining an educational program of authors, both "minores" and "majores," which he should study in order. The teacher outlines a rather ambitious reading course of twenty-one Latin authors, beginning with Donatus's grammar and then proceeding in the usual manner to "Cato" and Avianus; the *Eclogue of Theodulus* turns up in eighth position. The familiar programme is also evident in the so-called *Accessus ad auctores*, aids to study which give basic information about medieval authors and their works.[28] Huygens's edition of the *Accessus* summarises the authors and works treated in three manuscripts, and, despite the variations between the three, the sequence Cato-Avianus-Maximian, Latin *Iliad*, *Eclogue of Theodulus* is clearly recognisable. In the thirteenth century, a long and detailed list of school-authors is given in the *Laborintus* of Eberhard of Bremen, a teacher at the cathedral school; again it is headed by "Cato," the *Eclogue of Theodulus*, Avianus, "Aesop" (identifiable by verbal allusion as the version of Phaedrus's fables in elegiac verse),[29]

Maximian, Claudian's *Rape of Proserpina*, and the *Achilleis* of Statius, but continues at great length through other classical and medieval authors.[30]

The lists of authors could on occasion assume more fanciful forms—as, for example, in the thirteenth-century poem lamenting a dead teacher of grammar called Ambrose, in which the school-texts that he taught are represented as weeping for his loss.[31] In a long list of names, "Cato," Statius, Claudian, the *Facetus*, the *Eclogue of Theodulus*, Maximian, "Aesop," and Avianus all put in an appearance. Another flight of fancy takes the form of a pseudo-autobiographical poem in Old French, in which a jongleur laments the progressive loss of all his books through obsessive gambling.[32] The order in which the books have supposedly been lost corresponds to the order in which they would have been read, so that the educational curriculum is comically transformed into a kind of rake's progress. The list begins with the ABC and the Pater Noster, followed by the Creed, psalter, and liturgical manuscripts. Next comes the familiar sequence of the *libri catoniani:*

| | |
|---|---|
| Grant partie de mes auctors | I left many of my authors |
| Lessai à Saint-Martin de Tors. | at Saint-Martin of Tours. |
| Et mes Donès est à Orliens, | And my Donatus is at Orléans, |
| Et mes Chatonès à Amiens, | and my Cato is at Amiens, |
| A Chartres mes Theodelet, | my *Theodulus* is at Chartres, |
| A Roem mes Avionès. | and my Avianus at Rouen. |
| | (35–40) |

The familiar authors also appear in the *Battle of the Seven Arts* by the thirteenth-century poet Henri d'Andeli, a comic dramatization of the struggle between "Grammar," the humanist literature studied at Orléans, and "Dialectic," the Aristotelian logic which was displacing the study of classical literature in Paris. Cato, Avianus, the *Eclogue* of Theodulus, and the *Achilleis* of Statius fight together on the side of Grammar.[33]

The longest and fullest reading programme is contained in the *Registrum multorum auctorum* of Hugo of Trimberg, a thirteenth- or early fourteenth-century teacher at Bamberg, which groups authors for study according to chronology or type, and gives their opening words as an aid to identification (a librarian's dream).[34] Hugo's work is divided into three sections ("distinctiones"), the third of which lists "auctores minores." It begins with "Cato," "Aesop" (identifiable as the elegiac *Romulus*), Avianus, and Maximian. Next comes a group of Latin *comediae*, twelfth-century works in dramatic form (though probably intended for reading rather than acting). The first one named is the *Pamphilus*, which is the name of its hero;[35] it recounts his wooing of a girl named Galatea. This was an enormously popular work in the Middle Ages, surviving in at least fifty-nine complete manuscripts and represented in numerous florilegia.[36] There are verbal parallels between the *Pamphilus* and the *Facetus* "Moribus et vita" (the amatory one);[37] it is tempting to see the latter as the theoretical codification of the *Pamphilus*'s practice. And indeed the amatory *Facetus* appears only a little later in Hugo's list. The "moral" *Facetus* ("Cum nihil utilius") appears in the second part of Hugo's third "distinctio," where it is followed by a "Novus Facetus" (also called *Phagifacetus*),[38] which is another work on social etiquette, especially table manners, a "Novus Cato" (an adaptation of "Cato" into leonine hexameters),[39] and a "Novus Aesopus," which is said to improve on the old Aesop by interpolating many proverbs (this last is unidentifiable, since no work beginning with the first line given by Hugo is known).

These last works exemplify a notable feature of the medieval educational curriculum—namely, the way in which it was continually renewed and updated by the production of new texts which followed the old models but recast them into different verse forms, brought in new material, or provided replacements which fulfilled similar functions to the originals.[40] Thus, for example, the *Pamphilus* could be seen as an updating of Maximian, preserving an erotic element in the curriculum to hold the interest of the young (male) reader. The *Facetus* "Moribus et vita" likewise caters to this erotic interest, but combines it with the instructional mode of "Cato." The *Distichs of Cato* themselves inspired a long series of later imitations and competitors, some of which, like the *Facetus* "Cum nihil utilius," aimed to supplement "Cato," whereas others were intended to supplant it with material of a more Christian complexion. One way of doing this was to assemble collections of proverbs from the Solomonic books of the Bible; an example dating from the mid-eleventh century is the *Delicie cleri* of Arnulf of Orléans, where the Solomonic proverbs are cast into hexameter distichs—that is, into the verse-form of "Cato."[41] Otloh of St. Emmeran, a teacher at a monastic school, makes clear that his *Proverbia* are a Christian version of "Cato"; he reproves teachers who customarily use the fables of Avianus and the *Distichs of Cato* as first texts for their pupils, "not paying attention to the fact that to the young as well as to the elders among the faithful in Christ, Christian rather than pagan rudiments should be first set forth," so that once they have a secure grasp of the good, they can proceed safely to secular literature.[42] Attempts were also made to "Christianize" "Cato" by means of commentaries accompanying his text.[43] But not all the imitations of "Cato" were of this Christianizing sort. For example, the *Fecunda ratis* of Egbert of Liège, an eleventh-century schoolteacher,[44] is a kind of expansion of and replacement for both "Cato" and Avianus: it moves from one-line proverbs to two-line proverbs, apparently drawn from popular speech, and thence to short fables and narrative anecdotes. Egbert tells us in his preface that his work was written for boys to memorize, so that "when the teachers are from time to time absent, and the group of boys babble empty jingles among themselves, as if they would sharpen their wits by the recitation of these chants, then they should make use of these instead."[45] The twelfth century saw the production of the proverb-collection written by Peter Abelard for his son Astrolabe,[46] the proverbs of Serlo of Wilton (a teacher at Paris and at Oxford),[47] and the *Parabolae* of Alan of Lille.[48] One of the manuscripts of this last work is University of Notre Dame, MS 55. Completely different from the *Facetus* manuscript, it is a fifteenth-century paper manuscript, written in an impeccably neat and tidy hand with the text in a single column, leaving wide and empty margins (contrast the *Facetus* manuscript, where the upper and lower margins are crammed with additions). So far from representing the untidy world of everyday manuscript use, the *Parabolae* manuscript seems to reflect the age of print. And indeed, Alan's *Parabolae* was one of the so-called "Auctores octo," a revised, print-age version of the *liber Catonis* grouping, which was first printed at Lyons in 1488 and went through fifty editions by 1544.[49] In this revised group, "Cato" and the *Eclogue of Theodulus* hold their place, but Claudian, Maximian, and so on have been replaced by medieval works: the *Facetus* "Cum nihil utilius," Alan's *Parabolae*, the *Tobias* of Matthew of Vendôme,[50] a poem in the "contemptus mundi" tradition beginning "Cartula nostra,"[51] and the *Floretus*, a verse summary of basic Christian dogma, such as the Creed, the Ten Commandments, the Seven Deadly Sins, and so on.[52]

The other genres represented in the *Liber catonis* group were likewise constantly renewed through variations on the old themes. The *Eclogue of Theodulus* was probably an inspiration for the numerous Latin debate-poems written in the twelfth and thirteenth centuries.[53] Fable-collections proliferated. Medieval epics, such as the *Alexandreis* of Walter of Châtillon and the *Fall of Troy* by Joseph of Exeter, decked out antique themes with all the embellishments of modern (that is, medieval) rhetoric.[54] A present-day academic must stand awed by the energy and productiveness of medieval pedagogues, who without tenure review or research assessment exercises to spur them on, poured forth this stream of educational textbooks.

But what was the effect of all this educational activity on medieval literature—other than the obvious fact that generation after generation of students learned to read and write Latin? In the space remaining to me, I want to consider some of the ways in which these Latin school-texts left their mark on Middle English literature. I shall mostly be talking about the *Canterbury Tales*, but I shall end with a brief reference to *Piers Plowman*.

The *Canterbury Tales* are saturated with references to medieval school-texts. It is not surprising, given Chaucer's love of proverbs, that he often quotes the *Distichs of Cato*, sometimes anonymously, sometimes by name.[55] In the *Nun's Priest's Tale*, Pertelote quotes "Cato" in support of her advice to "take no heed of dreams" (2940–41; *Distichs of Cato* II.31). In the *Merchant's Tale*, Cato's injunction to maintain a dignified silence in the face of a wife's scolding tongue—

> Uxoris linguam, si frugi est, ferre memento;
> namque malum est non velle pati nec posse tacere.
> (III.23)

> Remember to put up with your wife's tongue, if she is thrifty, for it is a bad thing to be unwilling to suffer and to be unable to keep silence.

—is ironically applied to masculine helplessness in the face of wifely nagging:

Suffre thy wyves tonge, as Catoun bit;
She shal comande, and thou shalt suffren it.
(1377–78)

When the suspicious Canon and his Yeoman unexpectedly join the Canterbury pilgrims as they near their goal, a proverb from "Cato" is used to explain the Canon's suspicion of what his servant is saying to the Host:

Whil this Yeman was thus in his talkyng,
This Chanoun drough hym neer and herde al thyng
Which this Yeman spak, for suspecioun
Of mennes speche evere hadde this Chanoun.
For Catoun seith that he that gilty is
Demeth alle thyng be spoke of hym, ywis.
(684–89)

Ne cures, si quis tacito sermone loquatur:
conscius ipse sibi de se putat omnia dici.
(*Distichs of Cato* I.17)

Take no notice if someone is speaking sotto voce; a self-conscious person thinks that he is the subject of every conversation.

I pass over other examples where "Cato" is quoted without being mentioned by name but shall return to one such example later on.

Other school-text proverb-collections also put in an appearance in the *Canterbury Tales.* We have already seen that the *Facetus* is cited in the *Miller's Tale*; Alan of Lille's *Parabolae* is clearly the source of a pair of familiar proverbs which appear in exactly the same order in the *Canon's Yeoman's Tale*:

But al thyng which that shineth as the gold
Nis nat gold, as that I have herd told;
Ne every appul that is fair at eye
Ne is nat good, what so men clappe or crye.
(962–65)

Though these are familiar English proverbs, the source of these lines is evidently Alan:

> Non teneas aurum totum quod splendet ut aurum
> nec pulchrum pomum quodlibet esse bonum.
> (*Parabolae* III.217–18)

> Don't think that everything that shines like gold is gold, and don't think that every beautiful apple is a good one.

A Latin gloss in the margin of the Ellesmere manuscript of Chaucer clinches the allusion by quoting the first few words of each of these lines.

These examples demonstrate how the memorization that played so great a part in medieval education made the proverbs of "Cato" and later writers part of everyone's mental furniture; proverbs that we would associate with oral culture are stamped with a textual and Latinate character. They are the stock-in-trade of "clerkes." This is made very clear in the longest passage of the *Canterbury Tales* to draw on "Cato," the ending of the *Manciple's Tale.* This is the story about the talking crow who tells his master, the god Phebus, of his wife's adultery, and who is punished for his blunt truth-telling by being turned from white to black and having his beautiful singing voice turned into a pitiful squawk. The Manciple draws from this tale the simple moral that one should in general keep one's mouth shut.

> Lordynges, by this ensample I yow preye,
> Beth war, and taketh kep what that ye seye:
> Ne telleth nevere no man in youre lyf
> How that another man hath dight his wyf;
> He wol yow haten mortally, certeyn.
> (309–13)

This is a lesson that he claims was taught him by his mother, and he goes on to quote her words to him at length. The fictional address by the mother licenses the frequent use of the phrase "my sone," and so casts the passage into the form traditional in both the Solomonic books of the Bible and in secular wisdom-literature, the admonition by a father to a son or teacher to a pupil.[56] The precepts quoted by the Manciple interestingly blend Solomon with "Cato" in the manner that we have seen to be characteristic of the proverb-tradition as a whole: quotations from the Book of Proverbs are interwoven with renderings of the *Distichs of Cato.*

Daun Salomon, as wise clerkes seyn,
Techeth a man to kepe his tonge weel. [Prov. 21:23]
But, as I sayde, I am noght textueel.
But nathelees, thus taughte me my dame:
"My sone, thenk on the crowe, a Goddes name!
My sone, kepe wel thy tonge, and keep thy freend . . .
My sone, God of his endelees goodnesse
Walled a tonge with teeth and lippes eke,
For man shold hym avyse what he speeke.
My sone, ful ofte, for to muche speche
Hath many a man been spilt, as clerkes teche,
But for litel speche avysely
Is no man shent, to speke generally. [*Distichs of Cato* I.12b]
My sone, thy tonge sholdestow restreyne
At alle tymes, but whan thou doost thy peyne
To speke of God, in honour and preyere.
The firste vertu, sone, if thou wolt leere,
Is to restreyne and kepe wel thy tonge; [*Distichs of Cato* I.3]
Thus lerne children whan that they been yonge.
My sone, of muchel spekyng yvele avysed,
Ther lasse spekyng hadde ynough suffised,
Comth muchel harm; thus was me toold and taught.
In muchel speche synne wanteth naught. [Prov. 10:19]
Wostow wherof a rakel tonge serveth?
Right as a swerd forkutteth and forkerveth
An arm a-two, my deere sone, right so
A tonge kutteth freendshipe al a-two.
A jangler is to God abhomynable. [Prov. 6:17]
Reed Salomon, so wys and honurable;
Reed David in his psalmes; reed Senekke.

My sone, spek nat, but with thyn heed thou bekke . . .
My sone, be war, and be noon auctour newe
Of tidynges, wheither they been false or trewe. [*Distichs of Cato* I.12a]
Whereso thou come, amonges hye or lowe,
Kepe wel thy tonge and thenk upon the crowe.

(314–19, 322–46, 359–62)

At the heart of this passage is one of the earliest Catonian distichs:

Virtutem primam esse puto, compescere linguam:
proximus ille deo est qui scit ratione tacere.

(I.3)

In my view the first virtue is to hold one's tongue; he who knows how to keep a wise silence is akin to God.

Preceding and following this distich are the two halves of I.12:

Rumores fuge neu studeas novus auctor haberi;
nam nulli tacuisse nocet, nocet esse locutum.

Flee gossip and do not set it going, for it harms no one to have kept silent, but it does to have spoken.

The origin of this proverbial wisdom in the early learning situation is repeatedly emphasised by such phrases as "as wise clerkes seyn" (314), "as clerkes teche" (326), or "Thus lerne children whan that they been yonge" (334).[57]

The role assigned to "Cato" in this passage is rather a depressing one. That is, it closes down speech and truncates linguistic expression, reducing communication to rudimentary words and gestures (346). It is, of course, ironic that the Manciple takes so many words to warn against excessive speech, so that his admonitions undermine their own content. But it remains true that it is the minimalist character of proverbs that is important here. The beauty and creativity that characterise both Phebus and his crow at the beginning of the tale are destroyed by the end: Phebus has broken his musical instruments in remorse at having killed his wife, and he has reduced the bird's musicality, as I said before, to an ugly squawk. Art and beauty are, it seems, an illusion, simply ways of masking the ugly reality that the crow communicates to his master in the lowest common denominator of language, the jeering "Cokkow! Cokkow! Cokkow!" with which he informs him that he has been cuckolded. In this context, the final appeal to "Cato" is a similar return to basics, to the threadbare, everyday morality that best fits a cynical view of the world.

Against this bleak picture, however, we can set the more positive example of the *Franklin's Tale*, where the simple proverb "Patience conquers" becomes the foundation of a richly human ethic, exemplified in the loving marriage of Dorigen and Arveragus. Having related Arveragus's offer to relinquish the power that a medieval husband might legitimately claim over his wife, Chaucer praises this voluntary surrender as an example of patience.

> Pacience is an heigh vertu, certeyn,
> For it venquysseth, as thise clerkes seyn,
> Thynges that rigour sholde nevere atteyne.
> For every word men may nat chide or pleyne.
> Lerneth to suffre, or elles, so moot I goon,
> Ye shul it lerne, wher so ye wole or noon.
>
> (773–78)

At the centre of this passage is the familiar proverb "Patientia vincit" ("Patience conquers"). In the *Distichs of Cato* it appears in a somewhat elaborated form which fits it to the usual hexameter couplet:

> Quem superare potes interdum vince ferendo;
> maxima enim est hominum semper patientia virtus.
>
> (I.38)

> If you are able to conquer anyone, you should sometimes conquer him by yielding; for patience is always the greatest human virtue.

Numerous manuscripts of the *Distichs* gloss these lines with an elegiac couplet that had an independent circulation as a proverb:

Nobile vincendi genus est paciencia. Vincit
qui patitur. Si vis vincere, disce pati.[58]

Patience is a noble form of conquering. He who suffers, conquers.
If you wish to conquer, learn to suffer.

The Latin phrase "disce pati" is very close to Chaucer's "Lerneth to suffer."[59] I have argued before that this idea of "active patience"—that is, the willed acceptance of adversity, on every level from the heroic renunciation of Griselda to the minute adjustments of mood and behaviour envisaged in this passage of the *Franklin's Tale*—is Chaucer's most serious ideal of human behaviour.[60] It is not simply the inculcation of patience, but the mysterious paradox that patience conquers, that his narratives represent. As with the references to Cato in the *Manciple's Tale*, the clerical origins of this dictum are emphasised: Patience vanquishes "*as thise clerkes seyn.*" But it is not something to be known with the intellect alone; rather, it is internalised through experience, whether the hard way or the easy way.

Lerneth to suffre, or elles, so moot I goon,
Ye shul it lerne, wher so ye wole or noon.
(777–78)

I shall return to proverbs at my close, when glancing briefly at *Piers Plowman.* For the moment, I want to turn to other medieval school-texts that put in an appearance in the *Canterbury Tales.* The references to Avianus and the *Eclogue of Theodulus* are tantalisingly oblique.[61] With Maximian and Claudian, however, the allusions are clear and unequivocal.[62] Maximian is the source of one of the most haunting figures in the *Canterbury Tales,* the old man in the *Pardoner's Tale* who is encountered by the three profligate youths ("riotoures," as Chaucer calls them) who have set out to find and slay the scoundrel called Death, because he has killed one of their fellows. The old man too is looking for death, which always eludes him. To their mindless question as to why he is so old, he replies that it is because he cannot find a young man willing to swap ages with him, and also because Death will not take his life.

"Thus walke I, lyk a restelees kaityf,
And on the ground, which is my moodres gate,
I knokke with my staf, bothe erly and late,
And seye, 'Leeve mooder, leet me in!
Lo how I vanysshe, flessh, and blood, and skyn!
Allas, whan shul my bones been at reste?
Mooder, with yow wolde I chaunge my cheste
That in my chambre longe tyme hath be,
Ye, for an heyre clowt to wrappe me!'
But yet to me she wol nat do that grace,
For which ful pale and welked is my face."

(728–38)

These lines clearly echo a passage in Maximian's first elegy, as G. L. Kittredge long ago pointed out.[63] In this elegy, Maximian laments his old age and looks forward to death as a relief.

Aemula quid cessas finem properare senectus?
  cur et in hoc fesso corpore tarda venis?
solve precor miseram tali de carcere vitam:
  mors est iam requies, vivere poena mihi.

(1–4)

Jealous old age, why are you slow to hasten the end? And why do you come so late to my tired body? I beg you, release my wretched life from this prison: to me, death is now peace, and life a punishment.

He recalls the glories of his youth, his success as an orator, as a hunter, as an athlete, as a tragic actor. He remembers his physical hardiness, his ability to eat little and drink a lot. He dwells at length on how attractive he was to women, and how picky he could afford to be in choosing only the most perfect specimens of female beauty for his erotic enjoyment. Nowadays, however, all his senses are enfeebled—sight, hearing, smell, taste, and touch. His complexion is blotched, his skin stiff and dry, his eyes sunken, and his hands claw-like. Switching to a third-person description of a typical old man, his clothes too big for his shrunken limbs, he describes him, like the old man in the *Pardoner's Tale*, as striking on the earth with his staff and begging to be taken into it.

> ortus cuncta suos repetunt matremque requirunt,
> et redit ad nihilum, quod fuit ante nihil.
> hinc est quod baculo incumbens ruitura senectus
> assiduo pigram verbere pulsat humum
> et numerosa movens certo vestigia plausu
> talia rugato creditur ore loqui:
> "suscipe me, genetrix, nati miserere laborum:
> membra peto gremio fessa fovere tuo.
> horrent me pueri, nequeo velut ante videri:
> horrendos partus cur sinis esse tuos?
> nil mihi cum superis: explevi munera vitae:
> redde precor patrio mortua membra solo.
> quid miseros variis prodest extendere poenis?
> non est materni pectoris ista pati."
>
> (221–34)

> All things return to their origins, and seek out their mother, and that which was first nothing becomes nothing again. So it is that the old man, on the brink of destruction, leaning on his staff, strikes the inert earth with frequent blows; shuffling his many footsteps to its steady beat, he is imagined speaking thus with his wrinkled lips: "Receive me, O mother; take pity on the travails of your son. I seek to rest my tired limbs in your bosom. Children are afraid of me; my former looks are gone. Why do you allow your children to become monstrous? I have nothing to do with the world; I have exhausted life's gifts. I beg you, take back my dead limbs to their natal earth. What use is it to torture the wretched with multiple sufferings? It is not in the nature of a mother's heart to allow this."

One of the Middle English lyrics in Oxford, Bodleian Library, MS Digby 86 (ff. 134v–136v) is a free rendering of this elegy of Maximian, but it reduces the striking image of the old man beating on the earth to a simple wish to die.[64] Chaucer, however, seized on this image and introduced it into the *Pardoner's Tale*, where it takes on a sinister quality that makes it the central enigma of the tale. Some critics have tried to solve this enigma by suggesting that the old man *is* Death, unrecognized by the three youths who are searching for him.[65] But this interpretation blurs a central point of the tale, which is precisely that death is not a substance (in linguistic terms, a substantive); in searching for a personified death, the rioters are guilty of an obtusely literal approach to language. One "finds death" only by *being dead;* the end of the search is the obliteration of the searcher. In this sense, the rioters certainly find death. The old man directs them to a heap of gold, and they murder each other in the hope of increasing their share of it. In one of the analogues of the *Pardoner's Tale*, the rioters learn of the heap of gold by encountering a hermit who is fleeing from it and crying "Death! death!"[66] The hermit's response is a conventionally moral one. Chaucer's replacement of this figure with Maximian's picture of the old man who seeks in vain to die is a more imaginatively powerful way of indicating the complex human relationship to death as simultaneous presence and absence.

Claudian's *Rape of Proserpina* is similarly transformed by context in the *Merchant's Tale*.[67] Like the *Miller's Tale*, this is a story about an old man, January, who is cuckolded by his young wife, May. January is, however, not only old but also blind, and keeps his hand on his wife at all times, which makes adultery difficult. She manages to trick him by arranging a rendezvous with her lover Damian in a pear-tree, which she will climb, ostensibly for the pears, while January embraces its trunk (unaware that Damian is already up in the tree). At this point Chaucer unexpectedly introduces into the narrative the figures of Pluto and Proserpina, who, equally unexpectedly, are said to be the King and Queen of Fairyland. Despite this claim, it is evident that their origins are in Claudian's text, to which Chaucer explicitly refers.

And so bifel, that brighte morwe-tyde
That in that gardyn, in the ferther syde,
Pluto, that is kyng of Fayerye,
And many a lady in his compaignye,
Folwynge his wyf, the queene Proserpyna,
Which that he ravysshed out of [Ethna]

Whil that she gadered floures in the mede—
In Claudyan ye may the stories rede,
How in his grisely carte he hire fette—
(2225–33)

The scene to which Chaucer alludes is a dramatic and terrifying one. Pluto's chariot bursts up out of the underworld with the explosive power of a volcano, terrifying not only Proserpina and her companions, but all who hear it. He snatches her up and whirls her away, "like a lion," says Claudian, "when he has seized upon a heifer . . . and has torn with his claws the defenceless flesh and has sated his fury on all its limbs, and so stands befouled with clotted blood and shakes his tangled mane and scorns the shepherds' feeble rage."[68] Hair streaming in the wind, beating her arms in lamentation, Proserpina bewails her fate, calling on Jupiter for pity. Moved by her distress, Pluto attempts to comfort her by wiping away her tears and promising her a rosy future as Queen of the Underworld. In the *Merchant's Tale*, much time has clearly passed; Pluto and Proserpina have turned into an old married couple, with Pluto as pompously complacent husband and Proserpina as nagging wife. Observing May on the point of committing adultery, Pluto reflects sententiously on female duplicity.

This kyng of Fairye thanne adoun hym sette
Upon a bench of turves, fressh and grene,
And right anon thus seyde he to his queene:
"My wyf," quod he, "ther may no wight seye nay;
Th'experience so preveth every day
The tresons whiche that wommen doon to man.
Ten hondred thousand [tales] tellen I kan
Notable of your untrouthe and brotilnesse . . ."
(2234–41)

As I have pointed out elsewhere, *this is a rapist talking*.[69] The recollection of the scene in Claudian is essential to the perception of the irony here. The treasons done by women pale in comparison with acts of male aggression. And the scene in Claudian is also essential to the reader's appreciation of

Proserpina's reply. For the helpless victim of Claudian's narrative has now, it seems, very definitely got the upper hand. In response to Pluto's declaration that he will restore January's sight so that he can see his wife's treachery, she asserts that in that case she will grant May the ability to talk herself out of trouble. As for her husband's views on women, she replies with a long tirade against all the male "authorities," of whom Solomon is the prime example, who blame women for defects that are all their own. Pluto is reduced to weary resignation.

> "Dame," quod this Pluto, "be no lenger wrooth;
> I yeve it up!"
>
> (2311–12)

As I have also said before, he presents the ludicrous figure of a henpecked rapist.[70] This transformation of rapist and victim into henpecked husband and domineering wife is not intended to convince us that rape stories can have happy endings, but to show that female shrewishness, so far from being a natural condition, is a fair response to male aggression. Claudian's text is indispensable to perceiving the interdependence of these stereotyped gender roles, and Chaucer must have relied on his reader's knowledge of this text as a basis for understanding this comic scene.

From the ridiculous to the sublime—that is, Passus XVIII of *Piers Plowman,* in which Langland recounts Christ's Harrowing of Hell, and in which Alan of Lille's *Parabolae* play a surprising role. The Harrowing itself is preceded by a debate between the Four Daughters of God—Truth and Righteousness, Mercy and Peace—on the question of whether humankind can be saved from the damnation that is the inexorable consequence of Adam's sin. Mercy argues that they can, on the principle that "venom destroys venom," and so Christ's death will destroy death, and his guile will nullify the guile of the devil.

> And right as thorugh gilours gile bigiled was man formest,
> So shal grace that al bigan make a good ende
> And bigile the gilour—and that is good sleighte:
> *Ars ut artem falleret.*
>
> (XVIII 159–61)[71]

The Latin phrase is taken from a famous hymn by Venantius Fortunatus ("Pange, lingua"), but the English recalls the proverb that is the "moral" of Chaucer's *Reeve's Tale*: "A gylour shal himself bigyled be" (4321). This is a proverb represented in "Cato":

> Qui simulat verbis nec corde est fidus amicus,
> tu quoque fac simules: sic ars deluditur arte.
> (I.26)
>
> If anyone dissembles in his speech and is no true friend in his heart,
> see that you dissemble too; so guile is beguiled.

A Middle English translation of "Cato" renders this in the familiar form: "So gyle with gyle shal gyled be."[72] This proverb of "Cato" is quoted much earlier in *Piers Plowman* by the allegorical figure Dame Study, who judges its sentiment "un-Christian."

> "In oother science it seith—I seigh it in Catoun—
> *Qui simulat verbis, nec corde est fidus amicus,*
> *Tu quoque fac simile; sic ars deluditur arte:*
> Whoso gloseth as gylours doon, go me to the same,
> And so shaltow fals folk and feithlees bigile—
> This is Catons kennyng to clerkes that he lereth.
> Ac Theologie techeth noght so, whoso taketh yeme;
> He kenneth us be as bretheren, and bidde for oure enemys,
> And loven hem that lyen on us, and lene hem whan hem nedeth,
> And do good ayein yvel—God hymself it hoteth.
> (X 191–201)

In Passus XVIII, however, the beguiling of the beguiler takes on a more positive aspect; *ars ut artem falleret* is the Christian answer to Cato's *ars deluditur arte.*[73] Mercy's explanation founds the Redemption in a schoolboy game of tit-for-tat, which, as Christ later makes clear in his speech to Lucifer, coincides with the Old Testament law of a tooth for a tooth, an eye for an eye.

The Olde Lawe graunteth
That gilours be bigiled—and that is good reson:
*Dentem pro dente et oculum pro oculo.*
(XVIII 339–40)

The rationale for this appeal to the Old Testament is, as Christ goes on to say in the words of Matt. 5:17, "I am come not to destroy the Law but to fulfil it." But in the convergence of "Cato," Venantius Fortunatus, and the Bible, we may well wonder if we have here the Christianization of the pagan or the paganization of the Christian.

In the dramatic Harrowing of Hell, Lucifer is blinded and the gates of Hell are burst open and its inhabitants led forth. Angels rejoice with song and harp, and Peace celebrates the victory with a "note of poesie":

Thanne pipede Pees of poesie a note:
"*Clarior est solito post maxima nebula Phebus;*
*Post inimicias clarior est et amor.*
After sharpest shoures," quod Pees, "moost shene is the sonne;
Is no weder warmer than after watry cloudes;
Ne no love levere, ne lever frendes
Than after werre and wo, whan love and pees ben maistres."
(XVIII 410–14)

The pentameter couplet that Peace quotes is from Alan of Lille's *Parabolae* (33–34). The mighty drama of the Redemption culminates in the simplicity of this schoolboy proverb, which is then translated into an English that evokes the everyday experience of English weather. You are probably expecting me to quote T. S. Eliot: 'We shall not cease from exploration / And the end of all our exploring / Will be to arrive where we started / And know the place for the first time." It is true that *Piers Plowman* often seems to call these lines to mind, but I think I would rather end by stressing once again the union of the clerkly and the experiential here. Which comes first, the homely vernacular proverb or its Latin verse formulation? They are chicken-and-egg. For the Middle Ages, learning epitomized experience and experience validated learning. To a cleric like Langland, one of the best things about the Redemption is finding out that one's schoolbooks are true.

## ❧ 67 ❧
## "He Knew Nat Catoun"

### NOTES

1. Quotations from Chaucer are taken from *The Riverside Chaucer*, ed. Larry D. Benson (Boston, 1987).

2. See *Der kleine Pauly*, ed. Konrat Ziegler and Walther Sontheimer, 5 vols. (Munich, 1979), s.v. Dicta Catonis. The standard edition of the *Disticha Catonis* is that by M. Boas and H. J. Botschuyver (Amsterdam, 1952); a Latin text with facing English translation is available in the Loeb Classical Library, *Minor Latin Poets*, trans. J. Wight Duff and Arnold M. Duff (Cambridge, Mass., 1982), 2:585–633. See also the translations in Ian Thomson and Louis Perraud, *Ten Latin Schooltexts of the Later Middle Ages: Translated Selections* (Lewiston, N.Y., 1990), 49–80, and in Ronald E. Pepin, *An English Translation of Auctores Octo: A Medieval Reader* (Lewiston, N.Y., 1999), 5–24.

3. For discussion of the program of elementary education, see, for example, Nicholas Orme, *English Schools in the Middle Ages* (London, 1973), 59–63, 102–6; Pierre Riché, *Les écoles et l'enseignement dans l'Occident chrétien de la fin du Ve siècle au milieu du XIe siècle* (Paris, 1979), 222–36; Jo Ann Hoeppner Moran, *The Growth of English Schooling, 1340–1548* (Princeton, N.J., 1985), chapter 2; Suzanne Reynolds, *Medieval Reading: Grammar, Rhetoric and the Classical Text* (Cambridge, 1996), chapter 2.

In the following discussion, I confine myself to Latin school-texts in the interests of compactness, but it may be noted here that vernacular translations and imitations of these texts proliferated throughout the Middle Ages.

4. The title is given to the work in the medieval manuscripts. The Latin text was edited (along with numerous medieval German translations) by Carl Schroeder, *Der deutsche Facetus*, Palaestra 86 (Berlin, 1911), 3–28, and also (along with five medieval French translations) by J. Morawski, *Le Facet en françoys* (Poznan, 1923), 3–19. Pepin, *Auctores octo*, provides an English translation of a version of the *Facetus* contained in a printed edition of the *Auctores octo* (see above, 52). I cite the *Facetus* by reference to the couplet numbers in Morawski's edition (those in Schroeder follow a different order).

5. Morawski attempts to isolate the various later interpolations; see *Le Facet en françoys*, xxiii–xxiv, 12–15.

6. See Morawski, *Le Facet en françoys*, x–xii; J. W. Nicholls, *The Matter of Courtesy: A Study of Medieval Courtesy-Books and the Gawain-Poet* (Woodbridge, 1985), 146–48.

7. The identification was first made by Thomas Tyrwhitt; see Aage Brusendorff, "He Knew Nat Catoun for His Wit was Rude," in *Studies in English Philology: A Miscellany in Honor of Frederick Klaeber*, ed. Kemp Malone and Martin B. Rudd (Minneapolis, 1929), 320–39, at 337. Brusendorff suggests an alternative source in

Walter Burley's *Liber de vita et moribus philosophorum* (338), but the parallel is in my view less close.

8. Unless otherwise stated, all translations from Latin are my own.

9. For an accessible text of the *Facetus* "Moribus et vita," accompanied by a translation, see Alison Goddard Elliott, "The *Facetus*: or, The Art of Courtly Living," *Allegorica* 2.2 (1977): 27–51.

10. See Nicholls, *Matter of Courtesy*, 146.

11. See further n. 35 below.

12. Nicholls, *Matter of Courtesy*, 181, gives an avowedly selective list of 22 manuscripts, but does not include this one. A further thirteen manuscripts, including Notre Dame 6, can be found in the CD-ROM database *In Principio* (Turnhout, 2002).

13. On the verso of the last leaf, a sixteenth-century hand has written the following:

> Post deum petro laudes
> Et heluecijs gratias
> Vnitas helueciorum heroum
> errorum propulsatrix.

I am grateful to Tony Edwards for checking and improving my description of the manuscript, and to Richard Beadle for verifying my transcriptions.

14. M. Boas, "De librorum catonianorum historia atque compositione," *Mnemosyne*, n.s., 42 (1914): 17–46. The six texts named here appear as a group in the list of books bequeathed by William Ravenstone, a schoolmaster of St Paul's, in 1358; see Edith Rickert, *Chaucer's World*, ed. Clair C. Olson and Martin M. Crow (New York, 1948), 123, and for a fuller account, Edith Rickert, "Chaucer at School," *Modern Philology* 29 (1932): 257–74.

15. The most recent edition is by Francesco Mosetti Casaretto, *Teodulo, Ecloga: Il canto della verità e della menzogna* (Florence, 1997), with Italian translation and full introduction and commentary. Casaretto's text is, however, based on the much older critical edition in *Theoduli ecloga*, ed. J. Osternacher (Urfahr, 1902), as revised by R. B. C. Huygens in his edition of Bernard of Utrecht's commentary on the poem, *Commentum in Theodulum (1076–1099)* (Spoleto, 1977). There is also an *editio minor*, based on a single manuscript, by R. P. H. Green, *Seven Versions of Carolingian Pastoral* (Reading, 1980). For English translations, see Thomson and Perraud, *Ten Latin Schooltexts*, 110–57, and Pepin, *Auctores octo*, 25–40. On the role of the *Eclogue* in the school-text tradition, see George L. Hamilton, "Theodulus: A Mediaeval Textbook," *Modern Philology* 7 (1909–10): 169–85.

16. *Aviani Fabulae*, ed. Antonio Guaglianone (Turin, 1958). An English translation is provided in the Loeb *Minor Latin Poets*, ed., Duff and Duff, 2:669–749.

17. *The Elegies of Maximian*, ed. R. Webster (Princeton, N.J., 1900). For an English translation, see L. R. Lind, *Gabriele Zerbi, Gerontocomia, On the Care of the Aged, and Maximianus, Elegies on Old Age and Love* (Philadelphia, Pa., 1988).

18. *De raptu Prosperinae*, ed. J. B. Hall (Cambridge, 1969). A facing English translation is provided in the Loeb Classical Library, *Claudian*, trans. by Maurice Platnauer, 2 vols. (London, 1963), 2:293–377.

19. See Hall, *De raptu Prosperinae*, edition, 69–73; Moran, *Growth of English Schooling*, 35n.39. The author of the comment was apparently the owner of the book, Ralph Savage, who describes himself as "bonus puer."

20. For an edition of the *Achilleis* that focusses on its role as a school-text, see *The Medieval Achilleid of Statius*, ed. Paul M. Clogan (Leiden, 1968). A facing English translation is provided in the Loeb Classical Library, *Statius*, trans. by J. H. Mozley (London, 1961), 2:508–95.

21. Rino Avesani, "Il primo ritmo per la morte del grammatico Ambrogio e il cosidetto 'Liber Catonianus'," *Studi medievali*, ser. 3, 6 (1965): 455–88.

22. "Les 'Remedia amoris' d'Ovide, texte scolaire médiéval," *Bibliothèque de l'école des chartes* 115 (1957): 172–79.

23. Tony Hunt, *Teaching and Learning Latin in Thirteenth-Century England*, 3 vols. (Cambridge, 1991), 1:59–79. For further lists of manuscripts of this type, see Eva Matthews Sanford, "The Use of Classical Latin Authors in the Libri Manuales," *Transactions and Proceedings of the American Philological Association* 55 (1924): 190–248; Brother Bonaventure, F. S. C., "The Teaching of Latin in Later Medieval England," *Mediaeval Studies* 23 (1961): 1–20; and David Thomson, *A Descriptive Catalogue of Middle English Grammatical Texts* (New York, 1979).

24. See the edition by Harry F. Reijnders, "Aimericus, *Ars Lectoria*," *Vivarium* 9 (1971): 119–37; *Vivarium* 10 (1972): 41–101, 124–76 (the lists of authors are on page 170).

25. *Baebii Italici Ilias Latina*, ed. Marco Scaffai, with facing Italian translation (Bologna, 1982). "Homerus latinus" was often found among the *libri catoniani;* see Boas, "De librorum catonianorum historia."

26. The *Romulus* exists in several versions. For editions, see Léopold Hervieux, *Les fabulistes latins*, 5 vols., 2nd ed. (Paris, 1893–99; repr. New York, n.d.), 2:195–233, and Georg Thiele, *Der lateinische Äsop und die Prosa-Fassungen des Phädrus* (Heidelberg, 1910). For the use of Aesopic fables as medieval school-texts, see Klaus Grubmüller, *Meister Esopus: Untersuchungen zu Geschichte und Funktion der Fabel im Mittelalter* (Munich, 1977), and Edward Wheatley, *Mastering Aesop: Medieval*

*Education, Chaucer, and his Followers* (Gainesville, Fla., 2000). Grubmüller discusses the various *Romulus* collections on 67–85.

27. R. B. C. Huygens, ed., *Accessus ad auctores, Bernard d'Utrecht, Conrad d'Hirsau: Dialogus super auctores; Édition critique* (Leiden, 1970); extracts from the *Dialogue* are translated in *Medieval Literary Theory and Criticism, c. 1100–c. 1375*, ed. A. J. Minnis and A. B. Scott, with the assistance of David Wallace, rev. ed. (Oxford, 1988), 39–64. The translation given here is my own.

28. The *Accessus* have been edited by Huygens (see preceding note).

29. Since Hervieux's attribution of this fable-collection to one "Walter of England" (Galterus Anglicus) is based on the flimsiest of grounds, I refer to it as the elegiac *Romulus*. (The older reference to the author as the Anonymus Neveleti is also sometimes found.) The large number of surviving manuscripts (well over one hundred) of this work, and the degree of variation in the text, have prevented the production of a fully critical edition; the nearest approach to it is the text presented by Wendelin Foerster as an accompaniment to a medieval French version, *Lyoner Yzopet* (Heilbronn, 1882), 96–137, which is based on six manuscripts. For an *editio minor*, based on a fifteenth-century manuscript containing interlinear glosses and a prose commentary, apparently for schoolroom use, see Aaron E. Wright, *The Fables of 'Walter of England'* (Toronto, 1997). For an English translation, see Pepin, *Auctores octo*, 177–212.

30. Edmond Faral, ed., *Les arts poétiques du XIIe et du XIIIe siècle* (Paris, 1962), 358–61, lines 599–686. The *libri catoniani* appear in lines 602–21; two twelfth-century *comediae*, *Pamphilus* and *Geta* (see above, 51), appear between Maximian and Claudian. Another witness to the elementary reading program is Jacques de Vitry (1160/70–1240), who in a sermon addressed "ad scholares" recommends "libri Catonis, Theodosi [Theoduli?] et Aviani, Prudentii, Sedulii, Prosperi, Physiologi, et alii multi, praecipue Biblia versificata" (*Sermones vulgares* 16, *Analecta novissima*, ed. J. B. Pitra, 2 vols. ([Paris], 1885–88), 2:365–72, at 366.

31. The poem is printed by Avesani, "Il primo ritmo," 468–73.

32. J. Engels, "L''autobiographie' du jongleur dans un Dit du ms. Paris, B. N. f. fr. 837," *Vivarium* 7 (1969): 68–79.

33. Louis John Paetow, ed. and trans., *The Battle of the Seven Arts* (Berkeley, Calif., 1914), 56. *Pamphilus* is also included in this group (see above, 51). "Homer" (i.e., the Latin *Iliad*) and Claudian appear rather earlier (*Battle of the Seven Arts*, 39).

34. *Das "Registrum Multorum Auctorum" des Hugo von Trimberg: Untersuchungen und kommentierte Textausgabe*, ed. Karl Langosch, Germanische Studien 235 (Berlin, 1942).

35. *Pamphilus: Prolegomena zum Pamphilus (de amore) und kritische Textausgabe*, ed. Franz G. Becker, Beihefte zum Mittellatteinischen Jahrbuch 9 (Ratingen, 1972).

See also the edition by Stefano Pittaluga (with Italian translation) in *Commedie latine del XII e XIII secolo,* general ed. Ferruccio Bertini (Genoa, 1980), 13–137. For English translations, see Thomas Jay Garbaty, "*Pamphilus, De Amore*: An Introduction and Translation," *Chaucer Review* 2 (1967): 108–34; *Seven Medieval Latin Comedies,* trans. Alison Goddard Elliott (New York, 1984), 1–25; Thomson and Perraud, *Ten Latin Schooltexts,* 158–91.

Chaucer certainly knew the *Pamphilus,* since he refers to it at *Franklin's Tale* 110. Garbaty has argued for its influence on *Troilus and Criseyde*; see "The *Pamphilus* Tradition in Ruiz and Chaucer," *Philological Quarterly* 46 (1967): 457–70. In my view, its influence is much more evident in the *Miller's Tale,* where Nicholas's aggressive wooing is reminiscent of Pamphilus's amatory approach, and Alisoun's "Do wey youre handes!" echoes Galatea's "Pamphile, tolle manus!" See the discussion in my *Feminizing Chaucer* (Cambridge, 2002; a revised edition of *Geoffrey Chaucer* [Atlantic Highlands, N.J., 1991]), 76–80. For a discussion of the erotic aggression of *Pamphilus* in the context of other school-texts, see Marjorie Curry Woods, "Rape and the Pedagogical Rhetoric of Sexual Violence," in *Criticism and Dissent in the Middle Ages,* ed. Rita Copeland (Cambridge, 1996), 56–86.

36. See Becker's edition (cited in previous note), 11–117. Becker also identifies more than twenty manuscripts which are now lost (118–24).

37. See Alison Elliott's notes to her translation of the *Facetus* "Moribus et vita" (cited in n. 9 above), 56–57.

38. Hugo Lemcke, ed., *Reineri Phagifacetus sive de facetia comedendi libellus, addita versione Sebastiani Brantii* (Stettin, 1880).

39. For an edition, see F. Zarncke, "Zwei gereimte Uebertragungen der s.g. Disticha Catonis," *Berichte über die Verhandlungen der königlichen sächsischen Gesellschaft der Wissenschaften zu Leipzig, phil.-hist. klasse* 15 (1863): 23–78, at 24–48. The second text published by Zarncke is a "Cato Rhythmicus" (written, that is, in accentual metre, in rhyming quatrains).

40. See Ernst Voigt, "Das erste Lesebuch des Triviums in den Kloster- und Stiftsschulen des Mittelalters (11–15 Jahrhundert)," *Mitteilungen der Gesellschaft für deutsche Erziehung und Schulgeschichte* 1.1 (1891): 42–53.

41. The text was edited by Johann Huemer, "Zur Geschichte der mittellateinischen Dichtung Arnulfi delicie cleri," *Romanische Forschungen* 2 (1886): 211–46; for corrections by Ernst Voigt, see 383–90 in the same volume.

42. "[N]on attendentes quia tam paruulis quam senioribus Christi fidelibus sacra potius quam gentilia rudimenta primitus sunt exhibenda"; *Othloni Libellus Proverbiorum,* ed. W. C. Korfmacher (Chicago, 1936), 2, 16. Otloh's *Proverbia* are also available in *PL* 146: 299–338.

43. Richard Hazelton, "The Christianization of 'Cato': The *Disticha Catonis* in the Light of Late Mediaeval Commentaries," *Mediaeval Studies* 19 (1957): 157–73.

44. Egbert probably taught at the cathedral school of Liège. The *Fecunda ratis* was edited by Ernst Voigt (Halle A. S., 1889).

45. "[D]um absentibus interdum preceptoribus illa manus inpuberum quasdam inter se (nullas tamen in re) nenias aggarriret uti in his exercendis et crebro cantandis uersiculis quodammodo acueret, tum istis potius uteretur" (Voigt, 2).

46. J. M. A. Rubingh-Bosscher, ed., *Carmen ad Astralabium: A Critical Edition* (Groningen, 1987). Also available in *PL* 178, cols. 1759–66.

47. *Serlon de Wilton: Poèmes latins*, ed. Jan Öberg (Stockholm, 1965), 113–20; A. C. Friend, "The Proverbs of Serlo of Wilton," *Mediaeval Studies* 16 (1954): 179–218. Serlo's proverbs are Latinizations of medieval French proverbs.

48. *Liber Parabolarum*, ed. Oronzo Limone (Lecce, 1993); also available in *PL* 210:581–94. For English translations, see Thomson and Perraud, *Ten Latin Schooltexts*, 281–325, and Pepin, *Auctores octo*, 149–75.

49. See Rino Avesani, *Quattro miscellanee medioevali e umanistiche* (Rome, 1967), Introduzione, esp. 21.

50. *Mathei Vindocinensis Opera*, ed. Franco Munari (Rome, 1982), 160–255 (also in *PL* 205:933–80). For English translations, see Thomson and Perraud, *Ten Latin Schooltexts*, 237–68, and Pepin, *Auctores octo*, 79–148.

51. For an edition, see Edward Schröder (with a medieval German version), "Ein niederrheinischer 'Contemptus mundi' und seine Quelle," *Nachrichten von der königlichen Gesellschaft der Wissenschaften zu Göttingen, phil.-hist. klasse* (1910), 335–74 (also available in *PL* 184:1307–14). See also Robert Bultot, "La *Chartula* et l'enseignement du mépris du monde dans les écoles et les universités médiévales," *Studi medievali*, 3rd ser., 8 (1967): 787–834. For an English translation, see Pepin, *Auctores octo*, 55–77.

52. *Liber Floretus*, ed. Árpád Orbán (Kastellaun, 1978). For an English translation, see Pepin, *Auctores octo*, 213–57.

53. The classic study is Hans Walther, *Das Streitgedicht in der lateinischen Literatur des Mittelalters*, rev. Paul Gerhard Schmidt (Hildesheim, 1984).

54. For an edition of the *Alexandreis*, see *Galteri de Castellione Alexandreis*, ed. Marvin L. Colker (Padua, 1978). There is a prose translation in *The Alexandreis*, trans. R. Telfryn Pritchard (Toronto, 1986), and a verse translation in *The Alexandreis of Walter of Châtillon: A Twelfth Century Epic*, trans. David Townsend (Philadelphia, Pa., 1996). For an edition of Joseph of Exeter's poem, see *Joseph Iscanus: Werke und Briefe*, ed. Ludwig Gompf (Leiden, 1970); for an English translation, see *Joseph of Exeter: The Iliad of Dares Phrygius*, trans. Gildas Roberts (Cape Town, 1970). Books

1–3 have also been translated (with parallel Latin text) in A. K. Bate, ed. and trans., *Trojan War, I–III* (Warminster, 1986).

55. For a full discussion, which includes consideration of medieval commentaries on and Middle English translations of "Cato," see Richard Hazelton, "Chaucer and Cato," *Speculum* 35 (1960): 357–80.

56. Richard Hazelton, "The *Manciple's Tale*: Parody and Critique," *Journal of English and Germanic Philology* 62 (1963): 1–31, at 24, suggests that Chaucer is parodying the constant iteration of "my sone" by the confessor Genius in Gower's *Confessio amantis.* This might be an extra allusion, but it does not contradict the association with wisdom-literature.

57. Cf. *Troilus and Criseyde*, III 292–94.

58. See Hazelton, "Chaucer and Cato," 367. For the proverbial circulation of this couplet, see Hans Walther, *Proverbia sententiaeque Latinitatis Medii Aevi*, 5 vols. (Göttingen, 1963–67), no. 16974; and for English versions, B. J. Whiting, *Proverbs, Sentences, and Proverbial Phrases from English Writings mainly before 1500* (Baltimore Md., 1911; repr. New York, 1967) no. S865. As Hazelton notes, Criseyde's "the suffrant overcomith" (IV 1584) is an obvious translation of "Vincit qui patitur."

59. Cf. *Parson's Tale* 661: "If thou wolt venquysse thyn enemy, lerne to suffre."

60. See my *Feminizing Chaucer*, 89–99, 114–20, 125–28, 168–69.

61. For example, the Wife of Bath's famous question, "Who peyntede the leon, tel me who?" (692), ultimately derives from a fable of Avianus (no. 24), which tells of a quarrel between a man and a lion as to which was stronger. In support of his case, the man shows the lion a sculpted tombstone on which a man is overpowering a lion. The lion drily replies that if lions could carve tombstones, the picture would look very different. Later Latin fable-collections substitute a painting for a sculpture, and it may be one of these that Chaucer has in mind. The Latin gloss "Quis pinxit leonem?", which appears in the margin of the Ellesmere manuscript, suggests that a Latin source is more probable than the *Fables* of Marie de France, which were suggested by Robert A. Pratt, ed., *The Tales of Canterbury* (Boston, 1974), 269, n. to line 692. Chaucer's reference to "daun Pseustis" in the *House of Fame* (1227) is usually interpreted as an allusion to the *Eclogue of Theodulus.*

62. See George Lyman Kittredge, "Chaucer and Maximianus," *American Journal of Philology* 9 (1888): 84–85, and Robert A. Pratt, "Chaucer's Claudian," *Speculum* 22 (1947): 419–29.

63. See preceding note. Relevant passages from *Elegy* I are printed with facing English translation in Robert M. Correale and Mary Hamel, eds., *Sources and Analogues of the Canterbury Tales*, 2 vols. (Cambridge, 2001–5), 1:312–19.

64. Carleton Brown, ed., *English Lyrics of the XIIIth Century* (Oxford, 1932), no. 51. The closest lines to this passage are 202–3: "Ich wolde ich were on rest/ Wel lowe leiid in a chest." The lyric also appears in London, British Library, MS Harley 2253 (ff. 82r–82v). For a discussion of this lyric in relation to Maximian and Chaucer: see George R. Coffman, "Old Age from Horace to Chaucer: Some Literary Affinities and Adventures of an Idea," *Speculum* 9 (1934): 249–77.

65. For convenient summaries of critical views of the Old Man, see Alfred David, "Criticism and the Old Man in Chaucer's Pardoner's Tale," *College English* 27 (1965): 139–44, and Christopher Dean, "Salvation, Damnation and the Role of the Old Man in the *Pardoner's Tale*," *Chaucer Review* 3 (1968–69): 44–49.

66. The story exists in several versions; see Correale and Hamel, *Sources and Analogues*, 1:286–89, 290–93.

67. Chaucer also alludes to or echoes Claudian in the *House of Fame* (445–50, 1507–12), the *Parliament of Fowls* (99–105), and the *Legend of Good Women* (G 280).

68. I quote the translation in the Loeb edition (see n. 18 above).

69. Mann, *Feminizing Chaucer*, 53.

70. Ibid., 54.

71. Quotations of *Piers Plowman* are taken from the edition by A. V. C. Schmidt, *The Vision of Piers Plowman: A Critical Edition of the B-Text Based on Trinity College Cambridge MS B.15.17*, 2nd ed. (London, 1995).

72. Hazelton, "Chaucer and Cato," 376.

73. The two texts have been connected by Andrew Galloway, "Two Notes on Langland's Cato: *Piers Plowman* B I.88–91; IV.20–23," *English Language Notes* 25.2 (1987–88): 9–12. Galloway states that Cato's distich was typically glossed with Venantius's hymn, but he does not give any documentation.

# Computing Cynewulf

## The *Judith*-Connection

ANDY ORCHARD

SCHOLARS OF OLD ENGLISH HAVE FOR MORE THAN FOUR DECADES been generally both keen and able to use computers in their work,[1] and indeed the speed of technological development has been such that even surveys of such computistical tools produced less than ten years ago can now seem distinctly dated.[2] Within that period, there has been a huge level of increased activity associated with the World Wide Web, and scholars of Anglo-Saxon England now have a vast and bewildering array of electronic tools at their disposal.[3] Quite apart from the proliferation of more or less well-informed discussion-groups and the possibility of almost instantaneous communication with colleagues and students all over the world,[4] the modern scholar has access to a huge range of electronic manuscript facsimiles,[5] machine-readable corpora, bibliographies, sound-files, texts, and hypertexts,[6] as well as a plethora of online databases and other ongoing research-projects.[7] The widespread availability of a combination of machine-readable texts and electronic concordance-packages has likewise made the generation of customized concordances of individual texts, authors, or groups of texts quick and efficient, thereby hugely facilitating the process of textual comparison.[8]

Meanwhile, the past half-century has seen a similar revolution in the perception of Old English verse, with an ever-increasing focus on putative techniques of composition. Although the essentially formulaic nature of much of the surviving literature from Anglo-Saxon England has long been noted, attempts to assess the frequency, type, distribution, and purpose of such formulas have generally been too narrowly focussed to be of wide or lasting significance. The study of formulas, begun in the late nineteenth century to demonstrate conscious literary borrowing from one author to another,[9] paradoxically became after 1953 the tool used to demonstrate an inherited "oral-formulaic" tradition in Old English verse.[10] Since then, it has been comprehensively demonstrated that Anglo-Saxons from literate backgrounds (and composing in Latin) were also capable of producing highly formulaic texts,[11] and the close study of formulas has in general been relegated to the critical backwater. However, the use of machine-readable texts, computer-generated concordances, and electronic databases now offers the modern critic an opportunity to examine the formulas in Anglo-Saxon literature at a level and intensity previously unfeasible, and has effectively revitalized the whole issue of addressing the possibility of the direct influence of one Old English poem or poet on another in a much more comprehensive way than ever before.[12]

Some direct connection between *Beowulf* and *Andreas* is perhaps still the most strongly asserted, most recently in a connected series of doctoral dissertations by Anita Riedinger, Carol Hughes Funk, and Alison Powell.[13] In the course of her work, based on a detailed comparison of formulaic phrasing derived from customized computer-generated concordances, Powell in particular gives details and analyses of nearly ninety parallels unique in the extant poetic corpus to *Beowulf* and *Andreas*, and nearly 150 unique to *Andreas* and Cynewulf.[14] For the *Andreas*-poet at least, we seem more and more able to track down "the tradition" within which he worked. The suggested connection to Cynewulf is all the more interesting in that there is also a substantial amount of evidence linking *Andreas* to *Guthlac B*, the poem (presently unsigned but lacking a conclusion) that seems most likely also to have been composed by Cynewulf.[15] Both the Vercelli Book (Vercelli, Biblioteca Capitolare, MS CXVII), which contains the signed poems

*Fates of the Apostles* and *Elene*, as well as *Andreas*, and the Exeter Book (Exeter, Cathedral Library, MS 3501), which contains the signed poems *Christ II* and *Juliana*, as well as *Guthlac B*, have clear links with Cynewulf. Such widespread influence should perhaps encourage further speculation about the extent to which Cynewulf can be connected with the other two surviving major codices containing Old English verse, namely the Junius Manuscript (Oxford, Bodleian Library, MS Junius 11) and the *Beowulf* manuscript (London, British Library, MS Cotton Vitellius A.xv). In fact, although several earlier scholars (notably Claes Schaar) had argued that Cynewulf was influenced both by *Beowulf* and several of the biblical poems of the Junius Manuscript,[16] widespread early acceptance of the implications of the so-called "oral-formulaic" theory (namely that there once existed a large body of now lost Old English verse, composed using a common stock of traditional formulas) effectively curtailed all discussion of direct links between individual poems. It is striking to note the extent to which (for example) editions produced before and after the watershed year of 1953 treat parallel phrasing in different poems.[17]

A test-case for an assessment of the significance of verbal overlap between poems is provided by the verbal parallels that link *Judith* (in the *Beowulf* manuscript) and *Elene* (in the Vercelli Book). Both poems are clearly the works of literate poets, to the extent that both rely more or less heavily on identifiable Latin sources, but both nonetheless are demonstrably "formulaic," and evidently rely on traditional techniques of composition.[18] The overall differences in style and diction between *Judith* and *Elene*, moreover, are such as to preclude the possibility of common authorship.[19] A strong case can be made, however, for a more specific connection between the two poems than a series of common selections from a shared pool of traditional diction might imply. With the aid of a computer-generated concordance, it is possible to identify every single example of parallel phrasing between *Judith* and *Elene* extending the length of a half-line or more.[20] There are in fact some thirty-three such examples, which can be presented as follows:

[1] *Jud* 5 gefriðode, frymða waldend. Hyre ðæs *fæder on roderum*
*Ele* 1150 gefullæste, *fæder on roderum*

[2] *Jud* 10 ealle ða yldestan ðegnas; hie ðæt *ofstum miclum*
*Jud* 70 ut of ðam inne *ofstum miclum*

| | | |
|---|---|---|
| | *Ele* 44 | under earhfære *ofstum myclum* |
| | *Ele* 102 | geiewed wearð, *ofstum myclum* |
| | *Ele* 999 | *ofstum myclum* eft gearwian |
| [3] | *Jud* 13 | þæs ðe Iudith hyne, *gleaw on geðonce* |
| | *Ele* 806 | Iudas maþelode, *gleaw in geþance* |
| [4] | *Jud* 22 | *goldwine gumena,* on gytesalum |
| | *Ele* 201 | *goldwine gumena* in godes þeowdom |
| [5] | *Jud* 30 | swiðmod *sinces brytta,* oððþæt hie on swiman lagon |
| | *Ele* 194 | Ða wæs on sælum *sinces brytta* |
| [6] | *Jud* 41 | *fundon ferhðgleawe,* ond ða fromlice |
| | *Ele* 327 | *fundon ferhðgleawra,* þa þe fyrngemynd |
| [7] | *Jud* 49 | mihte wlitan þurh, *wigena baldor* |
| | *Ele* 344 | ond þæt word gecwæþ *wigona baldor* |
| [8] | *Jud* 60 | geðafian, *þrymmes hyrde,* ac he him þæs ðinges gestyrde |
| | *Ele* 348 | *þrymmes hyrde;* þanon ic ne wende |
| | *Ele* 858 | geþrowode, *þrymmes hyrde* |
| [9] | *Jud* 62 | galferhð *gumena ðreate* |
| | *Ele* 254 | hwonne heo sio guðcwen *gumena þreate* |
| | *Ele* 1095 | Glædmod eode *gumena þreate* |
| [10] | *Jud* 67 | wunode under *wolcna hrofe.* Gefeol ða wine swa druncen |
| | *Ele* 89 | wliti wuldres treo ofer *wolcna hrof* |
| [11] | *Jud* 81 | *be naman nemnan,* nergend ealra |
| | *Ele* 78 | ond *be naman nemde,* (nihthelm toglad) |
| [12] | *Jud* 82 | woruldbuendra, *ond þæt word acwæð* |
| | *Jud* 151 | þurh ðæs wealles geat, *ond þæt word acwæð* |
| | *Jud* 283 | *ond þæt word acwæð* to ðam wiggendum |
| | *Ele* 1071 | onwrige wuldorgifum, *ond þæt word acwæð* |
| [13] | *Jud* 83 | *Ic* ðe, *frymða god* ond frofre gæst |
| | *Jud* 189 | fysan to gefeohte. *Syððan frymða god* |

*Ele* 345 *Ic frumþa god* fore sceawode
*Ele* 502 folca to frofre, *syððan* him *frymða god*

[14] *Jud* 83 Ic ðe, frymða god ond *frofre gæst*
*Ele* 1036 fæst on ferhðe, siððan *frofre gast*
*Ele* 1105 fæder, *frofre gast,* ðurh fyres bleo

[15] *Jud* 84 *bearn* alwaldan, *biddan wylle*
*Jud* 187 þyssa burgleoda *biddan wylle*
*Ele* 789 þurg þæt beorhte gesceap *biddan wille*
*Ele* 813 Nu ic þe, *bearn* godes, *biddan wille*

[16] *Jud* 86 *ðrynesse ðrym.* Þearle ys me nu ða
*Ele* 177 in *þrynesse þrymme* geweorðad

[17] *Jud* 95 ædre mid elne onbryrde, swa he deð *anra gehwylcne*
*Ele* 1287 in fyres feng folc *anra gehwylc*

[18] *Jud* 118 *þystrum forðylmed,* þæt he ðonan mote
*Ele* 766 *þeostrum forþylmed.* He þinum wiðsoc

[19] *Jud* 134 oðþæt hie becomon, *collenferhðe*
*Ele* 247 *collenferhðe,* cwen siðes gefeah
*Ele* 378 *collenferhðe,* swa him sio cwen bead
*Ele* 848 *collenferhðe.* Cwen weorces gefeah

[20] *Jud* 155 *cyninga wuldor;* þæt gecyðed *wearð*
*Ele* 5 acenned *wearð,* *cyninga wuldor*
*Ele* 178 acenned *wearð,* *cyninga wuldor*

[21] *Jud* 155 cyninga wuldor; *þæt gecyðed wearð*
*Ele* 1049 Criste gecweme. *Þæt gecyðed wearð*

[22] *Jud* 169 *eft to eðle,* ond ða ofostlice
*Ele* 1219 *eft to eðle,* ond þa eallum bebead

[23] *Jud* 203 *hæleð* under helmum, of *ðære haligan byrig*
*Ele* 1005 *hæleð* hwætmode, *to þære halgan byrig*
*Ele* 1053 *hæleða* gerædum *to þære halgan byrig*
*Ele* 1203 *hæleða* cynnes, *to þære halgan byrig*

[24] *Jud* 206 *wulf* in *walde*, ond se wanna hrefn
*Ele* 28 *wulf* on *wealde*, wælrune ne mað

[25] *Jud* 210 *earn* ætes georn, *urigfeðera*
*Ele* 29 *Urigfeðera* *earn* sang ahof
*Ele* 111 *urigfeðra*, *earn* sið beheold

[26] *Jud* 221 leton forð fleogan *flana scuras*
*Ele* 117 On þæt fæge folc *flana scuras*

[27] *Jud* 222 *hildenædran*, of hornbogan
*Ele* 119 hetend heorugrimme, *hildenædran*
*Ele* 141 *hildenædran*. Heap wæs gescyrded

[28] *Jud* 237 *ehton elðeoda* ealle þrage
*Ele* 139 *ehton elþeoda* oð þæt æfen forð

[29] *Jud* 280 *lifes belidenne*. He þa lungre gefeoll
*Ele* 877 *life belidenes* lic on eorðan

[30] *Jud* 310 *laðan* cynnes. *Lythwon becom*
*Ele* 142 *laðra* lindwered. *Lythwon becwom*

[31] *Jud* 326 to *ðære beorhtan byrig*, Bethuliam
*Ele* 821 in *þære beorhtan byrig*, þær is broðor min

[32] *Jud* 336 *eorlas æscrofe*, Holofernes
*Ele* 275 *eorlas æscrofe* mid þa æðelan cwen

[33] *Jud* 344 *sigorlean in swegles* wuldre, þæs þe heo ahte soðne geleafan
*Ele* 623 *sigorlean in swegle*, saga ricene me

While several of these parallels are certainly more striking than others, the degree of overlap seems notable in several ways. Some thirty-six lines of *Judith* (or a little over 10 percent) apparently contain parallels with *Elene*, and in two cases both half-lines of verses in *Judith* can be matched in *Elene*.[21] From the alternative perspective, some forty-eight lines of *Elene* (or about 3.5 percent) apparently contain parallels with *Judith*. Such figures are of themselves of little value, but when these parallels are measured against the entire surviving corpus of Old English poetry, a rather more intriguing picture begins to emerge.

No fewer than eleven of the thirty-three parallels highlighted here are in fact uniquely shared by these two poems within the extant corpus,[22] and a further two are paralleled elsewhere only among other signed poems of Cynewulf.[23] In another nine cases, the parallels are found outside *Judith* and the signed poems of Cynewulf in only one other poem each (and one of the other poems in question, *Guthlac B*, has in fact a good claim to be considered also written by Cynewulf).[24] Even in the case of the remaining parallels, it is striking the extent to which the phrases in question are found elsewhere largely in the same limited set of poems:[25] *Andreas* and *Beowulf* in particular both feature prominently. The frequent overlap in repeated diction between these two poems is perhaps less surprising given that it has been argued not only that the *Andreas*-poet knew and consciously echoed both *Beowulf* and the works of Cynewulf, but that Cynewulf himself knew and consciously echoed *Beowulf*.[26] In fact, it might well be concluded from the available evidence that only one of the verbal parallels linking *Judith* and *Elene* has any widespread currency in the extant poetic corpus of Old English, appearing in a further seventeen sources.[27]

Even if one takes the view that what is important in the context of identifying patterns of formulaic usage is not only precise verbal correlation but also the extent to which similar phrasing can be identified by so-called formulaic "systems,"[28] it is surely striking how often the closest parallels within such systems surviving in the extant corpus are again for the most part to be found within the same highly limited set of poems.[29] Likewise, it is interesting to note the extent to which the parallels detected here between *Judith* and *Elene* are evidently clustered, a feature which can best be illustrated simply by detailing their distribution in fifty-line sections of each text:[30]

| | *No. of 'unique' parallels* | *No. of parallels* |
|---|---|---|
| *Judith* 1–50 | 4 | [7] |
| *Judith* 51–100 | 3 | [10] |
| *Judith* 101–50 | 1 | [2] |
| *Judith* 151–200 | 1 | [5] |
| *Judith* 201–50 | 3 | [6] |
| *Judith* 251–300 | 1 | [2] |
| *Judith* 301–50 | 3 | [4] |
| **TOTAL** | **16** | **[36]** |

| *(cont.)* | *No. of 'unique' parallels* | *No. of parallels* |
|---|---|---|
| *Elene* 1–50 | 0 | [4] |
| *Elene* 51–100 | 0 | [2] |
| *Elene* 101–50 | 5 | [7] |
| *Elene* 151–200 | 0 | [3] |
| *Elene* 201–50 | 0 | [2] |
| *Elene* 251–300 | 2 | [2] |
| *Elene* 301–50 | 4 | [4] |
| *Elene* 351–400 | 0 | [1] |
| *Elene* 401–50 | 0 | [0] |
| *Elene* 451–500 | 0 | [0] |
| *Elene* 501–50 | 1 | [1] |
| *Elene* 551–600 | 0 | [0] |
| *Elene* 601–50 | 1 | [1] |
| *Elene* 651–700 | 0 | [0] |
| *Elene* 701–50 | 0 | [0] |
| *Elene* 751–800 | 1 | [2] |
| *Elene* 801–50 | 1 | [4] |
| *Elene* 851–900 | 1 | [1] |
| *Elene* 901–50 | 0 | [0] |
| *Elene* 951–1000 | 0 | [1] |
| *Elene* 1001–1050 | 0 | [3] |
| *Elene* 1051–1100 | 0 | [3] |
| *Elene* 1101–1150 | 1 | [2] |
| *Elene* 1151–1200 | 0 | [0] |
| *Elene* 1201–1250 | 0 | [2] |
| *Elene* 1251–1300 | 0 | [3] |
| *Elene* 1301–1321 | 0 | [0] |
| **TOTAL** | 17 | **[48]** |

In *Judith*, the clustering of these parallels at the beginning of the poem is clear: nearly half of the parallels (whether "unique" or not) appear in the first 100 lines, which describe the feast of Holofernes, the bringing of Judith to his tent, her call for divine aid, and her intention to kill him.[31] A further cluster occurs in the passage from lines 201–50 (actually 203–37), which describes a battle between the Jews and the Assyrians in a manner unparalleled in the Vulgate source, and a final cluster occurs in the final lines of the poem (actually 326–44), describing the return of the victorious Jews and praise of Judith. The clustering of parallels in *Elene* seems still more localized, being more or less restricted to one section in lines 101–50 (actually 102–42), describing Constantine's battle against the Huns, and another in lines 301–50 (actually 327–48), describing how Elene summoned the wisest of the Jews in order to locate the Cross.

The densest passage of overlapping diction occurs in *Judith* just before the eponymous heroine decapitates her would-be rapist, when she somewhat anachronistically prays for strength to the Trinity (parallel phrasing is italicized):[32]

Ongan ða swegles weard
*be naman nemnan*, nergend ealra
woruldbuendra, *ond þæt word acwæð:*
"Ic ðe, *frymða god* ond *frofre gæst*,
bearn alwaldan, *biddan wylle*
miltse þinre me þearfendre,
*ðrynesse ðrym.*"

(*Judith* 80b–86)

> Then she began to call by name the guardian of glory, the saviour of all those who live in the world, and spoke these words: "I will ask you, God of creation, Spirit of comfort, Child of the Almighty, for your mercy for me in need, the power of the Trinity."

That fully five of the six lines of this passage should overlap in diction with *Elene* is surely striking, the more so since their diction is so obviously not drawn from the Old Testament source. While the Vulgate certainly has Judith pray at this point, there is of course no reference to the Trinity; the parallel passage simply notes "And Judith stood before the bed praying with tears, and the motion of her lips in silence, Saying: Strengthen me, O Lord God of Israel" ("Stetitque Iudith ante lectum orans cum lacrimis et labiorum motu in silentio dicens confirma me Domine Deus Israhel" [Judith 13:6–7]). Although none of the six parallels in these five lines is uniquely shared by these two poems in the extant corpus, three of them are found outside *Elene* and *Judith* only elsewhere in the works of Cynewulf or one other poem.[33] In fact, the closest parallel for the invocation of the Trinity found in *Judith* is another Cynewulf-inspired poem, *Andreas*, at the end of which the eponymous hero describes heaven (emphasis mine):[34]

> þær *fæder ond sunu*   *ond frofre gast*
> *in þrinnesse*   *þrymme* wealdeð
> in woruld worulda   wuldorgestealda.
>
> (*Andreas* 1684–86)

> Where Father and Son and Spirit of comfort rule in the power of the Trinity those glorious regions for ever and ever.

It is of course possible that in this case the *Andreas*-poet is simply borrowing directly from *Judith*, as he apparently does from both Cynewulf and *Beowulf*;[35] at all events, despite the clear extent of overlap, none of the parallels is sufficiently restricted in circulation to allow this passage to be used on its own as evidence of a direct relationship between *Judith* and *Elene*.

A much more promising link is provided by the passage describing how Holofernes' men brought Judith to his bed, since in the space of twenty-six-and-a-half lines there are no fewer than four half-lines shared with *Elene*, three of them uniquely in the extant corpus (indicated below by bold italics), and the fourth found elsewhere only in another of Cynewulf's signed poems (indicated below in italics):

> Hie hraðe fremedon,
> anbyhtscealcas,   swa him heora ealdor bebead,
> byrnwigena brego:   bearhtme stopon
> to ðam gysterne,   þær hie Iudithðe
> ***fundon ferhðgleawe,***   ond ða fromlice
> lindwiggende   lædan ongunnon
> þa torhtan mægð   to træfe þam hean,
> þær se rica hyne   reste on symbel
> nihtes inne,   nergende lað,

Holofernus. Þær wæs eallgylden
fleohnet fæger ymbe þæs folctogan
bed ahongen, þæt se bealofulla
mihte wlitan þurh, ***wigena baldor,***
on æghwylcne þe ðær inne com
hæleða bearna, ond on hyne nænig
monna cynnes, nymðe se modiga hwæne
niðe rofra him þe near hete
rinca to rune gegangan. Hie ða on reste gebrohton
snude ða snoteran idese; eodon ða stercedferhðe,
hæleð heora hearran cyðan þæt wæs seo halige meowle
gebroht on his burgetelde. Þa wearð se brema on mode
bliðe, burga ealdor, þohte ða beorhtan idese
mid widle ond mid womme besmitan. Ne wolde þæt wuldres dema
geðafian, *þrymmes hyrde,* ac he him þæs ðinges gestyrde,
dryhten, dugeða waldend. Gewat ða se deofulcunda,
galferhð ***gumena ðreate,***
bealofull his beddes neosan, þær he sceolde his blæd forleosan
ædre binnan anre nihte.

(*Judith* 37b-64a)

They quickly acted, the retainers, as their lord commanded them, the leader of mail-shirted warriors: they advanced in tumult to the guest-house, where they found Judith, wise in spirit, and then promptly the shield-warriors began to lead that shining woman to the high pavilion, wherein the powerful one always rested for the night, the one hateful to the Savior, Holofernes. There was a beautiful fly-net, all-golden, hung around the commander's bed, so that the evil one, the prince of warriors, might look through on each of the children of men who came therein, but none of mankind on him, unless the proud one ordered some battle-brave person of his men to step closer for consultation. They quickly brought to his bed the wise lady; then the stout-hearted men went to tell their leader that the holy woman had been brought to his private chamber. Then was the famous one happy in his heart, the prince of cities; he thought to besmirch that bright lady with filth and sin. The judge of glory, the shepherd of splendour, would not allow that, but restrained him from that deed, the lord, the ruler of hosts. Then the devilish one, lusting in heart, went with a band of men to go to his bed, where he was to lose his life swiftly inside a single night.

What is intriguing about this passage is that again it has no real basis in the biblical source, except for the allusion to Holofernes' fly-net, which is not only misplaced from its position in the narrative sequence of the Vulgate, but considerably elaborated here.[36] As such, the passage represents a conscious decision on the part of the poet to depart from the source and exercise more freely his poetic talents.[37]

The parallel passage from *Elene* describes how the eponymous heroine summons the wisest of the Jews in her search for the buried Cross. In the course of twenty-two lines, there are no fewer than six half-lines shared with *Judith* (indicated here in italics) three of them directly matched in the passage from *Judith* just cited (indicated here in bold italics):[38]

Hio þa on þreate  þusendo manna
***fundon ferhðgleawra,***  þa þe fyrngemynd
mid Iudeum  gearwast cuðon;
þrungon þa on þreate  þær on þrymme bad
in cynestole  caseres mæg,
geatolic guðcwen  golde gehyrsted.
Elene maþelode  ond for eorlum spræc:
"Gehyrað, higegleawe,  halige rune,
word ond wisdom.  Hwæt, ge witgena
lare onfengon,  hu se liffruma
in cildes had  cenned wurde,
mihta wealdend  be þam Moyses sang,
*ond þæt word gecwæð*  weard Israhela:
'Eow acenned bið  cniht on degle,
mihtum mære,  swa þæs modor ne bið
wæstmum geeacnod  þurh weres frige.'
Be ðam Dauid cyning  dryhtleoð agol,

frod fyrnweota, fæder Salomones,
*ond þæt word gecwæþ* ***wigona baldor:***
'Ic *frumþa god* fore sceawode,
sigora dryhten; he on gesyhðe wæs,
mægena wealdend, min on þa swiðran,
***þrymmes hyrde;*** þanon ic ne wende
æfre to aldre onsion mine.' "

(*Elene* 326–49)

Then they found in a crowd a thousand men wise in spirit, who most readily among the Jews knew ancient tradition; then they thronged in a crowd to where the emperor's kinswoman waited in might on a royal throne, a magnificent warrior-queen adorned with gold. Elene made a speech and spoke before the men: "Hear, you wise in heart, holy mysteries, words and wisdom; listen, you have received the teachings of the prophets, how the giver of life would be born in the guise of a child, the ruler of powers about whom Moses sang, and the guardian of Israel spoke these words: 'There shall be born unto you a boy in secret, glorious in power, whose mother shall not be made great in increase through a man's love;' about whom King David, the wise ancient prophet, father of Solomon, chanted a lordly song, and the prince of warriors spoke these words: 'I beheld before the God of creation, Lord of victories he was in that vision, the ruler of powers, on my right-hand side, the shepherd of splendour; from there I did not ever turn my face.' "

It is surely noteworthy that the three half-lines these two passages share should occur in precisely the same order in each (*fundon ferhðgleawra . . . wigona baldor . . . þrymmes hyrde* in *Elene*; *fundon ferhðgleawe . . . wigena baldor . . . þrymmes hyrde* in *Judith*), and that the first two of these parallels should be found uniquely in these two passages in the extant corpus. One might also note the overlap between the opening of Elene's address here (*ond þæt word gecwæþ . . . Ic frumþa god, Elene* 344a and 345a) and Judith's prayer before decapitating Holofernes, cited above (*ond þæt word acwæð / Ic . . . frymða god, Judith* 82b–83a),[39] as well as the curious circumstance that

Elene's speech begins with a fourfold invocation of God in clearly parallel phrasing (*frumþa god . . . sigora dryhten . . . mægena wealdend . . . þrymmes hyrde*, *Elene* 345a, 346a, 347a, and 348a) that bears more than a passing resemblance to a similar fourfold invocation of God in the parallel passage in *Judith* (*wuldres dema . . . þrymmes hyrde . . . dryhten, dugeða waldend*, *Judith*, 59b, 60a, and 61a). Unless one is to posit the existence of an oral-formulaic "summoning of Jews" theme that happens to be attested only in these two poems in the extant corpus, one must surely suppose that there is a direct link between *Elene* and *Judith*, albeit that they are clearly composed by different poets and survive in different manuscripts.

The direction of borrowing seems to be indicated by the fact that whereas the extended details of the summoning of Judith to Holofernes' tent (as with the references to the Trinity in *Judith* cited above) are not found in the Vulgate, there does seem a basis in Cynewulf's Latin source for the relatively elaborate description of the summoning of the wise Jews in *Elene*. An immediate difficulty, however, is the problem of identifying precisely what Cynewulf's Latin source might have been: Michael Lapidge's recent work on identifying a Latin source-text for Cynewulf's *Juliana* closer than any found so far has highlighted the difficulties implicit in any such analysis.[40] All critics agree that *Elene* is based on some version of the *Inuentio Crucis* legend, usually referred to as the *Acta Cyriaci*,[41] but recent scholarship has shown just how complex was the transmission of that text.[42] Nonetheless, all versions of the *Inuentio Crucis* contain a description of the summoning of the wise Jews that must underlie Cynewulf's rendering. The most widely circulating version of the relevant passage reads as follows:[43]

> Inuenerunt qui dicebant se scire legem, uiros numero mille. Et adducentes eos ad beatam Helenam statuerunt testimonium perhibentes eos legis scientiam multam habere. Helena autem dixit ad ipsos: "Audite mea uerba et auribus percipite meos sermones. Non enim intellexistis in sermonibus prophetarum, quemadmodum prophetauerunt de aduentu Christi? Pro hoc ergo uos hodie interrogo. Quia prior Moyses dixit quia: 'Puer nascetur et mater eius uirum non cognoscet.' Et iterum laudationum conscriptor David: 'Praeuidebam Dominum in conspectu meo semper, quoniam a dextris meis est, ut non commouear.' "

> They found men who said that they knew the law, a thousand in number. And leading them to Saint Helena, they made their case, bearing witness that they had great knowledge of the law. But Helena said to them: "Hear my words and receive my declarations in your ears. For have you not understood in the declarations of the prophets, how they prophesied about the coming of Christ? Therefore I ask you for this thing today. Because first Moses said that: 'A boy will be born and his mother will not know a man.' And again David, the author of adulations: 'I always saw the Lord before me in my sight, for he is on my right, so that I may not be moved.'"

Variant readings in the critical apparatus are in some cases undoubtedly closer to what Cynewulf must have had before him: one tenth-century manuscript (Karlsruhe, Badische Landesbibliothek, MS Aug. perg. 91) apparently has Moses be more specific about the boy who is to be born, saying that *Puer uobis in secreto nascebatur* ("A boy was born to you in secret"), and such a reading (but with the tense of the verb in the future, as elsewhere) surely underlies Cynewulf's assertion that *Eow acenned bið cniht on degle* (*Elene* 339: "A boy will be born to you in secret"). But whatever the precise Latin source, it remains unquestionable that, whereas Cynewulf was working directly from such a Latin text in crafting this passage, the parallel passage from *Judith* has no such extensive and obvious direct Latin source. Surely the likeliest explanation for the overlapping diction between *Judith* and *Elene* at this point, including parallel half-lines unique in the extant corpus and appearing in the same order, is that the *Judith*-poet has in this case been directly influenced by *Elene*.

Certainly, another pair of parallel passages in *Judith* and *Elene* strongly suggests the notion of a direct connection between the two texts. Both poems famously contain extended battle-sequences that represent considerable expansion of material in their respective Latin sources, and therefore in each case the poet is thrown back on his own resources, as well as, one might argue, on "the tradition."[44] The passage from *Judith* is briefer, and might be quoted first (layout mine):

> Þa wearð snelra werod   snude gegearewod,
> cenra to campe.

Stopon cynerofe
secgas ond gesiðas,   bæron sigeþufas,
foron to gefeohte   forð on gerihte,
hæleð under helmum,   of ðære haligan byrig
on ðæt dægred sylf.
Dynedan scildas,
hlude hlummon.   Þæs se hlanca gefeah
wulf in walde,   ond se wanna hrefn,
wælgifre fugel.   Wistan begen
þæt him ða þeodguman   þohton tilian
fylle on fægum;   ac him fleah on last
earn ætes georn,   urigfeðera,
salowigpada   sang hildeleoð,
hyrnednebba.
Stopon heaðorincas,
beornas to beadowe,   bordum beðeahte,
hwealfum lindum,   þa ðe hwile ær
elðeodigra   edwit þoledon,
hæðenra hosp.   Him þæt hearde wearð
æt ðam æscplegan   eallum forgolden,
Assyrium,   syððan Ebreas
under guðfanum   gegan hæfdon
to ðam fyrdwicum.
Hie ða fromlice
leton forð fleogan   flana scuras,
hildenædran,   of hornbogan,
strælas stedehearde;   styrmdon hlude
grame guðfrecan,   garas sendon
in heardra gemang.   Hæleð wæron yrre,
landbuende,   laðum cynne.

Stopon styrnmode,   stercedferhðe,
wrehton unsofte   ealdgeniðlan
medowerige;   mundum brugdon
scealcas of sceaðum   scirmæled swyrd,

ecgum gecoste, slogon eornoste
Assiria oretmæcgas,
niðhycgende, nanne ne sparedon
þæs herefolces, heanne ne ricne,
cwicera manna þe hie ofercuman mihton.

Swa ða magoþegnas on ða morgentid
ehton elðeoda ealle þrage,
oðþæt ongeaton ða ðe grame wæron,
ðæs herefolces heafodweardas,
þæt him swyrdgeswing swiðlic eowdon
weras Ebrisce.

(*Judith* 199–241a)

Then a troop of eager ones was quickly prepared, keen for battle; the very brave ones advanced, men and retainers, bore victory-banners; they went to the fight, straight ahead, heroes under helmets, from that holy stronghold, at the very break of day. Shields clattered, resounded loud. At that the lean wolf in the wood rejoiced, and the dark raven, carrion-keen bird; they both knew that those mighty men thought to supply them with their fill of the fey; but there flew in their wake an eagle eager for food, dewy-feathered; the dark-coated one sang a war-song, the one with horned beak. The battle-troops advanced, warriors to the fray, protected by bucklers, hollow shields, those who previously had endured the scorn of foreigners, the heathens' contempt. That was harshly paid back to them at the ash-play, to all the Assyrians, after the Jews under war-banners had reached the encampment. Then they promptly let fly forth showers of darts, battle-adders from horn bows, firm-fixed arrows. They stormed loud, the fierce war-fighters, sent spears into the throng of the hard ones. The warriors were angry, the land's inhabitants, with the hostile race; they advanced stern-hearted, resolute in spirit; they woke up unsoftly the ancient enemies, weary from drinking. With their hands the troops drew from their sheaths the brightly decorated swords, trusty of edge, slew the Assyrian warriors,

> evil-schemers. They spared none of that army, high or low, of living men that they could overcome. So those noble thegns throughout the morning pursued the foreigners the whole time, until that army's body-guards, those who were fierce, perceived that the Jewish men mightily showed them sword-strokes.

The battle-scene itself has only the mildest warrant in the Scriptural source.[45] The first half (lines 199–220a), detailing the preparations for battle, can perhaps be seen as an imaginative elaboration of Judith 14:7 ("Mox autem ut ortus est dies, suspenderunt super muros caput Holofernis, accepitque unusquisque vir arma sua, et egressi sunt cum grandi strepitu et ululatu." ["And immediately at break of day, they hung up the head of Holofernes upon the walls, and every man took his arms, they went out with a great noise and shouting."]). The second half of the scene (lines 220b–241a) has no grounding in the Vulgate whatsoever.[46] The passage from *Judith* is widely celebrated for its use of incremental repetition,[47] the anaphoric repetition of key words or phrases to mark off successive phases of a narrative, as seen in *Beowulf* in the famous description of Grendel's approach to Heorot (*com . . . com . . . com* [he came . . . he came . . . he came]) in the same manuscript.[48] Here, successive verse-paragraphs begin with the finite verb *stopon* + compound (for example, *stopon cynerofe* [the royally brave ones advanced], line 200b; *stopon heaðorincas* [the battle-warriors advanced], line 212b; *stopon styrnmode* [the stern-hearted ones advanced], line 227a); only the last of this group carries the main alliteration, and the continued use of compounds (*stercedferhðe . . . ealdgeniðlan . . . medowerige*) underlines the force of expression at this peak of the battle.[49] The fact that four of these compounds should be packed together in a single dense passage of only two-and-a-half lines (lines 227–29a), and that two of the three compounds combined in the *stopon . . . stopon . . . stopon* sequence should be repeated elsewhere in *Judith*, seems to indicate that their disposition here is both deliberate and artful,[50] so rendering their repetition elsewhere in the corpus in a distinctly limited range of poems (with *Andreas* again prominent) all the more intriguing.[51]

When one compares this passage from *Judith* with the matching battle-scene from *Elene*, a number of parallels emerge. Half-lines unique in the extant corpus to these two passages are given in bold italics, overlapping words and phrases are given in italics only; significant repetitions within the passage itself are indicated by underlining:

<u>Heht þa</u> onlice æðelinga <u>hleo,</u>
beorna beaggifa, swa he þæt beacen geseah,
heria hildfruma, þæt him on heofonum ær
geiewed wearð, ofstum myclum,
Constantinus, Cristes rode,
tireadig cyning, tacen gewyrcan.

<u>Heht þa</u> on uhtan mid ærdæge
wigend wreccan, ond wæpenþræce
hebban heorucumbul, ond <u>þæt halige treo</u>
him beforan ferian *on* feonda *gemang*,
beran beacen godes.
Byman *sungon*
*hlude* for hergum. *Hrefn* weorces *gefeah*,
***urigfeðra,*** ***earn*** sið beheold,
wælhreowra wig. *Wulf sang* ahof,
holtes gehleða. Hildegesa stod.

Þær wæs borda gebrec ond beorna geþrec,
heard handgeswing ond herga gring,
syððan heo earhfære ærest metton.
On þæt fæge folc ***flana scuras,***
garas ofer geolorand *on* gramra *gemang*,
hetend heorugrimme, ***hildenædran,***
þurh fingra geweald *forð* on*sendan.*

*Stopon* stiðhidige, stundum wræcon,
bræcon bordhreðan, bil in dufan,
þrungon þræchearde. Þa wæs þuf hafen.
segn for sweotum, sigeleoð galen.
Gylden grima, garas lixtan
on herefelda. Hæðene grungon,
feollon friðelease. Flugon instæpes

Huna leode, wa þæt halige treo
aræran heht Romwara cyning,
heaðofremmende. Wurdon heardingas
wide towrecene.
Sume wig fornam.
Sume unsofte aldor generedon
on þam heresiðe. Sume healfcwice
flugon on fæsten ond feore burgon
æfter stanclifum, stede weardedon
ymb Danubie. Sume drenc fornam
on lagostreame lifes æt ende.

Ða wæs modigra mægen on luste,
***ehton elþeoda*** oð þæt æfen forð
fram dæges orde. Daroðæsc flugon,
***hildenædran.*** Heap wæs gescyrded,
laðra lindwered. Lythwon becwom
Huna herges ham eft þanon.
Þa wæs gesyne þæt sige forgeaf
Constantino cyning ælmihtig
æt þam dægweorce, domweorðunga,
rice under roderum, þurh his rode treo.

Gewat þa heriga helm ham eft þanon,
huðe hremig, (hild wæs gesceaden),
wigge geweorðod. Com þa wigena hleo
þegna þreate þryðbold secan,
beadurof cyning burga neosan.

(*Elene* 99–152)

Then he ordered likewise, the protector of princes, ring-giver of warriors, just as he saw that sign, the war-leader of hosts, which had been shown to him in the heavens, with great haste, the glorious king, Constantine, Christ's cross, to be made a symbol. Then he ordered at dawn, with the break of day, warriors to waken and in that weapon-storm to raise the battle-standard and to carry that holy

> tree before them into the throng of foes, to bear the sign of god. Trumpets sang, loudly before the hosts, the raven rejoiced in the deed, the dewy-feathered eagle beheld the foray, the battle of the slaughter-fierce ones; the wolf raised up a song, the wood's companion; battle-terror reared. There was the clash of shields and the thrash of men; the hard hand-swing and the crash of hosts, after they first found the arrows' flight. Onto that doomed folk dire enemies sent forth showers of darts, spears over the yellow shields into the throng of fierce ones, battle-adders through fingers' force. Bold-hearted they advanced, at times pressed on, broke through the shield-cover, plunged in the blade, thronged on hard in fray. Then was the banner raised, the sign over the troops, the song of victory sung. The golden helmet and spears shone on the field of war. The heathens perished, fell without peace. All at once they fled, the people of the Huns, as that holy tree the king of the Romans ordered raised, doing battle. The bold ones were widely split asunder. Some battle took off, some unsoftly saved their lives in that war-fray, some half-dead fled into the fastness and saved their lives along the stone cliffs, took their places around the Danube, some drowning took off in the water-stream at their life's end. Then was the force of the brave ones in hot spirits; they pursued the foreigners right up to the evening from the start of the day: ash-darts flew, battle-adders. The army was destroyed, the shield-troop of foes: few of the force of the Huns reached thence home again. Then it was clear that the almighty king granted victory to Constantine in that day's work, mighty honours, powerful under the heavens, through his rood-tree. Then the defender of hosts went thence home again, exulting in booty (the battle was settled), made worthy by war. The protector of warriors then went to seek his mighty abode, the battle-brave king, to visit the strongholds, with a band of thegns.

That there are (counting only once the two occurrences here of the half-line *hildenædran*) four parallels (three of them unique) linking this section of *Elene* to the matching scene in *Judith* may seem striking enough, the more so when it is realized that (as earlier) the four parallels appear in the same order in each. But it is only when one factors in the non-unique parallels that the true extent of the overlap becomes clear:[52] there are no fewer than twenty-one elements common to both passages, again appearing in substantially the same order.[53] Though to be sure there are parallels to both battle-scenes elsewhere in surviving Old English poetry,[54] none is quite so extensive or specific. We can see this simply with respect to the so-called "Beasts of Battle" motif: of the sixteen examples of this theme surveyed by Mark Griffith, no two are so similar to each other (and so different from the rest) as these.[55]

But what is perhaps most interesting in comparing these two passages is the way that, despite much common material, each poet has managed to make his piece his own. The passage from *Elene* is a much more artful piece, employing a greater range of rhetorical effects: incremental repetition introduces two verse-paragraphs which focus on the cross as Constantine's banner (*Heht þa* . . . *Heht þa*, lines 99a and 105a), before we find a beautifully compact Beasts of Battle scene (lines 109b–113), leading into the battle itself, introduced by rhyme (lines 114–15: *gebrec . . . geþrec . . . handgeswing . . . herga gring*) and highlighted at its centre by precisely the same mechanism found in the parallel passage from *Judith*, namely *stopon* + compound (*stopon stiðhidige*, line 121a). The fact that the expression *stopon* + compound is not found at all elsewhere in surviving Old English verse only serves to heighten the parallel.[56] In the rest of the passage from *Elene*, essentially the same set of rhymes as before are repeated here (lines 121–23: *wræcon bræcon . . . þræchearde;* cf. line 114: *gebrec . . . geþrec*). And here also Cynewulf introduces his favoured technique of what might be termed "clashing verbs," emphasizing action: finite verbs are found juxtaposed at the end of one line and the beginning of the next (lines 120–27: *onsendan / stopon; wræcon / bræcon; dufan / þrungon; grungon / feollon*); it is perhaps worth highlighting the fact that if this is the only place in this passage where "clashing verbs" occur, they are entirely absent from the parallel passage in *Judith*.[57] Here too Cynewulf employs another favoured technique: beginning and ending consecutive lines with bisyllabic words of similar structure (a-lines: *stopon : bræcon : þrungon : segen* [manuscript *segn*] *: gylden;* b-lines: *wræcon : dufan : hafen : galen : lixtan : grungon*). Even after the battle-scene, Cynewulf shows a greater control over his material than the *Judith*-poet, concluding with a familiar *sum . . . sum . . . sum* passage (lines 131b–137),[58] and two verse-paragraphs tracing the routes home of the opposing armies, linked by the repeated phrase *ham eft þanon* ("back home thence," lines 143b and 148b).

But if this passage is undoubtedly a set-piece *tour de force* in which Cynewulf is exercising his poetic talents to the full, it must also be observed that in this case (as previously) there is rather more warrant in the Latin source than there is for the parallel passage in *Judith*. The relevant passage in the *Inuentio Crucis* reads as follows:[59]

> Et surgens impetum fecit contra barbaros, et fecit antecedere signum, et superueniens cum suo exercitu super barbaros coepit concidere eos proxima luce. Et timuerunt barbari et dederunt fugam per ripas Danobii, et mortua est non minima multitudo. Et dedit Deus in illa die uictoriam regi Constantino per uirtutem crucis. Veniens autem rex Constantinus in suam ciuitatem . . .

> And rising up he made an attack against the barbarians, and had the sign [of the Cross] go before, and coming upon the barbarians with his army he began to slaughter them at break of day. And the barbarians were afraid, and fled along the banks of the Danube, and no small multitude was killed. And God gave King Constantine the victory that day through the power of the Cross. But King Constantine coming into his own city . . .

To be sure, the battle-scene in *Elene* represents a considerable (and considerably artistic) expansion on the bare hints supplied by this passage, but at least in the *Inuentio Crucis* there is specific mention of a battle, a subsequent rout, and a triumphal return: in *Judith* the parallel battle-scene has been described as "a complete invention by the poet."[60] In the light of the preceding evidence, it might be suggested that the *Judith*-poet consciously chose to augment his Latin biblical source at this point from a vernacular verse-source apparently well-known to him—and that direct source was *Elene.*

Close analysis of those passages where parallel half-lines from *Elene* and *Judith* cluster has led us to focus on three sections of *Judith* where the poet seems deliberately to have departed from his source;[61] in each case, there is a tissue of verbal parallels connecting *Judith* to *Elene*, and in two of the three cases the unique parallels shared by the passages in question appear in the same order. To suggest that the poets of *Judith* and *Elene* should both stumble upon the same sequence of unique formulations independently would surely "outrage probability."[62] The evidence appears to indicate that Cynewulf embellished his Latin source, and that the poet of *Judith* then employed a number of Cynewulf's distinctive formulations in *Elene* in embellishing his own. Given that both Cynewulf and the *Judith*-poet were to some extent drawing on Latin learning and a Latin source, such a suggestion is simply in line with the known parallel mode of poetic composition employed by Anglo-Latin poets throughout the pre-Conquest period, namely, formulaic composition based in part on recycling a common stock of poetic formulas from curriculum-authors so widely scattered in the extant verse as to be simply part of the tradition, coupled with the conscious coining of idiosyncratic formulas by individual poets whose own phrasing was deliberately echoed by later generations.[63] Such was the technique employed by (for example) Aldhelm, Bede, Boniface, Alcuin, Aediluulf, Wulfstan of Winchester, and (so far as we can judge) every single Anglo-Saxon who ever chose to compose Latin verse.

The possibility of such direct and deliberate echoing of other texts and other authors makes the careful collection and analysis of formulaic phrasing in extant Old English verse (itself a task made much easier by the use of machine-readable texts and computer-generated concordances) a matter of high priority: only then can we come to a more considered assessment of the significance of the striking parallels of phrasing that link poems both within and across separate manuscripts.[64] To argue that Old English poets deliberately echoed each other's works is of course to return to the state of scholarly debate prior to the application of oral-formulaic theory to Anglo-Saxon studies in 1953, and in particular to question the underlying assumption that if only more Old English verse had survived, many parallels of phrasing unique in the extant corpus today would be recognized as mere commonplace. But if the arguments presented above that *Judith* borrows directly from *Elene* are accepted, then there is evidence that not only (as is widely acknowledged) are there clear overlaps between the Exeter Book and the Vercelli Book (in the shape of *Soul and Body I* and *II*) on the one hand, and between the Exeter Book and the Junius Manuscript (in the shape of *Daniel* and *Azarias*) on the other, but that Cynewulf and his influence extend to three of the four surviving major Old English poetic codices. Given such a pattern of survival, the notion that vast screeds of Old English poetry composed in the "classical" style have been lost is surely suspect. It is time to re-examine the assumptions of comparative chronology and the direct influence of one poem or poet on another that comprised so much of Anglo-Saxon scholarship for a century or so prior to 1953, even if with all the sophisticated panoply of computistical aids we end up simply repeating old conclusions that were set aside as a result of the impact of oral-formulaic theory. After all, as generations of Anglo-Saxon poets composing in the alternate literary languages of Latin and Old English seem to have agreed: if a thing is worth saying, it is probably worth saying again.[65]

## NOTES

1. A pioneering work is Jess B. Bessinger, Jr., "Computer Techniques for an Old English Concordance," *American Documentation* 12 (1961): 227–29; see too Angus Cameron, Roberta Frank, and John Leyerle, eds., *Computers and Old English Concordances* (Toronto, 1970).

2. See, for example, the excellent overview by Peter S. Baker, "Old English and Computing: A Guided Tour," in *Reading Old English Texts*, ed. Katherine O'Brien O'Keeffe (Cambridge, 1997), 192–215.

3. A useful index to such sites can be found at the "Old English Pages" site maintained by Cathy Ball, http://www.georgetown.edu/cball/oe/old_english.html. Other excellent examples of "clearing-houses" of Anglo-Saxon electronic research are the websites maintained by Simon Keynes, http://www.trin.cam.ac.uk/sdk13/sdk13home.html, and by TOEBI, http://www.hcu.ox.ac.uk/toebi/. These sites, like all the others mentioned in this essay, were last accessed in January 2005.

4. The first and still most prolific discussion-group is ANSAX-L, based at listserv@wvnvm.wvnet.edu; previous discussions are archived at http://www.mun.ca/Ansaxdat/.

5. So far, poetry has been extremely well-served: the best model available to date is Kevin S. Kiernan et al., eds., *Electronic Beowulf*, 2 CDs (London, 2000); a CD containing facsimiles and texts of the Exeter Book has been in preparation by Bernard J. Muir for some time. The Bodleian Library has put a complete facsimile of the Junius Manuscript on the web at http://image.ox.ac.uk/show?collection=bodleian&manuscript=msjunius11 and issued a CD: see Bernard J. Muir, ed., *MS Junius 11*, Bodleian Digital Texts 1 (Oxford, 2004).

6. Among the more promising examples of hypertexts available on the web are two which focus on Wulfstan's sermons: an electronic *Sermo Lupi ad Anglos*

produced by Melissa J. Bernstein at http://english3.fsu.edu/~wulfstan, and a version of the first six of Wulfstan's sermons by Joyce Tally Lionarons at http://webpages.ursinus.edu/jlionarons/wulfstan/wulfstan.html.

7. The entire extant corpus of Old English, as defined by the ongoing Dictionary of Old English project (itself with a website at http://www.doe.utoronto.ca), is to be found at http://ets.umdl.umich.edu/o/oec. Two large projects that have useful websites include "Fontes Anglo-Saxonici" (at http://fontes.english.ox.ac.uk) and "SASLC, Sources of Anglo-Saxon Literary Culture" at http://www.wmich.edu/medieval/research/saslc.

8. A now rather clunky-looking but still extremely effective DOS-based concordance-program is Micro-OCP, first released by the Oxford University Computing Service through Oxford University Press in 1988. Perhaps the best of the new generation of Windows-based concordance-programs is Concordance, available through http://www.rjcw.freeserve.co.uk. It is notable that among the first attempts to employ computers in Old English were two published concordances: Jess B. Bessinger, *A Concordance to Beowulf*, programmed by Philip H. Smith (Ithaca, N.Y., 1969), and Jess B. Bessinger, *A Concordance to the Anglo-Saxon Poetic Records*, programmed by Philip H. Smith (Ithaca, N.Y., 1978).

9. Representative studies include Arthur Fritzsche, "Das angelsächsische Gedicht *Andreas* und Cynewulf," *Anglia* 2 (1879): 441–96; Gregor Sarrazin, "*Beowulf* und Kynewulf," *Anglia* 9 (1886): 515–50; Gregor Sarrazin, *Beowulf-Studien: Ein Beitrag zur Geschichte altgermanischer Sage und Dichtung* (Berlin, 1888); Johannes Kail, "Über die Parallelstellen in der angelsächsischen Poesie," *Anglia* 12 (1889): 21–40; Gregor Sarrazin, "Parallelstellen in altenglischer Dichtung," *Anglia* 14 (1892): 186–92. See too Phoebe M. Luehrs, "A Summary of Sarrazin's 'Studies in Beowulf,'" *Western Reserve University Bulletin* 7 (1904): 146–65.

10. Francis P. Magoun, Jr., "The Oral-Formulaic Character of Anglo-Saxon Narrative Poetry," *Speculum* 28 (1953): 446–67. For overviews, see Alexandra Hennessey Olsen, "Oral-Formulaic Research in Old English Studies: I," *Oral Tradition* 1 (1986): 548–606, and "Oral-Formulaic Research in Old English Studies: II," *Oral Tradition* 3 (1988): 138–90; Andy Orchard, "Oral Tradition," in *Reading Old English Texts*, ed. O'Keeffe, 101–23; and John Miles Foley, ed., *Oral-Formulaic Theory and Research: An Introduction and Annotated Bibliography* (New York, 1985). A web-based version of Foley's *Bibliography*, updated through 1992, can be found at http://www.missouri.edu/~csottime/biblio.html.

11. The key study is Larry D. Benson, "The Literary Character of Anglo-Saxon Formulaic Poetry," *Publications of the Modern Language Association* 81 (1966): 334–41, although an early dissenting view is that of Claes Schaar, "On a New Theory of Old English Poetic Diction," *Neophilologus* 40 (1956): 301–5. Other stud-

ies which extend the analysis beyond Old English verse include Michael Lapidge, "Aldhelm's Latin Poetry and Old English Verse," *Comparative Literature* 31 (1979): 249–314; Andy Orchard, "Crying Wolf: Oral Style and the *Sermones Lupi*," *Anglo-Saxon England* 21 (1992): 239–64; Andy Orchard, *The Poetic Art of Aldhelm*, Cambridge Studies in Anglo-Saxon England 8 (Cambridge, 1994), 73–125; Andy Orchard, "Old Sources, New Resources: Finding the Right Formula for Boniface," *Anglo-Saxon England* 30 (2001): 15–38; and Andy Orchard, "Both Style and Substance: The Case for Cynewulf," in *Anglo-Saxon Styles*, ed. G. H. Brown and C. Karkov (Albany, N.Y., 2003), 271–305.

12. I have in progress a project entitled "An Anglo-Saxon Formulary" which seeks to identify and catalogue formulaic diction in four key areas of Anglo-Saxon literature in both Latin and Old English prose and verse dating from the seventh century to the eleventh, namely Old English verse, Anglo-Latin hexameter poetry, Wulfstan's sermons and the Old English anonymous homiletic tradition, and the Latin letters of the Bonifatian correspondence. The results will eventually be presented on the web in an online database. In providing the chance for researchers to analyse formulas by any combination of texts, authors, scribes, or manuscripts, "An Anglo-Saxon Formulary" will complement a number of major international projects currently concentrating on the literary culture of Anglo-Saxon England (such as *Fontes* or *SASLC*; see n. 7 above), and will provide a powerful tool for a deeper understanding of Anglo-Saxon literature (whether composed in Latin or Old English) as a whole.

13. Anita Riedinger, "The Poetic Formula in *Andreas*, *Beowulf* and the Tradition" (PhD diss., New York University, 1985); Carole Hughes Funk, "History of *Andreas* and *Beowulf*: Comparative Scholarship" (PhD diss., University of Denver, 1997); Alison M. Powell, "Verbal Parallels in *Andreas* and its Relationship to *Beowulf* and Cynewulf" (PhD dissertation, University of Cambridge, 2002). Anita Riedinger has also published a series of pertinent articles, including "The Old English Formula in Context," *Speculum* 60 (1985): 294–317; "*Andreas* and the Formula in Transition," in *Hermeneutics and Medieval Culture*, ed. P. J. Gallacher and H. Damico (Albany, N.Y., 1989), 183–91; and "The Formulaic Relationship Between *Beowulf* and *Andreas*," in *Heroic Poetry in the Anglo-Saxon Period: Studies in Honor of Jess B. Bessinger, Jr.*, ed. H. Damico and J. Leyerle, Studies in Medieval Culture 32 (Kalamazoo, Mich., 1993), 283–312. See also Andy Orchard, *A Critical Companion to Beowulf* (Cambridge, 2003), 163–66.

14. Powell, "Verbal Parallels in *Andreas*," 273–82 (listing eighty-nine parallels uniquely shared by *Andreas* and *Beowulf*) and 283–99 (listing 149 parallels uniquely shared by *Andreas* and the four signed poems of Cynewulf). See too, Orchard, "Both Style and Substance."

15. See Andy Orchard, *The Poetic Craft of Cynewulf,* Cambridge Studies in Anglo-Saxon England 35 (Cambridge, forthcoming).

16. Claes Schaar, *Critical Studies in the Cynewulf Group,* Lund Studies in English 17 (Lund, 1949; repr. New York, 1967), esp. 235–56 and 291–95.

17. Compare, for example, George P. Krapp, ed., *Andreas and the Fates of the Apostles: Two Anglo-Saxon Narrative Poems* (Boston, 1906), lvi–lvii (listing many parallels between *Andreas* and a range of poems, and deducing direct relationships between them), and Kenneth R. Brooks, ed., *Andreas, and the Fates of the Apostles* (Oxford, 1961), xxii–xxvii (where a handful of parallels are distinctly underplayed).

18. Mark Griffith, ed., *Judith* (Exeter, 1997), offers an exemplary edition; *Cynewulf's Elene,* ed. P. O. E. Gradon (Exeter, 1977), gives a much less full account. Still useful, especially in the present context, are Albert S. Cook, ed., *Judith, an Old English Epic Fragment* (Boston, 1893); T. Gregory Foster, *Judith: Studies in Metre, Language, and Style* (Strassburg, 1892); *Cynewulf's Elene,* ed. Charles W. Kent (Boston, 1889); and *Cynewulf's Elene,* 3rd ed., ed. F. Holthausen (Heidelberg, 1914).

19. For a detailed analysis of the diction and style of *Judith,* tracing both its similarities to and differences from the style and diction of Cynewulf, see Foster, *Judith,* 67–93.

20. In identifying these parallels, I have attempted to be as inclusive as possible, and have therefore counted what might be considered "natural" combinations of (for example) infinitive + auxiliary verb combinations (such as [15]), as well as cases where the half-line in question consists of a single (compound) word (such as [19] and [27]).

21. See parallels [2], [13], and [15] for cases where the same phrase matched in *Elene* occurs in more than one line of *Judith,* and parallels [13]–[14] and [20]–[21] for cases where both half-lines of an individual verse in *Judith* can be matched in *Elene.*

22. The parallels in question are [3], [6], [7], [9], [18], [26], [27], [28], [30], [32], and [33].

23. The parallels in question are [1] and [8]: the phrase *fæder on roderum* also occurs in *Christ B* 758b, and *þrymmes hyrde* likewise occurs in *Juliana* 280a.

24. The parallels in question are [2] (cf. *Genesis A* 2673b: *ofstum miclum*), [4] (cf. *Beowulf* 1171a, 1476a, and 1602a: *goldwine gumena*), [10] (cf. *Exodus* 298b: *wolcna hrof*), [11] (cf. *Paris Psalter* 67.4.5: *naman nemned*), [13] (cf. *Guthlac B* 820b: *frymþa god*), [16] (cf. *Guthlac A* 646a and *Christ B* 599a: *þrynesse þrym; Juliana* 726b: *þrynis þrymsittende*); [23] (cf. *Christ B* 461: *hæleð mid hlaford to þære halgan byrg; Christ B* 534: *hæleð hygerofe in þa halgan burg; Guthlac A* 812b: *in þa halgan burg*); [24] (cf. *Battle of Brunanburh* 65a: *wulf on wealde*); [25] (cf. *Seafarer* 24b–25a: *earn . . . urigfeþra*); [29] (cf. *Guthlac B* 1338a: *life bilidene*). For the argument that *Guthlac B*

is written by Cynewulf, see Orchard, "Both Style and Substance," and Orchard, *The Poetic Craft of Cynewulf.*

25. So, for example, the phrase *sinces brytta* or equivalent (parallel [5]) is found in *Genesis A* 1857b, 2642a, and 2728b; *Beowulf* 607b, 1170a, 1922a, and 2071a; *Wanderer* 25b; and *Preface to Gregory's Dialogues* 24b. The phrase *ond þæt word acwæð* or equivalent (parallel [12]) is found in *Genesis A* 1110b; *Genesis B* 639a; *Christ A* 316b; *Christ B* 474a and 714b; *Guthlac B* 1347b; *Azarias* 4b; *Juliana* 45a, 143b, 631b, and 640a; *Beowulf* 654b and 2046b; and *Wanderer* 91b. The phrase *frofre gæst* or equivalent (parallel [14]) is found in *Andreas* 906b and 1684b, *Christ A* 207b, *Christ B* 728b, *Guthlac A* 136b, *Guthlac B* 936b, *Juliana* 724a, and *Metrical Charm* 11.10. The phrase *biddan wille* or equivalent (parallel [15]) is found in *Andreas* 84b, *Juliana* 272b and 278b, *Beowulf* 427b, and *Kentish Psalm* 68b. The compound *collenferhð* or equivalent (parallel [19]) is found in *Andreas* 349b, 538a, 1108a, and 1578a; *Beowulf* 1806a and 2785a; *Fates of the Apostles* 54a; *Wanderer* 71a; and *Whale* 17a. The phrase *cyninga wuldor* (parallel [20]) is found in *Andreas* 171b, 555b, 854b, and 1411a; *Christ B* 508a; *Juliana* 279b; *Resignation* 21a; and *Menologium* 1b. The phrase *þæt gecyðed wearð* or equivalent (parallel [21]) is found in *Andreas* 90b and *Menologium* 52b. The phrase *eft to eðle* or equivalent (parallel [22]) is found in *Guthlac A* 355a and *Solomon and Saturn* 418a. The phrase *to ðære beorhtan byrig* or equivalent (parallel [31]) is found in *Andreas* 1649a, *Guthlac B* 1191a, *Beowulf* 1199a, and *Christ B* 519a.

26. See further Powell, "Verbal Parallels in *Andreas*," 105–232, and Schaar, *Critical Studies*, 239–51 and 261–87.

27. The phrase *anra gehwylc(ne)* or equivalent (parallel [17]) also occurs in *Genesis A* 2490; *Exodus* 187; *Daniel* 369; *Christ and Satan* 430; *Andreas* 933 and 1283; *Soul and Body I* 98; *Dream of the Rood* 108; *Christ C* 1025 and 1029; *Phoenix* 503, 522, and 534; *Riddle* 13.5; *Judgement Day I* 3; *Beowulf* 732 and 784; *Paris Psalter* 60.4.3; *Metres of Boethius* 11.83, 18.3, 20.65, 20.228, 25.20, 25.63, and 26.95; *Rune Poem* 60; *Solomon and Saturn* 234 and 357; *Judgement Day II* 96.

28. For the concept of the formulaic system, see further Donald K. Fry, "Old English Formulas and Systems," *English Studies* 48 (1967): 193–204; John D. Niles, "Formula and Formulaic System in *Beowulf*," in *Oral Traditional Literature: A Festschrift for Albert Bates Lord*, ed. John Miles Foley (Columbus, Ohio, 1981), 394–415; and Anita R. Riedinger, "The Old English Formula in Context," *Speculum* 60 (1985): 294–317.

29. So, for example, one might posit the existence of a system "X (x) (*on/in*) *geþance/geþonce*" which might generate parallel [3] above. In fact, apart from the lines from *Judith* and *Elene* indicated, only the half-lines *þriste on geþance* (found in *Andreas* 237a and *Elene* 267a) and *þriste geþoncge* (found in *Juliana* 358a) in the extant

corpus match the requirements of the system. This is not to deny the usefulness of studying formulaic systems, simply to re-assert the extent to which such study should give particular weight to verbatim repetitions. On the parallel use of what might be termed formulaic systems in Anglo-Latin hexameter verse, see Andy Orchard, "After Aldhelm: The Teaching and Transmission of the Anglo-Latin Hexameter," *Journal of Medieval Latin* 2 (1992): 96–133, at 113, where I show that in his *Vita metrica S. Cuthberti* Bede uses the matching phrases *perculsus corda pauore* (line 235), *uibratur corda timore* (line 663), and *perculsus corda tremore* (line 929), all signifying how a character was "struck with fear."

30. In counting 'unique' parallels here, I have included those where the parallel in question is either only found in *Elene* and *Judith* or where it is only found in *Elene*, *Judith*, and the poems of Cynewulf; in the latter category I have included *Guthlac B* alongside the four signed poems.

31. A useful breakdown of the structure of *Judith* is found in Cook, *Judith*, xxxix.

32. The parallels in question are nos. [11]–[16] above.

33. See nn. 24 and 25 above.

34. A less close parallel is found in *Metrical Charm* 11.10: *ac gehæle me ælmihtig and sunu and frofre gast.*

35. See n. 14 above.

36. Cf. Carl T. Berkhout and James F. Doubleday, "The Net in *Judith* 46b–54a," *Neuphilologische Mitteilungen* 74 (1973): 630–34. The allusion to Holofernes's fly-net derives from Judith 10:19, whereas the passage preceding the one cited is drawn from Judith 13:1, and that following from 13:4.

37. For a useful description of the relationship of *Judith* to its source, see Griffith, *Judith*, 47–61, esp. 59–60, which discuss this very passage.

38. The manuscript has the normal Latin abbreviation for *mille* ("a thousand") at line 327b, although the alliteration clearly requires the Old English *þusendo;* the word *word* is missing at line 338a, but again is clearly required by the alliteration and by the parallel with line 344a; and the manuscript reads the nonsensical *weno* at line 348b.

39. See parallel [13] and n. 24 above; the phrase *frumþa god* (or equivalent) only occurs outside these two poems in the extant corpus in *Guthlac B.*

40. Michael Lapidge, "Cynewulf and the *Passio S. Iulianae*," in *Unlocking the Wordhoard: Anglo-Saxon Studies in Memory of Edward B. Irving, Jr.*, ed. Mark Amodio and Katherine O'Brien O'Keeffe (Toronto, 2003), 147–71.

41. For a fair if somewhat dated account, see *Cynewulf's Elene*, ed. Gradon 15–22.

42. See Stephan Borgehammar, *How the Holy Cross Was Found: From Event to Medieval Legend*, Bibliotheca Theologiae Practicae 47 (Stockholm, 1991). The older discussion by A. Holder, ed., *Inventio Sanctae Crucis* (Leipzig, 1889) is still useful.

43. Borgehammar, *How the Holy Cross Was Found*, 259–60 (lines 59–67).

44. Cf. Griffith, *Judith*, 62–63.

45. Cf. Griffith, *Judith*, 62.

46. As Griffith, *Judith*, 62, puts it, the scene is "a complete invention by the poet, being an imminent rather than actual event in the source."

47. The standard study remains that of Kenneth Jackson, "Incremental Repetition in the Early Welsh *Englyn*," *Speculum* 16 (1941): 304–21; see too Adeline Courtney Bartlett, *The Larger Rhetorical Patterns in Anglo-Saxon Poetry* (New York, 1935), 4–61.

48. Orchard, *Critical Companion*, 78–79 and 189–91.

49. Of these compounds, *cynerof*, *heaðorinc*, *stercedferhð*, and *ealdgeniðla* are confined to poetry, and *styrnmod* and *medowerig* are unique to *Judith* within the extant corpus, the latter occurring twice, in lines 229a and 245a.

50. So, for example, the compound *cynerof* occurs in lines 200b and 311b (the latter in a context which is a clear echo of its former appearance), and *heaðorinc* in lines 179a and 212b. It also seems noteworthy that the compound *stercedferhð* also occurs twice in *Judith*, in lines 55b and 227b.

51. Two of these compounds are uniquely shared in the extant corpus by *Judith* and *Andreas*: *cynerof* appears in *Andreas* 484a and 585a, as well as in *Judith* 200b and 311b, whilst *ealdgeniðla* appears in *Andreas* 1048b and 1341b, as well as in *Judith* 228b. Forms of the compound *stercedferhð* are uniquely shared in the extant corpus by *Andreas* (line 1233b), *Elene* (line 38a), and *Judith* (lines 55b and 227b).

52. One might add here parallels [23] and [24] above from the battle-scene in *Judith*, although in each case they are neither specific to the poems in question nor matched in the battle-scene in *Elene*.

53. Consider, for example, the following sequences: *hlude . . . gefeah wulf . . . hrefn earn . . . urigfeðera . . . sang . . . stopon . . . forð . . . flana scuras hildenædran . . . garas sendon in heardra gemang . . . stopon . . . unsofte . . . ehton elðeoda* (*Judith*); *sungon . . . hlude . . . hrefn . . . gefeah urigfeðra earn . . . wulf . . . sang . . . flana scuras garas . . . on gramra gemang . . . hildenædran . . . forð onsendan stopon . . . unsofte . . . ehton elþeoda* (*Elene*).

54. Cf. Griffith, *Judith*, 62–63.

55. Mark S. Griffith, "Convention and Originality in the Old English 'Beasts of Battle' Typescene," *Anglo-Saxon England* 22 (1993): 179–99.

56. As with the compounds associated with *stopon* in *Judith*, the compound *stiðhidig* is rare within the extant corpus, being found elsewhere only in *Genesis A*

2897a and Cynewulf's *Juliana* 654a. One might also cite in this context the only other repetition of the verb *stopon* in *Elene* 716, where again it alliterates with a rare *stið*-compound: *Stopon ða to þære stowe stiðhycgende.*

57. Indeed, there seem to be only two examples of "clashing verbs" in all of *Judith*, at lines 175–76 (*gespeow/spræc*) and lines 277–78 (*fordraf/funde*).

58. See further, Matti Rissanen, "'Sum' in Old English Poetry," in *Modes of Interpretation in Old English Literature: Essays in Honour of Stanley B. Greenfield*, ed. Phyllis Rugg Brown, Georgia Ronan Crampton, and Fred C. Robinson (Toronto, 1986), 197–225.

59. Borgehammar, *How the Holy Cross Was Found*, 256 (lines 14–19).

60. Griffith, *Judith*, 62 (and cf. n. 46 above).

61. It is worth noting that in a fourth passage from *Judith* identified above as containing a cluster of parallels with *Elene*, namely, *Judith* 326–44, which comes right at the end of the poem as it now survives, two of the three parallels identified in this brief (nineteen-line) passage are uniquely shared in the extant corpus by the poems in question. The parallels are given as [31]–[33] above.

62. The phrase is Robert E. Kaske's, quoted first in Frederick M. Biggs, Thomas D. Hill, and Paul E. Szarmach, eds., *Anglo-Saxon Literary Culture: A Trial Version*, Medieval and Renaissance Texts and Studies 74 (Binghamton, 1990), xvi, and again by Christine Rauer, *Beowulf and the Dragon: Parallels and Analogues* (Cambridge, 2000), 10, in the middle of a useful discussion of the difference between sources and analogues.

63. For the model, see, for example, Andy Orchard, "After Aldhelm."

64. So, for example, one might note that a line that appears twice in *Andreas* (*Nu ðu miht gehyran, hyse leofesta* [*Andreas* 595 and 811]) appears to echo elements of both *The Dream of the Rood* (*Nu ðu miht gehyran, hæleð min se leofa* [78]) and *Elene* (*Nu ðu meaht gehyran, hæleð min se leofa* [511] and *hyse leofesta* [523a]); no other extant poem provides so close a match, and of course all three poems are contained in the Vercelli Book.

65. I am grateful to Tom Hall and Samantha Zacher for their help and advice in producing this paper; my greatest debt remains to Michael Lapidge, for his instruction and inspiration over more than two decades.

# The Contexts of Notre Dame 67

A. S. G. EDWARDS

THE MANUSCRIPT SOLD AT CHRISTIE'S ON 11 JULY 2000, LOT 73, from the collection of William and Christina Foyle,[1] and subsequently purchased by the University of Notre Dame, is one of unusual interest to students of Middle English devotional literature, as well as to cultural historians of broader preoccupation. Since it has been in private hands until recently,[2] the manuscript has never been the subject of study.[3] My concern is to offer a brief account of the likely date and site of production of the manuscript, to discuss the contemporary environment of its ownership, and to indicate what this suggests about the lay reading communities within which it must have circulated.

It may be helpful to begin by briefly describing the primary contents of the manuscript: these are two Middle English prose devotional works, *A Mirror to Devout People* (ff. 1r–108r), and *The Craft of Dying* (ff. 109v–126r). The first of these is clearly of Carthusian authorship. The beginning of the *Mirror* explains that while contemplating his own work the author (who is never named) became aware of "a man of our ordoure" (the only other manuscript of this work is more precise in specifying "a man of oure ordyr of charturhowse") who had translated into English "a booke of þe same matier þe which is called Vita Cristi" (f. 1r). This is a clear reference to the Pseudo-Bonaventure *Meditationes Vitae Christi*, translated into Middle English prose as the *Mirror of the Blessed Life of Jesus Christ* by Nicholas Love, the prior of the Carthusian abbey of Mount Grace, in Yorkshire—a work that is clearly the most popular and widely circulating evidence of the order's interest in the production of devotional works in England.[4]

Love's translation was completed by 1409 and licensed in London by Archbishop Arundel in the following year. Awareness of Love's work must have spread quite rapidly within metropolitan circles after this date, to judge from the evidence of the surviving copies, which include one by the so-called "Delta scribe."[5] It would have been hard for the *Mirror*-author to have remained in ignorance of the existence of Love's *Mirror of the Blessed Life of Jesus Christ* for long even if he resided in a sequestered environment, which leads one to suppose that the *Mirror to Devout People* was probably begun quite soon after 1410. How long it took to complete and to disseminate are not easy questions to answer. University of Notre Dame, MS 67 is probably the earliest surviving copy of the *Mirror to Devout People.* Indeed, as I have said already, only one other copy is extant, in what is now Cambridge University Library, MS Gg. 1. 6, ff. 1–144. It is possibly later than the Foyle copy and certainly inferior in material form. It is on paper, rather than vellum as is Foyle, with no decoration apart from a little rubrication, again very different from Foyle. It was produced for the Carthusian house at Sheen, in Middlesex.[6] A note at the beginning identifies it as "liber domus Ihesu de Bethleem ordinis cartusiensis de Shene" and identifies the scribe as "Willielmus plenus amoris" (f. iii), apparently William Mede (d. 1473), a monk of the house and the copyist of a number of manuscripts.[7]

The *Mirror* is addressed to a "gostely sustre in Ihesu criste" and characterizes itself as "a meditacioun of þe passioun of our lorde." It is essentially a compilation of passages from devotional writings such as Suso's *Orologium sapientiae* and the revelations of St. Bridget, Catherine of Siena, Elizabeth of Töss ("Hungary"), and Mechtild of Hackeborn.[8] In view of its envisioned audience the particular emphasis on such devotional figures is unsurprising. And perhaps such a gender specific audience goes some way towards accounting for its limited circulation. By the early fifteenth century the circulation of works specifically for such readers was still a regional phenomenon: some manuscripts of the writings of Rolle and Hilton spring most obviously to mind and will have some relevance to my narrative. Certainly it seems to have lacked the broadly based appeal of Love's work.

The other Middle English prose work in Notre Dame 67, *The Craft of Dying*, is a translation of a Latin treatise in the *ars moriendi* tradition that became increasingly widespread in England in the early fifteenth century, in both verse and prose. The present work was seemingly composed initially in Latin at the time of the Council of Constance in 1418, possibly by a Dominican,[9] and subsequently translated into various vernaculars, including French, German, Italian, Catalan, and, of course, Middle English.[10]

Unlike the *Mirror*, which clearly suffered from the competition of Love's work, *The Craft of Dying* was popular in Middle English. Fourteen other copies survive,[11] and all of those whose early provenance is establishable can be associated with either individuals or institutions within the metropolitan area or its environs. A number can be linked to religious houses there: thus London, British Library, MSS Harley 1706 and Additional 10596 are associated with Barking Abbey, a house of Benedictine nuns; Oxford, Bodleian Library, MS Douce 322 with Dartford Abbey, a house of Dominican nuns. At least four (London, British Library, MS Harley 4011; Cambridge, Trinity College, MS R. 3. 21; Oxford Bodleian Library, MS Rawlinson C. 894; and Oxford, Corpus Christi College, MS 220) were in lay ownership in London at an early date.[12] The text of *The Craft of Dying* in Notre Dame 67 is written by a different scribe from the one who copied the *Mirror*; the *Mirror*-scribe is most readily distinguished by the fact that he regularly dots the letter y, and also employs distinctive scrolled catchwords which are absent from the section containing *The Craft of Dying*. The decoration, however, seems consistent across the whole manuscript. Such circumstances may suggest that the commissioning of *The Craft of Dying* was contemplated only some time after the first scribe completed his stint, since he was not available to copy the second text.

The availability of such resources, in particular the quality of the decoration, together with the indications of the origins of other copies of both texts suggest that Notre Dame 67 was produced in the London area.[13] The links that seem to have existed between monks who were scribes at the Charterhouse at Sheen and the secular book trade may provide a conduit for the transmission of its texts between devotional and commercial environments.[14] For example, one monk there, Stephen Dodesham, who copied two manuscripts of Love's *Mirror* while he was at Sheen, evidently worked as a commercial scribe at an earlier stage of his life and was the scribe for one of the manuscripts of *The Craft of Dying*: Oxford, Bodleian Library, MS Bodley 423.[15]

But if Notre Dame 67 may have been produced in London, when was it produced and for whom? Clearly on the evidence of *The Craft of Dying* it could not have come into existence before the 1420s at the very earliest and possibly not for some time after that. The hands and decoration both seem to suggest a date around the middle of the century, probably towards the end of the second quarter. Such an approximate dating is supported by other manuscript evidence concerning its earliest owners and presumed commissioners. On its opening page there appear, within an initial, the arms of two families (see plate 1): those of the Scropes *azure*, a bend *or* with label *argent*, impaling those of Chaworth; more precisely the arms of John, 4th Baron Scrope of Masham and his wife Elizabeth Chaworth, who were married some time before 24 August 1418. John predeceased his wife, dying in 1455. She lived until 1466/7. Since the arms seem integral to the manuscript, rather than a later addition, one can date the manuscript within this period, most probably towards the end of it.[16]

It would be tempting to suggest that the collocation of texts is linked specifically to the identities and circumstances of the manuscript's owners and presumed commissioners. The *Mirror to Devout People* assumes a female audience. *The Craft of Dying* is a work obviously relevant to one conscious of the imminence of death. John Scrope cannot have had long to study the latter text, should he have wished to. Such speculation can be fleshed out and perhaps strengthened by some consideration not just of the biographies of Elizabeth and John, but also of the environments of reading and book collecting in which they and—equally crucially—their immediate families can be situated. Who were these owners, evidently literate persons of some affluence, with an apparent interest in devotional vernacular literature?

One may begin with Elizabeth. She is the daughter of Sir Thomas Chaworth (1380–1459), a member of the Nottinghamshire gentry sufficiently prominent to be characterized as "the wealthiest of the county's knights"[17] and a member of Parliament.[18] He was also a notable book collector, one who has left us substantial evidence of his interests. This evidence includes his will, in English, which contains a number of bequests of books. His daughter, Elizabeth Scrope, receives only a single book, "a fair Mesboke." But other bequests are more extensive. His son, William, receives "a boke of Englissh ye which is called Policonicon [presumably Trevisa's translation of Higden's *Polychronicon*], another boke of Notes of Fynes . . . another olde Messe boke with a boke of Placebo and Dirige . . . the lesce Antiphoner of iiij, a Graile, a Manuell, a litel Portose, the which the saide Thomas toke w^t hym always when he rode, a Sauter with Placebo and Dirige, and an Hympner in the same."

Clearly this bequest is a judicious mixture of the pious and the useful: what look like two Psalters, an Antiphonal, a Manual, and a breviary, as well as a legal ("Notes of Fynes") and an historical work ("Policonicon"). Where one places "a Graile" is unclear; its immediate context suggests most probably that it here means a Gradual, a service book with chants for the Mass, but the Scropes did possess an Arthurian manuscript at a later date.[19]

But these were not Thomas's only bequests. His cousin, Robert Clifton, gets "a newe boke of Inglisse, y^e which begynnyth with y^e lyffe of Seynt Albon and Amphibell and other mony dyuers lyfeȝ and thynges in y^e same boke," possibly San Marino, Calif., Huntington Library, MS HM 140.[20] And another cousin, Richard Willoughby, receives "an Englisse boke called Grace de Dieu,"—that is, a copy of *The Pilgrimage of the Soul*, a quite widely circulating Middle English translation of Deguileville's *Pelerinage de l'Ame*. And outside his family, he bequeaths to William, Archbishop of York, "an Englissh boke called Orilogium Sapiencie," while to "maister Gull" he leaves "a boke written in Latin called Policronicon."[21] Several other books survive, both pious and historical, containing his arms, that are not mentioned in his will. The most notable of the former is the massive Wollaton Antiphonal (590 x 400 mm), now Nottingham, University Library, MS 250.[22] There are also two books in English: a copy of Trevisa's translation of Bartholomaeus Anglicus's *De proprietatibus rerum*, now New York, Columbia University Library, MS Plimpton 263,[23] and one of Lydgate's *Troy Book*, now London, British Library, MS Cotton Augustus A. iv.[24] These last are all large and handsome books, which testify to the scale and scope of Chaworth's book collecting. Evidently Thomas Chaworth was a substantial bibliophile, one to whom both the quality as well as the quantity of his books mattered.

But the immediate contexts of the Chaworth collection are more suggestive in relation to Notre Dame 67. The family is associated with various kinds of books, including pious ones in the vernacular. It is perhaps noteworthy that one of the books Thomas Chaworth owned was "an Englissh boke called Orilogium Sapiencie," a work that was a source for the *Mirror to Devout People*, and another, "an Englisse boke called Grace de Dieu," is to recur in the history of the Scropes as book collectors.[25]

Neither of these works seems to have circulated in England before the early fifteenth century. And a number of the books of which we have a record have a distinctly contemporary feel to them, the "newe boke of Inglisse" for example, and the Trevisa translations, which again seem to have been copied by commercial scribes only from the fifteenth century. But Thomas may have been influenced to some degree by family traditions of collecting. There are grounds for suspecting that not all the books he owned were his own acquisitions, and that he inherited some sort of library from his forebears. Evidence for this comes from yet another book, one seemingly in the family's possession from the fourteenth century. This is a recently identified genealogical roll of the Kings of England, originally composed in the fourteenth century and extending to the reign of Edward II, but enlarged in the early fifteenth century down to the reign of Henry IV. This manuscript, now in a private collection in London,[26] may have been made for Maud de Chaworth (d. before December 1322), wife of Henry, Earl of Lancaster. It hints at a more extended tradition of book collecting within the family.

In general, however, the rather arriviste feel of Thomas Chaworth as a book collector stands in striking contrast to the activities of members of the house of Scrope into which Elizabeth Chaworth married. This house, with its distinct but related lines of Masham (in North Yorkshire) and of Bolton (in the West Riding of Yorkshire), came into being in the fourteenth century and "contributed a large number of the realm's justices, exchequer officials, soldiers and ambassadors."[27] The Masham branch of the family achieved the apogee of its influence in the late fourteenth and early fifteenth centuries. Richard Scrope (b. 1350?), younger brother of Stephen, 2nd Lord Scrope of Masham, became Archbishop of York in 1398. His resistance to Henry IV made him an early political martyr to Lancastrian Realpolitik with his execution in a field outside York on 18 June 1405.[28] Shakespeare's view of Richard as "an iron man . . . / Cheering a rout of rebels with your drum / Turning the word to sword, and life to death" (2 *Henry IV*, IV.i.236–38) does not seem to have been shared in the north of England in the fifteenth century, where he was still, some generations after his execution "holy bisshope Scrope, the blyssed confessour,"[29] and where evidence of devotion to his memory is extensive: in painting,[30] stained glass,[31] verse, and song.[32] This devotion extended to his relics, including his books. Thus, in 1459, one Thomas Dautre bequeathed to "magistro Willelmo Langton, spirituali patri meo, usum unius libri . . . quem librum Beatus Ricardus le Scrop habuit et gerebat in sinu suo tempore suae decollacionis."[33] This book cannot now be identified, nor are there, with one exception, other surviving indications of Richard's library. This exception is an ordinal, which now forms part (ff. 355–95) of London, British Library, MS Stowe 12. It has Richard's arms in an historiated initial on the opening leaf.

In contrast, the execution for treason of his nephew, Henry, 3rd Baron Scrope, Treasurer of England, a decade later, on 5 August 1415 at Southampton, prior to Henry V's departure to France, provided the opportunity for an extensive record of his book collecting. One consequence of the death of this "cruel, / Ingrateful, savage and inhuman creature," as one of Shakespeare's characters was to term him (*Henry V*, II.ii.91–92), was the forfeiture of much of his massive wealth. The records of this forfeiture survive, as does Henry's will. These documents together paint a picture of a very substantial private library. In total they record about eighty separate books, and this may not be the full picture of his collecting.[34] What is striking is the evidence of interest, particularly in his will, in devotional and pious books and the circles associated with them.[35] Many of these were bequeathed to members of his family. To his mother Margaret he left "omnes libros Capellae" as well as "unum Portiforium, & unum Missale de usu Eborum, & unum Librum de Vitis Sanctorum in Gallicis" (276). His brother Stephen, archdeacon of Richmond, to whom I will return, received "unum Librum de Omeliis Sancti Gregorii, & alium Librum de Omeliis Sancti Remigii, & alium Librum de Omeliis venerabilis Bedae . . . & unum Librum de Revelationibus Sanctae Brigidae" (276–77); to the last of these he adds a note, "quem emi Beverlaci" (277). Henry Fitzhugh, another brother, received copies of Rolle's *Incendium amoris* and *Judica me deus*, the latter described as "unum Quaternion parvum . . . quod Richardus Heremita composuit & scripsit" (276), a characterization that at least suggests the possibility of a Rolle holograph. To his sister, Matilda, a minoress in London, he bequeathed the sole identifiable Middle English work: "unum Librum in Anglicis, qui vocatur Stimulus Conscientie, coopertum in albo," that is, the extremely popular verse *Prick of Conscience*, together with other devotional books in Latin (277). There are other bequests of like kind, including one to his brother John, his successor and joint owner of Notre Dame 67, who receives "unum Psalterium novum glossatum . . . cum Armis meis & Uxoris meae" (277). John was to follow his brother in joining his own arms with his wife's in Notre Dame 67.

This account does not exhaust the evidence of Henry Scrope's library. A number of other books are specified in the inventories of forfeited materials.[36] Many are service books, including multiple copies, like "iiij magna Antiphonaria" and "iij parua Antiphonaria" (93) and "vi gradualia" (94), but including such works as "j magnam Legendam temporalem" (93) and "vnum librum de vita Sancte Brigid" (94), perhaps the one specified in his bequest to his brother Stephen, as well as volumes that relate to a particular local or regional piety, as with "vnum librum pro missa et matutinis de sancto Johanne Bridlyngton" (94), the Yorkshire Augustinian prior (d. 1379) who was canonized in 1401.

But it is possible that Henry Scrope's library may have included even more remarkable treasures. Longleat House, MS 24 (John de Burgh, *Pupilla oculi*) contains arms that seem identifiable with those of Henry.[37] What makes this fact particularly interesting is the existence of links between this manuscript and one of the most remarkable of the early fifteenth century: Cambridge, Corpus Christi College, MS 61, Chaucer's *Troilus and Criseyde.* This manuscript is linked to the Longleat one, and hence to Henry Scrope, by the fact that they were decorated by the same hand. That the links extended to Henry's ownership of Corpus 61 must remain speculation; but it is attractive speculation. Corpus 61 contains only a single, extraordinarily ambitious, full-page miniature. But space was left for eighty-nine further miniatures; if completed it would have been one of the most sumptuous vernacular manuscripts of the early fifteenth century.[38] This kind of lavishness would have demanded a patron of very great wealth. And the sudden abandoning of such an elaborately conceived decorative scheme suggests an abrupt loss of patronage. Such circumstances are consistent with both Henry's status and his sudden fall from power.

This must remain speculation. But the links between wealth, power, and vernacular book production can be documented elsewhere in fifteenth-century England, and Henry was evidently a collector of considerable stature.

By the mid-fifteenth century, their barony having been restored in 1425, the Scropes had re-established themselves as members of the lesser nobility, figures of power and influence but less politically central than they had been in earlier periods.[39] What happened to Henry's books is unclear.[40] But evidently books remained in the family.[41] Henry's heir was Stephen Scrope, archdeacon of Richmond, in Yorkshire, who died on 5 September 1418,[42] before the restoration of the barony. Some books of Stephen's survive, such as Oxford, Balliol College, MS 227, a manuscript of the *Gesta sanctorum* and other works;[43] a copy of Fitzralph's sermons, apparently made for Stephen;[44] and a copy of Jacobus de Cessolis, *De ludo scacchorum*, now Cambridge, Trinity College, MS B. 14. 12.[45] His will specified other books including a Catholicon, a copy of the Decretals, a Decreta, and Hostiensis in Lectura, but not any of those mentioned in his brother's bequest to him, which presumably passed to the Crown as attaindered property.[46]

We know of only one of Henry's books that passed to his brother, John, who ultimately succeeded him as 4th Baron Scrope of Masham, and that is the Psalter specified in Henry's will. We do not know whether Elizabeth Chaworth brought any books with her on the occasion of her marriage to him, before August 1418. But it is against such respective familial bibliophile environments that we can situate Notre Dame 67 in which their joint arms appear.

As I have already suggested, it is possible that Notre Dame 67 was intended for Elizabeth's use and intended to include only the *Mirror to Devout People*, since the work was addressed to women readers. But Elizabeth's husband John seems to have had some interest of his own in English devotional books, which may serve to strengthen the related possibility that *The Craft of Dying* was commissioned specifically for him. In his will, in 1455, for example, he bequeathed to his daughter, Eleanor "ane Englissh boke of ye Pater Noster, glosid, with Matynes of ye Passion," as well as some *de luxe*–sounding service books: "j Porthas couered in blew cloyth of damask of siluer [and ] j olde Masse Boke with Scrope armes in y^e^ begynnyng"[47] (this last sounds as if it could be an inherited book).

However, it has to be said that the main evidence for an interest in pious vernacular books in the Scrope family is to be found in the later fifteenth century in the female line. Elizabeth Chaworth, after her husband's death in November 1455, took the veil. It was possibly she who bequeathed Cambridge, Clare College, MS 5, a book of prayers, perhaps to some monastic house. It incorporates at the end of the manuscript a Middle English verse bookplate requesting prayers for "my lady scrope":

> he that lust for to loke
> or for to rede on this boke
> Be he of cyte toun or thrope
> Pray he for my lady scrope
> And thinke ȝe neuir to done amys
> But þenke on hym that gaf ȝow this
> For ihesu loue haue hym in mynde
> That this sette on ȝowre boke behynde
> (f. 147)[48]

The presence of a vernacular prayer may suggest something about Elizabeth's association with devotional works in English.

Either Elizabeth passed on books to her children or they were collectors in their own right, seemingly with some interest in Middle English religious manuscripts. For example, another Elizabeth Scrope, one of the daughters of Richard, younger son of Henry and Elizabeth, subsequently became, by her third marriage, Elizabeth de Vere, countess of Oxford. She owned, among other books,[49] London, British Library, MS Harley 1706, a substantial collection of Middle English verse and prose, including a copy of *The Craft of Dying* treatise that appears in Notre Dame 67 and a translation of Rolle's *Emendatio vitae*, which is interesting given the Scropes' earlier evident interest in his works.[50] She may have been the same "elyzabeth scrop" whose signature appears in Cambridge, University Library, MS Dd. 6. 1, a handsome late-fifteenth-century Sarum Hours.[51]

Comparison with the Scropes of Masham suggests the emulative nature of bibliophile interests in the collateral line of Scrope of Bolton. John, 5th Baron Scrope of Bolton (1435–1498) was the son of Henry, 4th Baron, and Elizabeth, daughter of Henry's kinsman, John, 4th Baron Scrope of Masham. The fifth Baron married three times, and two of these marriages are of some bibliographical moment. His second wife, Elizabeth St. John, came from a family of notable book collectors, particularly of English books.[52] His last marriage was to Anne Harling, who bequeathed a copy of "a Frenche booke called the Pistill of Othea" in 1498 to "my lord of Surrey," and "to my nevew sir Edward, a Frenche boke," and to "dame Jane Blakeney my white booke of Prayers."[53] She was a woman of some literary taste in other respects. She borrowed John Paston's manuscript of *Troilus and Criseyde* and also owned at least one English devotional book, a copy of the *Clensyng of Mans Soul* and other texts, now London, British Library, MS Harley 4012.[54]

Such traditions of female book ownership continued in the female Bolton line. Anne Harling/Scrope's daughter, Agnes, became, by her second marriage, wife of Sir Richard Ratcliffe (d. at Bosworth). She owned another vernacular devotional book, what is now New York Public Library, MS Spencer 19, a spectacularly decorated and illustrated copy of the Middle English *Pilgrimage of the Soul,* a translation of Deguileville's *Pelerinage de l'Ame*, a work already met in this account.[55] She bequeathed the manuscript to Marrick Abbey, York, a Priory of Benedictine Nuns.[56] Yet another Elizabeth, the widow of the 6th Baron Scrope of Bolton, bequeathed "a Primer & a Sauter" of distinguished provenance "which boke I had of the gifte of the most excellent princes King Henry the Seventh his mother,"[57] that is, the redoubtable Margaret Beaufort, patron of Caxton and owner of a substantial number of books in both manuscript and print, most of them of a devotional cast, including a copy of the first printed edition of Walter Hilton's *Scale of Perfection* (1494).[58]

Occasionally this branch of the Scrope family functioned as patrons not just of books but also of authors. John Skelton's *Philip Sparrow,* composed in the first decade of the sixteenth century, while he was vicar at

Diss, in Norfolk, was addressed to Jane Scrope, daughter of Sir Richard Scrope, a younger son of Henry, 4th Baron Scrope of Bolton.

The ranks of the family included some writers of its own: Stephen Scrope (1396?–1472), son-in-law of Sir John Fastolf, and translator for him of Christine de Pisan and other works;[59] and Thomas Scrope (d. 1491), bishop of Dromore, possibly an illegitimate scion of the Bolton line and the author of several works on the Carmelite order. At least one book survives from Thomas's library, a copy of Nicholas of Lyra's *Postilla*, now Cambridge, University Library, MS Ii. 4. 14, with his ex libris: "Liber iste constat Thome Scropp Episcop Dromoreum" (f. 1v).[60]

This is a lot of names and certainly far too many books.[61] But possibly at least some broad patterns emerge which bear on our understanding of Notre Dame 67. The most recurrent and most obvious is the evidence not just of literacy but of active book collecting among provincial nobility and gentry by the early years of the fifteenth century. We have yet to fully understand how books mattered in such secular environments but the simple fact of the incorporation of the Scrope/Chaworth arms suggests an insistence on the identification between owners and texts that gives such insistence both publicity and permanence. Such display does not, in itself, seem mere ostentation. Henry Scrope, John's father, and Thomas Chaworth, Elizabeth's father, both represented new kinds of secular book collectors, who, however their personal predilections diverge, collected in serious and sustained ways. Their children's efforts seem, on the evidence of Notre Dame 67, less ambitious but equally serious. And, in particular, it suggests another equally significant phenomenon: the emergence of forms of lay, literary piety associated with women readership. We have seen how such piety goes back, in the Scrope male line, to the mid-fourteenth century and their interest in Rolle. But it is only in the later fifteenth century, after Notre Dame 67, that we see its emergence in the female lines of the Scropes of both Masham and Bolton. It is possible to suggest that Notre Dame 67 is a key work in the development of such gendered interest in vernacular devotional texts within a family and region.

But it is perhaps appropriate to conclude somewhere near where we began. The *Mirror to Devout People* failed to circulate widely, I suggested, because of the more broadly based appeal of Love's *Mirror of the Blessed Life of Jesus Christ*. It is a curious coincidence that, among the manuscripts included in the Foyle sale with the *Mirror* was a copy of Love's work. It was owned by Sibilla de Felton, abbess of Barking Abbey at the time of her death in 1419, who owned a number of other devotional books.[62] Her copy of Love's work seems to have remained at the Abbey until the sixteenth century, when an inscription records the manuscript's bequest to one Agnes Gowldewell, by a nun of Barking. The nun's name is Margaret Scrowpe. She was a cousin of Elizabeth de Vere, formerly Scrope.

Margaret Scrowpe was still a nun at the Abbey when it was dissolved in November 1539, but her subsequent fate is unknown. She disappears from history carrying with her the last evidence of the primary role of female Scropes in the fostering of the interests of both branches of the family in devotional books in the later fifteenth and early sixteenth centuries. It was a pleasing accident of history that, at the millennium, brought this, the last of the Scrope books, together with one of their most important, the Foyle *Mirror.*[63]

# APPENDIX

## Summary Description of University of Notre Dame, MS 67

300 mm x 210 mm. Writing space 205 mm x 140 mm.
Parchment, ff. ii + 127 + i. 27 lines to a column; ruled in black ink.
Collation: ii, $1–15^8$, $16^8$ (wants 8, probably blank), i

Contents

ff. 1r–108r: *A Mirror to Devout People* (*IPMEP* 254).

Inc. "Gostely sustre in Ihesu criste I trowe it be noght ʒit from your mynde . . ." Expl. "And also aboute þe myddes. to þe worshype of þe holy trynyte. one euerlastyng verrey and almyghty god. To whome be all worship ioye and preysynge nowe and withoute ony endynge."

f. 108r: colophon.

Finito libro sit laus et gloria christo.
Soluite nunc mentem pro W. H. ad omnipotentem.
De uita christi libro finis datur isti
Paruos lactabit solidos quasi pane cibabit.
De bethlem pratum dedit hos Jhesu tibi flores
Post hunc ergo statum reddas sibi semper honores.

ff. 108r–108v: Oracio bona et deuota ad beatam uirginem mariam matrem domini nostri Ihesu Christi et beatum Iohannem Euangelistam.

Inc. "O intemerata et in eternum benedicta singularis . . ." Expl. "consubstancialis et coeternus cum eis et in eis viuit et regnat omnipotens deus Per omnia secula seculorum. Amen."

(This prayer is a standard component of Books of Hours; for a critical text and discussion, see A. Wilmart, *Auteurs spirituels et textes dévots du Moyen Age latin* [Paris, 1932], 474–504; for a translation, see Roger S. Wieck, *Time Sanctified: The Book of Hours in Medieval Art and Life* [New York, 1988], 164.)

f. 109r: colophon.

Nos tibi uirgo pia semper commendo maria;
Nos rogo conserues Christi dilecte Iohannes.
Virgo maria dei genitrix quam scriptor honorat
Sis pia semper ei prout hic te sperat et orat
Ex aliaque uice Iohannes christi dulcis amice
Da sibi solamen cum sanctis omnibus. Amen.

In omni tribulacione temptacione necessitate et angustia succurre nobis piissima uirgo maria.

AMEN.

(The word "christi" in line 5 renders the line unmetrical and is probably a gloss that has become embedded into the text at some point.)

ff 109v-126r: *The Craft of Dying* (Jolliffe L 4(a); *IPMEP* 234).

Inc.: "For alsmoche as þe passage of deth oute of the wrytchednesse of the exile of this world . . ." Expl. "euerlastyngly by þe mediacyon of our Lord Ihesu cryste þat is mediatour bytwix god and man. Amen.

f. 126r: three colophons.

Esto memor mortis nam porta fit omnibus ortis
Sepe sibi iuuenes accipit ante senes.

(These are the first two lines of a macaronic poem in Latin and Middle English; see *IMEV* 3122; Albert E. Hartung, ed., *A Manual of the Writings in Middle English, 1050–1500*, vol. 9 (New Haven, Conn., 1993) XXII.356; and Walther, *Initia* 5892.)

Non homo leteris tibi copia si fluat eris
Hic non semper eris memor esto quod morieris
Es euanebit quod habes tunc alter habebit
Corpus putrebit quod agis tecum permanebit.

(Walther, *Initia*, 12072; also a longer version (9 lines) in C. Horstmann, ed., *Richard Rolle of Hampole and his Followers*, 2 vols. (London, 1895–96; repr. Rochester, N.Y., 1999), I, 431, lines 496 ff.)

Finem siste pia mortis michi virgo maria
Es quia regina Manfeld defende ruina. Amen.

Contemporary doeskin binding over boards.

Copied by two scribes, the first responsible for ff. 1r–109r, the second for the remainder of the manuscript.

Decoration: Full page border, f. 1r; two historiated initials, ff. 1r, 109v, at the beginning of each of the Middle English texts, the first incorporating the Scrope/Chaworth arms (see below: Provenance), the second, a recumbent figure at prayer, with below, in a separate compartment, a figure with cope and mitre, pointing towards it. There is also an historiated initial on f. 108r of the Virgin and Child and St. John. See plates 1–3.

Provenance: Apparently produced at some point in the second quarter of the fifteenth century within the London area and acquired by John, 4th Baron Scrope of Masham and his wife Elizabeth Chaworth; their arms appear in the opening initial on f. 1r. The subsequent history of the manuscript is unknown until 1946 when it was sold at Sotheby's, 3 June, lot 112, the property of Mrs. Bertram Bell. It passed to the Foyle collection from which it was sold at Christie's, 11 July 2000, lot 73. It was acquired there by Quaritch who sold it to the University of Notre Dame.

## NOTES

1. See the Christie's catalogue, *The Library of William Foyle, Part I: Medieval and Renaissance Manuscripts, Tuesday 11 July 2000* (London, 2000), 221–3.

2. It seems to have first appeared on the market in Mrs. Bertram Bell's sale at Sotheby's, 3 June 1946, lot 112, whence it passed to the Foyle collection. At the Christie's sale on 11 July 2000, it was acquired by Quaritch who sold it to the University of Notre Dame.

3. Peter Jolliffe, for instance, in his *Check-list of Middle English Prose Writings of Spiritual Guidance* (Toronto, 1974), 225, notes that he was unable to examine it.

4. On this commitment see Michael Sargent, "The Transmission by the English Carthusians of some Late Medieval Spiritual Writings," *Journal of Ecclesiastical History* 27 (1976): 225–40, and the further references cited there.

5. On the so-called Delta scribe, see A. I. Doyle and M. B. Parkes, "The Production of Copies of the *Canterbury Tales* and the *Confessio Amantis* in the Early Fifteenth Century," in *Medieval Scribes, Manuscripts and Libraries: Essays Presented to N. R. Ker*, ed. M. B. Parkes and Andrew G. Watson (London, 1978), 206–8.

6. See N. R. Ker, *Medieval Libraries of Great Britain*, 2nd ed. (London, 1964), 178.

7. On this manuscript and Mede's obit see A. I. Doyle, "Book Production by the Monastic Orders in England (*c.* 1375–1530): Assessing the Evidence," in *Medieval Book Production: Assessing the Evidence*, ed. Linda Brownrigg (Los Altos Hills, Calif., 1990), 13 and fig. 8 (for a plate of Mede's hand in this manuscript). Other manuscripts he is known to have copied in whole or in part are London, British Library, MS Cotton Vespasian D. ix; Oxford, Bodleian Library, MSS Bodley 117 and Hatton 14; and Dublin, Trinity College, MS 241; on these see Ker, *Medieval Libraries*, 305; see also E. Margaret Thompson, *The Carthusian Order in England* (London, 1930), 332–33. I am also grateful to Professor Julia Boffey for access to her notes on Mede.

8. For discussion of the work's sources see Jonathan Hughes, *Pastors and Visionaries: Religion and Secular Life in Late Medieval Yorkshire* (Woodbridge, 1988), 105, and the appendix to Vincent Gillespie's article in the present volume.

9. On the genesis of this treatise see Mary C. O'Connor, *The Art of Dying Well* (New York, 1942), 50–60. For a detailed summary of its content see Nancy Lee Beaty, *The Craft of Dying: A Study of the Literary Tradition of the Ars Moriendi in England* (New Haven, Conn., 1970), 7–53.

10. For details of the various manuscript translations see O'Connor, *Art of Dying Well* 61–112.

11. For details see Jolliffe, L 4(a), 123, who lists thirteen other copies; R. Raymo, "Works of Religious and Philosophical Instruction," in *A Manual of the Writings in Middle English*, vol. 7, general ed. A. E. Hartung (New Haven, Conn., 1996), XX.216, adds University of Illinois, MS 80, ff. 6–8.

12. See Vincent Gillespie, "Vernacular Books of Religion," in *Book Production and Publishing in Britain, 1375–1475*, ed. J. Griffiths and D. Pearsall (Cambridge, 1989), 317–44, at 327, 342, nn. 50–51, who points to connections between *The Craft of Dying* and *A Treatise of Ghostly Battle* (Jolliffe H3). As Gillespie notes, two manuscripts containing both these texts are by the same scribe (London, British Library, MS Royal 17. C. XVIII and Oxford, Corpus Christi College, MS 220); also all eighteen texts in the Royal manuscript occur in the same order in Oxford, Bodleian Library, MS Rawlinson C. 894. In the present context it is interesting that in one manuscript, Manchester, Rylands Library, MS Eng. 94, *The Craft of Dying* occurs with Love's *Mirror of the Blessed Life of Jesus Christ.*

13. On the decoration as a basis for dating and localizing the manuscript, see Jessica Brantley's essay in this volume. Against the assumption of metropolitan origin must be set one piece of evidence. At the end of *The Craft of Dying*, on f. 126r opposite the second Latin colophon, occur the large initials "W. M." Just below this are two lines that read: "Finem siste pia / mortis michi Virgo maria / Es quia regina / Manfeld defende ruina. Amen." "Manfeld" is certainly William Manfeld, who in John Lord Scrope's last will dated 18 March 1453 is described as "my secretar" and also designated as one of the executors of his estate (see *Testamenta Eboracensia*, Part II, Surtees Society [London, 1855], 192). What is less clear is whether these lines indicate Manfeld is the scribe of the latter part of Notre Dame 67. Nor do they shed any light on where this part of the manuscript was copied and decorated. Without countervailing evidence London or its environs still seem the most likely origin for the manuscript.

14. For further speculation on the role of Syon as such a conduit, see Vincent Gillespie's essay in this volume.

15. For discussion with a full list of manuscripts copied by him and further references see A. I. Doyle, "Stephen Dodesham of Witham and Sheen," in *Of the Making of Books: Medieval Manuscripts, their Scribes and Readers; Essays Presented to M. B. Parkes*, ed. P. R. Robinson and Rivkah Zim (Aldershot, 1997), 94–115.

16. It is worth noting that this was not the first time the Scropes and Chaworths can be associated in an important bibliophiliac undertaking, though the other link is more tenous. Previous generations of the families can be linked to Sir Geoffrey Luttrell (d. 1345), whose son and heir Andrew married Beatrice Scrope. Sir Geoffrey was also on intimate terms with the Chaworths: his will includes a bequest to Thomas Chaworth "armigero meo," and he is named as co-executor with Andrew Luttrell; his will also includes a bequest to William Chaworth "camerario meo," possibly Thomas's son. Geoffrey Luttrell is best known to history as the commissioner of the Luttrell Psalter (now London, British Library, MS Additional 42130); for the text of his will see Eric G. Millar, *The Luttrell Psalter* (London, 1932), 52–54.

17. Simon Payling, *Political Society in Lancastrian England* (Oxford, 1991), 101; Payling's study contains much helpful discussion of Chaworth's political role.

18. For Chaworth's career see J. C. Wedgwood, *History of Parliament: Biographies of the Members of the Commons House, 1439–1509*, 2 vols. (London, 1936), 1:175–76.

19. It may be worth noting that, in the early sixteenth century, one Alys Scrope owned a manuscript of Lancelot romances which is now Oxford, Bodleian Library, MS Rawlinson Q.b.6; for description and further references see O. Pächt

and J. J. G. Alexander, *Illuminated Manuscripts in the Bodleian Library, Oxford, I* (Oxford, 1966), no. 586.

20. For description see C. Dutschke et al., *Guide to Medieval and Renaissance Manuscripts in the Huntington Library*, 2 vols. (San Marino, Calif., 1989), 1:185–90 (description of items 1–9).

21. For the text of this will see *Testamenta Eboracensia*, Part II, 225, 227, 228; for some discussion of this will see Thorlac Turville-Petre, "Some Medieval English Manuscripts in the North-East Midlands," in *Manuscripts and Readers in Fifteenth-Century England*, ed. Derek Pearsall (Cambridge, 1983), 132–33.

22. For a description, see N. R. Ker, *Medieval Manuscripts in British Libraries, IV: Paisley-York* (Oxford, 1992), 667–68.

23. For a description (not wholly accurate) see *On the Properties of Things: John Trevisa's Translation of Bartholomaeus Anglicus De Proprietatibus Rerum*, ed. M. C. Seymour et al., vol. 3 (Oxford, 1988), 19–22.

24. For description see *Lydgate's Troy Book*, Part IV, ed. H. Bergen, EETS e.s. 126 (London, 1935), 1–4.

25. Sir John le Scrope (d. 1405/6), younger brother of Stephen, second Lord Scrope of Masham, bequeathed "Elizabethae filiae meae unum librum de gallico vocatum Grace Dieu" (*Testamenta Eboracensia*, Part I, Surtees Society [London, 1836], 339), a copy of a French version.

26. The manuscript is described in Sam Fogg Rare Books, *Medieval Manuscripts*, Catalogue 12 (London, 1989), no. 10 (with plate); the description notes that "the roll remained in the possession of the Chaworth family until 1988." This manuscript was sold again in May 2005 by Sam Fogg to a private collector in London.

27. Lorraine C. Attreed, "An Indenture between Richard Duke of Gloucester and the Scrope Family of Masham and Upsall," *Speculum* 58 (1983): 1018–25, at 1019.

28. See J. W. McKenna, "Popular Canonization as Political Propaganda: The Cult of Archbishop Scrope," *Speculum* 45 (1970): 608–23.

29. "A Political Retrospect (1462)," in *Historical Poems of the XIVth and XVth Centuries*, ed. R. H. Robbins (New York, 1959), 223, line 14. York Minster MS Add. 67 contains a prayer (f. 102r–v) to "Sancto Ricardo scrupe martire."

30. For description and plate see O. Pächt and J. J. G. Alexander, *Illuminated Manuscripts in the Bodleian Library Oxford, III* (Oxford, 1973), no. 795 and Plate 77; for some reservations about this attribution see Kathleen L. Scott, *A Survey of Manuscripts Illuminated in the British Isles: Later Gothic Manuscripts, 1390–1490*, 2 vols. (London, 1996), 2:89–92, esp. 91–92.

31. See David O'Connor and Jeremy Haselock, "The Stained Glass," in G. E. Aylmer and Reginald Cant, eds., *A History of York Minster* (Oxford, 1977), 365, 378.

32. For a carol on Scrope's death, see R. L. Greene, ed., *The Early English Carols*, 2nd ed. (Oxford, 1977), no. 425.

33. *Testamenta Eboracensia*, Part II, 231. Dautre appears to be the son of Thomas Dautre, whose will appears ibid., 57–59 and who left a number of books; see further, Hughes, *Pastors and Visionaries*, 294.

34. For details and discussion of Scrope's forfeited books see C. L. Kingsford, "Two Forfeitures in the Year of Agincourt," *Archaeologia*, 2nd ser., 20 (1918–20): 71–100, especially 81–83, 93–94, 99; for some brief but characteristically astute comments on his book collecting, see K. B. McFarlane, *The Nobility of Later Medieval England* (Oxford, 1973), 237–38.

35. For Scrope's will, dated 23 June 1415, see T. Rymer, ed., *Foedera*, IX (London, 1709), 272–78; references to bequests are cited parenthetically in the text.

36. Kingsford, "Two Forfeitures," 82; references to bequests are cited parenthetically within the text.

37. See Kate Harris, "The Patronage and Dating of Longleat House MS 24, A Prestige Copy of the *Pupilla Oculi* Illuminated by the Master of the Troilus Frontispiece," in *Prestige, Authority and Power in Late Medieval Manuscripts and Texts*, ed. Felicity Riddy (Woodbridge, 2000), 36–54, esp. 42–54, and Kathleen L. Scott, "Limner-Power: A Book Artist in England c. 1420," in the same volume, 55–75.

38. For description see Scott, *Later Gothic Manuscripts*, 2:182–85 and the further references cited there.

39. For analysis of the Scropes' regional political role in the later fifteenth century, see A. J. Pollard, *North-Eastern England During the Wars of the Roses* (Oxford, 1990), esp. ch. 4, "Landed Society," 81–120; for some wider consideration of their political functions see J. Watts, *Henry VI and the Politics of Kingship* (Cambridge, 1996), passim.

40. Some of them were apparently forfeited and given to the choir of Royal Chapel of St. George at Windsor; see Ker, *Medieval Libraries*, 202.

41. The Scropes figure at various points in P. J. P. Goldberg, "Lay Book Ownership in Late Medieval York: The Evidence of Wills," *The Library*, 6th ser., 16 (1994): 181–89 (see esp. 185–187), but his observations are occasionally erroneous, and he seems unaware that much of his material (at least insofar as it relates to the Scropes) has already been published in *Testamenta Eboracensia*, Part IV, Surtees Society (London, 1869).

42. Payling, *Political Society in Lancastrian England*, 101.

43. For Stephen Scrope's biography see A. B. Emden, *A Biographical Register of the University of Oxford*, 3 vols. (Oxford, 1959), 3:1659–60, and *A Biographical Register of the University of Cambridge* (Cambridge, 1963), 515. For description of the Balliol manuscript see R. A. B. Mynors, *Catalogue of the Manuscripts of Balliol College*,

*Oxford* (Oxford, 1963), 226–30. It has the inscription "Liber quondam m. J. de Fandoun et nunc M. S. le Scrop" (f. 267v).

44. Oxford, New College, MS 90; see Emden, *Oxford*, 1660. However, in his *Cambridge*, 514, Emden ascribes ownership of this book to Richard Scrope, Archbishop of York.

45. For description, see M. R. James, *The Western Manuscripts in the Library of Trinity College, Cambridge: A Descriptive Catalogue*, 4 vols. (Cambridge, 1900–1904), 1:414; his name appears in an inscription on an end flyleaf. (I owe this reference to the kindness of Dr. Kathleen Scott.)

46. *Testamenta Eboracensia*, Part I, 388–89.

47. *Testamenta Eboracensia*, Part II, 190.

48. *IMEV*, 4104; printed in M. R. James, *A Descriptive Catalogue of the Western Manuscripts in the Library of Clare College, Cambridge* (Cambridge, 1905), 7; for description of this manuscript, see 7–11. James observes: "The indications are that it was given by lady Scrope to a monastery probably in Yorkshire" (7).

49. She owned, for example, Oxford, Bodleian Library, MS Rawlinson liturg. f. 37 (SC 15814), a Latin Psalter, given to her by her first husband, William, viscount Beaumont, on 5 March 1498/9: "Memorandum that I willyam viscount Beaumount the v[th] daye of Marche the yere of our Lorde god m[l] ccccclxxxxviij geve vnto Elisabeth my wief this psalter book" (f. 105v).

50. The manuscript is described in A. I. Doyle, "Books Connected with the Vere Family and Barking Abbey," *Transactions of the Essex Archaeological Society* 35 (1958): 222–43, at 234–35.

51. See A. Arnould and Jean-Michel Massing, *Splendours of Flanders* (Cambridge, 1993), 130–131, no. 41; however, the signature appears on the lower, inner margin on the recto of the final leaf (f. 145), which is otherwise blank and which seems codicologically unclearly related to the rest of the volume.

52. For details of the St. Johns as book collectors, see Julia Boffey and A. S. G. Edwards, "Books Connected with Henry Parker, Lord Morley and his Family," in *"Triumphs of English": Henry Parker, Lord Morley, Translator to the Tudor Court; New Essays in Interpretation*, ed. Marie Axton and James P. Carley (London, 2000), 69–76.

53. *Testamenta Eboracensia*, Part IV, 152. In view of the original links between the *Mirror* and Syon it is perhaps interesting that she describes herself as a sister of that house in her will, dated 28 August 1498 (*Testamenta Eboracensia*, Part IV, 151).

54. For details see E. Wilson, "A Middle English Manuscript at Coughton Court, Warwickshire, and British Library MS. Harley 4012," *Notes and Queries*, n.s., 24 (1977): 295–303; the paper by Anne Dutton, "Piety, Politics, and Persona: MS Harley 4012 and Anne Harling," in *Prestige, Authority and Power in Late-Medieval*

*Manuscripts and Texts*, 133–46, is of nugatory value. Doyle, "Books Connected with the Vere Family and Barking Abbey," includes much valuable material on the later book-collecting activities of female members of the Scrope family; see especially 233–34.

55. For a full description see Scott, *Later Gothic Manuscripts*, 2:217–19 and references cited there. It has been suggested that this manuscript probably passed to her via the Percys, with whom her family had some connection; see Mary Erler, "Exchange of Books between Nuns and Laywomen: Three Surviving Examples," in *New Science out of Old Books: Studies in Manuscripts and Early Printed Books in Honour of A. I. Doyle*, ed. Richard Beadle and Alan Piper (Aldershot, 1995), 362–64.

56. Ker, *Medieval Libraries*, 129.

57. *Testamenta Eboracensia*, Part V, Surtees Society (London, 1884), 51.

58. On Margaret as book collector, see Susan Powell, "Lady Margaret Beaufort and her Books," *The Library*, 6th ser., 20 (1998): 197–240 and the further references there (not, however, noting this book).

59. On Stephen Scrope see Robert R. Raymo and Elaine E. Whitaker, eds., *The Mirroure of the Worlde* (Toronto, 2003), 18–25, and the further references cited there.

60. The following note is on the front flyleaf: "Liber iste constat Thome Scroppe episcopo Dromorensi cuius precium est quinque solidos. empto de decano capelle beate marie de campis in Norwic. A.D. 1462. Johann. Nelle." For description see *A Catalogue of Manuscripts Preserved in the Library of the University of Cambridge*, 6 vols. (Cambridge, 1856–67), 3:452–53. I owe this reference to the kindness of Dr. Kathleen Scott.

61. This may be the point to lay a possible ghost. Janet Backhouse, in *The Madresfield Hours: A Fifteenth-Century Manuscript in the Library of Earl Beauchamp* (Oxford, 1975), 27, suggests that this manuscript contains "a coat of arms of the Scrope family" on f. 156. She has kindly advised me that she no longer feels that this is correct.

62. Doyle, "Books Connected with the Vere Family and Barking Abbey," 240–41; see also N. R. Ker, "More Manuscripts from Essex Monastic Libraries: With Notes on Manuscripts Connected with Essex Parish Libraries," *Transactions of the Essex Archaeological Society*, n.s., 2 (1945), 298–310, at 310. The manuscript was sold at Christie's, 11 July 2000, lot 72 (see the Christie's catalogue, *The Library of William Foyle, Part I: Medieval and Renaissance Manuscripts* [London, 2000], 218–20), for £85,000 to Sam Fogg Rare Books and subsequently exported.

63. I am indebted to Ian Doyle for his efforts to save me from error.

# The Haunted Text

## Reflections in *A Mirror to Devout People*

VINCENT GILLESPIE

I

I am haunted by the tortoises. Not in a Captain Hook, ticking clock, looking over your shoulder sort of way, admittedly. But rather in a Pavlovian, associative sort of way. It began in 1977, a quarter of a century ago, when I first looked at the Foyle manuscript of the *Mirror to Devout People* (now University of Notre Dame, MS 67). To examine their manuscripts, it was necessary to travel to the Foyle country house far out from London in bleakest, dankest, and, as it turned out, coldest Essex, not far from the site of the heroic Anglo-Saxon Battle of Maldon. One had the feeling of being about as welcome at Beeleigh Abbey as the Viking invaders had been in 991 when they visited the area on the off chance of a spot of casual looting and pillage. Beeleigh is a magnificent half-timbered Tudor manor house welded onto the stone remains of what had been a house of Premonstratensian canons. The mid-winter landscape lay under a limp shroud of fog. I don't think there were bats wheeling in the sky as I walked up the drive, and I don't suppose that the door was creakingly opened by an Igor-figure, enquiring if I had rung, but that was pretty much how it felt.

At Beeleigh, manuscripts were read in the old stone chapter house of the abbey. Old, stone, bitterly cold, and, as I soon discovered, to be shared with a large number of tortoises in various stages of hibernation. Igor explained that it was not possible to heat the chapter house, but if the cold became so intense that I was in danger of losing fingers or, better still, whole limbs, it might be possible to provide a single-bar electric fire. I stuck out the intense cold for several hours, but eventually gave in and begged for mercy. A small fire was produced and I carried on reading the beautiful and textually very important copy of the *Speculum Christiani* that had been the main purpose behind my visit. Having finished that, I turned to the equally beautiful Foyle *Mirror to Devout People.* At this point, the tiny one-bar electric fire began minutely to raise the air temperature of the chapter house. As I turned the pages of the *Mirror*, reading of the life of Christ, taking in the author's puzzled but valiant attempts to keep his narrative on an even keel, registering his flickering and inconsistent success in defining and consistently addressing a coherent audience, I became aware that the tortoises were stirring. As I read of the nativity, the childhood of Christ, the joys and sorrows of Mary, and the final pains of the Passion, I tried to block out the increasingly unmistakable sound of tortoise shells rubbing against each other. At first, suspecting that the lack of food, drink, or even a glass of water (which would undoubtedly have frozen had it been offered) might be making me susceptible to visionary delusions, I tried to ignore the temptation. But gradually, ineluctably, I was forced to acknowledge that, yes, however much I tried to deny it, there was indeed a tortoise orgy going on in the pen next to where I sat. Needless to say, my attention to the finer points of the closing chapters of the *Mirror* was not perhaps what it might have been. Hardly surprising, then, that I am haunted by the tortoises, and that, re-reading the text on the microfilm generously supplied by the library at Notre Dame, I heard at my back not just time's winged chariot, but also the insistent grating of tortoise shells.

Now the moral of this is that context is everything. Even an author as apparently uncertain about his potential readership as the anonymous Carthusian author of the *Mirror* could not have envisaged or predicted the circumstances in which I would end up reading his text. As I pondered the sources and intended audiences of the text, and reflected on the way that those audiences had moved beyond the explicit addressee of the "ghostly sister" to embrace, by a process of textual *mouvance*, a readership of secular but devout men and women, a very different kind of embracing and *mouvance* was going on feet away from me. The widest possible horizon of expectation constructed by a reception theorist would fail to embrace the comic potential of that day at Beeleigh Abbey. So for me, the *Mirror to Devout People* is a haunted text. These days I might have been entitled to post-traumatic stress counselling. After all, I might have withdrawn into my shell.

## II

As a text originally composed in the second quarter of the fifteenth century and preserved in two copies from around and probably not much later than 1450, the circumstances of the composition and circulation of the *Mirror to Devout People* repay careful and discriminating attention. It is, I think, important to distinguish texts of this vintage from those produced in the first flush of enthusiasm for vernacular guides to godliness. Important not only because we have learned in recent years to attend much more carefully to the impact on such vernacular writings of the Arundel decrees of 1407–1409 but also because we need to understand more fully the ebb and flow of popular and institutional confidence in such writings. There is a model of the development of the market for vernacular religious texts that charts a steadily growing level of confidence and sophistication in the composition, production, circulation, and consumption of these works. This model sees the Arundel decrees as intervening in that development primarily by forcing a change from original composition in the vernacular into the more defensive compilation of approved texts attributed to approved authorities from before the time of Wyclif. Hence, the model goes, the renewed popularity of Rolle in compilations of the post-Arundelian years (Rolle being safely dead by 1349), and the wholesale attribution of spurious works to him to travel under his protective cloaking. We have grown familiar with the apparently dominant role of the English Carthusians, with sometimes a supporting appearance by the Bridgettines, in the production and circulation of such texts. The underlying message of this model has been one of consistent progress: vernacular works of growing sophistication, both intellectual and organisational, and a developing technology for information retrieval in such texts through the provision of apparatus, indices, and lists of chapters, thereby facilitating independent reading and selective consultation. The same model of improvement applies to discussions of readership and reception. Prologues, it is argued, increasingly address the broad and flexible range of readers that texts of this kind aspire to reach. Starting from the reflex, romance-driven formulaic invocations of "lered" and "lewed" in the catechetic and penitential texts of the late thirteenth and fourteenth centuries, one can point to a more serene recognition in later texts that the readership can expand from the named original recipient to other readers, from professed religious to committed laymen, from women to men, and vice versa. This is a fundamentally ameliorative model—things can only get better. Texts get smarter, readers more demanding, inscribed audiences more permissive and inclusive.[1]

It is probably time to inflect some aspects of this argument more carefully. This paper is offered as a small step in that process of re-assessment, and starts from two assumptions. First, that in London this model of democratization and ventriloquial empowerment of the laity applied only to a tight-knit spiritual aristocracy of well-born lay people or wealthy and socially mobile merchants and metropolitan secular priests (especially the powerful rectors of the city of London parishes), all often intimately related by close family and personal links with a small number of powerhouse religious institutions: the Bridgettines at Syon, the nuns of Dartford and Barking Abbey, and the Charterhouses of London and Sheen. It is not accidental that it is precisely these houses and these groups of readers that feature in the textual history of the two works in the Notre Dame manuscript.[2] (Sometimes considering the history of English vernacular religious writing in the first half of the fifteenth century is like watching one of Shakespeare's history plays performed by a cast of five or six actors, all valiantly rushing off stage only to reappear moments later in a different part and wearing a different hat.)

The second assumption is that part of the problem in adequately historicizing post-Arundelian religious writings, and particularly writing from the period 1410–1450, lies in the studied and sustained atemporality and anonymity to which much of it aspires, not just in its insistent reaching back to older writers like Rolle and its cautious reliance on Augustine, Gregory, and Jerome, but also in its coded and oblique engagement with the theological events of its period, and in the almost Chaucerian self-effacement of its religious authors. It is also important to register the "conservatism" that texts produced in this period often show, not just in theological matters, but in terms of their general ecclesiastical attitude to lay access to spiritual texts. While it is proper to stress the importance of the Arundel decrees as a potentially illiberal response to a perceived theological and political threat, for example, it is surprising how little attention has been paid in scholarly work on English texts to the decrees of the Council of Constance (1414–1417) and the far-reaching impact they had on pan-European attitudes, or to the impact on English theological thought and writing of the outspoken, prolific, widely read, and emphatically conservative Chancellor of the University of Paris, Jean Gerson. The founding in 1415 of Sheen and Syon, those "two chantries where the sad and solemn priests / Sing still for Richard's soul" (Shakespeare, *Henry V*, IV.i.301–2), as wealthy and favoured royal foundations committed to orthodoxy and standing as bastions against heresy, ought I think to be seen as a defining moment in the history of English religious writing at least as significant as the Arundelian decrees, and perhaps with more long-lasting effects on the intellectual timbre of English spirituality.[3] The founding, generous endowment and rapid growth of Syon and its libraries in the first half of the fifteenth century adds an important new vector to the dynamics of the textual transmission of religious texts.[4] We already know of a distinctive "London group" of Hilton manuscripts pivoting on Sheen and Syon, and of a "London group" of manuscripts of *The Imitation of Christ*, also with strong Sheen and Syon representation.[5] I suspect that Syon's intervention in the transmission of English spiritual writing was more decisive than has yet been realized or established.

I think this is partly because we have been working with too monolithic a view of the public role of the English Carthusian province in English spirituality in the fourteenth and fifteenth centuries. Ian Doyle's cautionary words that "we should not assume too omnipresent or intitiatory a role for the Carthusians in the circulation of writings not composed by their own members [because] we find them so frequently among the owners of spiritual texts" remind us that ownership is not the same as transmission.[6] We need to look more carefully at Carthusian interventions in contemporary spiritual writing and we must assess the evidence for textual circulation cautiously, without assuming that wide dissemination beyond an audience of confrères or fellow religious was ever a common intention of Carthusian scribes and authors. In most cases, I suspect that such circulation was by accident rather than design, and without deliberate agency on the part of the Carthusians themselves.[7] Marleen Cré, for example, has recently persuasively argued that the important collection of vernacular mystical and paramystical texts in the Amherst manuscript (London, British Library, MS Additional 37790) was not just produced within a Carthusian milieu (as had been widely accepted) but that it was also probably produced for a Carthusian audience.[8]

In the fifteenth century, of course, Carthusian intervention in public religious culture starts at a high water mark with the exception that perhaps proves the rule: the confident, almost glib control that Nicholas Love, in his *Mirror of the Blessed Life of Jesus Christ*, brings to his engagement with the *Meditationes Vitae Christi* of Iohannes de Caulibus. Love's text is supremely secure in its relationship to the *antiqui* and to the *moderni:* it patronizes its audience with its playpen spirituality, but it equally patronizes its sources in its selection, rejection, and modification of them. The result is a text with a notably harmonious overall tone and style, the product of a writer at ease with his material and with where it is going. It is dismissive of the Lollards and their views, refusing to enter into debate or contestation with them, preferring the rhetorical mode of simple confutation. His narrative sweeps along in a majestic display of confident narrative control, secure in its relationship to its audience, in its relationship to its sources, and, subsequently, in its relationship to ecclesiastical authority. Love's text was explicitly targeted at "lewde men & women & hem þat bene of symple vndirstondyng . . . þe whiche as childryn hauen nede to be fedde with mylke of lyȝte doctryne & not with sadde mete of grete clargye and of hye contemplacion."[9] Love is sufficiently assured in his role as an author to acknowledge the inevitability, even perhaps the desirability of his readers undertaking their own imaginative performance of the meditative catalysts he provides, confident that the good sense and obedience of his readers will keep them within the bounds of theological decency.[10] A similar quiet authority, though infinitely more self-effacing, is found slightly earlier in the writings of the *Cloud*-author, although his works were much more carefully controlled in their circulation, achieving only "a seemingly slow and tight diffusion through the Carthusians and other contemplative communities and individuals."[11]

But it seems to me that something happens to that confidence as the century progresses. Much later we get the introspective writings of Richard Methley and John Norton reflecting uneasily, indeed anxiously, on their own meditative and contemplative experiences; and the red annotator's self-conscious and perhaps self-justifying comments on the text of Margery Kempe. I have argued elsewhere that in the generation after Love we can see the charterhouses apparently collecting first-hand accounts describing the raw data of mystical experience, as well as accumulating texts to guide that process of *probatio* and *discretio* whose nascent technology was known in the *Cloud* corpus as "discretion of spirits." *The Book of Margery Kempe*, the 1456 Vision of Edmund Leversedge, the Short Text of Julian of Norwich, Margarete Porete, Ruusbroec, the mystical diaries of Norton and Methley: all are grist to the mill of Carthusian self-analysis, no doubt primarily to help in the calibration of their own processes of spiritual self-assessment, and perhaps also to equip them as spiritual advisors for other members of the community.[12] But the tightly controlled circulation of these texts within the order and their largely successful policing of them to prevent leakage into a potentially more volatile readership in the wider community suggest a more cautious approach to their making of books. Indeed in fifteenth-century England the movement of such texts is largely centripetal—in from the laity to the charterhouse by acquisition or testamentary bequest—rather than centrifugal—out from the charterhouse into lay circulation. The only version of Margery Kempe's book that saw the light of day before modern times was that highly edited and crafted set of printed excerpts that describe her as a recluse, and the circumstances of that printing have more than a whiff of Syon provenance about them.[13] The common-profit book extracts from Rolle and Hilton circulating among certain rich merchants and stationers in London in the mid-century years carefully select less volatile aspects of their teachings, and in any case derive from a textual milieu that again points strongly to Syon rather than the Carthusians as a point of origin or dissemination.[14]

Love's epigraph was St. Paul's (and Chaucer's) dictum that all that is written is written for our doctrine. The practice of his later confrères is much less inclusive, and much less trusting. In the decades immediately after Love, Carthusian textual production was much more focussed on books that provided for the needs of professed religious than on the needs of devout laymen.[15] That such laymen may eventually have come to own works produced in response to the needs of such religious should not lead us to infer too readily that the Carthusians were active parties to such a transfer. Recent work on lay reading and textual communities of well-born and noble women in London has suggested that their patterns of book ownership and reading are largely indistinguishable from those of their sisters and daughters who were professed nuns. In some cases, we know that books could be commissioned from stationers by laymen to be given to female family members in nunneries: the Barking Abbey and Dartford books explored in detail by Ian Doyle are well known.[16] But we know much less about the books and texts that leached out from circulation inside such religious houses to achieve wider readership and circulation in the general population. If, as I have suggested, the Carthusians were more cautious and perhaps more introspective in their book-making activities post-Arundel and post-Constance, we may need another conduit through which their works reached a wider readership. I suspect that in London the main such conduit, and a notably leaky one, was in fact Syon. I also suspect that, with or without the conscious consent or permission of the Carthusians over the river, the special circumstances of the Syon Brethren and the special configuration of the double convent at Syon led to books originating at Sheen being propelled into much wider circulation.

The standard scholarly accounts of the London transmission of the works of Richard Rolle and Walter Hilton often refer to a Sheen/Syon axis for the production, circulation, and transmission of those authors. The typical taxonomy of such explorations reveals that we have books written by named Carthusian scribes or otherwise identifiable as Carthusian being read or owned by named and identifiable Syon nuns, thus establishing a *de facto* (albeit enclosed and silent) textual community across both sides of the river. So, although the Syon/Sheen textual community comprises a group of monks serving the reading needs of a group of nuns, it is Carthusian monks primarily serving the needs of Bridgettine nuns. This emergent textual community has one striking oddity about it: it almost entirely effaces and marginalizes the Brethren of Syon. The role of the Brethren as producers of contemplative and other religious works is indeed modest when they are separated out from the male-Sheen/female-Syon axis.[17] In the first half-century of the house's existence, from the first enclosures in 1420 to the regularization of arrangements for the Brethren's library in 1471, *The Orcherd of Syon* and the *Mirror of Our Lady* are the only substantial works that can be confidently ascribed a Syon authorship, and both of these are targeted at an in-house audience of Syon nuns. No text that has been assigned a Sheen/Syon provenance by modern scholarship has Syon authorship claimed for it in the catalogue of the Brethren's library.[18] The only named Syon author in the vernacular in this period is Symon Wynter, to whom are ascribed sermons on the Syon indulgences, expositions of the Marian canticles and a *Life of Jerome* translated into English for one of his spiritual clients, Margaret, Duchess of Clarence. Now, if Sheen regularly made books for Syon, under commission and perhaps under the direction of the Syon Brethren, that does not mean that those books were designed or intended to circulate more widely than that very specific original audience. On the other hand, neither does it mean that the Syon Brethren would have felt under any constraint about facilitating such a wider circulation. In his life of Jerome, Wynter exhorts Margaret "that hit sholde lyke your ladyship first to rede hit & to do copye hit for yoursilf & syth to lete oþer rede hit & copye hit whoso wyll." Here is *prima facie* early evidence of textual transmission from Syon: the exemplar is to return to the abbey, but the copy made from it may itself be freely copied by whoever wishes access to it among the Duchess's circle of friends and contacts.[19]

## III

So where does that leave the *Mirror to Devout People*, and why have I described it as a haunted text? The *Mirror to Devout People*, or the *Speculum Devotorum* to give it the less permissive and socially inclusive title it wears in its religious rather than secular guise, treats the life, death, Resurrection, and Ascension of Christ in thirty-three chapters, one for each year of Christ's life on earth.[20] In the Cambridge copy, which has a Sheen *ex libris* inscription, the author indirectly identifies himself as a Carthusian by referring to Nicholas Love as "a man of oure ordyr of charturhowse." In the

Notre Dame copy the reference is, more enigmatically, to "a man of our ordoure" (f. 1r): the reference to the Charterhouse was either added for explicitness in the "religious" copy in Cambridge (or its antecedents) or deleted as irrelevant in the "secular" copy in Notre Dame (or its antecedents).[21] Colophons in both manuscripts elliptically refer to the House of Jesus of Bethlehem at Sheen, established across the river from Syon and soon to become the largest and richest house of the English Carthusian province.[22] The Cambridge manuscript was copied by William Mede, a professed Carthusian of Sheen, who was ordained as an acolyte in 1417 and died as sacrist in 1474. The colophon in Notre Dame has the initials "W. H.," perhaps an error for "W. M." or indicating the name of another Carthusian author or scribe—though I cannot find a Sheen monk with those initials in the (admittedly incomplete) obit lists for the first seventy years of the house's history—but possibly trying to pass off as the work's "oonlie begetter" that other Mr. W. H., the cautious and conservative Walter Hilton, whose works were valued at Sheen and Syon.[23] That the Notre Dame copy has moved some way from the text's place of conception is suggested by the Northern dialect of its scribe, in contrast to William Mede's "suthren tonge" localised as Surrey (in which county, of course, Sheen itself sat).[24]

Addressed to a "gostely sustre in Ihesu criste" (f. 1r) or "relygiouse sustre" (f. 5r), but one whose command of Latin is limited, the work purports to fulfill an earlier promise made to the ghostly sister to provide a meditation on the Passion of the Lord. "By counseill," that is on the advice of other spiritual and good men, primarily the Prior of his Charterhouse, the author has expanded that original plan to include the whole life: "I haue putte to mykyll more þan I behette yow" (f. 1r). The initial relationship between author and recipient, therefore, is clearly posited as personal, even intimate, perhaps one of spiritual director to advisee. It has been suggested that the ghostly sister is most probably a nun, and likely to be a nun of Syon.[25] I shall argue here that the evidence of the text strongly supports a nun of Syon as one of the intended audiences of the work. The extent of the contact between the Carthusian and the nun is unclear, as it invariably is in such cases, the most famous of which is the relationship between another later Sheen Carthusian, James Grenehalgh, and another later Syon nun, Joanne Sewell.[26] The Carthusian author refers to "when we spake laste to gidre" (f. 1r), but the relationship is configured as primarily textual, and the tone adopted echoes that of earlier letters of spiritual direction, and indeed of Hilton's *Scale of Perfection*, one of the sources explicitly cited by the *Mirror*-author. So one need not posit extensive meetings between the parties for there to have been a spiritual relationship. Indeed it might be possible to argue that the author's knowledge of similar texts would have allowed him to create in his work a series of gestures that positioned his text comfortably in the genre of such letters and in the privileged intimacy of writings such as Rolle's English epistles, the *Cloud* and *Privy Counselling*, and the opening of book 1 of *The Scale of Perfection* (which is the only book of Hilton's work of which the *Mirror*-author shows textual knowledge).

But it is soon clear that comfort and security are not the emotions uppermost in his mind in writing the prologue. Indeed the prologue presents a compelling portrait of a man haunted by his own sense of textual inadequacy, an inadequacy that goes well beyond conventional generic gestures of humility and incapacity. Although he apes the gestures of the "pore compilator," as his main source Iohannes de Caulibus (Pseudo-Bonaventure) and Nicholas Love had done before him, his textual insecurity is much more evident.[27] His main textual debt, he writes, is to "Boneauenture a cardynale and a worthi clerk," and he had often put off beginning his own work because of his own unworthiness and because he had "herde telle" that a man of his order had already translated Bonaventure into English; that man is, of course, Nicholas Love, first prior of Mount Grace. It is worth noting that he claims (and indeed displays) no first-hand knowledge of Love's book, nor does he even seem familiar with it despite its status as a widely circulated and popular text with the accolade of an *imprimatur* from the archbishop.[28] Instead he asks advice from "spyrituell and goode men" (f. 1r) and accepts the counsel of his prior and other "gostely faders" to continue with the work as best he can among his other duties and "excercyes" (f. 1v). Life in a Carthusian cell could be an isolated as well as a solitary affair, and it may have been only the priors who knew much of what was going on elsewhere in the order and in the wider world.

Indeed it was probably the prior who determined the allocation or destination of books copied inside his house and who approved commissions for copying coming from outside the house. The chronicle of the London Charterhouse records the book-making activities of John Homersley, a long-serving member of the London house from his profession in 1393 until his death in 1450. Homersley was an assiduous scribe, praised by the chronicle for his obedience to Guigo's exhortations in the order's *Consuetudines* that Carthusians should preach the word of God with their hands. "Carrying what he had written to the prior's cell, he did not take care that they should be lent to anyone or put anywhere, but leaving them there with the prior he returned in silence to his cell." Although these books may have been for the use of his own community, the chronicle also records that "a certain priest," presumably outside the house, used to supply Homersley with parchment for writing books and after death appeared to him with the Virgin Mary to point out an error in his copying and to urge him kindly to amend it.[29]

The Carthusian booklists offer only flimsy and fragmentary evidence of the order's book culture in the fifteenth century. Most evidence comes from surviving manuscripts that were in Carthusian hands or were produced by them.[30] Impressive though they can seem, we should be careful not to overstate the textual resources and knowledge inside the order early in the fifteenth century, and in particular we should beware of over-extrapolation from the holdings in one house to those in another. Although the fragmentary surviving booklists suggest that books moved round between the different houses of the order, it is striking that Love's *Mirror of the Blessed Life of Jesus Christ*, this mega-text of the English Carthusian province, appears in the *Mirror to Devout People* only as a ghostly absence of presence. This is all the more surprising as Henry V, as part of his founder's benevolence, had authorized an exchequer payment of one hundred pounds to Mount Grace "pro certis libris et aliis rebus" ("for certain books and other things") that had been sent to Sheen, presumably to build up the library of the new royal foundation. But in 1420 the General Chapter of the Carthusians was still instructing Sheen to acquire those books that it needed, so the collection must have been inadequate or at least incomplete.[31] In his last will (10 June 1421) Henry had also left most of his own substantial collection of sermons and books of meditation to be divided equally between Sheen and Syon, with Syon getting the preaching books because the Carthusians were forbidden to preach. Henry had also left to Sheen a copy of Gregory the Great that was already in their care. However, while there are grounds for believing that neither Sheen nor Syon received any of the promised royal books, the Syon library was quickly augmented by substantial private collections from its first Brethren, such as the Lincoln grammar master John Bracebridge (who gave well over one hundred books).[32] It is unlikely that any English charterhouse of this date had anything like the size of library enjoyed by the Brethren of Syon, even in the first quarter-century of that house's life.

Certainly not, it would appear, the nearest charterhouse to Syon. For, if we take this prologue at face value, it seems that Sheen did not have a copy of Nicholas Love at the time that the *Mirror to Devout People* was composed. The three copies of that work made by the Sheen Carthusian Stephen Dodesham all date from rather later in the fifteenth century.[33] But the author of the *Mirror to Devout People* was not without textual resources, as the list of sources in my appendix shows: in addition to the Pseudo-Bonaventure (itself a repertory of citations from Peter Comestor, Bernard, and others), he cites the *Historia Scholastica* of Peter Comestor; Nicholas of Lyra's literal Postills on the Gospels; sermons and other works by John Chrysostom, Clement, Augustine, Bede, Gregory, and Bernard; the first book of Hilton's *Scale of Perfection*; Suso's *Orologium sapientiae* (often the same passages as occur in the Carthusian Ludolph of Saxony's *Vita Christi*); *Legenda Aurea*; *The Three Kings of Cologne*; *Mandeville's Travels* (probably in English); one of the infancy Gospels; Richard of St. Victor; the Carthusian Adam of Dryburgh; miracles of the virgin; and other materials. In addition he draws on certain revelations of what he calls "approued women" (f. 3r), namely Mechtild of Hackeborn, Elizabeth of Töss, Catherine of Siena, and Bridget of Sweden. Despite this formidable array of sources (some carried through from the Pseudo-Bonaventure, but many not), the author is fearful of his own "vnkonnyng and vnworthynesse" (f. 1v), but hopeful that he may be excused by the merits of those who are profited by his "symple travayle".[34] His sources are not always very deftly handled and, unlike Love, he often steers his text towards the ascetic and pragmatic and away from the affective and imaginative. His array of sources, and his often clumsy marshalling of them, reveals more of the influence of anxiety rather than the anxiety of influence. Far from being a dwarf on the shoulders of giants, he is a dwarfish narrator lost among a sea of giant legs and often uncertain which leg to cling to.[35]

And he is a very anxious author. Early in the prologue he is already extending his inscribed audience beyond his ghostly sister, not in a permissive and confident way, but almost in the expectation of criticism. He answers "ony man" who may ask why he bothers to write another text after Bonaventure by hoping that his meditations, by the grace of God, may be "full profitable to deuoute cresten soules" (f. 2r), even though "he þat wrote friste þe meditacions folowyng were bot a symple man and of no reputacioun" (ff. 1v–2r).[36] He has avoided adding "ymaginaciouns" that might have appealed to carnal souls, but has added nothing of his "owne wytte" except things that he hopes may be conceived by "open resoun and goode conciens" (f. 3r).[37] As a compiler, augmenting Pseudo-Bonaventure, he has relied most heavily on Peter Comestor and Nicholas of Lyra:

> For þei gone moste nerest to þe story and to þe letterale vnderstondyng of ony doctores þat I haue redde noght wythstondyng I haue broght in other doctores in diuers places as to morall vertues. (f. 3r)

This is an altogether more ascetic text than other works in the *Meditationes* tradition.

Several interesting points emerge from these statements of humility. First, although his primary support came from his own prior, he also receives good advice and counsel from other "gostely faders." Who might they be? Possibly members of his own house, but perhaps also those "spyrituell and goode men" on the other side of the river, the thirteen priests, four deacons, and eight lay brothers who, at full strength, made up the Brethren of Syon, an austere and high-minded group into whose care the spiritual welfare of the sixty Syon nuns was entrusted by the Bridgettine rule.[38] As we shall see, there are a number of oblique comments in the text that may allude to the distinctive features of the Bridgettine foundation and to the role of the Brethren in it. If we can locate this text firmly and plausibly in a closed Sheen-Syon nexus, without an implied or achieved lay circulation as part of the author's intended audience for the text, then this will change the emphasis in our reading of the work and in our perception of the mechanics of its circulation. If Syon was the conduit and perhaps the commissioner of the work, then we will need to reconsider the agency of the Carthusians in the lay circulation witnessed by the Notre Dame manuscript, and perhaps modify or recontextualize our model of Carthusian involvement in the textual transmission of vernacular materials.

Second, he refers to himself as the man who "wrote friste" (f. 1v) the meditations following, perhaps implying that he envisages others copying the text after he has finished it. Is he perhaps haunted by the knowledge that any text sent to Syon stands a good chance of being copied and disseminated beyond the walls of that cloister, whatever its original intended audience? If so, his anxiety was well founded: the Notre Dame manuscript is copied elegantly but rather hastily and imperfectly. The text is full of corrections and emendations between the lines and in the margins. At the end of the *Mirror* there is a marginal note on the first blank line which reads "examinatur" (f. 109r): this copy has been corrected against an exemplar and its deficiencies supplied. Indeed, given that the marginal rulings for chapter headings and *marginalia* continue seamlessly on from the ruling for text, it may be that this copy was designed to replicate the *mise en page* of its exemplar.

Whatever the intentions expressed by the author in the prologue—presumably written last as it contains a table of the chapters in the work and offers, as Ian Johnson has shown ("Prologue and Practice"), a formal, *accessus*-like account of the whole work—the text of the *Mirror* itself reveals a plurality of inscribed audiences and readers. This plurality might support the assumption that the author envisaged the text reaching the hands and eyes of diverse lay readers. But it may be that his compositional practice was neither as systematic nor as apparently emancipatory as that. In some cases the plurality of possible reading positions reflects the haunting presence of reading postures envisaged by the sources employed at that point in the work. In other cases the internal logic of the exposition and the drift of his own reflections draws the author ineluctably into configuring his audience in a particular way. While the peroration implies an apparent authorial recognition of the inevitability of a wider readership, and of the possibility of the work being selectively read or copied when he addresses "yow here or ony other deuoute seruante of god þat is by his grace to rede þis booke or ony parte þer of" (f. 108r), this kind of selective devotional reading is similar to that encouraged at Syon, as we shall see below. We need to attend carefully to the *voces paginarum* and see what they tell us about the way that the text configures its readership or audience.

While the audience most explicitly addressed at the start and finish of chapters is the "gostely sustre," the dominant inscribed audience of the text is a less clearly specified religious woman. Chapter 18, discussing the events of Maundy Thursday, puts words into the mouth of his inscribed audience (f. 55r): "Here as me semeth yhe myght seye . . . I þat am a woman," questioning why she can only receive communion under the form of bread. But he ventriloquizes this question only to require her obediently to accept "þis litell þat I haue seide to yow," to avoid asking questions about the sacrament, and to put her faith generally in the faith of holy church along with "other comon peple" (f. 55r), "and þat is ynogh to yche meke cresten soule" (f. 55v). In the Passion chapters, the reader is configured, in typical Pseudo-Bonaventuran style, as one of the women who accompany Mary through the ordeal of the Crucifixion and its aftermath, encouraging her to imagine what service she would have offered to the virgin if she had been present with her.

Elsewhere in the text, he seems to acknowledge the possibility of female lay readership: the finding of the child Jesus in the temple (cap. 10) prompts a discussion of Mary's words to Christ when she says "Your father and I have been looking for you," citing Augustine on Mary's meekness in putting Joseph first in the sentence, and arguing that women, and particularly those that have husbands, should learn to be meek and not to prefer themselves in any thing. Elsewhere again he explains that Joseph lived as a "mayden" with Mary after the Visitation, for as doctors say they "bothe to gidre avowede virgynite" (f. 15v). He is much more emphatic about this than Pseudo-Bonaventure, perhaps reflecting the growth in popularity of such vows of married chastity in the fifteenth century (such as that taken by Margery and John Kempe) and the increasing number of widowed vowesses. Elizabeth Chaworth/Scrope, one of the original owners of Notre Dame, took the veil as a vowess after the death of her husband John Lord Scrope in 1455, and a number of high-born vowesses were associated with Syon in the fifteenth century.[39]

In keeping with thc feminine targeting of these audiences, a distinctive feature of the *Mirror* is the emphasis it gives to the actions, reactions, and emotions of the Virgin Mary. Much of this is highly conventional: on one level this is only a somewhat more restrained reflection of the role that Mary typically plays in the *Meditationes* tradition as the suffering subject, the inscribed point of view within the text that acts as an affective paradigm for the reactions of the reader. There are plenty of invitations throughout the text to feel pity, sorrow, grief, and imaginative engagement with Mary as she observes and meditates on the events of Christ's life. But there are also some interesting inflections of the tradition. Following Pseudo-Bonaventure, for example, the *Mirror* mounts a robust defense of the apocryphal tradition that Jesus appeared first to his mother on the morning of his Resurrection, coming to her in a parody of the Annunciation while she sits alone deep in meditation in the Upper Room on "Mounte Syon."[40] She is, as he comments, "a perfite ensample" and "a trewe myrour of perfeccioun to all wymmen as our lorde Ihesu to all men" (f. 12r). At the Annunciation, we are invited to imagine her as a nun-like figure, in her *cubiculum*, at her prayers as the Angel arrives, "for she was alwaye wele occupiede" (f. 9v; this detail is not in Pseudo-Bonaventure).[41]

But the *Mirror* goes rather further than this in its presentation of her as a model contemplative and a paradigm of reflection and meditation on the events that unfolded before her. He achieves this mainly through extensive borrowings from the writings of his "approued women," namely Mechtild of Hackeborn, Catherine of Siena, Elizabeth of Töss and, most extensively, Bridget of Sweden.[42] In the Nativity chapter (cap. 5), much influenced by Bridget, Mary stands "as þoff sche had be lifte vp in ane extasye or suownynge of contemplacioun yfillede with gostely swetnes"(f. 17v). Her lyric meditations and laments at the foot of the cross and at the deposition provide valuable, if basically conventional, formulae for the affective meditator to respond to and copy. The *Mirror* repeats and develops the assertion in Pseudo-Bonaventure and in Ludolph of Saxony that, on returning home after the burial of Christ, she stopped at the cross and reverenced it, becoming the first person so to do, emphasizing in two consecutive chapters that between the Crucifixion and the Resurrection "in hir alone \a/bode þe feyth of holy chirche þat tyme" (f. 82v; this detail is not in Pseudo-Bonaventure).[43] Most tellingly, in filling the void in the Gospels relating to the events of Holy Saturday, the *Mirror*, in a major expansion of the description in Pseudo-Bonaventure, reports that Mary undertakes a retrospective meditation on all the happenings that she has witnessed in the previous few days, and all the events of Christ's life on earth, offering a paradigm of the ideal reading process envisaged by the text for itself. This reflection takes place alone in the room where the Last Supper had been held, located, we are repeatedly told, in a part of Jerusalem called "Mello þat is to seye in Mounte Syon" (f. 82v). Elsewhere in the book, he repeats verbatim extracts from Bridget's revelations that record her first-person response to her showings, which he leaves as gendered direct speech so that the (implied female) reader can appropriate them for use as a personal meditation. So the female and contemplative strands in the book are quite prominent.

Interestingly, though, the text also addresses itself on occasion to male religious. Speaking of Mary's visitation to Elizabeth and the lessons in meekness it teaches, he writes that "þis is necessarie and profitable to yow and to other men and women þat lyuen in religion and haue forsaken your owne wyll" to live under the "meke and siker ȝoke of obedience" (f. 15r). (In the Notre Dame copy, this chapter's lengthy exposition of the kinds of meekness is closely monitored and signposted by extensive marginalia.) At the Last Supper, John's marvelling at Christ's words betokens that "men and women þat haue taken vp on hem þat state of contemplatyue lyuynge" should be busily and diligently occupied in "louynge" (meaning both loving and praising) of God and forget all worldly things (f. 57r). At the Purification, Mary's obedience to Mosaic law is a "feire ensample to all religiouse men and women howe gladly theye shulde obeye to þe obseruaunces of here reules and þe byddynges of here souereynes," as well as a "generale ensample" to all Christian people to obey the biddings and ordinances of Holy Church (ff. 26r–26v).

But the most extraneous audience invoked by the text is an audience of male religious who are both contemplatives and, most unusually, also preachers. Chapter 13, dealing with Christ's retreat into the desert and his temptations there, and chapter 14, covering the calling of the Apostles, are presented as a paradigm form of living for all preachers. These addresses to preachers are not found in Pseudo-Bonaventure, which refers at this point to an audience of "monachi."[44] Chapter 13 exhorts all preachers and teachers to follow Christ who withdrew into the desert of his own spirit:

> ¶ Also in þat he yaf ensample þat men þat wolde preche and teche goddis worde shuld firste vsen hem selfe to be mykell alone fro þe companyes of folke where they myghte ȝeue hem conueniently to holy meditacions and prayers, fastynge, wakynge and other holy exercyces by þe whiche helpynge þe grace of god þei myghte ouercome vices in hem selfe and þe sotell temptacyoun of þe fende. (f. 37r)

"And so wolde God," he continues, "alle prechoures walde do nowadayes" (f. 37v), a passage marked *Nota bene* in the margin of Notre Dame. Warming to his theme in chapter 14, he notes that when people hear or read the words of graduates, masters of divinity, or doctors of law, they have "grete deynte þer of" and "comenden it gretely." But if the words come from a "common letterde man" or a "deuoute man not graduate þat is to seye not degreede" they despise it and have little dainty of it (f. 41v). This is an odd passage and out of keeping with its context, and with its sources (it is not in Pseudo-Bonaventure), though its primary purpose is to explain the mix of learned and "lewd" men called by Jesus to be his apostles. But coming from the pen of a man who has been haunted by his own sense of inadequacy when faced with the textual authority of the cardinal and great clerk Bonaventure and of other doctors he has read and cited, and who describes himself as a "symple man and of no reputacioun" (f. 2r), it seems particularly heartfelt. On one level this is typical Carthusian intellectual modesty: consider the (probably Carthusian) translator's prologue to the vernacular version of Suso's *Orologium sapientiae* and his allegory of the sphere with three levels where the doctors and scholars miss out on the wisdom of God because they are puffed up with *scientia* and miss the *sapientia* that comes from the simple and total love of God, or the *Mirror*-author's statement in his prologue that meditation on the Passion of Christ makes unlearned men into learned men, and "unwise" men and idiots into masters not of the science that puffs up but of charity that edifies, a statement itself taken from Suso and also used by Ludolph of Saxony.[45]

But on the other hand I wonder if this concern with preachers who live lives of reclusion in the desert and with the popular preference for graduates and doctors over simple men does not perhaps reflect another level of anxiety, another haunting if you like: a possible sense of intellectual inadequacy in the face of the high-powered graduate community living just over the river in the desert of Syon who were by this date already winning praise and reputation for their learning and for their work as preachers to the laity. When he draws attention to the inauthentic and apocryphal material in the *Gospel of Nicodemus* he includes it with the words: "I commytte it to þe dome of þe reder whether he woll admytte it or none" (f. 91v). He here inscribes a male reader with the ability to exercise theological judgment and discrimination.

Does the *Mirror to Devout People* make more sense if it is seen as addressed to the totality of the community in Syon: religious sisters, contemplative fathers who were also preachers, and lay people living in the abbey or as spiritual clients of the Brethren? How does the text look if we put it in a Bridgettine rather than a Carthusian context? Can we more adequately account for the text's unusual features by placing it, initially at least, in a tight, specific, and conveniently local setting rather than in the looser framework of broad and increasing lay access to such materials?

## IV

The prominent and privileged position occupied by Mary in the *Mirror to Devout People*, though not unprecedented in the *Meditationes Vitae Christi* tradition and fairly commonplace in the meditations on the Passion that the *Mirror* author initially intended to write, is paralleled by the unusual prominence given to Mary in the constitution of the Bridgettine order:

> This religion þerfore I wyll sette & ordeyne fyrst & principally by women to the worshippe of my most dere beloued modir, whose ordir and statutys I shall declare most fully with myn owne mowthe.

"Per mulieres primum et principaliter" (for women first and foremost).[46] These are the words of Christ in the preamble to the *Regula Salvatoris* dictated by him to Bridget. A postulant for admission at Syon was preceded into the church by a red banner with images of Mary on one side and the crucified Christ on the other. The bishop draws her attention to the banner saying that the image of Christ teaches patience and poverty while the image of Mary teaches chastity and meekness. The manner of the Bridgettine life is equally clearly stated in the Rule:

> The begynnyng of this religion and of helth ys very mekenes and pure chastite and wylfull pouerte.
>
> Principium itaque huius religionis et salutis est vera humilitas, pura castitas atque voluntaria paupertas.[47]

Meekness, chastity, patience, and poverty of spirit are repeatedly singled out by the author of the *Mirror to Devout People* as the dominant virtues inculcated by his text (though these are, of course, commonplaces of meditative writing), especially in his discussion of Mary's behaviour at the Visitation to Elizabeth. The ascetic contemplative life of Syon is well matched in the controlled tone of the *Mirror to Devout People*, which is notably less enthusiastic and affective and more cautious about "ymaginaciouns" than other texts in the *Meditationes* tradition. The office of the Syon sisters was based on the *Sermo Angelicus*, again dictated to Bridget and heavily focussed on the role of Mary in the economy of salvation, while the liturgical and paraliturgical prayer of both houses sent up a seamless hymn of praise to God and to his mother. The companion to the office, the *Mirror of Our Lady*, translated and glossed the Bridgettine Breviary for those of limited latinity and must have been composed in the same decades that produced our text.[48]

"By women for the worship of my most dearly beloved mother": the role of the nuns was to observe strict enclosure and to sing the praises of the Virgin, in a life of obedience to the abbess as "souereyn" of the house. Note how the language of the prologue to *The Orcherd of Syon* echoes the language used in the *Mirror*:

> Religyous modir & deuote sustren clepid & chosen bisily to laboure at the hous of Syon in the blessid vyneȝerd of oure holy Saueour, his parfite rewle which himsilf enditide to kepe contynuly to ȝoure lyues eende vndir þe gouernaunce of oure blessid Lady, hir seruise oonly to rede and to synge as hir special seruauntis and douȝtren, and sche ȝoure moost souereyne lady and cheef abbes of hir holy couent.[49]

The structure of the order—sixty nuns, thirteen priests (the apostles plus St. Paul), eight lay brothers, and four deacons (Ambrose, Gregory, Jerome, and Augustine), the total symbolizing the post-Ascension community of the Church—privileges the role of the abbess as the head of the community, with primacy over the whole business of the house and over the Brethren, who were in turn led by the Confessor-General, who was second in dignity, superior in spiritual matters and near coeval, much to be respected and admired, and sometimes to be yielded to by the Abbess.

The Syon Brethren had a more widely defined function:

> Thes thrittene preestis owe to entende oonly to dyuyne office and studie & prayer. And implie them with none oþere nedes or offices.

> Whiche also are bounde to expoune iche sonday the gospel of the same day in the same messe to all herers in ther modir tonge.[50]

They are also "opynly to preche" on solemn festivals. They also, of course, say Mass for the sisters and attend to their spiritual needs. At Syon, the acquisition of various indulgences and pardons, especially the *ad vincula* indulgence, soon gave further opportunities for public preaching by the Brethren, and it is at one such occasion that Margery Kempe is in attendance at the end of book two of her *Book.* There is evidence, however, from outside of the Rule to suggest that the Syon Brethren were also expected to accept confessions from outside the house, and the Brethren at Vadstena at least had the status of minor penitentiaries. There is also some evidence to suggest that they acted as spiritual directors for well-placed laymen and women, as Symon Wynter did for Margaret, Duchess of Clarence. The Brethren, many of whom entered Syon after careers as secular priests, academics, or administrators, and increasingly became a predominantly graduate community, also seem to have offered collegial hospitality to priests and laymen who wished to work in the library and share in the life of the house. And as the fifteenth century progressed they would have served as marketing managers for the Syon brand name, as the fame of the Syon pardon spread and crowds flocked to the indulgence sermons and bought the printed versions of the pardon and indulgences. Syon was a fashionable place to visit and the Brethren were in the front line of handling the masses of visitors, while the nuns were assiduously protected from exposure to them.[51] The lections added at Syon to the general martyrology at the end of the Brethren's *Martiloge* reveal a conception of the Brethren's role that is similarly high-minded, austere, and idealistic. The lections, added in the top and bottom margins and keyed to the daily readings from the martyrology, address themselves to the core priestly functions of preaching, teaching, confessional judgment, and pastoral and spiritual guidance. Usually only a couple of sentences long, they offer a daily infusion of sacerdotal theory to reinforce the commitment of the Brethren to their vocation. Preaching is to be plain but effective:

> Sermo sacerdotis debet esse purus, simplex et apertus, tractans de misterio legis, de doctrina fidei, de uirtute continentie, de disciplina

> iustitie, plenus grauitate et honestate, plenus suauitate et gracia. (London, British Library, MS Additional 22285, f. 78v)
>
> The sermon of the priest must be pure, simple, and open, dealing with the mystery of the Law, the teaching of the Faith, the virtue of restraint, the rule of justice, full of gravity and honesty, full of sweetness and grace.

Teaching must be carefully targeted at the needs and abilities of the audience:

> Prima prudentie uirtus est eam quam docere oporteat existimare personam. Rudibus populis seu carnalibus plana atque communia non summa atque ardua predicanda sunt ne immensitate doctrina opprimantur potius quam erudiantur. (ibid., f. 99r)
>
> The first feature of Prudence is to assess the character of those who are to be instructed. For simple and worldly people, those things to be preached must be plain and commonplace, not elevated or hard, lest they be weighted down with greater instruction than they can assimilate.

The emphasis is on the cultivation of humility and the avoidance of spiritual and intellectual pride, on the paramount importance of matching words and works—"tam doctrina quam uita" ["as the teaching so the life"] and of living what is taught—"Sacerdotis predicacio operibus confirmanda est ita ut quod docet verbo instruat exemplo" ["The preaching of the priest is to be confirmed by [his] works so that what he teaches by word he may demonstrate by example"] (ibid. f. 93v). Patient poverty, meekness, humility, and pragmatism are the touchstone of the *Regula Salvatoris*, as they are of the *Regula Sancti Augustini* which the order nominally took as its Rule.

Now, as well as the unusually insistent prominence of Mary in the *Mirror* version of the life of Christ, an even more striking oddity in this version is the emphasis given to St. John the Evangelist, culminating in an excursus in the last chapter of the work on his merits and the powers of his saintly intercession, especially in relation to the prayer *O intemerata* with which the *Mirror* closes, which describes Mary and John as "Ye two celestial jewels. Ye two lights divinely shining before God." The role of John is quietly built up throughout the *Mirror*: in the Last Supper passage, his silent marvelling at the words of Christ is figured as a paradigm of contemplative living for all men and women.[52] The commendation of Mary and John to each other by Christ on the cross is the subject of extended discussion, stressing John's role as protector and help to Mary after Christ's death. In the work's final chapter, John is noted for his four special privileges: his special loving of Christ, the incorruption of his body after death, his showing of "privetees," and the fact that God's mother was commended to his care. Citing at length from a sermon on John by the Carthusian Adam of Dryburgh, the *Mirror* explains that his symbol is a flying eagle, because of his ability to comprehend by cleanness of soul the high privities of everlasting mysteries.[53] John's position of near-equality with Mary is emphasized by the *Mirror*: as neither of them has any "souereyn" in the world because of their devoted virginity, so, the text argues, it is fitting that they be joined together in esteem. Moreover, John, we are told, was a great preacher who on the morning of his death went into his Church in Rome to preach to his beloved people: "byddynge hem þat þei shulde be stedfaste in þe feythe and feruente in þe kepynge of þe comaundementes of god" (f. 102v). He wins the triple aureole of martyrdom, preaching, and virginity. This strangely configured account of John, to whom, the author of the *Mirror* says, the ghostly sister has a special devotion, distorts the shape of the text and greatly extends the length of the final chapter. But, in the context of a close target audience of a Syon nun, it is easy to see it as figuring the special attributes of the contemplative, virgin preachers who made up the Brethren of Syon and were meant to stand as bastions of orthodoxy against the tides of heresy, and perhaps more specifically the Confessor-General, who served as the abbess's representative on earth and lived a life of reclusion interspersed with pastoral and business activities on behalf of the house.

There may be other oblique references to the special circumstances of the house. The odd little disquisition on Mary saying "Your father and I" at the finding of Jesus in the temple, with its moral that women should not put themselves before men, looks slightly different in the context of the constitution of Syon where the abbess, like Mary, has greater authority, but defers to the Confessor-General (configured as the loyal Joseph) in spiritual matters. Indeed the Syon Additions to the Rule describe them both as "fader and moder to the hole congregacion of sustres and Brethren."[54] The injunction to pray the *Pater Noster*, *Ave Maria*, and Creed at the beginning, middle, and end of the *Mirror*, although a common devotional gesture, exactly parallels the injunction in the Bridgettine Breviary, the *Mirror of Our Lady*, and the Additions for the nuns to preface most of their daily Hours with precisely those prayers, and the office of those nuns and lay-Brethren who could not read was to be entirely made up of those prayers. The discussion in the *Mirror to Devout People* of the Annunciation and Mary's undoing of Eve's wrongdoing, with its conventional play on Ave/Eva, parallels a very similar (but admittedly commonplace) discussion of the same tropes in the *Mirror of Our Lady*.[55] The chapter on how to distinguish between good and evil visions parallels similar discussions in the *Revelations* of St. Bridget and in *The Orcherd of Syon*.[56] The linking of the key episodes of Christ's Passion to the Hours of the Divine Office, although found in numerous Passion meditations in the Pseudo-Bonaventuran tradition, gains extra force from the knowledge that between the hours of Terce (the condemnation of Christ in the *Mirror*) and Sext (the Crucifixion in the *Mirror*), the nuns of Syon all visited the open grave that was kept in their enclosure to meditate on their own mortality. The lyric force of the tableaux meditations on Christ's love and mercy in chapter 24 of the *Mirror*, dealing with the opening of Christ's side, and the deposition from the cross in chapter 25 (linked with Evensong) are given extra potency as possible meditative aids for the sisters by the knowledge that before the hour of Evensong, the community of nuns met together to pray for forgiveness from God and each other for the sins they had committed. The account of Mary reverencing the cross and then returning alone to her cell to meditate on the Passion parallels much of what we know about the life and the reading of Syon nuns. Both the *Mirror of Our Lady* and the *Mirror to Devout People* encourage "devout beholding" in the mind and imagination of the reader, and both encourage a kind of meditation that is restrained and ascetic rather than affective and enthusiastic.

Moreover, the occasional references to married lay readers, or the acknowledgement of the possibility of such lay readers, need not imply that the text was originally designed to pass into a wide reading public: Syon had a large resident staff of laymen, including important postholders like the steward, whose families were often housed on the site. It was also a design feature of Bridgettine houses to include apartments for royal visitors. In addition, we know that it was the habit of pious and well-born men and women to hire lodgings in the precincts of Syon for various periods of time, and there may even have been lay vowesses living in the precincts alongside those postulants for admission to the community who chose to fulfill their year of external novitiate close to the house. From 1446 onwards, Syon also had strong links with the influential Guild of All Angels in nearby Isleworth, a guild with close connections to the world of the London common-profit books. Syon was a truly mixed, large, and diverse community, which, despite the strictness of its formal enclosures, was in many ways permeable and hospitable to the outside world.

Looked at as a text designed to address a mixed and varied audience in the world, as I have looked at it in the past, the final assessment has to be that the *Mirror to Devout People* is a failure: it fails to inflect its material adequately to encompass those readers who are not "goostly," and its references to the laity are clumsy and fleeting. So to argue that here is a text designed to serve the needs of multiple audiences is to argue that it has largely failed in its design. But to see it as a text addressing the very specific needs of a very specific community of nuns and priests configured in a manner that was unique in medieval Britain immediately resolves many of the inconsistencies and awkwardnesses of address. I would argue that the *Mirror* shows an allusive but genuine knowledge of the circumstances and spiritual life of the Bridgettines and avowedly seeks to address those circumstances and the Marian-centred nature of that spiritual life. A Bridgettine reader of the *Mirror to Devout People* would feel immediately at home in an imaginative world heavily colored by the revelations of Bridget (the nativity scenes in the *Mirror of Our Lady* are especially close to those in the *Mirror to Devout People*), Catherine of Siena, and Elizabeth of Töss. Both texts share a common emphasis on Mary as the sole guardian of the faith between Christ's death and Resurrection. In the *Mirror to Devout People*, Christ greets his mother in his apocryphal appearance to her on the morning of his Resurrection with the words *Salve sancta parens*, regularly recited by the nuns as part of their office, and also translated and glossed in the *Mirror of Our Lady*).[57]

The *Mirror of Our Lady* offers much sensible and enlightened advice to the nuns about how and when they should read books, and about the kinds of books they should employ for their differing moods and needs. Its purpose, apart from glossing the office, is to offer a mirror in which Mary can be seen so that the nuns can be stirred more devoutly to praise her:

> And therfore now moste dere and deuoute systres, ye that are the spouses of oure lorde Iesu chryste and the specyall chosen maydens and doughtres of his moste reuerende mother, lyfte up the eyen of youre soulles towarde youre souerayne lady and often and bysely loke and study in this her myrroure, and not lyghtely but contynually, not hastynge to rede moche atones but labouryng to knowe what you rede. (ed. Blunt, 4)

Devout reading is called one of the parts of contemplation, for it causes much grace and comfort to the soul if it is discreetly used. When you read alone, you should not be hasty and read too much at once, but should sometimes read a thing twice or three times. Similarly, *The Orcherd of Syon* has reordered Catherine of Siena's *Dialogo* for an audience of Syon nuns so that it can be dipped into and explored in sections, though the author recommends a complete reading first. Interestingly, the author of the *Mirror to Devout People* recommends exactly the same approach to his book, saying that he has designed a detailed list of chapters to allow navigation round the text and selective reading, "noghtwythstondyng hit were þe beste who so myght haue tyme and laysere þerto to rede hit all as hit is sett" (f. 1r).[58]

The advice on reading in the *Mirror of Our Lady* is designed to be applied to any kind of book encountered by the nuns. But singled out for comment are those books that

> ar made to enforme the vnderstondynge. & to tel how spiritual persones oughte to be gouerned in all theyr lyuynge that they may knowe what they shall leue & what they shall do. how they shulde laboure in clensyng of theyr conscyence. & in gettyng of vertewes how they shulde withstonde temptacyons & suffer trybulacyons & how they shall pray. & occupy them in gostly excercyse. with many suche other full holy doctrines. (Blunt, 68)

The reader of such books should seek to assess the extent to which their own life conforms to these models and precepts and, where deficiencies are identified,

> besely to kepe in mynde that lesson that so sheweth you to youre selfe & ofte to rede yt ageyne. & to loke theron. & on your selfe. with full purpose & wyll to amende you & to dresse youre lyfe ther-after. (ibid.)

Put in the specific context of reading at Syon, the *Mirror to Devout People* fits flawlessly into the scheme of reading recommended by the *Mirror of Our Lady.* Similar advice is repeated in other Syon books, while the Brethren's library contained a "tractatus de laude lecture divine" (N.67: SS1.921jj). Thomas Betson's *Right Profitable Treatise* (1500) cites Jerome's advice to religious women:

> Lete none see you from the seruyce of god or unoccupyed. In re-dynge of prophetes, epystles, gospelles, sayntes lyues and other dedes of vertue doynge, hauynge euer bokes in your handes, studyenge or wrytynge þat people seynge you may saye: Beholde here the seruaunt of god and the lanternes of the worlde.[59]

If the "goostly faders" that the author of the *Mirror to Devout People* had consulted before embarking on his work had indeed included Syon Brethren, the Syon ethos of improving reading might well have been part of the "counsell" that he received from them.

I have remarked above on the oddity that many of the texts and books known to have been owned by Syon nuns have a Carthusian provenance. Apart from the *Orcherd* and the *Mirror of Our Lady*, hardly any of their books seem to have come from the pens of the Syon Brethren. They of course had a public ministry of preaching and sacramental care, a public ministry that was denied to the Carthusians by statute. Instead the Carthusians preached with their hands by making books, becoming "heralds of the faith."[60] If, as I have argued, the peculiar shape and texture of the *Mirror to Devout People* can be explained and accounted for by defining its target audience as the community at Syon, broadly conceived, then we cannot consider this work as evidence of Carthusian intervention in facilitating greater lay access to materials of this kind. I suspect that the role of facilitator in this case probably rests with Syon, as may the role of commissioning the text in the first place: the initial audience may have been small, local and tightly defined. The Carthusians probably had no agency in its later expansion to include well-connected lay people like Elizabeth Chaworth/Scrope, whose husband's family had numerous connections to Syon and other metropolitan nunneries.[61]

But was it only "counsell" that the Carthusian author of the *Mirror to Devout People* might have received from Syon? We have noted that he had apparently not read Nicholas Love's *Mirror of the Blessed Life of Jesus Christ* but had only heard tell of it. Our author needed access to a wide range of texts to compose his work. Would he have found them in Sheen at the date he was working on his text? It is impossible to say. What we can say with certainty is that, with one exception, every major source he cites and uses in his work could have been found in the library of the Syon Brethren in copies that were probably in the library before 1450.[62] The library at Syon was a noted resource not only for the Brethren but for their many guests and visitors. The role of the Syon Brethren in the pastoral care of the nuns and of lay people may have extended to the lending of books to neighbouring houses, and certainly seems to have included the commissioning of books from Sheen for the use of the community. Those books were perhaps composed drawing on the resources of their own remarkable library and may subsequently have made their way or have been deliberately propelled into wider circulation. That model of transmission fits well with the known facts concerning the circulation of many religious texts in London in the fifteenth century. But a full consideration of the agency of Syon in such transmission is material for another paper, and I can already hear the sound of the tortoises at my back.

> "When we were little," the Mock Turtle went on . . . "we went to school in the sea. The master was an old Turtle—we used to call him Tortoise—." "Why did you call him Tortoise if he wasn't one?" Alice asked. "We called him Tortoise because he taught us," said the Mock Turtle angrily: "really you are very dull!"
>
> —*Alice's Adventures in Wonderland*[63]

## APPENDIX

### *A Myrrour to Deuote Peple*: List of Chapters and Authorities Cited in Text

***Prologue***: Suso; Bonaventure; Peter Comestor; Nicholas of Lyra; other "doctores" for "morall vertues"; revelations of "approued women."

Reader to say thrice Ave Maria, Pater Noster, Credo.

1. ***Creation and Fall***: Hilton, *Scale* 1.43.
2. ***God's Plan for the World***: John Chrysostom.
3. ***Annunciation***: Augustine; Jerome; Catherine of Siena.
4. ***Visitation***: John Chrysostom; Ambrose.
5. ***Nativity***: Three Kings of Cologne; "Book of the Youth of Our Lord"; Bridget of Sweden.
6. ***Circumcision***: Bernard; Richard of Saint-Victor; Petrus Ravenna.
7. ***Coming of the Magi***: Three Kings of Cologne; Gregory.
8. ***Purification***: Augustine, Sermon on Purification/Presentation; *Legenda Aurea.*
9. ***Flight into Egypt***: Master of Stories; Three Kings of Cologne; "Book of the Youth of Our Lord."
10. ***Finding in the Temple***: Augustine; Nicholas of Lyra.
11. ***Life of Christ from 12 until Baptism in Jordan***: Bridget of Sweden.
12. ***Baptism***: Bonaventure; Bernard; *Legenda Aurea*, Legends of Simon and Jude, incl. the miraculous image of Christ's face, King Aqbar; Master of Stories.
13. ***Temptations in the Desert***: Master of Stories; Nicholas of Lyra; Gregory, Homily for Lent 1.
14. ***Calling of the Apostles***: Nicholas of Lyra; Bernard; Gregory, *Moralia.*
15. ***The Miracles***: Nicholas of Lyra; Master of Stories; Augustine, *Soliloquies.*
16. ***Raising the Dead***: Augustine.

Reader to say thrice Ave Maria, Pater Noster, Credo

17. ***Palm Sunday***: Nicholas of Lyra.
18. ***Schir Thursday; Last Supper; Garden of Gethsemane***: Suso.
19. ***Capture and Scourging***: Nicholas of Lyra.
20. ***The Hour of Prime. Christ before Annas and Caiphas***: crowning with thorns (citing Mandeville "þat was a wele trauaylede knyghte"); Jerome; Master of Stories; Nicholas of Lyra.
21. ***The Hour of Terce. Christ before Pilate***: *Legenda Aurea*, cap. 67 (James the Less)
22. ***The Hour of Sext. Crucifixion***: two manners of crucifying (Bridget); Nicholas of Lyra; Gregory, Homily for Gospel of Quinquagesima Sunday.
23. ***The Hour of None. The Death of Christ; Laments of the Virgin***: Nicholas of Lyra; Gregory, Homily of the 12th Day.
24. ***"Aftir none." The Opening of the Side; Washing Clean from Sin***: Nicholas of Lyra; Gregory
25. ***The Hour of Evensong. Deposition***: Nicholas of Lyra; Bridget.
26. ***Compline. Burial***: Master of Stories.
27. ***Saturday***: no sources cited.
28. ***The Harrowing of Hell***: Master of Stories; sceptical references to Gospel of Nicodemus as "vnsiker"; Nicholas of Lyra "in a treatise of þe seyng of the beynge of God (?)"; Augustine, Sermon.
29. ***Resurrection and First (Apocryphal) Appearance to BVM***: Master of Stories; Augustine; Mechtild of Hackeborn, *Liber specialis gratiae* 1.xix (= *Booke of Gostly Graces* 181. 2–6); *Legenda Aurea*; Nicholas of Lyra.
30. ***First Five Authentic Appearances***: Gregory; Nicholas of Lyra; *Legenda Aurea*; Jerome.
31. ***Second Five Authentic Appearances***: Leo the Great, Sermon on Ascension; Gregory, Sermon on Ascension; Nicholas of Lyra.
32. ***Ascension***: Nicholas of Lyra; Peter Comestor; Augustine, *Soliloquies.*
33. ***Pentecost and Special Commendation of John the Evangelist***: Nicholas of Lyra; Gregory; Clement "in a pystell"; *Legenda Aurea*; Jerome, Prologue to John's Gospel and to Revelation;

Adam [Dryburgh] Cartusiensis "in a worthy sermone"; Bede, Sermon on John; Augustine on John's Gospel; Life of Elizabeth of Töss ["Hungary"]; Edmund of Abingdon and the Miracles of Our Lady regarding miraculous power of *O intemerata*; Gregory on the life of John.

Reader to say thrice Ave Maria, Pater Noster, Credo.
*O intemerata* and closing prayers and colophons.

## NOTES

1. The most recent and most influential articulation of the impact of the Arundel decrees on vernacular religious culture is the fine essay by N. Watson, "Censorship and Cultural Change in Late-Medieval England: Vernacular Theology, the Oxford Translation Debate, and Arundel's Constitutions of 1409," *Speculum* 70 (1995): 822–64. Earlier discussions tend to underplay the changes wrought by Arundel. See, for example, my "Vernacular Books of Religion," in *Book Production and Publishing in Britain, 1375–1475*, ed. J. Griffiths and D. Pearsall (Cambridge, 1989), 317–44, which now looks underhistoricized compared to the discussions in Watson or in *The Idea of the Vernacular: An Anthology of Middle English Literary Theory, 1280–1520*, ed. J. Wogan-Browne, N. Watson, A. Taylor, and R. Evans (Exeter, 1999), though some of those discussions also tend to the ameliorative model. But this paper wonders if the impact of Arundel needs more careful analysis, more local examination, and wider contextualization than it has perhaps hitherto received.

2. See further the article by A. S. G. Edwards in this volume. The other work in the Notre Dame manuscript, *The Craft of Dying*, addresses itself to an explicitly double audience of "lewed men" as well as religious and devout persons. Its Bernardine account of the Passion and of the deposition (f. 113v) has many similarities with cap. 24 of the *Mirror*. See Gillespie, "Vernacular Books," 327; R. Raymo, "Works of Religious and Philosophical Instruction," in *A Manual of the Writings in Middle English*, vol. 7, ed. A. E. Hartung (Hamden, Conn., 1986), XX.216; G. R. Morgan, "A Critical Edition of Caxton's *The Art and Craft to Know Well to Die* and *Ars Moriendi* together with the Antecedent Manuscript Material," (DPhil diss., Oxford, 1973), although unaware of the Foyle/Notre Dame copy, comments that *The Craft of Dying* "seems to have circulated among substantial lay families with strong religious connections in and around the metropolis during the second half of the fifteenth century" (127).

3. The standard account of the foundation of Syon is still G. J. Aungier, *The History and Antiquities of Syon Monastery, the Parish of Isleworth and the Chapelry of Hounslow* (London, 1840). More recently M. B. Tait, "The Brigittine Monastery of Syon (Middlesex) with Special Reference to its Monastic Uses" (DPhil diss., Oxford, 1975) studied much unprinted manuscript material and explored the spiritual and cultural life of the house. See also N. Beckett, "St. Bridget, Henry V and Syon Abbey," in *Studies in St. Birgitta and the Brigittine Order*, 2 vols., ed. J. Hogg, Analecta Cartusiana 35:19 (Salzburg, 1993), 2:125–50, for a recent perspective on the politics of the foundation. For discussion of the spirituality of the order (and especially of the nuns), see R. Ellis, *Viderunt eam filie syon: The Spirituality of the English House of a Medieval Contemplative Order from its beginnings to the present day*, Analecta Cartusiana 68 (Salzburg, 1984). On Sheen, see N. Beckett, "Sheen Charterhouse from its Foundation to its Dissolution" (DPhil diss., Oxford, 1992).

4. The standard (and masterly) discussion of the Syon libraries is now C. De Hamel, *Syon Abbey: The Library of the Bridgettine Nuns and their Peregrinations after the Reformation*, Roxburghe Club (Otley, 1991). The *registrum* of the library of the Brethren (ca. 1504) is now Cambridge, Corpus Christi College, MS 141. It was first edited by M. Bateson, *Catalogue of the Library of Syon Monastery Isleworth* (Cambridge, 1898). A more detailed edition is now available as *Syon Abbey*, edited by Vincent Gillespie, with *The Libraries of the Carthusians*, edited by A. I. Doyle, Corpus of British Medieval Library Catalogues 9 (London, 2001), which includes an introduction analyzing the history of the Brethren's library. References to this edition will give the alphabetical library mark (e.g., M.1) followed by the number for that entry in the Corpus (e.g., SS1.734). SS1 refers to the original *registrum*, SS2 to entries reconstructed from erasure and indices.

5. M. G. Sargent, "Walter Hilton's *Scale of Perfection*: The London Manuscript Group Reconsidered," *Medium Aevum* 52 (1983): 189–216; R. Lovatt, "The *Imitation of Christ* in Late Medieval England," *Transactions of the Royal Historical Society*, 5th ser., 18 (1968): 97–121; *The Imitation of Christ*, ed. B. J. H. Biggs, EETS o. s. 309 (Oxford, 1997), vii.

6. A. I. Doyle, "Carthusian Participation in the Movement of the Works of Richard Rolle between England and other parts of Europe in the 14th and 15th Centuries," in *Kartäusermystik und -Mystiker*, Analecta Cartusiana 55:2 (Salzburg, 1981): 109–20, at 116.

7. See the example printed by F. Wormald, "The Revelation of the Hundred Pater Nosters," *Laudate* 14 (1936): 165–82, at 180–181, where a devotional text passes from London Charterhouse to Mount Grace, from Mount Grace to a secular priest, and only then from secular priest into (perhaps memorial rather than textual) lay use. See my "Dial M for Mystic: Mystical Texts in the Library of

Syon Abbey and the Spirituality of the Syon Brethren," in *The Medieval Mystical Tradition: Exeter Symposium VI*, ed. M. Glasscoe (Cambridge, 1999), 241–68, esp. 249. On Carthusian involvement with and possible production of pastoral (rather than devotional) books, see my "Cura pastoralis in deserto," in *De Cella in Seculum: Religious and Secular Life and Devotion in Late Medieval England*, ed. M. G. Sargent (Cambridge, 1989), 161–81, and my "The Evolution of the *Speculum Christiani*," in *Latin and Vernacular: Studies in Late-Medieval Texts and Manuscripts*, ed. A. J. Minnis (Cambridge, 1989), 39–62.

8. M. Cré, "Vernacular Mysticism in the Charterhouse," (PhD diss., Fribourg, 2001); M. Cré, "Women in the Charterhouse," in *Writing Religious Women: Female Spiritual and Textual Practices in Late Medieval England*, ed. D. Renevey and C. Whitehead (Cardiff, 2000), 43–62. For a detailed recent description of this manuscript and an account of Grenehalgh's annotations, see M. G. Sargent, *James Grenehalgh as Textual Critic*, 2 vols., Analecta Cartusiana 85 (Salzburg, 1984), 2:499–510. On Ruusbroec, see M. G. Sargent, "Ruusbroec in England: *The Chastising of God's Children* and Related Works," in *Historia et Spiritualitas Cartusienses*, ed. J. de Grauwe (Ghent, 1983), 303–12; M. G. Sargent, "The Heneage Manuscript of *Calculus de Perfectione Filiorum Dei* and the Middle English *Treatise of Perfection of the Sons of God*," *Ons Geestelijk Erf* 59 (1985): 533–59.

9. *Nicholas Love's Mirror of the Blessed Life of Jesus Christ*, ed. M. G. Sargent (New York, 1992), 10.

10. On Love, see S. Oguro, R. Beadle, and M. G. Sargent, eds., *Nicholas Love at Waseda* (Cambridge, 1997) for an overview of recent scholarship. For a provocative reading of Love's disparaging attitudes to lay and therefore vernacular spirituality, see N. Watson, "Conceptions of the Word: The Mother Tongue and the Incarnation of God," *New Medieval Literatures* 1 (1997): 85–124, esp. 91–98.

11. A. I. Doyle, "Publication by Members of the Religious Orders," in *Book Production and Publishing in Britain*, ed. Griffiths and Pearsall, 109–23, at 113.

12. Gillespie, "Dial M for Mystic," 241–48; J. Hogg, "Mount Grace Charterhouse and Late Medieval English Spirituality," in *Collectanea Cartusiensia* 3, Analecta Cartusiana 82:3 (Salzburg, 1980), 43.

13. G. R. Keiser, "The Mystics and the Early English Printers: The Economics of Devotionalism," in *The Medieval Mystical Tradition in England: Exeter Symposium IV*, ed. M. Glasscoe (Cambridge, 1987), 9–26; S. E. Holbrook, "Margery Kempe and Wynkyn de Worde," ibid., 27–46.

14. The erased entry at M.26 (SS2.127) in the *registrum* of the Brethren's library at Syon has contents that parallel those of London, Lambeth Palace Library, MS 472 and are closely similar to another such common-profit volume. Lambeth was made from the goods of a wealthy London grocer, John Killum, one

of whose executors was John Colop, involved in the making of other similar volumes. Colop was a founder member of the Chapel and Guild of the Nine Orders of Angels in Isleworth, "juxta Syon" and with links to both Syon and Sheen: the foundation charter (1446) of the guild is printed in Aungier, *History and Antiquities*, 459–64 (and translated 215–25). See Gillespie, "Vernacular Books," 319–20; Gillespie, *Syon Abbey*, 469–70; Sargent, "London Manuscript Group"; W. Scase, "Reginald Pecock, John Carpenter and John Colop's 'Common-Profit' Books: Aspects of Book Ownership in Fifteenth-Century London," *Medium Aevum* 61 (1992): 261–74. The issue is further explored in Vincent Gillespie, "Walter Hilton at Syon Abbey," in *'Stand up to Godwards': Essays in Mystical and Monastic Theology in Honour of the Reverend John Clark on his Sixty-Fifth Birthday*, ed J. Hogg, Analecta Cartusiana 204 (Salzburg, 2002): 9–61, to which should be added the information that John Somerset was listed in the Syon *Martiloge* as one of the friends and special benefactors of the house, further strengthening the links between Syon and the fraternity. See also A. F. Sutton and L. Visser-Fuchs, "The Cult of Angels in Late Fifteenth-Century England: An Hours of the Guardian Angel presented to Queen Elizabeth Woodville," in *Women and the Book: Assessing the Visual Evidence*, ed. by L. Smith and J. Taylor (London, 1996): 230–65, which places the circumstances of the foundation of the fraternity into a wider devotional and social context.

15. There is some evidence of increasing lay (sometimes royal) access to charterhouses in the second half of the fifteenth century, mainly to participate in liturgical offices out of the sight of the monks. There is little sign of Carthusians systematically engaging in the spiritual direction of seculars, though some were granted letters of spiritual fraternity. See J. A. Gribbin, *Aspects of Carthusian Liturgical Practice in Later Medieval England*, Analecta Cartusiana 99:33 (Salzburg, 1995), 33–51; C. B. Rowntree, Studies in Carthusian History in Later Medieval England, with Special Reference to the Order's Relations with Secular Society, (PhD diss., York, 1981), 373 ff. On the pattern of Carthusian daily life, see B. Barrier, *Les activités du solitaire en chartreuse d'après ses plus anciens témoins*, Analecta Cartusiana 87 (Salzburg, 1981). But the purity of the life may have been challenged and somewhat eroded in the fifteenth century; see J. Hogg, "Everyday Life in the Charterhouse in the Fourteenth and Fifteenth Centuries," in *Klösterliche Sachkultur des Spätmittelalters*, Veröffentlichungen des Instituts für Mittelalterliche Realienkunde Österreichs 3 (Vienna, 1980), 113–46.

16. A. M. Hutchison, "Devotional Reading in the Monastery and in the Late Medieval Household," in *De Cella in Seculum*, ed. Sargent, 215–27; F. Riddy, "'Women talking about the things of God': A Late-Medieval Sub-culture," in *Women and Literature in Britain, 1150–1500*, ed. C. M. Meale, 2nd ed. (Cambridge, 1996), 104–27, and the essays by Julia Boffey and Carol Meale in the same volume;

A. I. Doyle, "Books Connected with the Vere Family and Barking Abbey," *Transactions of the Essex Archaeological Society* 25 (1958): 222–43. On London widows and monastic houses in general and on the connection with Syon of one merchant's widow in particular, see J. Stratford, "Joan Buckland (d. 1462)," in *Medieval London Widows: 1300–1500*, ed. C. M. Barron and A. F. Sutton (London, 1994), 113–28. The important new study by Mary Erler, *Women, Reading, and Piety in Late Medieval England* (Cambridge, 2002) appeared too late for me to take account of it in this paper, but its centre of gravity appears to be in the later fifteenth century.

17. The foundational survey of this material remains James Hogg's "The Contribution of the Brigittine Order to Late Medieval English Spirituality," in *Spiritualität Heute und Gestern*, Analecta Cartusiana 35 (Salzburg, 1983), 153–74. For recent discussion, see, for example, Keiser, "Economics of Devotionalism"; J. T. Rhodes, "Syon Abbey and its Religious Publications in the Sixteenth Century," *Journal of Ecclesiastical History* 44 (1993): 11–25; J. T. Rhodes, "Religious Instruction at Syon in the Early Sixteenth Century," in *Studies in St. Birgitta*, 2:151–69.

18. The important mid-fifteenth-century Latin compilation of contemplative materials known as *Speculum Spiritualium*, for example, is often attributed a Syon/Sheen provenance. But none of the five copies preserved in the Syon catalogue claims it as a Syon text. Indeed Betson's index explicitly attributes it to "Adam monachus Cartusiensis," while the entry describing the copy at M.60–61 states that the preceding rubrics were "ex compilacione dompni henrici Domus Cartusiensis de Bethleem monachi" (that is, the neighbouring house of Sheen). E. A. Jones, "A Chapter from Richard Rolle in Two Fifteenth-Century Compilations," *Leeds Studies in English*, n.s., 27 (1996): 139–62, gives the most recent list of manuscripts and editions. There is debate about the provenance of another mid-century compilation, the vernacular *Disce mori*, which may be the work of a Syon brother and which may be addressed to a vowess or postulant to the house. The evidence, which is not conclusive, is reviewed by E. A. Jones, "The Heresiarch, the Virgin, the Recluse, the Vowess, the Priest: Some Medieval Audiences for Pelagius's *Epistle to Demetrias*," *Leeds Studies in English*, n.s., 30 (2000): 205–27.

19. On Margaret's links with Syon (and those of other noble benefactors), see G. R. Keiser, "Patronage and Piety in Fifteenth-century England: Margaret, Duchess of Clarence, Symon Wynter and Beinecke MS 317," *Yale University Library Gazette* 60 (1985): 32–46; the quotation from Wynter is on p. 41. Some other powerful early friends of Syon are mentioned in F. R. Johnston, "Joan North, First Abbess of Syon, 1420–33," *Birgittiana* 1 (1996): 47–65; *The Incendium Amoris of Richard Rolle of Hampole*, ed. M. Deanesly (Manchester, 1915), 91–130. One of Margaret's gifts, a copy of Symon Wynter's *Sanctilogium Salvatoris*, originally items M.1 and M.2 (SS1.734–35) in Betson's catalogue, was copied by Stephen Dodesham,

later a Sheen Carthusian of some scribal productivity, though this may have been completed before his entry into religion when he may have worked as a professional scribe. A sermon on the Syon indulgences by Symon Wynter survives in London, British Library, MS Harley 2321, ff. 17r–62r, with shorter adaptations surviving elsewhere; S. Powell, "Preaching at Syon Abbey," *Working Papers in Literary and Cultural Studies* 29 (Salford, 1997) gives a full account of this text and of the popular appeal of the pardons.

20. The work is preserved in two copies: Cambridge, University Library, MS Gg. 1. 6 and Notre Dame, Indiana, University of Notre Dame, MS 67 (olim Foyle). There is an incomplete edition in *The Speculum Devotorum of an Anonymous Carthusian of Sheen*, ed. J. Hogg, Analecta Cartusiana 12 (Salzburg, 1973). An edition based on the Cambridge manuscript was produced by Bridget Ann Wilsher as a Master's thesis at University College, London, in 1956. An edition based on Notre Dame 67 (then Foyle) was completed by J. P. Banks as a Fordham University doctoral thesis (New York, 1959). Paul Patterson, a doctoral student at the University of Notre Dame, is working on a critical edition with commentary, based on Notre Dame 67 but also taking account of the Cambridge manuscript. The major recent discussions of the work are E. Salter, "Ludolphus of Saxony and his English Translators," *Medium Aevum* 33 (1964): 26–35; E. Salter, *Nicholas Love's "Myrrour of the Blessed Lyf of Jesu Christ,"* Analecta Cartusiana 10 (Salzburg, 1974), 106–10; I. Johnson, "Prologue and Practice: Middle English Lives of Christ," in *The Medieval Translator: The Theory and Practice of Translation in the Middle Ages*, ed. R. Ellis et al. (Cambridge, 1989), 69–85; M. G. Sargent, "Versions of the Life of Christ: Nicholas Love's *Mirror* and Related Works," *Poetica* 42 (1994): 39–70; G. R. Keiser, "Middle English Passion Narratives and their Contemporary Readers: The Vernacular Progeny of *Meditationes Vitae Christi*," in *The Mystical Tradition and the Carthusians*, ed J. Hogg, Analecta Cartusiana 130:10 (Salzburg, 1996), 85–99; and R. Salman, "Spirituality and Sex Change: *Horologium sapientiae* and *Speculum devotorum*," in *Writing Religious Women*, 63–79.

21. Also I haue bee sterred oftymes to haue lefte þis besynes both for myne vnworthynesse and also for Boneauenture a cardynale and a worthi clerk made a book of þe same matier þe which is called *Vita Cristi*. And moste of all when I herde tell þat a man of our ordoure hadde turned þe same booke in to englysshe (Prologue, Notre Dame 67, f. 1r.).

22. In Cambridge most of the colophon is now missing, with only the first sentence found on f. 144v. It survives intact in Notre Dame (for a text, see the appendix to Edwards's essay in this volume).

23. The *chartae* of the Carthusian order record that there are monks from other houses of the English province with the correct initials. William Hammond

died as a monk of Coventry in 1480. William Harrison, professed monk of Mountgrace, died as a guest at Axholme in 1504. The Dom William Heet, professed monk of Sheen who died at Hull Charterhouse in 1511, is much too late to have been our author. The closest match chronologically is William Hull (alias Parys) who dies as a monk of Witham in 1434. It is just possible that William Hull spent some time at the new foundation of Sheen before returning to Witham, and therefore just possible that he may be the author of the *Mirror*.

24. Professor Jeremy Smith of the University of Glasgow, who generously examined the language of the Notre Dame manuscript, describes it as "a somewhat colourless text with a sprinkling of regional forms." He suggests the forms co-locate most plausibly in East Anglia, specifically East Norfolk, though the presence of some Northern forms suggests a reserve placing of the Lincolnshire/Rutland/Leicestershire borders (personal communication, 5 May 2004). For the linguistic features of the Cambridge manuscript, see *LALME* 3:496–97.

25. See, for example, Salman, "Spirituality and Sex Change," 71, and Johnson, "Prologue and Practice," 75.

26. The fullest account of this relationship, along with a detailed analysis of Grenehalgh's textual work, is found in Sargent, *James Grenehalgh*.

27. *Iohannis de Caulibus Meditaciones Vite Christi olim S. Bonauenturo attributae*, ed. M. Stallings-Taney, CCCM 153 (Turnhout, 1997), hereafter *MVC*; S. McNamer, "Further Evidence for the Date of the Pseudo-Bonaventuran *Meditationes Vitae Christi*," *Franciscan Studies* 38 (1990): 235–61.

28. In this respect I differ from Michael Sargent, who argues that the author had both the *MVC* and Love's *Mirror* "constantly in mind in shaping his own work," "Versions of the Life of Christ," 65. I can see no need for him to have known Love's work in composing his own, nor can I discern any textual indebtedness to Love, except where Love is sharing *MVC* as a source. Rather I concur with J. P. Banks (cited in n. 20) that "the *Speculum* does not depend directly on either of them as sources, except in minor instances. But for its basic inspiration, its general tone and structure, the *Speculum* relies entirely on the *Meditationes*" (p. cxxxv; cited in Sargent, "Versions of the Life of Christ," 64).

29. W. St. J. Hope, *The History of the London Charterhouse from its Foundation until the Suppression of the Monastery* (London, 1925), 60, 62; cf. also E. M. Thompson, *The Carthusian Order in England* (London, 1930), 278–79.

30. The booklists are edited and annotated in Gillespie, *Syon Abbey*. On surviving Carthusian books, see N. R. Ker, *Medieval Libraries of Great Britain: A List of Surviving Books*, 2nd ed., Royal Historical Society Guides and Handbooks 3 (London, 1964); *Supplement*, ed. A. G. Watson, Royal Historical Society Guides and Handbooks 15 (London, 1987); A. I. Doyle, "English Carthusian Books Not

Yet Linked with a Charterhouse," in *A Miracle of Learning: Studies in Manuscripts and Irish Learning; Essays in Honour of William O'Sullivan*, ed. T. Barnard, Dáibhí Ó Cróinín, and Katherine Simms (Aldershot, 1998), 122–36.

31. Beckett, "Sheen Charterhouse," 78–79, citing exchequer document E403/621, m.1 and editions of the *chartae* for 1420 in Analecta Cartusiana 100:8 (1986), 12; 100:10, 45 and 100:21, 88. The *chartae* entry instructs Sheen to conform its practices concerning the Divine Office to those of the order "et iniungimus ei ut prouideant domui suae de libris ordini necessariis et sufficientibus" ["and we command them that they provide their house with those books that are necessary and sufficient for the order"]. The books may have been liturgical.

32. P. Strong and F. Strong, "The Last Will and Codicils of Henry V," *English Historical Review* 96 (1981): 79–102; Becket, "Sheen Charterhouse," 127–28. Bridget is included in the list of saints from whom suffrages are requested at the beginning of the will (Strong and Strong, "Last Will and Codicils," 89). K. B. McFarlane, *Lancastrian Kings and Lollard Knights* (Oxford, 1972), appendix C: "Henry V's Books," prints a list of the books taken after the siege of the Market of Meaux, apparently from one of the town's religious houses, which he suggests might have been destined for Syon or Sheen. The books passed initially into the personal custody of the Treasurer, John Stafford, finding their way into the Treasury itself only in 1427, when this list was made. Initially some and subsequently all were given to King's Hall Cambridge, where they are noted by 1440. No reason for overriding the provisions of the will and its codicils is given.

33. On Dodesham's output, see A. I. Doyle, "Stephen Dodesham of Witham and Sheen," in *Of the Making of Books: Medieval Manuscripts, Their Scribes and Readers; Essays presented to M. B. Parkes*, ed. P. R. Robinson and R. Zim (Aldershot, 1997), 94–115.

34. See the similar but less extended gesture in *MVC*, prologue, 9–10.

35. Keiser, "Passion Narratives," elegantly analyses the stylistic and structural inadequacies of the author.

36. And leste ony man þat myght efterwarde rede þe booke foloweyng shulde conceyue temptacyoun that I þat am bot a symple man shulde doo suche a werke eftre so worthi a man as Boneauenture was seth he wrote of þe same matier ¶ Hit myght be answered to þe satisfaccyoun of her concyences thus. Ther bene foure euangelistes þat wryten of þe manhode of our lorde. And yit all writen wele and treuly and þat one leueth another suppleth. ¶ Also þe doctures of holy chirche expownden þe same euangelyes þat þei wrote diuers wyses to þe comforte of cristen peple and yit all is goode to cresten peple and necessarye and profitable. And so þoff he þat wrote friste þe meditacions folowyng were bot a symple man and of no reputacioun in comparison of so worthi a clerke as Boneauenture was, ȝit þe

meditacions by þe grace of god mowe be full profitable to deuote cresten soules . . . þoff þe werke be bot symple ȝit þe entente of hym þat didde hit was full goode. And þerfore who so kanne noght excuse þe werke latt him excuse þe entente And for þe entente of him þat dedde it was to symple and deuote soules þat kan noght wele vnderstonde latyn, and also for þe thynkynge of our lordis passioun and manhode is þe grownde and þe waye to all trewe deuocyoun, this booke may be called *A Myrrour to deuote peple* (Prologue, Notre Dame 67, ff. 1v–2r.).

37. And I haue putte no thyng to of myne owne wytte bot þat I trowe may trewly be conceyved by open resoun and goode conciens for þat I holde þe sikereste. For þof þer myght haue bene putte to some ymaginaciouns þat happely myght haue bee dilectable to carnale soules, ȝit þat that is done aftre concience is sikerer þoffe þe meditaciouns myght haue be by such ymaginaciouns happely more comfortable to some carnale foulke (Prologue, Notre Dame 67, f. 3r).

38. On the spirituality of the Brethren in particular, see Ellis, *Viderunt eam filie Syon*, and R. Ellis, " Further Thoughts on the Spirituality of Syon Abbey," in *Mysticism and Spirituality in Medieval England*, ed. W. F. Pollard and R. Boenig (Cambridge, 1997), 219–43. See also my "'Hid Diunite': The Spirituality of the English Syon Brethren," in *The Medieval Mystical Tradition in England: Exeter Symposium VII*, ed. E. Jones (Cambridge, 2004), 189–206.

39. *MVC*, cap. 6, 29. Mary Erler has done important work on paramonastic women such as vowesses; see her "English Vowed Women at the End of the Middle Ages," *Mediaeval Studies* 57 (1995): 155–203; "Syon's 'Special Benefactors and Friends': Some Wowed [*sic*] Women," *Birgittiana* 2 (1996): 209–22. On Margery Kempe's vow of married chastity made before Bishop Philip Repingdon of Lincoln some time between June 1413 and February 1414, see *The Book of Margery Kempe*, ed. S. B. Meech and H. E. Allen, EETS o. s. 212 (London, 1940), cap. 14, 33–34 and notes. Repingdon considers the vow unusual because John Kempe is still alive, but proceeds to give Margery the mantle and ring after reassurances from her husband.

40. Contrast the less explicitly contemplative take on this passage in *MVC* cap. 82: "domi remansit et orabat" (300–301).

41. See Thomas Betson's exhortations to the nuns, printed below.

42. On the reception of the continental women mystics in England, see R. Voaden, ed., *Prophets Abroad: The Reception of Continental Holy Women in Late-Medieval England* (Cambridge, 1996). The cult of Bridget in England predates the foundation of Syon (and may indeed have been one of the drivers for it).

43. For Mary reverencing the cross, see *MVC*, cap. 80, 284.

44. *MVC*, cap. 17, 84–5. *MVC* contains an embedded treatise on the active and contemplative lives which follows on from the Martha and Mary story

(caps. 45–58, 171–216). Cap. 55 (200–203) deals with Christ in the desert but makes no mention of preachers or preaching.

45. K. Horstmann, "*Orologium sapientiae* or The Seven Poyntes of Trewe Wisdom aus MS. Douce 117," *Anglia* 10 (1887): 323–89; R. Lovatt, "Henry Suso and the Medieval Mystical Tradition," in *The Medieval Mystical Tradition in England: Exeter Symposium II*, ed. M. Glasscoe (Exeter, 1982), 47–62; Salman, "Spirituality and Sex Change." A new edition of this important text is in preparation by Professor Christina von Nolcken, using Aberystwyth, National Library of Wales, MS Porkington 19 as base text, where the prologue occupies pp. 7–13. For the use of this passage from Suso in Ludolph of Saxony's *Vita Christi*, see *Ludolphus de Saxonia: Vita Jesu Christi*, 4 vols., ed. L. M. Rigollot (Paris, 1878), 4:4–5.

46. *Regula Salvatoris*, cap. 1. The Middle English version is reproduced from Cambridge, University Library, Ff. 6. 33 in *The Rewyll of Seynt Sauioure and Other Middle English Brigittine Legislative Texts*, vols. 2–4 [all published], ed. J. Hogg, Salzburger Studien zur Anglistik und Amerikanistik, Bd. 6 (Salzburg, 1978–80), 2:1–58 at 8, which also reproduces a Latin text from Cambridge, St. John's College, MS 11 (A. 11). The standard edition of the versions of the Latin is *Regula Salvatoris*, ed. S. Eklund, *Den Heliga Birgitta Opera Minora* 1, Samlingar utgivna av Svenska Fornskriftsällskapet, Andra Serien, Latinska Skrifter, 8:1 (Lund, 1975). Four versions survive of the Additions to the Rule specially written for the English Syon in distinct versions for the Sisters and the Brethren: London, British Library, MS Arundel 146 (in Middle English, for the sisters); London, Guildhall Library, MS 25524 (in Middle English, for the Brethren); Cambridge, St. John's College, MS 11 (a fragmentary Latin text for the Brethren); and a post-medieval Latin version produced in Lisbon in 1607. The first three are reproduced or edited by Hogg. Fragments of the Rule and Additions were more recently identified among the manuscripts still in possession of the sisters (and now housed in Exeter University Library) in N. R. Ker and A. J. Piper, *Medieval Manuscripts in British Libraries*, 4 (Oxford, 1992), 348–49. Descriptions of the life at Syon in what follows are drawn from the *Rule*, the *Additions*, the *Breviary*, and the *Mirror of Our Lady*, and can be found in the editions already cited.

47. *Regula Salvatoris*, cap. 1, Hogg, 2:8–9. According to the *Additions for the Sisters*, cap. 17, eight days after profession, novices received an exhortation from the abbess that expounded on the meaning of "veray mekenes, pure chastite & wylful pouerte," Hogg, 4:99–101.

48. J. H. Blunt, ed., *The Myroure of Oure Ladye*, EETS e.s. 19 (London, 1873); A. J. Collins, *The Bridgettine Breviary of Syon Abbey*, Henry Bradshaw Society 96 (London, 1969). For an account of the life of the house, see Ellis,

*Viderunt eam filie Syon*, and Ann M. Hutchison, "What the Nuns Read: Literary Evidence from the English Bridgettine House, Syon Abbey," *Mediaeval Studies* 57 (1995): 205–22.

49. "The Translator's Prologue," in *The Orcherd of Syon*, ed. P. Hodgson and G. M. Liegey, EETS o.s. 258 (London, 1966), 1.

50. Hogg, *Rewyll of Seynt Sauioure*, 2:38; *Regula Salvatoris*, cap. 15, § 174 (Eklund, 121). For the passage in the text, see cap. 13, § 171 (Eklund, 161–62). On the complex development of the rule and its manifestations in England, see Ellis, *Viderunt eam filie Syon*, ch. 1.

51. The Syon *Additions for the Brethren* (Guildhall manuscript) record in a short chapter headed "Of the offices of the prechours" that "Eche of the prechours schal besyde the sermon day haue thre hole days at lest oute of the quyer to recorde hys sermon," Hogg, *Rewyll of Saint Savioure*, 3:122. On their penitential authority, see Johnston, "Joan North," 56, citing *Liber Privilegiorum Monasterii Vadstenensis*, ed. E. Nygren (Copenhagen, 1950), 236. The *Additions for the Brethren* contain many injunctions about protecting the enclosures.

52. Cf. *MVC*, cap. 73, 245–46, where Peter symbolizes the active life and John the contemplative. An interesting reflection of the linkage between Mary and John is found in a manuscript from the very earliest collection at Syon (G.17: SS1.450), given by Thomas Fishbourn, the first Confessor-General (d. 1428), containing two adjacent unidentified items ascribed to Peter Comestor: "de laude beate virginis" (perhaps one of the nine sermons on the Virgin ascribed to him) and "de laude Iohannis Euangeliste."

53. *PL* 198:299–309.

54. *Additions for the Sisters*, cap. 58, Hogg, 4:198, with a list of their ideal attributes that has much in common with those of Mary and John in the *Mirror*.

55. Blunt, *The Myroure of Oure Ladye*, 77–79.

56. The *probatio* tradition is discussed in R. Voaden, *God's Words, Women's Voices: The Discernment of Spirits in the Writing of Late-Medieval Women* (York, 1999).

57. Blunt, *The Myroure of Oure Ladye*, 299.

58. ¶ And I haue sett þe tytles of [þe chapeters] in a table eftre þis prefacioun of þe booke þat who so euer liketh to rede it may see shortly ther all þe matier of þe booke folowyng, and rede when him lyketh beste. And þat he maye þe sonner fynde þat he desireth moste and þe better kepe hit in mynde and also þe redyer fynde hit if him luste to see hit aȝen. Noghtwythstondyng hit were þe beste who so myght haue tyme and laysere þerto to rede hit all as hit is sett (Prologue, Notre Dame 67, f. 1r.).

59. *STC* 1978, repr. in facsimile (Cambridge, 1905): sig, c iv v.

60. In his *Consuetudines*, Guigo envisaged the making of books as the Order's distinctive contribution to the *cura animarum*. In his well-known dictum, borrowed

from Cassian, repeated by Adam of Dryburgh in the *Quadripartite Exercise of the Cell*, and reflected and refracted in many Carthusian legislative texts and commentaries throughout the medieval period, Guigo wrote: "Libros quippe tanquam sempiternum animarum nostrarum cibum cautissime custodiri et studiosissime volumus fieri, ut quia ore non possumus, dei verbum manibus predicemus." ["Because we desire that books should be made with the greatest zeal, and guarded with very great care, as a perpetual source of food for our souls, in order that we may preach with our hands the word of God, since we may not do so with the mouth."] Guigues 1er, *Coutumes de Chartreuse*, Sources Chrétiennes 313 (Paris, 1984), XXVIII.3.

61. John, fourth Lord Scrope was the heir of his older brother Henry, third Lord Scrope, executed in 1415. Henry had been supportive of the project that led to the foundation of Syon and Sheen (popularly thought to be in expiation of Henry IV's murder of Archbishop Richard Scrope, an uncle of Henry and John). Henry Scrope possessed many religious books, including an alleged autograph of Rolle and another Rolle book, both left to Henry FitzHugh, who was responsible for the first (failed) plantation of Bridgettines in England, and who remained a strong supporter of the Syon project. Interestingly, Syon later claimed to own an autograph of Rolle's *Melos amoris* (M. 27: SS1.760a). Henry Scrope also left to the Abbess of Syon a choice of books or vestments to the value of forty pounds, and made bequests to several other figures active in the foundation and early life of Syon, notably John London, the anchorite of Westminster, and Bishop Thomas Langley of Durham. See A. I. Doyle, "A Survey of the Origins and Circulation of Theological Writings in English in the 14th, 15th and Early 16th Centuries with Special Consideration of the Part of the Clergy Therein," 2 vols. (PhD diss., Cambridge, 1953), 1:151; 2:209, 302–3.

62. For a list of the sources explicitly cited in the text, see my appendix. The major exception is Adam of Dryburgh's Sermon on John the Evangelist (*PL* 198:299–307), which is not witnessed at Syon. As a Carthusian text, a copy might have been at Sheen: one of the major textual witnesses to his sermons is an early fifteenth-century manuscript formerly at London Charterhouse (Edinburgh, National Library of Scotland, MS 9999). Most of the citations of Bernard come through the *MVC*. Syon has multiple copies of all the major patristic sources used. In considering copies of the major post-patristic sources found at Syon, I have looked for evidence of early accession (pre-1450) as witnessed by the names of the donor, by external evidence, or by the absence of a recorded donor. What follows, therefore, is not a complete list of Syon's holdings of these works but a list restricted to relevant pre-1450 accessions: Iohannes de Caulibus, *Meditationes Vitae Christi* (M.6: SS1.739, given by Symon Wynter [d. 1448]; M.7: SS1.740, no donor, with other Passion meditations, erased at M.76: SS2.142); Peter Comestor, *Historia*

*Scholastica* (E.17: SS1.323a, with Richard of Saint-Victor, no donor, and erased at E.52: SS2.91); Heinrich Suso, *Orologium sapientiae* (O.3: SS1.945f, given by John Bracebridge); Nicholas of Lyra, *Postilla litteralis* (E.28–9: SS1.334–5, no donor, and erased copies in SS2); Jacobus de Voragine, *Legenda Aurea* (M.9: SS1.742, given by William Fitzthomas, at Syon by 1428); John of Hildesheim, *Historia trium regum [The Three Kings of Cologne]* (M.15: SS1.748m-n, no donor; M.17: SS1.750g, in English, no donor; this volume interestingly also contains a "Declaracio Regule Cartusie" [SS1.750f]); Walter Hilton, *The Scale of Perfection* (M.24: SS1.757b – c, in English, given by Fishbourn; erased at M.26: SS2.127a, no donor, and at M.110: SS2.147, no donor; the Latin translation by Thomas Fishlake is at M.25: SS1.758, no donor); *The Gospel of Nicodemus* (M.83: SS1.816a, given by Fishbourn; O.35: SS1.977l, given by Bracebridge); *Miracles of the Virgin*, though the contents of these collections varied widely (O.39: SS1.981d, given by Bracebridge). All the writings of the "approued women" included in the *Mirror* were demonstrably present at Syon: Bridget's revelations (M.64: SS1.797, now London, British Library, MS Harley 612, s.xv[1]; M.65: SS1.798, M.66: SS1.799, both were the gift of the first Confessor-General, Thomas Fishbourn [d. 1428]); Mechtild's *Booke* (M.47: SS1.780, no donor, perhaps in English, and M.94: SS1.827g, no donor); Elizabeth of Töss (in English and erased from the main catalogue at M.20: SS2.125); Catherine of Siena (M.71: SS1.804g, no donor, and of course through *The Orcherd of Syon*). There is even a copy of *Mandeville's Travels* at Syon (M.77: SS1.810g), but this appears to be a later, printed text given by Confessor-General Falkley, who died in 1497.

63. Without daring to suggest which is the Tortoise and which the Mock Turtle, I am deeply grateful to Dr. A. I. Doyle for his attempts to save me from heresy and vulgar error, and to Professor Jill Mann for the care and attention she has lavished on this essay. Being very dull, I of course remain solely responsible for the remaining errors.

# The Visual Environment of Carthusian Texts

## Decoration and Illustration in Notre Dame 67

JESSICA BRANTLEY

UNIVERSITY OF NOTRE DAME, MS 67, RECENTLY ACQUIRED FROM the sale of the Foyle collection,[1] includes a rare Middle English devotional text: *A Mirror to Devout People* (ff. 1–108).[2] We know that the *Mirror* was composed by a Carthusian monk, for its preface refers to Nicholas Love's translation of the Pseudo-Bonaventuran *Meditationes Vitae Christi* as the work of "a man of our ordoure." But—just as important—this vernacular *Mirror* is addressed to the writer's "gostely sustre in Ihesu criste."[3] What is more, the Notre Dame copy seems to have been commercially produced for aristocratic readers.[4] So although the origins of the *Mirror* can be traced to the environment of the charterhouse, its later life and readership can be definitively located elsewhere. This sort of diffusion is not unusual for Carthusian texts, which circulated widely in late medieval England and were often read outside the charterhouse, indeed outside of any monastic community.[5] Notre Dame 67 thus represents in particular terms the general tangle of lay and monastic interests characteristic of vernacular devotional texts associated with the Carthusian Order. I will address one aspect of that tangle here: the illustration and decoration of a Carthusian text in a manuscript made for the laity. Although this secular book might initially seem far removed from the austere surroundings of the charterhouse, the images in Notre Dame 67 work to negotiate the distance between the text's Carthusian exemplars and its new lay readership.

For a vernacular English book, this manuscript offers an unusual quantity of decoration. In addition to pen-flourishes and an accomplished full bar-frame border, there are three illuminated initials: a coat of arms (f. 1r; plate 1), the Virgin Mary and John the Evangelist (f. 108r; plate 2), and a dying man, with a bishop in a separate picture-space below (f. 109v; plate 3). Although the figural paintings are simple, their inclusion demonstrates that images are important to the environment of the devotional text. One way of measuring the rarity of these pictures is to compare Notre Dame 67 to the one other witness to the *Mirror to Devout People*: Cambridge, University Library, MS Gg. 1. 6. The Cambridge copy of the *Mirror* is known to have come from the charterhouse at Sheen, for it was written by Sheen scribe William Mede, and its inscription identifies it as: "liber dominus Ihesu de Willielmus ordinis cartusiensis de Shene."[6] The Carthusian manuscript is a far less luxurious object, written on paper and boasting only occasional rubrication, with no figural illustration at all. It would be easy to conclude that the monastic manuscript contrasts with the lay manuscript in precisely the ways one would expect: one is humbly devout, while the other is showily aristocratic. But the reality is more complicated, for the Carthusian visual environment was not as barren as one might assume, nor was the aristocratic world entirely untouched by charterhouse piety. Were the pictures added to Notre Dame 67 only when the text was copied for lay readers? Or is it possible that the original Carthusian exemplar of the *Mirror to Devout People*, written for a "gostely sustre," included illustration of some kind?

Unfortunately, we can ask more questions than we can answer about this lost exemplar, and about its images. For the visual environment of late medieval Carthusians in England is not easy to imagine or to reproduce. The first difficulty, of course, is the iconoclasm of the English Reformation, which resulted in the destruction of most devotional art apart from manuscript painting. Very little remains of what was certainly a lively and rich national artistic culture; consequently, one can never know with certainty what buildings, sculptures, or paintings English monks might have made (or even looked at), nor can one even draw definitive negative conclusions from negative evidence. Moreover, even on the Continent most extant Carthusian art is postmedieval; the canonization in 1623 of St. Bruno—the founder of the order—produced a great flourishing of baroque art and architecture in charterhouses, where relatively little had been produced before.[7] Accordingly, most scholarly attention to Carthusian art has focused on European rather than British examples, and those generally later than the fifteenth century.[8] But the most significant difficulty in investigating any kind of Carthusian art is more fundamental still: the Carthusian Order sought at its foundation to institute an extreme monastic asceticism, avoiding decoration of its churches and any sort of art object that could be considered *de luxe*. The earliest documents forbid precious ornament explicitly, and almost absolutely: for example, in his *Consuetudines* (1127) Prior Guigo I affirms: "We do not have any ornaments of gold or silver in the church, with the exception of the chalice and the reed by which the blood of the Savior is taken, nor do we have hangings or carpets."[9] The *Consuetudines* are the oldest codification of Carthusian life, but their prohibition of decoration is repeated, in varying forms, in the subsequent *Statuta Antiqua* (1259), *Statuta Nova* (1368), and *Tertia Compilatio* (1509).[10] It is difficult, given the strength of this early asceticism, to imagine that visual experience could have been very important for Carthusians of any time or place.

Yet even these early testaments from the charterhouses do not eschew the material world altogether; it is possible to detect in them a certain ambivalence towards the use of luxury materials. Guigo himself recognizes that gold and silver, in moderation, do honor to the furnishings of the Mass, and thus to the Lord whose sacrifice the Mass celebrates. The *Statuta Antiqua* loosen Guigo's strictures further to allow for some gold or silver, not exclusively on chalice and reed, but also on the priest's stole and maniple, and on bookmarkers.[11] In spite of the Order's basic asceticism, decorative extravagance seems to be admissible where it can be seen to do honor to God, rather than to reinforce the pride of man.[12] The pragmatic distinction implied here between acceptable and unacceptable forms of embellishment suggests that images can be used in this visually austere environment to further devotional purposes, and that, in practice, devotional art played a role in medieval Carthusian spirituality. As we explore the place of figural art in the charterhouse, it is worth remembering that the primary vocation of the Carthusians is not poverty, as for the followers of Francis, but solitude within monastic community.[13] The contradiction between the severity of their rule and their patronage of art is accordingly less stark, but the implications for their visual environment—both in the church and in the cell—are perhaps more surprising.

The artistic practices of late medieval charterhouses generally drew on the ambivalence of the early statutes towards visual display rather than on their stricter forms of asceticism. We can learn what was commonly done not so much from the measured idealism of the foundational documents as from what the later rules felt the need to forbid. By the time of the *Statuta Nova* in the mid-fourteenth century, pictures in charterhouses appear to have become so commonplace that they had to be explicitly prohibited, and their removal ordered. The statutes legislate gently against what was obviously a frequent transgression: "Let us not use any kind of tapestry, or cushions decorated with pictures or other extravagances; but decorative pictures, too, should be scraped away from our churches and houses, if it can be done without giving scandal; and new ones should not be allowed to be made."[14] The general chapter of 1424 specified more precisely the removal of the "curiously" painted pictures that had appeared on some charterhouse altars, and of other paintings that contained coats of arms and figures of women.[15] This concern for the abuse of imagery is echoed in the early sixteenth-century *Tertia Compilatio*, where visitators are particularly advised to watch for decorative indiscretion in churches and houses of the Order.[16]

These admonitions are revealing, for they indicate that a surprising variety of imagery indeed found its way into the ascetic charterhouse. They also record qualified objections to pictures—only those that might be taken away "without scandal" are to be removed. But the statutes illuminate too the ultimate source of some of the Carthusian concern about imagery, for they record, more precisely, objections to "curious" pictures of life outside the charterhouse. The repeated admonition against "curiosity" implies a discomfort with the level of ornamentation in particular artworks; a "curious" image is one too elaborately wrought, to no purpose other than aesthetic and formal pleasure.[17] Simplicity is a hallmark of art meant to serve the ends of prayer. But of course the objection here goes beyond excessive luxury, to encompass also the particular subjects of these figurative images:

lay life outside the charterhouse. Secular coats of arms and images of women are a far cry from Guigo's golden chalice.

As the anxieties of the statutes suggest, it was often secular influences that led in the fourteenth and fifteenth centuries to increased luxury—and more art—in the austere environment of the charterhouse. Monks increasingly prayed for the souls of wealthy benefactors, and also accepted those benefactors within the charterhouse walls, against all expectation of the Order's founders. In monasteries such as Champmol, Pavia, and Sheen, aristocratic (or even royal) founders demonstrated their piety, their wealth, and their power through their patronage of Carthusian art and architecture. At Champmol, in Dijon—perhaps the clearest example of the opulent effects of aristocratic patronage—Philippe de Bourgogne designed an elaborate artistic program to proclaim his associations with the fashionably eremitic order and to enhance the grandeur of his own burial-place.[18] The Charterhouse at Champmol was filled with art: from the High Altar retable carved by Jacques de Baerze and painted by Melchior Broederlam, to the *Martyrdom of St. Denis* painted by Jean Malouel and Henri Bellechose, to Claus Sluter's magnificent *Well of Moses* in the cloister, and finally Philippe's tomb itself, with its Carthusian mourners (see, for example, figure 6.1). Against the explicit direction of Guigo,[19] late medieval Carthusians allowed the tombs of their benefactors to be built in the monastic church, and the Duke of Burgundy symbolized his radical incorporation into the Charterhouse community by choosing to be buried in the habit of a Carthusian monk. Even (or especially) in death, the influence of aristocratic patrons on monastic churches was powerfully felt.

Less princely foundations responded to secular influences as well. The thirty-nine lay graves in the Coventry church, for example, contained men, women, children, and one executed felon.[20] As the Carthusians forsook their original remote "wildernesses," more numerous foundations in urban areas brought the monks into frequent contact with devout people of all kinds, and this contact, not surprisingly, had material consequences.[21] It is clear from the precision of the architectural wishes expressed in wills that lay people—even women—were inside Carthusian churches frequently.[22] As the laity worshipped in Carthusian churches, they exerted pressure on the form those churches took, instituting oratories and side-chapels that would serve their own devotional needs. Joseph A. Gribbin has explored

FIG. 6.1. A Carthusian mourner from the tomb of Philip the Bold, made for the Charterhouse of Champmol, Dijon (France). Detail from Claus Sluter, Claus de Werve, and Jean de Marville, *Tombeau de Phillippe le Hardi.* Musée des Beaux-Arts, Dijon (France). Photograph © Musée des Beaux-Arts de Dijon.

the ways in which the liturgy in London was affected by such contacts, and has claimed that outsiders turned the Charterhouse there into a "liturgical workshop."[23] Reformation accounts of the furnishings of the London church indeed show it to be indistinguishable from parish churches, the visual environment of the Carthusians impossible to differentiate from that of any late medieval worshipper.[24] Carthusian spiritual practice in the late Middle Ages was deeply influenced by the needs of the pious laity; and, as a result, the visual environment of monastic devotion—at least in such venues as the charterhouse church—was to some degree directed by the designs of the surrounding community.

It is easiest to see the effects of lay involvement with Carthusian life in the public buildings of the charterhouse, such as the church. The cenobitic buildings welcomed the world in the form of visitors from outside, as well as in the form of public displays of imagery: architecture, sculpture, and even less monumental artworks, such as rich altarpieces, announced the close relations of the charterhouse to temporal wealth and power.[25] But the increased influence on Carthusian life from the world outside was not only seen in the relatively public buildings of the charterhouse—it was felt also within the privacy of the monks' cells.[26] Luxurious donations from aristocratic patrons served not only for the construction of tombs and oratories. Smaller donations were sometimes domestic objects, sometimes luxurious clothes,[27] but they also occasionally comprised figurative images, whether in manuscript or panel paintings. At Champmol, for example, Philippe de Bourgogne arranged for each cell to have a saint's image in a stained glass window, and a devotional painting for the oratorium, such panels perhaps including the Crucifixion images by Jean de Beaumetz now in the Cleveland Museum of Art (figure 6.2) and the Louvre.[28] Benefactions to Mount Grace included this from Sir John Depeden to the prior in 1402: "a picture of the crucifixion."[29] The questions sent by the English province to the general convocations at the Grande Chartreuse record increasing anxiety about the propriety of patrons' gifts. The general chapter consistently returns the answer—based on Guigo's *Consuetudines*[30]—that such gifts are not allowed, certainly not if given to particular monks for their individual ownership, but the continual questions suggest that the problem arose repeatedly.[31] The tolerance of some luxurious objects within the

FIG. 6.2. Jean de Beaumetz, French, active 1361–died 1396. *The Crucifixion with a Carthusian Monk*, 1390–1395. Tempera and gold on wood, 56.6 x 45.7 cm. © The Cleveland Museum of Art, 2004. Leonard C. Hanna, Jr., Fund, 1964.454.

charterhouse for the purposes of individual consumption seems to have encouraged the temptations of private ownership.

But in spite of the opposition of the general chapter, individual use of some kinds of art objects served to clarify their purely devout purposes. Archaeological exacavations at Mount Grace have uncovered the most utilitarian of devotional images: an ivory head of Christ from the prior's cell and an indulgence with a picture of Christ as the Man of Sorrows from another.[32] Even Carthusian iconoclasts, defending their ascetic practice against the criticism of the orthodox,[33] make a place for devotional imagery in the cells while outlining their objections to art in public places. Guillaume d'Ivrée, author of the apologia *De origine et veritate perfectae religionis* (ca. 1313),[34] complicates our understanding of the visual asceticism of Carthusian life. He responds in this way to objections that the Carthusians have no painted images or sculptures:

> The Carthusians have in all their churches (and are bound to have, according to the institutions of their Order) one image of the Crucifixion in a solemn and eminent place, as well as many crosses over each altar. In the oratory of their cells they have generally had a crucifix and an image of the Virgin Mary, and also sometimes of other saints, according to the possibility and means that offer themselves. Their honest and poor religion mandates that they avoid expensive curiosities in painting and in sculpture and in varieties of grand and extravagant buildings, not consonant with the roughness of the solitary life. St. John Damascene taught that the images and pictures on the walls were as scriptures to the laity, and that those who did not know how to read in books, could understand through murals, as if through rough letters, what they could not understand in writing. And therefore it is commendable that such pictures should be made for churches where people frequently go, but would be useless and superfluous in Carthusian deserts where crowds (except for a few men) do not congregate. . . . Yet, as was said before, the Carthusians in their cells do not refuse nor reject devotional pictures, but accept and seek them freely and eagerly because they excite devotion and imagination, and augment devotional ideas.[35]

Guillaume cites John of Damascene as a defender of pictures for the instruction of the laity, but (as one might expect) he points out that such an argument does not apply so well to the devotion of learned, solitary monks. Pictures have a public life in "churches where people frequently go," but they should have no place in the Carthusian solitude. However, even Guillaume concedes the value of images in the monks' private meditations. A crucifix, an image of the Virgin, and images of particular saints are useful in individual devotion, not because of their didactic, but because of their affective, power. A photograph of a modern Carthusian monk at prayer, though clearly anachronistic, can give some idea of the ways in which artwork was used in the medieval cell to enhance private devotional experience (figure 6.3).[36]

The individual devotional experience pictured here is the subject, as well as the goal, of a surprising number of Carthusian medieval images, for the monks' representation of themselves in their art is both frequent and conspicuous. One might imagine that the monks were performing devotional acts by representing themselves at prayer, increasing their access to the divine by figuring it repeatedly in their pictures. As Yvette Carbonell-Lamothe has observed:

> No other order seems to have imposed its own image so confidently, to have been so insistent upon the representation of itself and upon its artistic translation.[37]

Her primary example is the altarpiece painted by Enguerrand de Quarton in the mid-fifteenth century, for the Carthusians of Villeneuve-lès-Avignon. It is probably the most celebrated example of Carthusian panel-painting, both for its beauty and for the detailed copy of the artist's commission that has been preserved. That commissioning document calls clearly for a depiction of "the cross of our Savior, and at the foot a praying Carthusian," and indeed Quarton has painted a tiny monk in prayer beneath the splendid Coronation of the Virgin (figure 6.4).[38] But the imposing retable with its memorable Carthusian figure is only one manifestation of the tradition of self-representation, for the depiction of the monks themselves in connection with their divine visions is widespread. Not only public paintings such as Quarton's altarpiece, but more private artworks, as well,

FIG. 6.3. Dom Benedict Lambres praying at the oratory in his cell in the second Great cloister of the Charterhouse of Farneta, in 1949. Printed by permission of Jan de Grauwe.

FIG. 6.4. Detail of the *Couronnement de la Vièrge.* Enguerrand Quarton. Retable painted for the Charterhouse of Villeneuve-lès-Avignon. Musée de l'Hospice, Villeneuve-les-Avignon, France.

included images of Carthusians at prayer before divine figures. As we have seen, the panel paintings in the cells at Champmol included a picture of a Carthusian monk praying before the cross, joining supplicant with Savior in a personalized devotional aid.[39] And the Carthusian monk Jan Vos seems to have commissioned two paintings featuring his own image in similar scenes, one for public display and the other for private devotions. An altarpiece for the charterhouses where Vos was prior (Genadedal, 1441–50, and Nieuwlicht, 1450–58) shows the monk praying to the Virgin and Child, flanked by Saints Barbara and Elizabeth; a smaller panel ostensibly for the prior's personal use shows substantially the same scene, omitting only St. Elizabeth.[40] Just as Philippe de Bourgogne imagined himself in monastic community by wearing a Carthusian habit to his grave, individual Carthusians imagined themselves in divine community through images such as these.

The ways in which private images could construct community within Carthusian solitude brings us to the manifestation of visual art in the cell most important for our purposes: images in books. Books constituted an exception to, or an acceptable way around, the isolation of the cell, as in Guigo's famous pronouncement that, in lieu of preaching with their mouths, the silent Carthusians would "preach with their hands"—that is, they would write and copy devotional texts.[41] Similarly, Carthusian bookmaking could require exceptions to strict poverty, and we might deduce that if any trace of material wealth is to be found in medieval charterhouses, it is to be found in the library. An early anecdote well illustrates both the material demands aristocratic patrons put on the monks' simplicity and the bibliographical resolution that was sometimes found. Guibert de Nogent relates the story of a gift to the Grande Chartreuse from the Count of Nevers:

> Let me show you how jealously they guard their poverty. This very year the Count of Nevers, a man whose piety is equal to his power, paid them a visit, driven by his own devoutness and their excellent reputation. He warned them repeatedly to guard against the accumulation of worldly goods. Once he returned home he thought anew about their poverty, which he had observed; but he did not heed his own warnings and sent them some silver vessels, such as cups and

> dishes of very great value. But they did not forget what he had told them; for once he made his intentions known he found himself fully refuted with his own words. "We have decided," they said, "to keep no riches that might come to us from outside, whether for our own upkeep or for furnishing our church; and if we are not to use them for either of these two purposes, what would it avail us to accept them?" Ashamed to have made a proposal that contradicted his own words, the count pretended not to have heard their refusal and instead sent a new offering of oxhides and parchments in abundance, for he knew that they would inevitably make use of these.[42]

This revealing episode demonstrates both the appeal of Carthusian asceticism to pious laypeople, as we have already seen, and the temptations to decorative extravagance offered by even the most well-meaning benefactors. But the story shows, too, that such external pressures were relieved—in this one case, at least—through the monks' determined bookishness. The gift of rich vessels from a wealthy outsider was accepted only when it was changed into oxhides and parchments, precious materials properly diverted towards devotional—and specifically literary—uses.

But if books themselves were acceptable luxury objects, the nature of Carthusian manuscript-painting remains as difficult to assess as other kinds of Carthusian art. Evidence of actual charterhouse illumination is more plentiful than other signs of artistic practice; we know that the monks sometimes decorated books, as well as wrote them, but it is difficult to attribute particular images securely to Carthusian illuminators, and their efforts did not usually go far beyond ornamented initials and rubrication.[43] Of course, illustrators who were not Carthusians also influenced Carthusian devotional experience. But the range of criteria by which books are linked to the Order is broad; simply identifying the volumes that reflect the imaginative life of the cell can be as difficult as understanding how they do so. Because books—as opposed to monumental sculpture—are easy to transport, it is particularly difficult to pin down their place of origin. It is unclear what kinds of internal evidence are significant, whether a marginal note recording the ownership of a charterhouse, for example, signifies more than, for example, pictures of Carthusian monks or the inclusion of Guigo's *Consuetudines*.[44] Nor is it obvious what to make of external signs of Carthusian book-ownership, such as a manuscript donation recorded in a will. Some "Carthusian books" were made by Carthusians, and so show the stamp of monastic piety as a reflection of their creation. Some were made for or given to them, and so reflect the interests either of Carthusians as readers or of their patrons in the secular world. These complications are important to keep in mind as we examine a few examples of manuscript illustration that—for one reason or another—can be called "Carthusian."

We have already seen that the late-medieval vogue for the Order among aristocrats led to the production of remarkably luxurious objects meant to celebrate monastic austerity—and illuminated books are no exception to this tendency. The most remarkable example is probably the *Belles Heures* of Jean, Duke of Berry, a sumptuous book made ca. 1408–9. The manuscript contains a series of beautiful paintings by the Limbourg brothers, which relate the story of St. Bruno's foundation of La Grande Chartreuse.[45] The series begins with the miraculous warnings of the theologian Diocres from beyond the grave and continues with the prophetic dream of Bishop Hugh of Grenoble, finally illustrating Bruno's response to these marvels: his establishment of a monastic community in the wilderness.[46] These images represent the Carthusian foundation-narrative, but they suggest important aspects of the Order's vocation, as well. For example, the scene of Bruno and his companions leaving the city (figure 6.5) balances as eloquently as any written testament the double commitment of the Carthusian monk to solitude within monastic community and to monastic community within the solitude of wilderness. A hermit in his cave and a lonely sepulchre on the hillside represent the death to life in this world that is the eremitic life, but the ecclesiastical edifice in the distance symbolizes—in an oddly proleptic way—the monastic community that would become the Grande Chartreuse. So although this series was commissioned by and for an aristocrat, and therefore gives little impression of how the monks themselves might have pictured their calling, it offers, nonetheless, an important perspective on Carthusian life.

Similar cycles adorned the walls of late medieval charterhouse churches, refectories, and cloisters,[47] and occasionally appear in books that can be more confidently located in monastic milieux. A version of the foundational narrative made its way, in the humbler form of a woodblock print, into a Carthusian book as practical and as widely disseminated as the 1510 Bâle edition

FIG. 6.5. St. Bruno leaving the city for the wilderness. *Belles Heures of Jean, Duke of Berry*, f. 95v. New York, The Metropolitan Museum of Art, The Cloisters Collection, 1954.

of the *Statutes* (figure 6.6).[48] The same narrative stands behind the illustrations of London, British Library, MS Additional 25042, a fifteenth-century Middle Dutch volume that describes and illustrates Carthusian ways of life, seemingly for the monks themselves.[49] The Dutch pictures are rougher and less accomplished than those of the Limbourgs, but they offer a more clearly Carthusian vision of their own history. The prophetic stars of the bishop's dream are pictured, for example, but they are juxtaposed with what must be a group of contemporary Carthusian monks (figure 6.7).[50] From this conflation of the Order's history and its present to the architectural specificity with which the cloister and the cells of the charterhouse buildings are depicted, these pictures do seem to reflect a Carthusian, rather than aristocratic, perspective. They offer not so much a fantastic myth of origins—although allusions are made to that compelling story—as a practical vision of what late medieval charterhouse life was like.

Although this second set of Carthusian manuscript images seems much more likely to have been seen by monks than Jean de Berry's *Belles Heures*, neither of these series was necessarily used in that way. A more certain (though less tangible) kind of evidence for Carthusian use of particular manuscripts derives from booklists.[51] There is definitive evidence of a close connection between a set of illustrated manuscripts and a specific Carthusian reader, for example, recorded in the list of items taken by the English chartermonk Thomas Golwynne from London to Mount Grace in 1519. This list includes a number of codices, some boasting "fayer" illuminations:

> Item a fayer wrytten yornale made by the cost of Master Saxby havynge a claspe of sylver and an Ymage of seynt Jerome gravyn theryn: the second lef. of Advent. begynneth *Jersalem Alleluis*; this boke standyth in makynge iij *li.*
>
> Item a fayer wrytten Sawter with a fayer ymage of seynt Jerome theryn in the begynnynge; the ijde lef of the sawter begynnyth *te erudimini.*
>
> Item a boke wrytten conteynynge certeyn masses with the canon of the masse and a kalender in the begynnynge of the boke with a fayer ymage of Jhesu standynge be for.

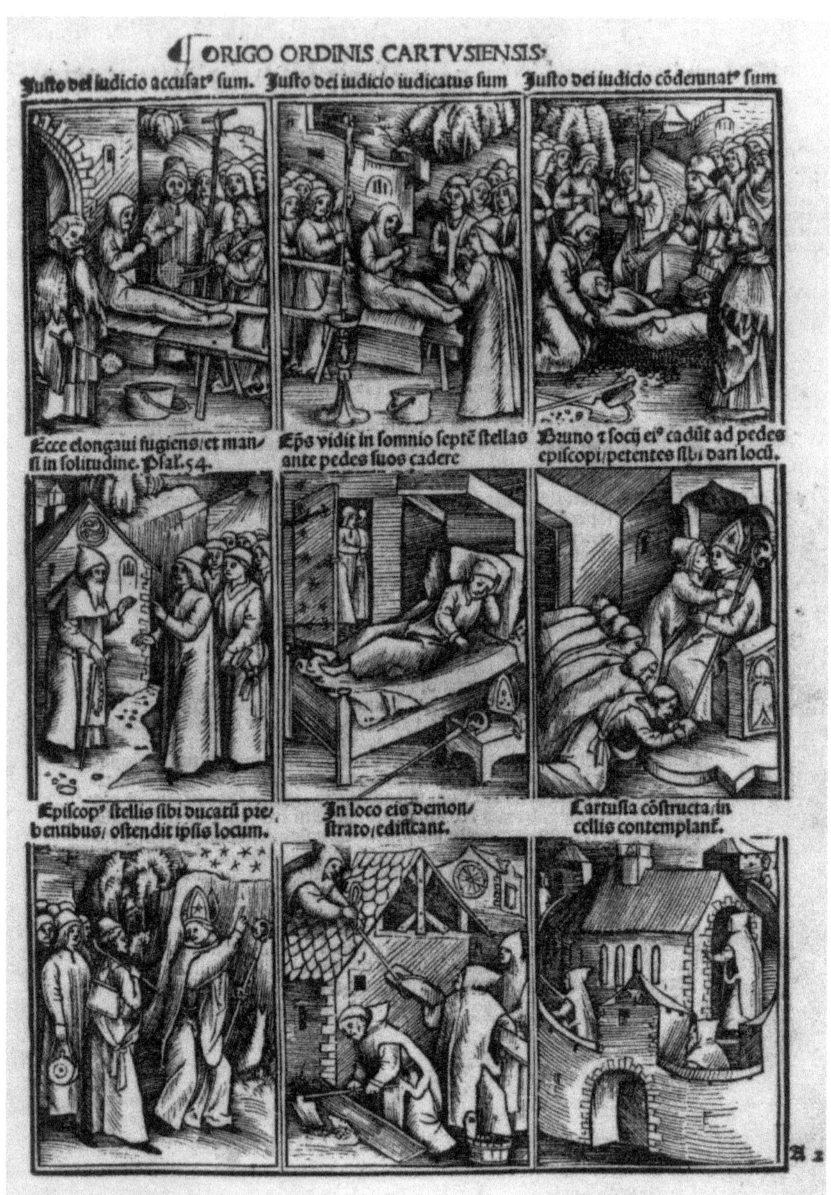


FIG. 6.6. Frontispiece narrating the foundation of the Carthusian Order. *Statuta Ordinis Cartusiensis* (Bâle, 1510). British Library shelfmark 704.h.21. Reproduced by permission of The British Library.

FIG. 6.7. Carthusians and the vision of the Seven Stars. London, British Library, MS Additional 25042, ff. 10v and 11r. Reproduced by permission of The British Library.

> Item a wrytten boke of prayers of diuerse seyntes with ymagys lymyd, and dirige wrytten theryn.
>
> Item a wryten boke of papyr with diuers storyes, and of Ars moriendi theryn.[52]

It is not remarkable, of course, to find a fair image of Jesus among Golwynne's books. Nor is it especially surprising that his collection contains two manuscript images of St. Jerome, who was the patron saint of hermits, and so perhaps especially beloved by the eremitic Carthusians.

But the last item on the list is particularly suggestive: "Item a wrytten boke of papyr with diuers storyes, and of Ars moriendi theryn." Although the identity of Golwynne's book could never be undisputed, the book as briefly described is similar to a Carthusian miscellany we know, if it is not the very volume. This book is London, British Library, MS Additional 37049: a miscellaneous Middle English manuscript written "of papyr" that certainly contains a multitude of "diuers storyes."[53] It also contains a number of texts that could be styled *Artes moriendi*, with memorable pictures of grinning skeletons. One example is the "Disputation between the Body and Worms," in which the dead body, still wearing its fashionable headdress from life, now debates with worms.[54] And there are several examples here of the late medieval *transi* tomb: a beautiful effigy above and a decomposing body below.[55] Finally, several deathbed-scenes offer tableaux in which a host of angelic and devilish figures vie for a human soul (figure 6.8).[56] The connection is weak, the identity unlikely, not least because Golwynne's description of this "wryten boke" makes no mention of illustrations.[57] But if Additional 37049 is not Golwynne's book, his booklist demonstrates that such a volume is not absolutely singular.

This richly illustrated miscellany is probably our most certain testimony to the activity of a Carthusian illustrator. It does not offer the certainty of a charterhouse colophon, but internal evidence both textual and visual points strongly to Carthusian use, and even to Carthusian production. A poem on the founding of the Carthusian Order praises it to the detriment of all others and is illustrated with a pictorial narrative—including the bishop's dream, his meeting with Bruno *et alios*, the movement into the wilderness, and the occupation of the completed charterhouse—related to the kind of series we saw earlier, in the *Belles Heures*.[58] The second image accompanying this poem depicts a Carthusian monk holding a book—a reference, it seems, to the bookmaking activities of the scribe and artist of this manuscript.[59] And the book is littered with numerous pictures of Carthusian monks at prayer: among them, a tiny monk gazing up at an enormous Crucifixion (f. 45r), a slightly larger monk meditating on Christ and his bleeding heart (f. 67v), and a remarkable image in which a monk prays before a Crucifixion-tableau growing quite literally out of the Holy Name (f. 36v). Like the small figure in Quarton's altarpiece, these images of readers respond meditatively to the devotional material they are reading, mirroring the activities of the monastic readers and viewers of the manuscript as they perform devotional acts. But—remarkably—even the strong evidence here for Carthusian production and use has not gone entirely unquestioned; other monastic orders and secular figures are also pictured in Additional 37049. In fact, the manuscript confuses the issue quite pointedly

FIG. 6.8. "Debate for the Soul." London, British Library, MS Additional 37049, f. 19r. Reproduced by permission of The British Library.

by representing monks and laypeople in precisely the same roles, as when the praying layman illustrating the lyric "O man vnkynde" on f. 20r is replaced by a praying Carthusian in the illustration of the same text, repeated on f. 24r (figures 6.9–6.10).

The difficulty of clearly distinguishing Carthusian from lay artifacts, even in this extreme case, brings us at last back to the images in Notre Dame 67. For, even though I have been describing visual culture in the late medieval charterhouse, it must be reiterated that the particular images that concern us here are "Carthusian" in only the most distant way. That is, Notre Dame 67 contains a Carthusian text, decorated and illustrated for lay readership. This is not a book that was read in the Sheen Charterhouse, where the text was probably composed, nor was this volume seen by the text's first audience, probably nuns in the Bridgettine monastery at Syon. Is there any reason then to think that the visual environment of the charterhouse, or of Carthusian books, was translated into this manuscript?

It would seem unlikely, at first glance, since in addition to the Carthusian *Mirror to Devout People*, the manuscript contains other texts that have no explicit connection to monastic devotion: the Latin prayer *O intemerata* (ff. 108r–109r) and *The Craft of Dying* (ff. 109v–126), the latter a popular didactic work on the proper manner of embracing death, surviving in this version in fourteen other copies.[60] Even though *The Craft of Dying* is apparently not elsewhere connected to the Order, it nonetheless reveals some connections with known Carthusian interests. Because medieval Carthusians spent most of their time in solitude, they, even more than other monks, thought of the profession of their vows as a kind of "death" to the world. We saw an emblem of this in the mountainside tomb towards which Bruno and his followers move in the illustration from the *Belles Heures.* And we have also seen a decided morbidity in the assortment of texts and images filling Additional 37049: threatening skeletons, decomposing bodies, deathbed struggles.[61] But if this text's interest in death is not inconsonant with Carthusian spirituality, similar interests are too widespread in late medieval England to provide a strong connection with charterhouse life. Two other manuscript copies of *The Craft of Dying* reflect its mortal preoccupations in pictorial terms, including a threatening figure of Death holding a spear and a bell, the ominous word "dethe" written repeatedly in the space around him (see Figure 6.11).[62]

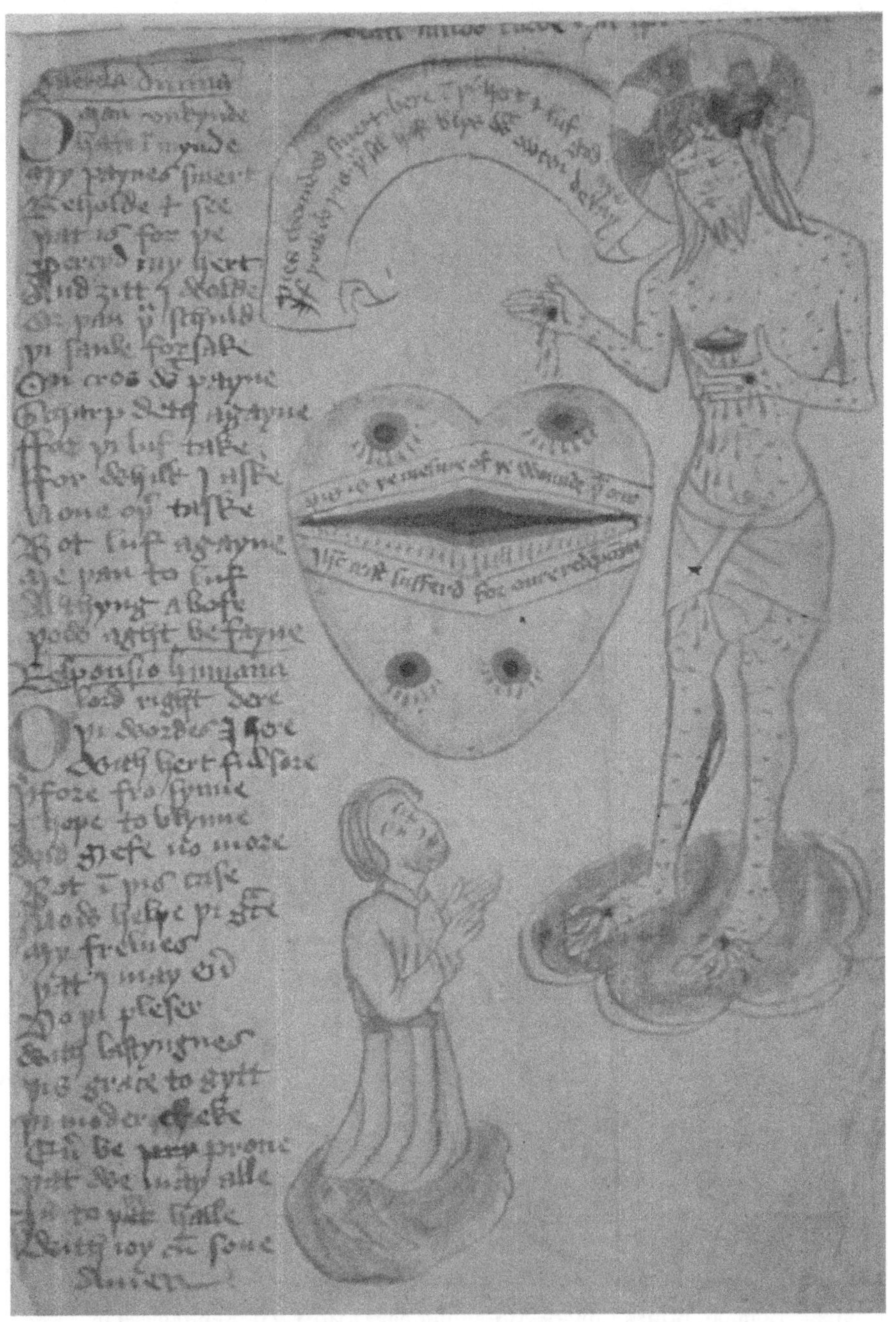


FIG. 6.9. *Querela divina-Responsio humana*; with Christ, wounded heart, and praying layman. London, British Library, MS Additional 37049, f. 20r. Reproduced by permission of The British Library.

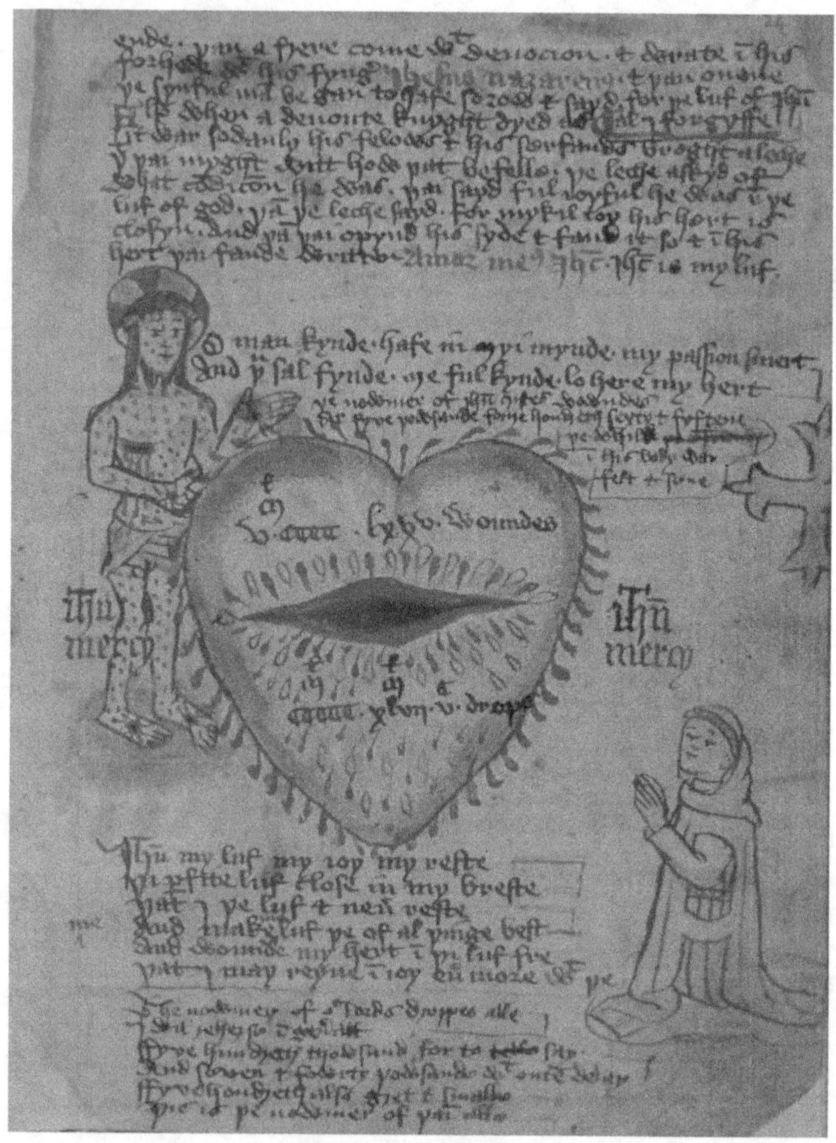

FIG. 6.10. *Querela divina*; with Christ, wounded heart, and praying Carthusian monk. London, British Library, MS Additional 37049, f. 24r. Reproduced by permission of The British Library.

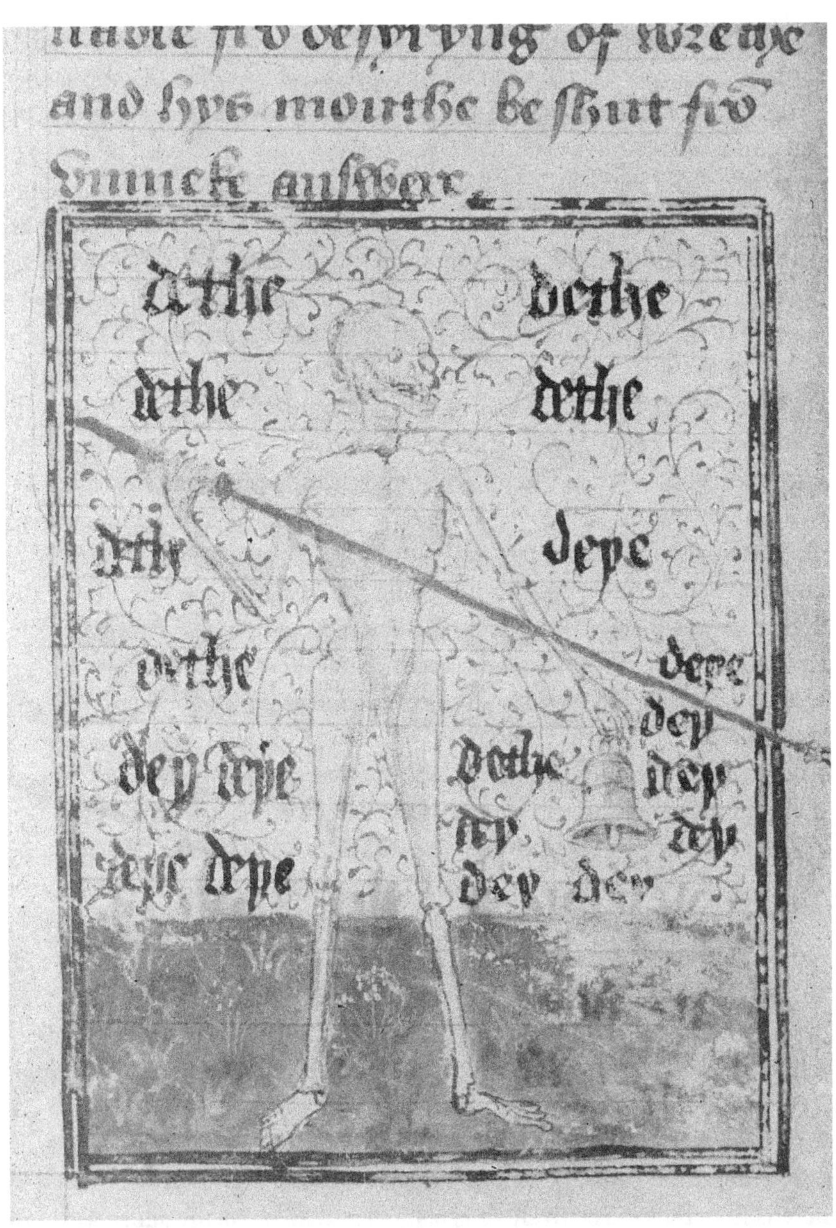


FIG. 6.11. Death with bell and spear. Oxford, Bodleian Library, MS Douce 322, f. 19v. Reproduced by permission of the Bodleian Library, University of Oxford.

In Notre Dame 67, this common fascination with envisioning death is manifested in two small illustrations that preface the *Craft of Dying* (Plate 3): in the first, a dying man lies peacefully in bed, hands clasped in prayer. One can almost make out a beatific smile crossing over his face. The focus of this historiated initial is entirely on the conduct ("the craft") of the dying person, and he seems to have absorbed well the instruction of the text that follows. Although the text mentions the terrible torments that will arrive in a person's last moments,[63] the deathbed scene from Additional 37049 comes far closer to representing that struggle (cf. figure 6.8). The Notre Dame image—in which death is entirely indistinguishable from sleep—reassures its readers of the text's primary emphasis: that one can die well, and peacefully, in perfect spiritual health. Below this initial is another small image: a bishop redirects our attention to the upper picture-space, in a visual demonstration of the way in which spiritual directors can guide the attention of a dying person towards his salvation. Although the majority of this treatise is concerned with preparing the dying person himself for the event, several chapters are devoted to the right conduct of friends, family, and religious advisors.[64] An historiated initial illustrating the text in Bodleian Library, MS Douce 322 also seems to represent this community (f. 27r; see figure 6.12).[65] If these pictures, simple as they are, do not establish a strong pictorial tradition surrounding *The Craft of Dying*, they do, nevertheless, reflect and interpret some of the crucial emphases of the text.

The prayer dividing the *Mirror to Devout People* from *The Craft of Dying* also opens with an historiated initial (plate 2). The text celebrates the intercessory powers of the Virgin Mary and St. John the Evangelist, and most often appears as an accessory prayer in books of hours.[66] In Notre Dame 67, it is added to the end of the *Mirror*, as the culmination of the author's Marian interests, and his "speciale commendacioun of the worshipfull apostell Seynte John euangeliste" (f. 96v).[67] The historiated initial depicts a Virgin and Child with St. John, who holds a chalice and what appears to be the palm of martyrdom. Although the Virgin and John are particularly important in the text of this prayer (and in the text of the *Mirror*), their depiction here is nonetheless relatively unusual. *O intemerata* usually addresses both the Virgin and John, but it is almost always illustrated by images representing the Virgin alone or the Virgin with her son—most often, a pietà.[68] The inclusion of John here, and the iconography that represents him,

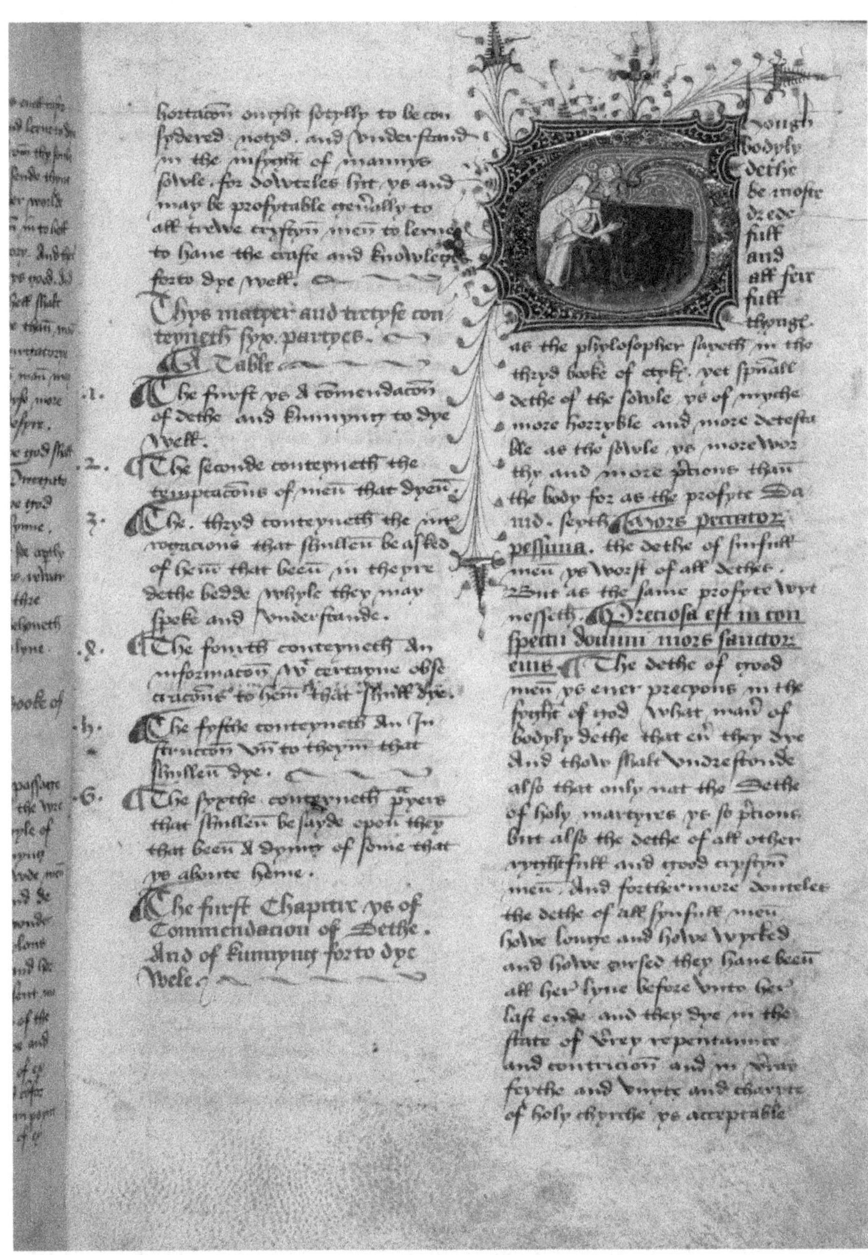

FIG. 6.12. Deathbed scene. Oxford, Bodleian Library, MS Douce 322, f. 27r. Reproduced by permission of the Bodleian Library, University of Oxford.

require further explanation. His chalice, though it does not contain the usual serpent, probably symbolizes the poisoned cup given to him by priests of Diana at Ephesus (or, in some legends, by Domitian). But the palm is a greater mystery, for John was not strictly a martyr. According to legend, he escaped death twice: once when he drank unharmed from the poisoned chalice, and once when he was merely refreshed by a bath in a cauldron of boiling oil outside the Latin Gate in Rome. Even though John was known to have died peacefully in his old age, these miraculous events transformed him into a martyr in popular imagination.

The *Mirror* reflects this belief in John's figurative martyrdom, explaining that he is praised "for þe redynes of soule þat was in hym to suffre martyrdome when he was caste in to þe forseide tonne [barrel]," and concluding "þerfore it is approuede and worshepede of holy chirche for a martyrdome" (f. 104v).[69] But one would expect an image of John in boiling oil to suggest this aspect of his legend, and indeed such pictures do appear in the iconographic tradition surrounding him.[70] An alternative explanation for the palm in the Notre Dame illustration derives from John's role as *Virginis custos*—the appointed guardian of Christ's mother, who was entrusted to him from the cross. In Christ's words, as reported by the *Mirror*, "Lette a virgyne take tente to a vyrgyne, John to Mary and Mary to John" (f. 102r). As the Virgin's surrogate son, John was often represented with the palm of paradise given to him by angels at her death, which he carried in her funeral procession.[71] So, rather than suggesting his own martyrdom, it is possible that the palm points towards his special relationship with her, a relationship that structures the text of the prayer *O intemerata.* Where one might have expected a conventional copy of a familiar exemplar—a standard pietà illustrating this standard prayer—one finds instead what looks like artistic innovation dependent on interpretation of the text. Whether it is the text of the *Mirror* that suggests John's martyrdom, or the text of *O intemerata* that suggests his role as guardian of the Virgin, the image seems to have developed from this artist's attention to the particular context of Notre Dame 67.

The final illustration to consider in Notre Dame 67 is the first, the illustration of the Carthusian *Mirror to Devout People* (plate 1). This "Carthusian" picture accompanying a Carthusian text is not illustrative, in the sense that the historiated initials are. It could more properly be called decoration, for it consists only of an armorial initial and a border of acanthus leaves. But if not truly pictorial, this decoration is nonetheless informative.

The mere presence of such an elaborate border indicates something about the prestige both of the book and of the text, for it dignifies a vernacular "myrrour" with ornamental loveliness that might have been reserved for other, Latinate uses. And the style of the border can help in dating and localizing the book, for it resembles those made in London in the mid-fifteenth century. Of the dated and datable borders surveyed by Kathleen Scott, the Notre Dame example most resembles a London copy of the *Nova statuta Angliae*, from 1445/6 (figure 6.13).[72] Both manuscripts show full bar-frame borders intertwined with pink and blue acanthus clusters, which are shaded with white striations. The spraywork between acanthus clusters is slightly more ornate in the *Nova statuta*, where floral motifs are organized by sections, and pinecones appear among the gold, green-lobed balls. Scott calls it "at the same time conventional and representative of first-rate London work in the favoured style at this period." If the Notre Dame border is less detailed, it seems to come from the same aesthetic environment. The figural style corroborates this provenance, for, though the figures are simple, they show similarities with contemporary metropolitan work. A comparison of the Marian initial with illustrations in a *Brut* chronicle now in private hands, for example, shows analogous figures seated in initials, and comparably plain lines in the facial features.[73] These comparisons indicate that Notre Dame 67 was decorated most probably by commercial artists working in London in the second quarter of the fifteenth century.

The decoration and illustration of Notre Dame 67 points to a London origin for the book, but a less accomplished volume in Scott's survey of borders provides an equally revealing comparison: a Sheen copy of Nicholas Love's *Mirror of the Blessed Life of Jesus Christ* (figure 6.14).[74] This book was written by the Carthusian scribe Stephen Dodesham in "the yer of Kynge Edwarde the iiij[the] xiij[the]," i.e., 1475, and although there is no certainty that the artist was also a Carthusian of Sheen, it seems likely that he was. The full border on f. 3v shows some of the standard features of English work: a bar-frame wrapped in acanthus leaves, spraywork with gold balls and green lobes. But this Sheen border has an archaic look, and if one didn't know the date of the manuscript one might have placed it three

FIG. 6.13. *Nova statuta Angliae.* London, Public Record Office E 164/10, f. 44r. Reproduced by permission of the National Archives, Kew.

Quecumque scripta sunt ad nostram doctrinam scripta sunt, ut per pacienciam et consolacionem scripturarum spem habeamus. Ad romanos xv°.

These ben the wordes of the gret doctour and holy apostle poule. consideryng that the gostly lyvynge of alle cristen trewe creatures in this worlde stant specialy in hope of the blisse and the lif that is to come in another worlde. And for as muche as twey thinges principaly norisshen and strengthen this hope in man. þat is pacience in herte. and ensample of vertues and good lyvyng of holy men writen in boke. and souereynly the wordes. and the dedes writen of oure lorde ihu crist verrey god and man. for the tyme of his bodely lyvyng here in erthe. therfore to strengthe us. and comforte us in this hope. spekith the apostle the wordes forsaide. to this entent seieng. that alle thinges that ben writen generaly in holichirche and specialy of oure lorde ihu crist. they ben writen to oure lore. that by pacience and comforte of holy scriptures we haue hope that is to say of the lif and blisse that is to come in another worlde. Herto accordyng spekith seynt Austyn thus. Goddys sone toke man. and in him he suffred that longith to man. and was made medicyne of man. and this medicyne is so mychel that it

FIG. 6.14. Nicholas Love, *Mirror of the Blessed Life of Jesus Christ.* Glasgow, University Library, MS Hunter 77 (T.3.15), f. 3v. Reproduced from Glasgow University Library, Department of Special Collections

decades earlier. This example alerts us that Carthusian manuscripts might follow London bookshop fashions, albeit many decades late. I will not suggest that Notre Dame 67 is also a late Sheen manuscript following London fashions, but the possibility of such imitation reminds us, once again, that not all monastic manuscripts are clearly segregated from secular ones.

The arms accompanying the Notre Dame *Mirror to Devout People* are even more informative than the border, for they indicate, in all likelihood, for whom and by whom the book was commissioned. It seems probable that John, fourth Baron Scrope of Masham (d. 1455) had the book made for his wife, Elizabeth: their arms (Scrope impaling Chaworth) are the two shown on the manuscript's opening page.[75] That these secular arms in this urbane book are connected with a Carthusian text may show simply that—as we have already repeatedly seen—late medieval aristocratic interest in Carthusian spirituality was often reflected in art objects. Notre Dame 67 confirms the multiple audiences that the *Mirror* itself expects, and its pictures, rather than replicating the visual environment of the charterhouse, represent the new lay environment in which the Carthusian text finds itself. But they have some relevance, too, to ways in which Carthusian devotion typically imagined itself in visual terms. The Scrope/Chaworth arms show an incorporation of the reader within the book not so different in kind—if very different in form—from the small figures of the praying monk that we have seen populating a more properly "Carthusian" manuscript. If the small monks at prayer in Additional 37049 bring the Carthusian reader into his book, making a visual emblem of the connection between text and audience, the images in Notre Dame 67 do precisely the same. Of course, secular arms do not replicate the meditative mechanisms of the monks at prayer; instead, they proclaim the importance of the owners, and only incidentally the piety of the readers. But both represent the self materially in the environment of a devotional text.

This representation of the lay self in the context of the charterhouse is not unique: one might think of Philippe de Bourgogne dressing his corpse in a Carthusian habit, or the "curious" pictures of women or coats of arms that the Carthusian general chapter objected to in 1424. Notre Dame 67 recalls that particular prohibition, for it incorporates the coats of arms of both a layman and a laywoman—Elizabeth Scrope—who was probably among the book's first readers. A. S. G. Edwards has noted that Elizabeth's partial ownership of this book is an interesting sign of things to come: the rise of female reading of vernacular devotional books.[76] Her ownership might be taken as a sign, too, of how far this manuscript has come from the text's Carthusian origins. Elizabeth Scrope's arms represent an intrusion inverted from the one that worried the general chapter, for instead of lay images threatening to trouble a monastic environment, here a Carthusian text seems anomalous in its secular setting. But even the monastic *Mirror* was originally designed for a "gostely sustre," and lay women occasionally entered the charterhouse church, an interaction of communities not so different from the interaction symbolized by Elizabeth Scrope's arms decorating this manuscript.

The visual association of the Scrope/Chaworth family with the *Mirror to Devout People* demonstrates in emblematic fashion the strong connection of Carthusian texts with lay reading that is crucial to understanding devotional Middle English literature. This illustrated book bears out in one particular instance what is crucial to the late medieval Carthusian visual experience in general: the continual oscillation between monastic meditation and lay piety. In spite of the monks' dedication to the solitary religious life, Carthusian spirituality also included a surprisingly public face. Connections between Carthusians and the laity in the late medieval period were crucial, both for the monks themselves and in very important ways for the aristocratic world. Notre Dame 67—although it was in all likelihood neither made nor used by Carthusian monks—forms a part, nonetheless, of the broad bibliographic and visual culture of the charterhouses. In spite of the monks' ascetic, eremitic goals, one cannot isolate Carthusian visual experience from the world around it, and that is what this manuscript finally shows.[77]

## NOTES

1. For a summary description of the manuscript, see the auction catalogue: Christie's, London, *The Library of William Foyle, Part I: Medieval and Renaissance Manuscripts, Tuesday 11 July 2000* (London, 2000), 221–23; see also the appendix to A. S. G. Edwards's essay in this volume.

2. *The Speculum Devotorum of an Anonymous Carthusian of Sheen*, ed. James Hogg, 2 vols., Analecta Cartusiana 12–13 (Salzburg, 1973–74).

3. Since there were no Carthusian nuns in medieval England, the female addressee must have been either a nun of another order or a pious laywoman. For an argument that the treatise was written for a nun of Syon, see the essay by Vincent Gillespie in this volume.

4. For a consideration of the people and books connected to the manuscript's lay readership, see the essay by A. S. G. Edwards in this volume.

5. A. I. Doyle was among the first to call attention to the movement of Carthusian books, in his much consulted Ph.D. thesis; see "A Survey of the Origins and Circulation of Theological Writings in English in the 14th, 15th, and Early 16th Centuries with Special Consideration of the Part of the Clergy Therein," 2 vols. (PhD diss., Cambridge, 1953). See also such foundational studies as Elizabeth Salter, *Nicholas Love's "Myrrour of the blessed lyf of Jesu Christ,"* Analecta Cartusiana 10 (Salzburg, 1974); Michael Sargent, "The Transmission by the English Carthusians of some Late Medieval Spiritual Writings," *Journal of Ecclesiastical History* 27 (1976): 225–40; and Vincent Gillespie, "*Cura pastoralis in deserto,*" in *De Cella in Seculum: Religious and Secular Life and Devotion in Late Medieval England,* ed. Michael Sargent (Cambridge, 1989), 161–81. Doyle and others have in more recent years cautioned against assuming too great a Carthusian influence on vernacular devotional reading; see, e.g., A. I. Doyle, "Carthusian Participation in the Movement of Works of Richard Rolle between England and other Parts of Europe in the 14th and 15th Centuries," in *Kartäusermystik und -mystiker,* vol. 2, Analecta Cartusiana 55 (Salzburg, 1981), 109–20. But although the mechanisms of transmission resist generalization, it remains true that late medieval Carthusian texts were widely read outside of charterhouses.

6. For a discussion of Mede and other Carthusian scribes, see A. I. Doyle, "Book Production by the Monastic Orders in England (*c.* 1375–1530)," in *Medieval Book Production: Assessing the Evidence,* ed. L. L. Browning (Los Altos Hills, 1990), 1–19, esp. 13–15.

7. Seventeenth-century Carthusian painting includes works by Zurbaràn and Carducho in Spain, and—most famously—Le Sueur's series of the life of St. Bruno painted for the Carthusians of Paris (1645–48). For an overview, see Joan Evans, *Monastic Iconography in France from the Renaissance to the Revolution* (Cambridge, 1970), 32–34. For a more specialized study of post-medieval imagery in a particular Charterhouse, see Sabine Fischer, *Das barocke Bibliotheksprogramm der ehemaligen Kartause Marienthron in Gaming,* Analecta Cartusiana 58:3 (Salzburg, 1986).

8. For a short introduction to medieval Carthusian art in France, see Joan Evans, *Art in Medieval France, 987–1498* (Oxford, 1948), 150–57. See also Augustin Devaux, "La décoration des chartreuses médievales," in *L'architecture dans l'Ordre des*

*Chartreux*, Analecta Cartusiana 146 (Sélignac, 1998), 119–41; and the short section concerning "Beaux Arts" in Albert Gruys, *Cartusiana: Un instrument heuristique*, 3 vols., (Paris, 1976), 1:34. In addition, several essay-collections devoted to Carthusian art show a decided Continental focus: Danel Le Blévec and Alain Girard, eds., *Les Chartreux et l'art: XIVe–XVIIIe siècles; Actes du Xe colloque internationale d'histoire et de spiritualité cartusiennes (Villeneuve-lès-Avignon, 15–18 septembre 1988)* (Paris, 1989); James Hogg, ed., *The Mystical Tradition and the Carthusians*, Analecta Cartusiana 130:13 (Salzburg, 1997); and (though not strictly devoted to the visual arts) James Hogg, Alain Girard, and Daniel Blévec, eds., *Die Kartäuser und die Künste ihrer Zeit*, 3 vols., Analecta Cartusiana 157 (Salzburg, 2001).

9. "Ornamenta aurea vel argentea, preter calicem et calamum quo sanguis domini sumitur, in ecclesia non habemus, pallia tapetiaque reliquimus." See Guigues 1er, *Coutumes de Chartreuse*, Sources Chrétiennes 313 (Paris, 1984), XL.1. All translations, unless otherwise noted, are my own.

10. For a facsimile reprint of the Carthusian statutes (Bâle, 1510) see James Hogg, *The Evolution of the Carthusian Statutes from the Consuetudines Guigonis to the Tertia Compilatio*, Analecta Cartusiana 99:1–4 (Salzburg, 1989). There is no modern critical edition, but a useful consideration of the editorial history of the *Statutes* can be found in Hubert Elie, *Les éditions des Statuts de l'Ordre des Chartreux* (Lausanne, 1943).

11. *Statuta Antiqua*, Part 2, XXXII. Cited by E. Margaret Thompson, *The Carthusian Order in England* (London, 1930), 184.

12. An emphasis upon the devotional utility of Carthusian art underscores most apologetic treatments of the subject; see, e.g., Alain Girard, "De l'image en Chartreuse," in *The Mystical Tradition and the Carthusians*, ed. Hogg, Analecta Cartusiana 130:3 (Salzburg, 1995), 145–55. For a consideration of general monastic attitudes to art, see Conrad Rudolph, *The 'Things of Greater Importance': Bernard of Clairvaux's Apologia and the Medieval Attitude Toward Art* (Philadelphia, 1990).

13. See Bernard Bligny, "Les premiers chartreux et la pauvreté," *Le moyen âge* 57 (1951): 27–60. Yvette Carbonell-Lamothe points out that the Carthusians had as great an influence on later art as the Franciscans did in the thirteenth and fourteenth centuries, but that such influence remains largely unexplored; see her "Conclusions," in *Les Chartreux et l'art*, ed. Le Blévec and Girard, 395–402, at 402.

14. *Statuta Nova*, Part 2, 1.7. "Tapetia universa et cussini picturati vel alias curiosi in usu apud nos non habeant: sed et picture curiose ubi sine scandalo fieri poterit de nostris ecclesiis et domibus eradantur: et nove de cetero fieri non permittant." Cf. Thompson, *Carthusian Order*, 129; I differ somewhat in my understanding of this passage. I am grateful to Traugott Lawler for advice concerning this translation.

15. See Oxford, Bodleian Library, MS Rawlinson D.318, transcribed in Michael Sargent and James Hogg, eds., *The Chartae of the Carthusian General Chapter*, Analecta Cartusiana 100 (1983), 2:77–223. Rawlinson MS D.318 and London, Lambeth Palace Library, MS 413 are cited by Thompson, *Carthusian Order*, 266.

16. *Tertia Compilatio*, III.5.

17. Rudolph translates "curiosus" as "unusually distractive," *'Things of Greater Importance'*, 176n.473. For an interesting discussion of the insistent use of the adjective, see Elie, "Appendice: le sense cartusien de l'adjectif *curiosus*," in his *Les éditions*, 193–200.

18. The involvement of so many known and accomplished artists in the decoration of Champmol makes it a particularly interesting—if not exactly representative—case in which to examine the visual environment of Carthusian spirituality. See Sherry C. M. Lindquist, "Accounting for the Status of Artists at the Chartreuse de Champmol," *Gesta* 41.1 (2002): 15–28. The standard study of Champmol is Cypren Monget, *La Chartreuse de Dijon*, 3 vols. (Tournai, 1898–1905); see also Sherry C. M. Lindquist, "Patronage, Piety, and Politics in the Art and Architectural Programs at the Charterhouse de Champmol in Dijon (France)" (PhD diss., Northwestern University, 1995), and Renate Prochno, *Die Kartause von Champmol: Grablege der burgundischen Herzöge, 1364–1477* (Munich, 2002). For a study of Champmol's most significant sculptor, see, e.g., Kathleen Morand, *Claus Sluter: Artist at the Court of Burgundy*, photographs by David Finn (Austin, Tex., 1991).

19. A single chapter of the *Consuetudines* (XLI) contains the prohibition against incorporating the "tombs of strangers" and the prohibitions against accepting gifts from and saying prayers for outsiders—multiple manifestations of the single problem of external influence on Carthusian life.

20. For a survey of burials in all English houses, see Glyn Coppack and Mick Aston, *Christ's Poor Men: The Carthusians in England* (Stroud, 2002), 65–68.

21. Guigo himself drew an analogy between cities and wealth: "Considera quomodo paupertas et vilitas in mediis urbibus solitudinem praestent, divitiae turbis heremos impleant." Guigues 1er, *Les Méditations (Recueil de Pensées)*, Sources Chrétiennes 308 (Paris, 1983), 307. ["Consider how poverty and squalor create solitude in the middle of cities, and wealth fills the desert with crowds." *The Meditations of Guigo I, Prior of the Charterhouse*, trans. A. Gordon Mursell, Cistercian Studies Series 155 (Kalamazoo, Mich., 1995).]

22. The General Chapter in 1438 reflected a concern about women in Carthusian churches, refusing to allow women to enter the church at Mount Grace for the burial of an important benefactor: "Priori domus Assumptionis Beate Marie in Monte Gratie non fit misericordia. Et sepulturam quam petit concedi-

mus, sed feminarum introitum denegamus." See Hogg and Sargent, *Chartae*, 3:27. See also Sherry C. M. Lindquist, "Women in the Charterhouse: The Liminality of Cloistered Spaces at the Chartreuse de Champmol in Dijon," in *Architecture and the Politics of Gender in Early Modern Europe*, ed. Helen Hills (Aldershot, 2003), 177–92.

23. Joseph A. Gribbin, "'Ex Oblatione Fidelium': The Liturgy of the London Charterhouse and the Laity," in *The Mystical Tradition and the Carthusians*, ed. James Hogg, Analecta Cartusiana 130:5 (1996), 83–104, at 85. See also Joseph A. Gribbin, *Aspects of Carthusian Liturgical Practice in Later Medieval England* (Salzburg, 1995).

24. The description of decoration and furnishings at London, made by Dr. Thomas Legh and Dr. Francis Cave in 1539, includes a number of paintings, as well as carvings in ivory and alabaster; see Coppack and Aston, *Christ's Poor Man*, esp. 53–55. See also Thompson, *Carthusian Order*, 182–84, and W. H. St. John Hope, *The History of the London Charterhouse from its Foundation until the Suppression of the Monastery* (London, 1925).

25. Marc Venard suggests that the common spaces of the charterhouses were the spaces deliberately given over to things of this world, and so were more likely spaces in which to display art objects; he even suggests that the Carthusians thought of their communal spaces as "sacrificed" to the world, a sacrifice made to preserve the privacy of their cells. See his "Conclusions," in *Les chartreux et l'art*, ed. Le Blévec and Girard, 403–10, at 409.

26. Observers, both medieval and modern, disagree on this point; cf. Daniel Le Blévec, "Les chartreux et l'art," in *Les chartreux et l'art*, ed. Le Blévec and Girard: "Alors que les murs de l'église et des chapelles, ceux de la salle capitulaire, de réfectoire, de l'hôtellerie se couvraient de tableaux, les ermitages des pères restaient, quant à eux, le refuge de l'austerité primitive" (14). An eighteenth-century monk upheld the distinction between what is appropriate in the church and what in the cell, warning his brothers: "We should avoid the childish weakness of those who decorate their cells like chapels." ("On doit éviter la faiblesse puérile de ceux qui ornent leur cellule comme des chappelles," quoted in Venard, "Conclusions," 408.) But even this condemnation (*pace* Venard and Le Blévec) testifies to some monks' tendencies towards private visual display.

27. For example, the inventory made in 1519 by the monk Thomas Golwynne of items he took with him on a journey from London to Mount Grace includes: "Item a wyde sloppe furryd to put over all my gere, of the gyfte of my Lady Conway," "Item a newe pylche of the gyft of Mr. Saxby," "Item a newe mantell by the gyfte of Syr John Rawson knyght of the Roodes," "Item a lytell brasyn morter with a pestyl gevyn by the gyfte of a frende of myne," "Item a new chafyngdysshe of laten gevyn to vs," "ij new tyne botylles gevyn by a kynsman of owrs," and "Item a

brasse panne of a galone gevyn to vs lyke wyse" (the full list is quoted in Thompson, *Carthusian Order*, 326–28); see also James Hogg, "Everyday Life in a Contemplative Order in the Fifteenth Century," *Kartäuserliturgie und Kartäuserschriftum*, Analecta Cartusiana 116:4 (1989), 95–109, esp. 100–101.

28. For these conjectures, see Charles Sterling, "Oeuvres retrouvées de Jean de Beaumetz, peintre de Philippe Le Hardi," *Bulletin Musées Royaux des Beaux Arts* 4 (1955): 57–82. I am grateful to Sherry Lindquist for this reference.

29. "I tabulam cum crucifixione pictam" (quoted in Thompson, *Carthusian Order*, 236).

30. "If clothing or another gift of that kind has been sent to one of us, converse or monk, by a friend or relative, it is not given to him, but rather to another, so that he does not seem to have something to himself alone." ("Si alicui nostrum sive laico sive monacho, ab aliquo vel amico vel propinquo vel vestis vel aliquid huiusmodi missum fuerit, non ei sed alii potius datur, ne quasi proprium habere videatur," *Consuetudines* LIX.1).

31. For example, this question of individual ownership was addressed from London to the Grande Chartreuse in 1494: "If anyone wished to give an old book or other thing to a particular person for life, might a prior license the latter to receive it?" (quoted in Thompson, *Carthusian Order*, 274). The answer was no. For other questions of this sort, see Joseph A. Gribbin, ed., *Liturgical and Miscellaneous Questions, Dubia, and Supplications to La Grande Chartreuse from the English Carthusian Province in the Later Middle Ages*, Analecta Cartusiana 100:32 (Salzburg, 1999).

32. See Coppack and Aston, *Christ's Poor Men*, 93. It is not known whether these items were gifts, but they do confirm the presence of private devotional imagery in the Carthusian cell.

33. There were other objections to the extremities of Carthusian asceticism: the monks' vegetarianism, for example, was feared to impede the treatment of the sick. See Thompson, *Carthusian Order*, 104.

34. For a thorough discussion of this tract, and questions surrounding its authorship, see James Hogg, "Guillelmus de Yporegia: *De Origine et Veritate Perfecte Religionis*," Analecta Cartusiana 82:2 (Salzburg, 1980), 84–118.

35. "Certum est enim quod Cartusienses in omnibus ecclesiis suis habent, et habere debent ex Ordinis sui institutis, imaginem Crucifixi in loco solemni et eminenti, et super pluria altaria plures cruces; in oratoriis quoque cellarum suarum generaliter consueverunt habere Crucifixum et imaginem Mariae Virginis, et etiam aliquando aliorum Sanctorum secundum quod se offert possibilitas et facultas. Honestati vero et paupertati Religionis attestatur ipsorum, si refugiunt curiositates sumptuosas in picturis et sculpturis et varietatibus aedificiorum solemnium et

mirabilium, quae rusticitati vitae solitariae non concordant. Secundum enim doctrinam Joannis Damasceni, imagines et picturae murorum sunt quasi quaedam scripturae et literae laicorum, ut qui in libris legere non noverunt, in murorum picturis quasi quibusdam literis grossis intelligunt, quae ipsi illiterati intelligere nequeunt in scripturis. Et ideo tales picturae laudabiliter fieri possunt in ecclesiis ubi concurrit frequentia populorum, quae frustra et superflue fierent in desertis Cartusiensium quo non consueverunt populi, licet aliquando pauci viri, convenire. . . . Ideo et praedicti Cartusienses in cellis suis, sicut praedictum est, devotas picturas non renuunt nec recusant, sed ad excitationem devotionis et imaginationis, et augmentum devotae conceptionis, easdem libenter et affectuose recipiunt et requirunt." See C. Le Couteulx, *Annales ordinis Cartusiensis ab anno 1084 ad annum 1429* (Montreuil-sur-Mer, 1887–1891), 1:276–77. Paraphrased from Oxford, Bodleian Library, MS Bodley 549 (ff. 25–85v) by Thompson, *Carthusian Order*, 106.

36. For a Charterhouse museum that reconstructs the artistic environment of the medieval and modern cell, see Michael Koller and Jürgen Lenssen, *Kartäusermuseum Tückelhausen: ein Museum der Diözese Würzburg* (Lindenberg, 1997).

37. "Aucun autre ordre ne paraît avoir aussi sûrement imposé sa propre image, avoir été aussi exigeant sur la représentation de lui-même et sur sa traduction artistique," Carbonell-Lamothe, "Conclusions," 400–401.

38. "La croix Nostre Seigneur, et au pié d'icelle aura ung priant chartreux." See Charles Sterling, *Enguerrand Quarton: le peintre de la Pietà d'Avignon* (Paris, 1983). Quarton was also a sometime painter of manuscripts, for example, New York, Pierpont Morgan Library, MS 358 (*Heures*); and Paris, Bibliothèque Nationale de France, Nouv. acq. lat. 2661 (*Missel de Jean des Martins*).

39. Hans Belting claims that the cell paintings at Champmol "always depicted the Crucifixion but also included a portrait of the cell's occupant"; see his *Likeness and Presence: A History of the Image Before the Era of Art*, trans. Edmund Jephcott (Chicago, 1994), 417. While this claim may seem unduly sweeping, it testifies to the regularity with which Carthusians depicted themselves at prayer.

40. The larger panel is 19 x 24 1/2 in., while the smaller one is 7 5/8 x 5 1/2 in. See Marian W. Ainsworth, with contributions by Maximilian P. J. Martens, *Petrus Christus: Renaissance Master of Bruges* (New York, 1994); and Joel M. Upton, *Petrus Christus: His Place in Fifteenth-century Flemish Painting* (University Park, 1990).

41. "Libros quippe tamquam sempiternum animarum nostrarum cibum cautissime custodiri et studiosissime volumus fieri, ut quia ore non possumus, dei verbum manibus predicemus," *Consuetudines* XXVIII.3 ["We desire that the books be made with the greatest attention and kept very carefully, like perpetual food for our souls, so because we are not able to preach the word of God with our mouths, we may do so with our hands"].

42. "Intantum, inquam, suae sunt custodes inopiae ut, hoc ipso quo agimus anno, Nevernensis comes, vir omnino religiosus et potens, eos, causa devotionis et optimae, quae hinc emanat, opinionis, inviserit multumque super seculari eos cupiditate, ut caverent inde, monuerit, cumque, regressus ad sua, eorum indigentiae, quam viderat, meminisset, et monitorum, quae eis intulerat, nequaquam memor esset, nescio quae argentea, sciphos videlicet et scutras, precii plurimi eis misit. Sed eorum quae dixerat illis nequaquam obliviosos invenit: communicato namque mox consilio, quaecumque dixerat ad integrum refutata recepit. 'Nos,' inquiunt, 'neque in expensis nostris neque in ecclesiae ornamentis, exterarum quippiam pecuniarum retinere delegimus. Et si in horum alterutro non expenditur, ut quid a nobis suscipitur?' Puduit itaque praevaricatoriae contra suum sermonem oblationis comitem et tamen, dissimulata aspernatione eorum, boum tergora et pergamena plurima retransmisit, quae pene inevitabiliter ipsis necessaria esse cognovit." See Guibert de Nogent, *Autobiographie*, ed. Edmond-René Labande (Paris, 1981), 68–70; *A Monk's Confession: The Memoirs of Guibert de Nogent*, trans. Paul J. Archambault (University Park, Pa., 1996), 32.

43. Few studies and exhibitions have addressed the question of Carthusian illumination directly, but see Dominique Mielle de Becdelièvre, *Prêcher en silence: Enquête codicologique sur les manuscrits du XIIe siècle provenant de la Grande Chartreuse* (Saint-Étienne, 2004), esp. 48–49, 116–21, 134–42, and 192–240; Françoise de Forbin, "Les manuscrits de la chartreuse de Villeneuve-lès-Avignon," in *Les chartreux et l'art*, ed. Le Blévec and Girard, 39–63; Margrit Früh, "Die Illustrationen in Guigo Engelherrs Manuskripten," in *Mystical Tradition*, Hogg, 35–69, Analecta Cartusiana 130:13; Christian de Merindol, "Les premières bibles peintes cartusiennes," in *La naissance des Chartreuses*, ed. Bernard Bligny and Gérald Chaix (Grenoble, 1986), 69–106; Musée de Dijon, *La Chartreuse de Champmol: foyer d'art au temps des ducs Valois* (Dijon, 1960); Pierre Vaillant, *Les enluminures des manuscrits cartusiens* (Grenoble, 1958); and Pierre Vaillant, *Les manuscrits de la Grande Chartreuse et leurs enluminures* (Grenoble, 1984). On English Carthusian illumination in particular, one will soon be able to consult Julian M. Luxford, "Precept and Practice: The Decoration of English Carthusian Books," in *Studies in Carthusian Monasticism in the Late Middle Ages*, ed. Julian M. Luxford (Turnhout, forthcoming). I thank Dr. Luxford for allowing me to see his essay in an early version.

44. The difficulties have been eased by A. I. Doyle's useful essay, "English Carthusian Books Not Yet Linked With a Charterhouse," in *A Miracle of Learning: Studies in Manuscripts and Irish Learning; Essays in Honour of William O'Sullivan*, ed. Toby Barnard, Dáibhí Ó Cróinín, and Katharine Simms (Aldershot, 1998), 122–36.

45. For a facsimile of the *Belles Heures*, now in the Cloisters Collection of the Metropolitan Museum of Art, see *The Belles Heures of Jean, Duke of Berry*, ed. Millard Meiss and Elizabeth H. Beatson (New York, 1974). Previous to this manuscript cycle, only four single scenes from Bruno's life are known.

46. The cycle consists of eight scenes: Diocres expounding the Scriptures (f. 94r), Diocres crying out from his bier (f. 94v), the burial of Diocres (f. 95r), Bruno's departure for the monastic wilderness (f. 95v), Bishop Hugh of Grenoble dreaming prophetically of seven stars (f. 96r), St. Hugh's audience with Bruno and his six companions (f. 96v), the new monks entering the Grande Chartreuse (f. 97r), and a view of the Grande Chartreuse itself (f. 97v).

47. The fourteenth-century paintings in the Paris charterhouse no longer survive, having been replaced in the seventeenth century by Le Sueur's grand twenty-two-part set, now in the Musée du Louvre. There were fifteenth-century cycles at Basel and Cologne. For a complete survey, see Margrit Früh, "Bilderzyklen mit dem Leben des Heiligen Bruno," in *La naissance des Chartreuses* 161–78; see also Werner Beutler, "Die beiden Brunozyklen der Kölner Kartause St. Barbara," *Die Kartäuser und ihre Welt: Kontakte und Gegenseitige Einflüsse*, Analecta Cartusiana 62:3 (Salzburg, 1993), 118–212; and Rudolf Riggenbach, "Die Wandbilder der Kartäuse," in *Kunstdenkmäler des Kantons Basel-Stadt*, vol. 3, *Die Kirchen, Kloster und Kapellen*, ed. Casimir Hermann Baer (Basel, 1941), 577–94.

48. For the version in the Basel *Statutes*, see Hogg, *Evolution of the Carthusian Statutes*, and Elie, *Les éditions*, esp. 50–58.

49. This manuscript contains a series of images that tell the Carthusian foundation-story, but also a series that appears to offer scenes from everyday monastic life. It contains a version of the Carthusian rule, which, though in Dutch rather than in Latin, suggests monastic readership. For a full description, see Willem de Vreese, *De Handschriften van Jan van Ruusbroec's Werken* (Ghent, 1900–1902), 518–24. See also British Library, *Catalogue of Additions to the Manuscripts in the British Museum, 1854–75*, vol. 2 (London, 1877) for a somewhat less detailed account.

50. The number of monks is too great to represent Bruno and his companions.

51. On Carthusian library booklists, see Thompson, *Carthusian Order*, 313–34; and J. A. Large, "The Libraries of the Carthusian Order in Medieval England," *Library History* 3 (1975): 191–203; both now superseded by A. I. Doyle, "The Carthusians," in *Syon Abbey*, edited by Vincent Gillespie, with *The Libraries of the Carthusians*, edited by A. I. Doyle, Corpus of British Medieval Library Catalogues 9 (London, 2001), 607–52. An important single list is John Blacman's donation, recorded in Oxford, Bodleian Library, MSS Laud misc. 152 and 154; see Roger Lovatt, "The Library of John Blacman and Contemporary Carthusian Spirituality," *Journal of Ecclesiastical History* 43 (1992): 195–230.

52. Thompson, *Carthusian Order*, 328. See also n. 27 above.

53. BL MS Add. 37049 forms the subject of my book-in-progress, *Reading in the Wilderness: Devotional Performances in a Late-Medieval Carthusian Miscellany.* Most of the folios in the manuscript have been published in James Hogg, ed., *An Illustrated Yorkshire Carthusian Religious Miscellany, British Library London MS Additional 37049: The Illustrations*, vol. 3, Analecta Cartusiana 95 (Salzburg, 1981).

54. BL MS Add. 37049, f. 33r. For editions of this text, see Karl Brunner, "Mittelenglische Todesgeschichte," *Archiv für das Studium der neueren Sprachen und Literaturen* 167 (1935): 20–35; and John W. Conlee, *Middle English Debate Poetry: A Critical Anthology* (East Lansing, Mich., 1991), 50–62.

55. This sort of image appears on ff. 32v and 87r of Additional 37049. Francis Wormald relates the design to sculptural *transi* tombs, such as the tomb in Lincoln Cathedral of Bishop Richard Fleming, d. 1431. See Francis Wormald, "Some Popular Miniatures and their Rich Relations," in *Miscellanea pro Arte: Hermann Schnitzler zur Vollendung des 60. Lebensjahres am 13. Januar 1965* (Düsseldorf, 1965), 279–85, at 283–84. Further, see Kathleen Cohen, *The Metamorphosis of a Death Symbol: The Transi Tomb* (Berkeley, Calif., 1973); Marlene Villalobos Hennessy, "The Remains of the Royal Dead in an English Carthusian Manuscript, London, British Library, MS Additional 37049," *Viator* 33 (2002): 310–54; Klaus P. Jankovsky, "A View into the Grave: *A Disputacion Betwyx þe Body and Wormes* in British Museum Ms. Ad. 37049," *Texas A & I University Studies* 7 (1974): 137–59; and Marjorie Malvern, "An Earnest 'Monyscyon' and 'þinge Delectabyll' Realized Verbally and Visually in 'A Discputacion Betwyx þe Body and Wormes,' A Middle English Poem Inspired by Tomb Art and Northern Spirituality," *Viator* 13 (1982): 415–43.

56. Such scenes appear twice in the manuscript: on f. 19r, where the Virgin and the crucified Christ intercede with God on behalf of the dying soul, and on f. 28v, where a single monk represents the forces of good.

57. It is possible that "storyes" here could refer to pictorial or sculptural representations, as well as texts; s.v. *MED* storie (n.1), 3. The specificity with which Golwynne's list describes other manuscript illuminations makes this interpretation unlikely, however.

58. See R. H. Bowers, "Middle English Verses on the Founding of the Carthusian Order," *Speculum* 42 (1967): 710–13.

59. The close physical connection of text and image suggests that in this manuscript scribe and artist were probably the same.

60. See *Boke of Craft of Dying*, in Robert R. Raymo, "Works of Religious and Philosophical Instruction," in *A Manual of the Writings in Middle English, 1050–1500*, ed. Albert E. Hartung, vol. 7 (New Haven, Conn., 1986), XX.216.

61. See Hennessy, "Royal Dead," and James Hogg, "A Morbid Preoccupation with Mortality? The Carthusian London British Library MS Additional 37049," in *Zeit, Tod, und Ewigkeit in der Renaissance Literatur*, Analecta Cartusiana 117:2 (Salzburg, 1986), 139–89.

62. London, British Library, MS Harley 1706 (f. 19v), and Oxford, Bodleian Library, MS Douce 322 (f. 19v).

63. See especially chapter 2, which concerns "the temptacions of men that dyene." For an edition of the text, see C. Horstmann, ed., *Yorkshire Writers: Richard Rolle of Hampole and his Followers* (1895; repr. Cambridge, 1976, 1999), 406–20.

64. Chapters 3 and 6 are particularly addressed, not to the dying man, but to "som man that is abowt him."

65. See Kathleen L. Scott, ed., *An Index of Images in English Manuscripts from the Time of Chaucer to Henry VIII, c. 1380–c. 1509. The Bodleian Library, Oxford*, vol. 2 (London, 2001). The *Index* describes the image on f. 27r as "nude woman in bed with arms crossed; man beside bed with arms crossed" (39).

66. On the complex textual history of *O intemerata*, see A. Wilmart, *Auteurs spirituels et textes dévots du Moyen Age latin* (Paris, 1932), 474–504. For a translation of the text, see Roger S. Wieck, *Time Sanctified: The Book of Hours in Medieval Art and Life* (New York, 1988), 164.

67. See the essay by Gillespie in this volume.

68. An alternative text omits to mention St. John; see Wilmart, *Auteurs spirituels*, 493–5. Among the most popular subjects for illustrating *O intemerata* are the Holy Family; the Virgin herself, perhaps crowned, holding a book, or weaving; the Virgin with saints and angels; or a Pietà. See Wieck, *Time Sanctified*, 95–96, and Roger S. Wieck, *Painted Prayers: The Book of Hours in Medieval and Renaissance Art* (New York, 1997), 86–90.

69. The *Mirror* does not, however, mention the episode of the poisoned chalice.

70. Louis Réau, *Iconographie de l'art chrétien*, 3 vols. in 6 (Paris, 1955–59), 3.2:708–20.

71. Ibid., 3.2:712.

72. London, Public Record Office E 164/10, f. 44r; Kathleen L. Scott, *Dated and Datable English Manuscript Borders, c. 1395–1499* (London, 2002), 64, pl. 18.

73. The *Brut* manuscript is in the library of Professor Robert G. Heyneman, in Chapel Hill, N.C. For a description of it, see Kathleen L. Scott, *A Survey of Manuscripts Illuminated in the British Isles: Later Gothic Manuscripts, 1390–1490*, 2 vols. (London, 1996), no. 77. The comparison is suggested by the Christie's sale catalogue.

74. Glasgow, University Library, MS Hunter 77 (T.3.15), f. 3v; Scott, *Dated and Datable English Manuscript Borders*, 95, pl. 31b.

75. For a full discussion of the Scropes and their books, see the essay by Edwards in this volume.

76. See the essay by Edwards in this volume.

77. I would like to thank Jill Mann for her learned and generous assistance with this essay at all stages.

# The Knight and The Rose

## French Manuscripts in the Notre Dame Library

MAUREEN BOULTON

COMPARED TO SPECIALISTS IN OLD AND MIDDLE ENGLISH, students of medieval French literature are not nearly as well-served with facsimiles of important manuscripts. The University of Notre Dame is therefore particularly fortunate to have in its possession two actual manuscripts preserving medieval French literary texts of considerable interest. The two volumes date from the same period—the second half of the fifteenth century—but otherwise present striking contrasts. One (now designated University of Notre Dame, MS 51) contains a version of a verse chronicle in the form of an epic poem composed in the late fourteenth century, and based on events of the Hundred Years' War. The other (now University of Notre Dame, MS 34) contains a copy of the *Roman de la Rose*, composed in two different periods of the thirteenth century, and from the time of its appearance until the early sixteenth century one of the most influential literary works in any language. In addition to containing significant texts, both manuscripts are interesting paleographically. I shall examine each of these manuscripts in turn, discussing both their contents and their form.

The sole text included in Notre Dame 51 is the *Chanson de Bertrand du Guesclin*, a verse chronicle or *chanson de geste* devoted to the greatest French military hero of the fourteenth century, composed by a rather obscure writer known only by his surname, Cuvelier. For an Anglophone audience nourished on Shakespeare's history plays, the idea of a French military hero in this period may seem an oxymoron, but the French perspective was entirely different, and Cuvelier's poem is an important historical witness to that view.

In recounting the life of a military commander who was seen by contemporaries as a paragon of chivalry, Cuvelier's epic is an example of the "chivalric biography," a genre first established in the thirteenth century by the Anglo-Norman poem on the *Histoire de Guillaume le Maréchal*.[1] The genre became popular only in the context of the Hundred Years' War, with the biographies of rival heroes. Chandos Herald's verse *Vie du Prince Noir*, written ca. 1385, was exactly contemporary with Cuvelier's poem and celebrated English chivalry in the person of the Black Prince and his companions.[2] Cuvelier's poem may have been either the inspiration for, or a response to, the celebration of the English heroes. Cuvelier's praise of Bertrand du Guesclin also anticipated the biographies of fifteenth-century French heroes such as Marshal Boucicaut and Jacques de Lalaing.[3]

Bertrand du Guesclin, who lived from 1323 to 1380, was a minor Breton nobleman who in 1370 was appointed by the French king Charles V to the high office of Constable of France, and given the supreme command of the French armies that that office entailed. Like his better-known contemporary Froissart, Cuvelier was a serious historian who, in addition to relying on earlier sources, also collected accounts from witnesses to the events, particularly from Du Guesclin's companions in arms. Using the life span of his hero as a frame, the poet consulted historical sources such as the *Chronique de Saint Denis* in order to construct accounts of the War of the Breton Succession (1341–64), the French intervention in the civil war in Spain (between Pedro the Cruel and his half-brother Enrique de Trastámara, 1355–70), and the reconquest of France at the end of the first stage of the Hundred Years' War (1370–80).[4] On the other hand, in his effort to cast his hero as an exemplar of the contemporary ideals of chivalry, Cuvelier was also guilty of betraying the historical record, as well as of strategic omissions.[5]

We know virtually nothing about Cuvelier, who identified himself near the beginning of the poem, in lines omitted in the Notre Dame manuscript. He was apparently associated with the court of Charles VI, but is probably not to be identified (as has been suggested) either with the "poor troubadour" referred to by Philippe de Mézières, or with the similarly obscure composer of *ars subtilior* songs.[6] He must have begun his work shortly after the death of his hero in 1380, and must have completed it before 1387, when Jean d'Estouteville commissioned a prose version of the work.[7] The seven surviving copies of the original verse form,[8] and the thirteen of the prose version, attest to the popularity of the subject.[9] The prose chronicle was also printed several times in the late fifteenth and sixteenth centuries, and continues to serve as the principal source for biographies of Du Guesclin, the most recent of which was published in 1999.[10]

The rather greater popularity of the prose rendering of the life of Du Guesclin raises the question of the poetic form chosen by Cuvelier for his subject. The poem has not been popular with literary critics, who accuse it of tedium and prolixity. At more than twenty-four thousand lines, it is undeniably long, and it certainly makes too much use of line-fillers in its pursuit of rhyme. Nevertheless, the poet's choice of the epic verse-form was both deliberate and effective: by casting his story in the form of the twelfth- and thirteenth-century *chansons de geste*, he glorified his hero and associated Du Guesclin with Charlemagne's heroic warriors. The defeats at Crécy and Poitiers were serious blows to French self-esteem, while the ransom of Jean II after his capture at the latter battle was a political and economic disaster as well. Jean's ransom (originally four million écus, eventually reduced to three million) exceeded the fiscal capacity of the kingdom after the territorial inroads made by the English.[11] The successful reign of Charles V, aided by his constable, did much to restore order, prosperity, and national pride to his countrymen. During his father's captivity (1356–60), Charles acted as the regent of France. It was probably during this period that Charles first encountered Du Guesclin. As king, Charles adopted a military policy of strategic retreats and small skirmishes in place of pitched battles. These tactics, which had served the English well, may have been borrowed from those of English captains like Robert Knolles and Sir John Chandos.[12]

Du Guesclin's rise from the minor nobility to the head of the French armies was unparalleled, and was due both to his unprecedented military career and to the changing nature of the war. Having no group of vassals to lead on campaign, Du Guesclin became the head of a band of adventurers and engaged in guerilla warfare against the English in Britanny and lower Normandy. In the 1360s his expedition to Spain at the head of the "great companies" served to remove these marauders from the French countryside (though its effect on Spain was less happy).[13] His strengths included the ability to execute rapid movements over long distances and to concentrate his forces at critical points. His control over the undisciplined armies of the period has been described as "legendary," and he was also a good strategist.[14] His major weakness—a reckless and undisciplined courage in pitched battles—was ironically the very quality that earned him the respect and admiration of the upper nobility.[15] Virtually from the moment of his death Bertrand du Guesclin became the subject of legend. Cuvelier's contribution was to turn Du Guesclin into a new type of noble hero, devoted to the service of the king and the state, and his poem not only glorified its protagonist but defended and glorified the French monarchy itself. The latter needed all the help it could get during the reign of Charles VI, which began in 1380, and the civil wars and defeats of the next fifty years help to explain the continued copying of Cuvelier's epic.

Notre Dame 51, copied (according to the colophon on the last page) in 1464, contains 298 paper leaves measuring 280 by 202 mm. Watermarks in three different patterns (unicorn entire, P augmented with trefoil, anchor augmented with ball and cross), are visible on almost half of the leaves. The watermarks correspond closely, but not perfectly, to examples in Briquet's *Les Filigranes*, and are typical of papers produced in northern France in the second half of the fifteenth century.[16]

The volume has been foliated in the upper right-hand corner in pencil in a modern hand. The twenty-two gatherings consist in most cases of sixteen leaves, but the second and sixth have eighteen leaves, gatherings fifteen to nineteen have twelve, and the last two gatherings are a bifolium and a quaternion. All but the first and last gatherings are marked by a quire signature in the lower left margin of the recto of the first leaf. The collation is complete, but five leaves have been misbound.[17] In the first quire, the second bifolium (ff. 2 and 15) has been reversed, and its final leaf (f. 16) became detached and is now bound into the third gathering, after f. 35; another bifolium from the end of the manuscript (ff. 289–90) has been reversed and inserted into the tenth gathering after f. 151. The ruling, guided by pricking in the outer margins, was done with a stylus; both pricking and ruling are occasionally visible in the latter part of the book. The text is laid out as a single column of verse, with between 34 and 40 lines per page, and is written in a small, neat cursive script.[18] Paper manuscripts are obviously not deluxe volumes, so it is not surprising that the decoration in the book is limited to two-line initials placed at the beginning of each stanza. The two initials (one blue and one red) on the first page are smaller, finer, and ornamented with contrasting filigree. Of the remaining initials, all but two are in red ink, and most are unornamented and fairly crude. The indicator letters are often visible, but on four occasions the rubricator has nevertheless filled in the wrong letter.[19] In the manner of most French verse manuscripts in the fourteenth and fifteenth centuries, the initial letter of each line of verse is highlighted with a stroke of yellow, as are occasional words within the line. The volume seems to have been written by a single scribe, differences in the appearance of various pages being due to changes of ink or pen. In addition, most of the corrections were made by the same scribe. Some slips he corrected immediately by striking out and substituting the correct word, but other corrections were made later above the line of writing.[20] The text has very little punctuation, mainly a point to separate the two halves of the alexandrine line, but the punctuation increases from f. 266 to the end.

The dialect of the text shows frequent Picardisms, more in fact than any of the other manuscripts. These examples from ff. 248v–49r are characteristic, and typical of the scribe's language: *chinquant* (v. 3, for *cinquant*), *ochis* (v. 8, for *occis*), *cheux* (v. 41, for *ceux*), *escapper* (v. 43, for *eschapper*), *le moitié* (v. 8, for la).[21] On the other hand, Francien forms like *champs* (v. 109), *cheval* (v. 85), *chastel* (v. 90), *France* (v. 210), show that the scribe did not systematically rewrite it in Picard, and the dialect provides no evidence to suggest a specific provenance. The opening words of the second folio are sometimes used in medieval catalogues to identify particular volumes. The opening words of the second folio in Notre Dame 51 ("Et estoit a par lui") do not coincide with any in published medieval booklists, and so the Notre Dame volume cannot be attributed to a specific medieval collection.[22] The signatures of one early owner (Antoinette du Bronc) on the last page have been covered over with a pasted sheet, but her mottoes "Jonesse enporte" and "Jonesse m'abuse" (youth carries me away, youth mistreats me) remain at the top of the page. It is interesting that an early owner, and perhaps the first, of this book of chivalric exploits was a woman. In the eighteenth century, the manuscript was in the possession of the duke of Bournonville (1662–1705), whose books were sold in 1706.[23] The seventeenth-century binding is of mottled calf, with gilt border-lines and gilt ornaments between the welts on the spine; the three flyleaves at each end of the volume differ from the paper of the text-block and probably date from the same period as the binding.

In the nineteenth century, Notre Dame 51 formed part of the famous collection of Sir Thomas Phillipps of Cheltenham, and Phillipps's number (8194) is inscribed inside the front cover. Phillipps owned two copies of the poem, but the whereabouts of the other, illustrated copy are currently unknown. The Notre Dame volume was auctioned by Sotheby's in 1966, and the University of Notre Dame acquired it two years later from H. P. Kraus for $5,800.

The *Chanson de Bertrand du Guesclin* has been edited twice, first in 1839 on the basis of two manuscripts, and most recently by Jean-Claude Faucon on the basis of a third copy, to which he supplied significant variants from all the other manuscripts.[24] From the point of view of an editor seeking to establish Cuvelier's text, or at least an approximation of it, Notre Dame 51 is obviously less important than the other copies. Not only is it substantially later than the other manuscripts, but its text is also one of the most divergent. Overall the Notre Dame copy is about 1,800 lines shorter than the critical edition, but it also contains substantial interpolations.[25] For a critic interested in the *mouvance* of a medieval text, however, or in the rewriting of history, the reworkings of Notre Dame 51 make it particularly interesting. The episodes expanded in Notre Dame 51 are precisely those—where Du Guesclin was not personally involved—that did not interest Cuvelier.

As these comments suggest, the versions of the poem transmitted by the various manuscripts differ markedly from each other, to such a degree that one can speak of several redactions. Aside from the normal variants, one finds whole episodes introduced or omitted, and individual adventures recounted more fully, as well as similar material recounted in stanzas of different rhymes. As one would expect in such circumstances, the text of the Notre Dame manuscript does not correspond closely to any of the redactions represented in the printed editions, although it agrees with all of them at different points.[26] One passage occurs in a different order,[27] but the manuscript also contains several passages not found in any of the other published texts. Beginning on f. 248v and continuing for fully ten leaves is a passage of more than 900 lines unique to this version. The additional material consists of elaborations on events that the other copies dispatch in a few lines. The death of the marshal Arnoul d'Audrehem at Saumur in 1370 is recounted in two stanzas (79 lines), whereas Charrière's version reports it in three lines.[28] The passage continues with a long account of naval expeditions: Owen Lawgoch's taking of Guernsey, and the defeat of the Earl of Pembroke's fleet at La Rochelle in 1372.[29] One of the most dramatic of the additional incidents in this passage is the account of a confrontation between Du Guesclin and his king, who has failed to raise the money necessary to pay the army and continue the war into Guyenne in 1371. Summoned to Paris, Bertrand reproaches the king for taxing the poor excessively, and recommends that he summon the "chapperons fourrés"—the prelates and lawyers who wear fur-lined hoods—and raise money from those who have it.[30]

Another passage unique to this manuscript underscores Cuvelier's theme of royal service. In recounting the death of Jean de Grailly, captal de Buch—one of the greatest Gascon allies of the English—the redactor of Notre Dame 51 portrays the captal at his death repenting his departure from the service of the Valois king.[31]

The ending of the poem in the Notre Dame manuscript also differs from that of the published versions: it is longer (six stanzas containing 145 verses instead of four with 124 verses), and all of its stanzas have rhymes different from those in the other versions.[32] Although the same events are covered in all versions, the emphasis is different. Du Guesclin's last exploit was the capture of the castle of Chateauneuf-Randon; although mortally wounded, Du Guesclin bluffed the English garrison into surrendering. The Notre Dame manuscript notes that the tent where the dying constable was lying caught fire so that he had to be carried to a safer place. While the published versions quote Du Guesclin's instructions to his marshal, Notre Dame 51 omits this speech; instead, it inserts, at the end of the incident, a conversation between Du Guesclin and the English captain absent from the other versions. The Englishman's chagrin at finding himself surrendering to a dying man is fully captured in Notre Dame 51. In both versions the dying Du Guesclin takes leave of his wife, of King Charles, of the king's brothers (the dukes of Anjou, Burgundy, and Berry), and of his cousin, the duke of Bourbon. The Notre Dame manuscript names in addition his companions-in-arms Olivier de Clisson (who succeeded Du Guesclin as constable) and Jean de Beaumont. The added names help to carry the history forward into the next century. In the final stanza describing his burial, all versions note that Du Guesclin was buried in the abbey of St. Denis; the published versions observe that Charles V died soon afterwards. The Notre Dame manuscript is much more specific in its account: the constable's body was embalmed and his entrails delivered to his wife, who buried them "nobly" within his fief, while the body was buried in the abbey, "at the foot of the king."[33] Lugubrious as these details may seem to a modern audience, the procedure described was fairly typical of funerals of high-ranking noblemen.[34]

While it does not drastically alter our understanding of Cuvelier's epic, Notre Dame 51 stands as an interesting witness to the process of rewriting history shortly after the conclusion of an often inglorious war.

As I indicated above, Notre Dame's other French manuscript, Notre Dame 34, is a copy of the *Roman de la Rose*—the best-known and most influential work of medieval French literature. In the first section of roughly four thousand lines, Guillaume de Lorris (writing ca. 1230) used an allegorical dream-vision to recount his own love story. His poem broke off with his beloved's Fair Welcome imprisoned in the castle of Jealousy. Some forty years later Jean de Meun wrote an eighteen-thousand-line continuation to the poem, overwhelming Guillaume's elegant fiction with learned digressions on history, cosmology, natural philosophy, and moral philosophy, before relating the successful assault on the castle and the plucking of the rose. The *Roman de la Rose* was translated into English by Chaucer, as well as into German and Dutch by less famous poets. The *Fiore*, a translation into Italian, is sometimes attributed to Dante.[35] In its original form in Old French, it survives in more than three hundred manuscripts.

Notre Dame's manuscript is a good quality but not deluxe copy, made in the second half of the fifteenth century. It is composed of 140 parchment leaves measuring 280 x 203 mm, foliated in brown ink in the upper right corner. The parchment flyleaves (three at the beginning, one at the end) differ in color and thickness from the leaves of the text, and may date from the sixteenth century. The collation of the volume is complete: there are sixteen gatherings, mainly of eight leaves, although the ninth and the last have only four leaves. Most of the gatherings are marked with catchwords written vertically downwards on the ruling for the right margin in a small cursive script.[36] Leaf signatures are occasionally visible in the lower right corner of the recto.[37] The text was written in a fifteenth-century vernacular textura by a single scribe who also made most of the annotations, and it is laid out in two columns of 39 lines, guided by rulings in red.[38] The volume contains 21,636 lines, or the entire romance;[39] the first part ends at f. 26vb, and the second begins immediately after a rubric announcing the change.

The manuscript contains a single miniature, at the top of the first column, set into the initial M. There are three figures, one seated, with two others standing at his left, all wearing similar garments. The seated figure wears a long round-necked gown without a collar, with narrow sleeves; over it he wears a short ermine cape split in front; his hair is cut to mid-neck length; and he is wearing a hat of the style known as a "turkey bonnet."[40] The standing figures wear robes of similar cut, but less sumptuous material. It is possible that the seated figure represents the reader or owner of the manuscript, while the others might be images of the two authors. The two books on a stand under the window behind them may represent the two parts of the poem.[41] On the basis of the clothing, it may be possible to narrow the dating to the last third of the century.[42] The miniature is supplemented by a narrow foliate half-border, and in the bottom margin is a shield of arms, perhaps of the first owner. Divisions in the text are marked with two-line initials in gold paint on a red or blue ground, for which the indicator letters are frequently visible.[43] The initials of each line are highlighted with yellow, but are not set off in a column.

Since the text is laid out in two columns with a single verse per line in a column, there is relatively little punctuation. Rubrics mark major divisions in the text, which are further divided into sections by the gold initials. Most of the instructions to the rubricator were removed, but one set remains on f. 74v. Breaks in thought are marked with a mark resembling a modern semicolon (*punctus versus*), lesser pauses by a check mark (perhaps a form of the *virgula suspensiva*), and a stronger medial pause by a *punctus.*[44] Checking sample lines on f. 40r with the text of Poirion's edition, the punctuation in the manuscript corresponds closely to that chosen by the editor.[45] Although running titles are not systematic, indications of the content of the page are frequent and increase towards the end of the volume.

The manuscript was rebound in the sixteenth century in Italian brown morocco over oak boards, and has two green silk ribbons. Both covers are ornamented with broad arabesque borders enclosing an ornamented lozenge.[46]

The dialect of the text shows occasional Picard traits, but the arms on the shield on the first folio (a red shield with three silver scallop shells or gules three escallops argent in the language of blazon) match those of the Norman family of Fraidel in the so-called *Armorial de Navarre.*[47] Since the armorial was compiled between 1368 and 1375, the individual listed there was probably an ancestor of the owner of the manuscript. In the nineteenth century, the manuscript was owned by Ambroise-Firmin Didot, a French publisher and book collector whose firm published the volumes of the Société des Anciens Textes Français, as well as important series devoted to historical documents.[48] Part of this collection was sold in 1881, and Notre Dame 34 was bought in the twentieth century by James P. R. Lyell of London, whose collection was sold in its turn at his death in 1949.[49] Notre Dame's *Rose* was among those bought at that time by Bernard Quaritch, and re-sold by him in 1952. Like its companion, Notre Dame's *Rose* was acquired in 1968 from H. P. Kraus.

The version of the *Roman de la Rose* in Notre Dame 34 is slightly shorter than the text of the standard edition: the first part is sixty lines shorter, mainly due to the omission of couplets or single lines and it is at least 150 lines shorter by the end.[50] Langlois did not discuss this volume in his classification of the manuscripts: according to his criteria, however, the first section belongs to the deviant group II, while the second part corresponds to the more correct group I.[51] Since its variants do not correspond exactly to any of his other criteria, I was unable to classify either section more precisely.[52]

As is typical of many *Rose* manuscripts, Notre Dame 34 exhibits an elaborate system of annotations. Most of these were written in the same hand as the text, but often the color of the ink is different. A few annotations in the second part were added by a second hand, but they are not qualitatively different from the others.[53] Major divisions in the text are marked by rubrics. At the end of the first part of the romance the rubricator misidentified its author as "Guillaume de St. Amour" rather than Guillaume de Lorris. Although I cannot explain the rubricator's attribution of the poem to an important master of the University of Paris, it recurs later in the manuscript. On f. 74va, the mention of Guillaume de St. Amour in the text (Poirion edition, vv. 11506–7) is labelled in the margin "De l'exil de mestre Guillaume de Saincte Amour qui conmença ce livre" ["On the exile of master William of St. Amour, who began this book"].[54]

Within the different sections of the poem, marginal notes identify speakers and scenes, while the content of a column or page is often indicated at the top. On f. 37v, for example, the top of the left column bears the label "Come on doit eviter Fortune" ["How one must avoid Fortune"], while the right column is marked "De fortune come on ne la doit pas doubter" ["About Fortune: how one must not fear her"]. In the left margin, notes mark the speeches of "Amant" and "Raison." The marginal notes in the second part also identify sources, gloss unfamiliar words, and explain classical allusions.[55] Further down on f. 37v, for example, the references to "Socrates" at v. 5847 and "Solin" (i.e., Solon) at v. 5857 are marked; between these notations there is a symbol consisting of three dots with a hook below that draws attention to the whole passage. Such notation of the authors paraphrased by Jean de Meun made it possible to use the volume as a vernacular compendium of Latin learning.[56]

In the second part of the poem, the annotations are more frequent as well as longer. As a point of comparison, the first four-thousand-line section of the poem, copied on twenty-six leaves, contains fifty annotations. Half of these identify speakers, while the other half label the content of passages.[57] In the seven and a half leaves devoted to the discourse of Faux

Semblant [False Seeming]—a passage a little more than a quarter of the length of the Guillaume de Lorris section of the romance—there are forty-nine annotations in the margins.[58] Seventeen of these are indications of the speaker; three others gloss obscure words.[59] Only five of the marginal notes are neutral indications of the content, for example, "Des ypocrites" (f. 75rb, ["About hypocrites"]). The twenty-one remaining annotations draw attention to, or respond to, the content of the text, particularly where it deals with the failures of religious (f. 72vb: "Come religieux contempnent povres gens" ["How the religious despise poor people"]) the issue of mendicancy (f. 74rb: "Come nule apostre ne mendia," ["How no apostle begged"]), and religious hypocrisy (f. 77va: "Come le faint religieux qui ayme le monde resemble le chien qui vomit," ["How the sham religious who loves the world resembles a dog that vomits"]). Three of the annotations in this section are in Latin—two of these quote the biblical sources of the text, while the third cites a decretal that contradicts the text.[60] Other passages are highlighted, without comment, by the figure of three dots with a hook below. Such careful annotation, mainly in the hand of the principal scribe, suggests that the book was prepared for a reader familiar with Latin, and one who took a critical view of the failings of members of religious orders.

The annotations continue in later sections of the romance. In one case, the lines "Dire vos os tout en apert / Que n'est pas voir quan qu'il apert" (Poirion, vv. 12217–18 ["I dare tell you openly, that it is not true however it appears"]) are marked in the margin with a pointing finger, drawing the reader's attention to false appearances. The long speech of La Vieille [The Old Woman] is annotated almost as heavily as that of Faux Semblant. Copied on eleven leaves (ff. 83r–93v; vv. 12740–14711 of Poirion's edition), the nearly two thousand lines of La Vieille's speech contain seventy-five annotations. Two of these identify sources (f. 83va; Platon = Plato; f. 90va; Orace = Horace). All of the rest mark the various and scandalous teachings of the Old Woman, for example, "Come la vielle preuve par une similitude que on se puet perjurer en amours" (f. 85ra: ["How the old woman proves by a comparison that one may perjure oneself in love"]). Such attention to the wicked Old Woman is not necessarily incompatible with the implicit condemnation of religious hypocrisy of the annotations to Faux Semblant's speech. The annotations here provide a convenient catalogue of the vices of women, and might have appealed to a misogynist reader.

The annotations in the discourses of Nature (ff. 102v–105r, ff. 108r–124r) are different from those in the earlier passages. Some of them are philosophical in character, as for example the note on f. 104rb:

> Comme nul ne sauroit descripre ne paindre Nature, la cause est telle: Car Nature est la cause et le commence[ment] de mouvoir et reposer les corps mobiles ou active[ment] ou passivement. Ore . . . est manifeste que le[s] corps naturelx mouv[ent] et reposent et qui le prouveroit, ce soit par choses mayns manifestes. Mays c'est une chose fole et rude de prouver une chose congneue par raisons mayns cogneues. Don[c] rude choze est de vouloir soy enquerir que Nature soit.

> How no one would be able to describe or paint Nature, the cause is this: For Nature is the cause and the beginning of the moving and the resting of moving bodies, either actively or passively. Now it is manifest that the natural bodies move and rest, and whoever would prove it, he does it by things less manifest. But it is a rude and foolish thing to prove a known thing by things less known. Therefore it is a rude thing to wish to seek what Nature may be.

Folio 110rb, next to the passage in Nature's confession to Genius dealing with predestination and free will, contains the longest annotation in the manuscript.[61] The entire right margin is filled with a long, complicated (and not very clear) explanation of the nature of destiny: "Destinee est une disposicion qui est es choses mobiles par laquelle la divine providence par les secundes causes qui sont causes des destinees annexe a ces disposicions et ordres . . ." ["Destiny is a disposition in moving things through which providence, by means of second causes which are the causes of destinies attached to these dispositions and orders . . ."]. The character of these philosophical glosses helps to round out our impression of the personality of the commissioner of Notre Dame 34 as a serious, well-educated, and perhaps misogynist reader.

Each of these manuscripts presents features and problems—both physical and textual—typical of its genre and period. They illustrate the ordering of gatherings by various systems (catchword, quire signatures, leaf signatures). The physical state of the books, with misbound leaves, replaced bindings, and leaf repairs, also reflects their rather checkered history since the time of their production. Since each manuscript is a late copy of the text it preserves, neither is crucial to the establishment of a critical edition. Nevertheless, these two manuscripts illustrate vividly how medieval texts were altered, adapted, and annotated to suit the needs and interests of different readers in different periods. Notre Dame 34, with glosses supplied by the main scribe of the text, shows a late medieval book-producer highlighting and commenting on particular aspects of a text written more than two centuries earlier. The content of the annotations suggests that the original recipient of this copy of the *Roman de la Rose* was literate in Latin as well as French, was familiar with canon law, was critical of the religious orders, and was inclined to think ill of women. In contrast, the interpolated redaction of the *Chanson de Bertrand du Guesclin* in Notre Dame 51 reveals how a text may evolve in response to changed historical circumstances. While Cuvelier's poem commemorated the hero who had transformed the fortunes of the French in the 1370s, the Notre Dame redaction produced a century later shows its protagonist standing up to his king. This shift in emphasis probably reflects the troubled reigns that followed the poem's composition. In each case, a close examination of the textual changes introduced in these late copies documents the varying reception and interpretation of texts over time.

## NOTES

1. Elisabeth Gaucher, *La biographie chevaleresque: Typologie d'un genre (XIII^e–XV^e siècle)* (Paris, 1994). On Guillame le Maréchal, see Ruth J. Dean and Maureen Boulton, *Anglo-Norman Literature: A Guide to Texts and Manuscripts*, Anglo-Norman Text Society Occasional Publications 3 (London, 1999), no. 57.

2. Dean and Boulton, *Anglo-Norman Literature*, no. 72; see also Geneviève Hasenohr and Michel Zink, eds., *Dictionnaire des lettres françaises: Le moyen âge*, 2nd ed. (Paris, 1992), 677–78 (hereafter *DLF*[2]).

3. *DLF*[2], 951, 951–52; Gaucher, *La biographie chevaleresque*, 624–27, 627–32, and passim.

4. Marianne Gbenoba and Gisela Seiffert-Busch, eds., *La littérature historiographique des origines à 1500: Partie documentaire*, vol. 11.2 of *Grundriss der Romanischen Literaturen des Mittelalters* (Heidelberg, 1993), 95, no. 13873.

5. Gaucher, *La biographie chevaleresque*, 456–57, 463–65, 474. Cf. Jean-Claude Faucon, "La Chanson de Bertrand du Guesclin," *Perspectives médiévales* 12 (1986): 13–17 for a positive estimate of Cuvelier's historical merit. Among his omissions is any reference to what Raymond Cazelles refers to as the "disgrace" of Du Guesclin's final months; see Raymond Cazelles, *Société politique, noblesse et couronne sous Jean le Bon et Charles V*, Mémoires et documents publiés par la Société de l'Ecole des Chartes 28 (Geneva, 1982), 551–53.

6. *DLF*[2], 363.

7. See Gaucher, *La biographie chevaleresque*, p. 223. Jean d'Estouteville was a squire to Charles V and Charles VI; he served as Captain of Vernon with Du Guesclin, who gave him the lordship of Charlesmesnil (Seine-Maritime). For his dates of service in the French army (1373–1416), see John Bell Henneman, *Olivier de Clisson and Political Society in France under Charles V and Charles VI* (Philadelphia, 1996), 216.

8. One of the copies was divided, and the two parts are now Montpellier, Bibl. Interuniv., MS H 250 and Paris, Bibliothèque Nationale de France, MS nouv. acq. fr. 993; see Jean-Claude Faucon, "Note sur deux manuscrits de la *Chanson de du Guesclin* par Cuvelier," *Revue d'histoire des textes* 8 (1978): 319–23. The other manuscripts are Paris, Arsenal, MS 3141 (early 15th cent.); Le Mans, Bibl. mun., MS 14 (15th cent., some pages recopied in the 16th); London, British Library, MS Additional 20850 (ca. 1400); Aix-en-Provence, Bibl. Méjanes, MS 248 (1441); Paris, Bibliothèque Nationale de France, MS fr. 850 (15th cent.).

9. Francisque Michel, ed., *Chronique de du Guesclin* (Paris, 1830), 10–18.

10. Yves Jacob, *Bertrand du Guesclin: connétable de France* (Paris, 1999). See also Richard Vernier, *The Flower of Chivalry: Bertrand du Guesclin and the Hundred Years War* (Woodbridge, 2003). For the early editions of the prose chronicle, see Jacques-Charles Brunet, *Manuel du libraire et de lamateur de livres*, 6 vols. (Paris, 1860), "Du Guesclin (Bertrand)," vol. 2, cols. 869–70.

11. On the ransom, see Cazelles, *Société politique*, 360–61.

12. On the avoidance of pitched battles, a policy that may have been advised by Olivier de Clisson, see Henneman, *Olivier de Clisson*, 56, 59.

13. *Encyclopaedia Britannica*, 11th ed. (New York, 1910), "Du Guesclin," 8:648. See also Edouard Perroy, *The Hundred Years War*, trans. W. B. Wells (New York, 1965), 155–57.

14. Jonathan Sumption, *The Hundred Years War*, vol. 2, *Trial by Fire* (Philadelpia, 1999), 506.

15. Henneman, *Olivier de Clisson*, 57.

16. On watermarks, see C. M. Briquet, *Les Filigranes: Dictionnaire historique des marques du papier*, 4 vols. (Leipzig, 1923): unicorn, no. 10008; P, no. 8605; anchor, nos. 365–88; *Supplementary Material* (Amsterdam, 1968). See also Gerhard Piccard, *Die Wasserzeichen Piccard im Hauptsarchiv Stuttgart* (Stuttgart, 1961–): vol. 4, *Wasserzeichen Buchstabe P*, 2 (1977), vol. 6 *Wasserzeichen Anker* (1978); vol. 10 *Wasserzeichen Fabeltiere* (1980); and Vladimir Mošin, *Anchor Watermarks* (Amsterdam, 1973), 4–5, type Fr. I 1.c: unencircled anchor with circumflex flukes, surmounted by a cross, pls. 5–6.

The unicorn watermark is the most frequent in Notre Dame MS 51 and is found on at least 95 leaves, including ff. 2, 10, 20, 30, 43, 55, 65, 76, 86, 95, 200, 220, 230, 250, 261, 271, 281, 290. The augmented P occurs some 25 times, including ff. 150, 165, 175, 185, 196, 211. The anchor occurs some 24 times, including ff. 101, 111, 120, 132, 140, 156.

17. Collation: $1^{16}$ (1–16: f. 2 follows f. 14, f. 15 follows f. 1, f. 16 misbound after f. 35), $2^{18}$ (ff. 17–34), $3–5^{16}$ (ff. 35–82), $6^{18}$ (ff. 83–100), $7–14^{16}$ (ff. 101–228), $15–19^{12}$ (ff. 229–88), $20^{2}$ (ff. 289–90: misbound after f. 151), $21^{8}$ (ff. 291–98).

18. On the gothic system of scripts, see Michelle P. Brown, *A Guide to Western Historical Scripts from Antiquity to 1600* (Toronto, 1990), 80–81. For French examples of this cursive script (*cursiva*), see Jacques Stiennon, *Paléographie du moyen âge* (Paris, 1973), 119–20.

19. Folios 44v (L for S), 51r (S for B), 53r (E for T), 290r (E for T); on f. 290v the indicator letter (a) is wrong, and the rubricator has correctly filled in I; on f. 151r the initial was not filled in.

20. For example, on f. 10r, l. 12 the verb form by insertion; on f. 49v Meullen was three times corrected to Melun; on f. 99v the end of the line is corrected, but the error was not struck out.

21. For a transcription of this passage, see Jean-Claude Faucon, ed., *La Chanson de Bertrand du Guesclin de Cuvelier*, 3 vols. (Toulouse, 1990–91), 2:449 and following.

22. There are two entries for *Bertrand du Guesclin* in inventories of the libraries of the Dukes of Burgundy. One refers to a parchment copy of the prose version (now Brussels, Bibliothèque royale, MS 10230); see Georges Doutrepont, *La littérature française à la cour de Bourgogne*, (Paris, 1909), 410. The other entry, no. 235 of the inventory of 1420, is not full enough to determine whether the volume contains the prose version or Cuvelier's poem; see Georges Doutrepont, *Inventaire de la "Librairie" de Philippe Le Bon, 1420* (Brussels, 1906), 159.

23. On the provenance of Notre Dame 51 see *Bibliotheca Phillippica*, II (London, 1966), 85–87, no. 70.

24. E. Charrière, ed., *Chronique de Bertrand du Guesclin par Cuvelier, trouvère du XIVe siècle*, 2 vols., Collection de documents inédits, Première série, histoire politique (Paris, 1839) relied on Paris, Bibliothèque Nationale de France, MS fr. 850 giving long variant passages from Paris, MS Arsenal 3141 in the notes. Faucon, *La Chanson*, used Montpellier, Bibl. Interuniv., MS H 250 and Paris, Bibliothèque Nationale de France, MS nouv. acq. fr. 993 (originally a single volume) as a base.

25. Faucon, *La Chanson*, 2:445–98 and 3:339–41. There is a brief description of Notre Dame 51 in 3:327–28.

26. According to Faucon, it agrees most closely with MS C (Le Mans, Bibliothèque municipale, MS 14).

27. *Bibliotheca Phillippica*, 86 refers to a passage of two hundred lines beginning on f. 49r ("Or fu au Pontorson avoecques sa maisnie . . .") as an addition not found in the published versions. In fact, although the first stanza is unique to Notre Dame 51, the rest of the passage beginning on f. 49v ("Le duc de Normendie manda de sez ami . . .") corresponds to a passage in Charrière's edition beginning at v. 3510.

28. Notre Dame 51, f. 249r–v, Faucon, *La Chanson*, 2:450–51.

29. Notre Dame 51, ff. 254v–260r; Faucon, *La Chanson*, 2:461–71. On this battle, see Jean Favier, *La Guerre de Cent Ans* (Paris, 1980), 335–37; on Owen, see 344.

30. Notre Dame 51, f. 254v; Faucon, *La Chanson*, 2:460, vv. 475–80.

31. Notre Dame 51, ff. 281v–282r; Faucon, *La Chanson*, 2:476–77.

32. Notre Dame 51, ff. 296v–298v; Faucon, *La Chanson*, 2:493–96.

33. Notre Dame 51, f. 298 r–v; Faucon, *La Chanson*, 2:496, vv. 137, 143.

34. Cf., for example, Christopher Allmand, *Henry V* (Berkeley, 1992), 174.

35. Santa Casciani and Christopher Kleinhenz, eds. and trans., *The Fiore and Detto d'Amore: A Late 13th-century Italian Translation of the Roman de la Rose attributable to Dante, with Introduction and Notes*, Devers Series in Dante Studies 4 (Notre Dame, 2000); see also Zygmunt Barański and Patrick Boyde, eds., *The Fiore in Context: Dante, France, Tuscany*, Devers Series in Dante Studies 2 (Notre Dame, 1997).

36. Folios 8, 16, 32, 40, 48, 56, 64, 76, 84, 92.

37. For example, ff. 3, 4, 69–72, 121–24.

38. The best examples of French vernacular scripts are found in Henri-Jean Martin and Jean Vézin, eds., *Mise en page et mise en text du livre manuscrit* (Paris, 1990), 231–88.

39. The text has been numbered every ten lines, in black ink, in a modern (probably nineteenth-century) hand.

40. C. Willett and Phillis Cunnington, *Handbook of English Mediaeval Costume* (London, 1952; revised 1973), 149 (b).

41. I am grateful to Michel Zink for making these suggestions to me during his visit to the University of Notre Dame in April 2002.

42. Willet and Cunningham, *Handbook*, 142: long roundnecked gown, without collar [1425–1500]. Gowns similar to the ones in Notre Dame 34 are found in Paris, Bibliothèque Nationale de France, MS fr. 18, f. 234v, dated between 1469 and 1473; see François Avril and Nicole Reynaud, *Les manuscrits à peintures en France, 1440–1520* (Paris, 1995), 49–50. Similar hats and haircuts are found in Paris, Bibliothèque Nationale de France, MS fr. 19819, f. 1r, dated 1470 (ibid., 143). Two examples of the split capelet are found in miniatures in printed books of the 1480s; see Alain Arnould and Jean Michel Massing, *Splendours of Flanders* (Cambridge, 1993), 164–65, 168–70, 182–83, nos. 55, 57.

43. The artist has made several mistakes, e.g., at ff. 72vb, 85vb, 137va.

44. On punctuation in manuscripts, see M. B. Parkes, *Pause and Effect: An Introduction to the History of Punctuation in the West* (Berkeley, 1993), esp. 41–49, "The Development of the General Repertory of Punctuation."

45. Daniel Poirion, ed., *Guillaume de Lorris et Jean de Meun, Le Roman de la Rose* (Paris, 1974). ND 6079: Par quoy sont aux honneurs venus (*punctus elevatus;* = Poirion 6284: period). ND 6085: S'il en eussent eu le pouair (*punctus elevatus;* = Poirion 6290: period). ND 6091: Fors par flebesse ou par defaut (*punctus elevatus;* = Poirion 6296: period). ND 6094: Car ainxi le dit l'escriture (*punctus medius;* = Poirion 6299: semicolon).

46. There are two bookplates (A. F. Didot and P. R. Lyell) inside the front cover. On the recto of the first flyleaf a printed description from an unidentified English sale catalogue is pasted in. On the second flyleaf is a title page lettered in Roman capitals and lowercase letters, giving the title, authors, and the date "MCCC ou environ." The description of the work in French on the third flyleaf probably dates from the nineteenth century.

47. The French version of this blazon is listed in the Norman section of the *Armorial de Navarre*; see Michel Popoff, ed., *Marche d'Armes. II Normandie*, (Paris, 1985), 22, no. 85; on page 115, no. 346, the bearer is identified in the list of knights bachelor as M. Robert de Fraidel. In England, the same arms were borne in this period by successive barons Dacre, but it is unlikely that the manuscript was owned by an Englishman. I thank my husband, D'A. J. D. Boulton, for his assistance with the identification of the arms and with the dating of the clothing.

48. On the Didot firm and A.-F. Didot, see *Grand dictionnaire universel du XIXe siècle*, (Paris, 1870), 6:776–77.

49. On Lyell's collection, see Albinia de la Mare, *Catalogue of the Collection of Medieval Manuscripts bequeathed to the Bodleian Library Oxford by James P. R. Lyell* (Oxford, 1971), xv–xxix. According to De la Mare, Lyell's manuscripts are identifiable by his bookplate; in addition, the inside cover usually contains in Lyell's hand the date of purchase, the initial of the bookseller, and the price in cipher; a number in a circle in pencil is the number of the inventory made at his death (no. 64).

50. For example, vv. 77–78, 323–24, 1029–30, 1036, 1189–90, 1475–76, 1533–34, 1595–96, 1823–24, 1969–70, 2075, and 2135–36 of Poirion's edition are omitted from MS 34.

51. Ernest Langlois, *Les manuscrits du Roman de la Rose: Description et classement* (Lille, 1910), 241–44.

52. Ibid., 265–68: Notre Dame 34 does not have the variant in v. 2834 (= ND 2790), but it does have two lines interpolated between vv. 2836–37. Its reading at vv. 109–10 (= ND 108–9) "Descendoit l'eaue fort et roide / Clere estoet l'eaue et aussi froide" does not correspond to any of the 21 possibilities he lists. It has at least one variant ["une ymage" at v. 20799 (= ND 20665)], but not most of the others typical of group A. It has the interpolation between vv. 4228–29 (= ND 4169–70) typical of group B, but none of the other interpolations common to that group; see Langlois, *Les manuscrits*, 352–53, 359–60.

For the second part, ibid., 351–52; Notre Dame 34 lacks the interpolation between vv. 8178–79 (= ND 7967–68). It does, however, contain a version of the interpolation into the speech of Faux Semblant (f. 72rb; Poirion, *Le Roman de la Rose* 312–15); see Langlois, *Les manuscrits*, 426–30.

53. The second hand appears in annotations on ff. 72rb, 75va, and 77va, and perhaps on 86va and 111ra.

54. The nineteenth-century sale catalogue remarks: "Par une singulière distraction, le rubricateur s'est trompé sur le nom du premier auteur de ce poème," *Catalogue des livres précieux, manuscrits et imprimés . . . . M. Ambroise Firmin-Didot* (Paris, 1881), 3:27.

55. On f. 37rb, the reference to Echo (cf. Poirion, *Le Roman de la Rose*, v. 5808) is glossed: "Equo est la deesse des eaux" ["Echo is the goddess of the waters"].

56. Sylvia Huot, "Rose, Roman de la" in W. W. Kibler and Grover Zinn, eds., *The Encyclopedia of Medieval France* (New York, 1995), 821–23. For a fuller discussion of annotation in *Rose* manuscripts see Huot, *The Romance of the Rose and its Medieval Readers: Interpretation, Reception, Manuscript Transmission* (Cambridge, 1993).

57. For example, on f. 14rb: "le premier commande[ment]" ["the first commandment"]; "Le second commande[ment]" ["the second commandment"].

58. Folios 70rb-77vb: vv. 10952–12010 in Poirion's edition.

59. For example, f. 75ra "Fimbries, c'est la superfluité d'ung loing vestement, come ce qui trayne a terre" ["Fringe, that is the excess of a long garment, as what drags on the ground"]; see Poirion, v. 11626.

60. Folio 75va: *Nichil habentes, omnia possidentes* (2 Cor. 6:10) is the source for v. 11678 "Ceus qui tout ont sanz rienz avoir" ["Those who have everything without having anything"].

Folio 75vb: *Intrinsecus sunt lupi rapaces* (Matt. 7:15) is the source for v. 11718 "Dedenz sommes lou ravissable" ["Inside we are ravishing wolves"].

Folio 72rb: "Come aucuns portans habis de religion font a croire aux simples gens qui soufist d'estre confes [. . .] a eux, qui est contre la decretale qui se comence *Omnis utriusque sexus*" ["How some wearing the habit of religion make simple people think that it suffices to confess to them, which is against the decretal that begins *Omnis utriusque sexus*"].

61. See vv. 17077–17115 of Poirion's edition.

# The *Meditations on the Life of Christ*

## An Illuminated Fourteenth-Century Italian Manuscript at the University of Notre Dame

DIANNE PHILLIPS

THE TEXT KNOWN AS THE *MEDITATIONES VITAE CHRISTI* (*MVC*) has long been accorded a central role in the history of late medieval culture. A devotional guide that retells the life of Christ, it enjoyed immediate success as a medieval bestseller, as testified by the more than two hundred manuscript copies still extant.[1] Its appeal owes as much, no doubt, to its style as to its subject. Drawing on diverse medieval literary traditions, ranging from the apocryphal gospels to the sermons of Bernard of Clairvaux, the author of the *Meditationes* transformed his primary source material—the laconic scriptural accounts of Christ's life—into an emotionally charged and vivid narrative, peppered with excursus into the spiritual meanings and religious lessons to be derived from its Christological contents. The profoundly visual character that suffuses the resultant amalgam of the affective and didactic has proved irresistible to art historians in search of explanations both for the proliferation of new iconographies and for the stylistic shifts towards greater naturalism and emotional expressiveness that are the hallmarks of the Trecento.[2]

Scholarly consensus has held that the text was written in Latin ca. 1300 by a Franciscan friar for a Poor Clare, and that in its original form it was a work of about one hundred chapters, narrating the entire life of Christ from the celestial events preceding the Annunciation right through to Pentecost, interrupted in the middle, at the point when Christ visits Martha and Mary in Bethany, by a treatise on the active and contemplative lives.[3] Mary Stallings-Taney, who published the critical edition in 1997, generally adheres to this view, though she endorses the identification of the author, first made in the eighteenth century, as Iohannes de Caulibus.[4] From the fifteenth through the mid-nineteenth centuries the work was regularly attributed to Bonaventure; throughout the twentieth century its authorship was most often relegated to an unknown Pseudo-Bonaventure. In both her introduction to the critical edition and a subsequent article, Stallings-Taney has acknowledged the validity of the arguments advanced by Sarah McNamer in 1990 for a redating of the text from ca. 1300 to the second half of the 1330s.[5] McNamer argues that the *Revelations* that are cited as a source for the early life of the Virgin in the *MVC* should be attributed not to Elizabeth of Hungary but to Elizabeth of Töss, a Dominican nun whose *Vita* was probably written by her follower, Elsbet Stagel. In McNamer's view, Elizabeth of Töss's death in 1336 thus constitutes a *terminus post quem* for the *MVC*, with the composition around 1364 of Niccolò di Mino Cicerchia's poem on the Passion, which derives from the *MVC*, providing a *terminus ante quem*.[6] Despite her acceptance of McNamer's redating, Stallings-Taney does not even gesture towards its implications. For art historians, among others, it would be of enormous consequence, given the near-universal view that the text was essential to the emergence of new stylistic impulses and iconographies at the dawn of the Trecento.

Stallings-Taney neither concedes nor acknowledges McNamer's other hypotheses regarding the origins of the text. The most salient of these depends on the observation that the shorter versions in Latin of the ninety-six-chapter text, designated by Fischer as the "*kleine*" text (in contrast to the "*grosse*" version), are not at all a uniform group. However, according to McNamer, there is a group of forty-one-chapter texts in Italian that is demonstrably consistent, and she raises the possibility that such a version might very well be prior to the long Latin text.[7] Stallings-Taney has never directly addressed the latter hypothesis nor acknowledged the radical revision of conventional views that it would necessitate. From her editorial work, she remains firm in her conviction that in its origins the text was a work of over one hundred chapters and was composed in Latin; she considers its occasional Latinization of Italian words as proof of this point.[8] While McNamer has not completed her study of the shorter Italian version of the *MVC*, her review of Stallings-Taney's critical edition persists in questioning the grounds for the unequivocal assertion that the original language of the *MVC* was Latin.[9]

These recent developments in textual scholarship on the *MVC* bear directly upon the significance and interpretation of an unsigned and undated manuscript of the *Meditationes* in the collection of the Snite Museum of Art at the University of Notre Dame.[10] Written in Italian in the *littera rotunda* typical of fourteenth-century Bologna, it was originally a book of 128 folios, of which 121 survive, and consists of forty-three chapters plus a prologue.[11] The chapters fall into three almost equal categories, devoted respectively to Mary's early life and Christ's Infancy, his Passion, and his post-Passion appearances; there are no chapters devoted to his adult ministry nor the treatise on the active and contemplative lives. Essentially, it would appear to belong to McNamer's category of the Italian forty-one-chapter versions of the *MVC*. Interestingly, the Snite manuscript concludes with a short anecdote relating a eucharistic vision of Albert the Great which immediately follows the list of chapters at the end of the *Meditationes* text.[12] That element, perhaps merely a product of the pronounced Dominican presence in Bologna, is intriguing in the light of McNamer's discernment of other Dominican traces in a text hitherto regarded as thoroughly Franciscan. For now, though, speculation on the place of the Snite manuscript in the history of the *MVC* text must be deferred until further study of the shorter Italian version is complete.

Bracketing the emergence of these new developments in the chronology of the *MVC*, the truisms that focus on the Franciscan background of its author and his sensitivity to the interests of his intended reader as essential to its innovative character remain valid. Attuned to his cloistered female audience, the author of the *Meditationes* exploited sensory experience to make the story at once concrete and compelling, not only describing scenes rich in visual (and often homely) detail and dramatic in emotional content, but also exhorting his reader to imagine herself as though actually present, as a reverent eye-witness to, and even a vicarious participant in, the life and death of Christ. Those qualities are all apparent in the Snite text even though subtle adjustments in wording, which appear throughout the manuscript, suggest an awareness that its particular readers were both male and female and that they dwelt in the secular world, a likelihood confirmed by the illuminator's approach to the text's illustrations.[13]

In light of the oft-remarked imaginative and visual character of the *Meditationes*, it is perplexing that so few manuscripts are illuminated; only two extensively illustrated fourteenth-century examples have hitherto been identified. One of these, Bibliothèque Nationale de France, MS ital. 115, is widely familiar through Ragusa and Green's translation of its Italian text and reproduction of its extensive, though incomplete, program of illustrations (193 of the 297 that were planned were executed).[14] Probably produced in Tuscany in the fifth decade of the fourteenth century, the Paris manuscript in both its text and pictures seems the consummate example of an *MVC* intended for a cloistered female audience.[15] Much less well-known—at least among art historians—is the illuminated manuscript at Oxford, Corpus Christi College, MS 410.[16] Like the Paris manuscript, it is an example of the long *MVC* but is written in Latin and decorated with a complete cycle of 154 miniatures.[17] It seems to have been produced in central Italy around the mid-fourteenth century and may have been made for a noblewoman. Though a comparison of the illustrations in these two manuscripts indicates no standard pictorial program, in their comprehensive approaches the artists do share a notable attentiveness to the particularities of the text.

Given the small number of illuminated fourteenth-century *Meditationes* that have been identified,[18] the Snite manuscript represents a significant discovery. Because it is a shorter text, it includes fewer pictures, but its forty-eight extant illuminations still constitute an ambitious pictorial program;[19] in comparison, the illuminated *Decretum Gratiani* manuscripts, for which Bologna is justifiably famous, normally include thirty-eight miniatures.[20] For the most part, the text of each chapter is preceded by a large miniature appropriate to the episode that it narrates, though with somewhat less fidelity to textual specifics than the illustrations of the Paris and Oxford manuscripts. The Snite manuscript is the smallest of the three, its leaves measuring 180 x 125 mm and its miniatures averaging 75 x 80 mm. In size it resembles a Book of Hours, a manuscript type not as widespread in Italy as elsewhere, though an example in Kremsmünster, illuminated by Niccolò da Bologna and dated to 1349, bears some resemblance to the Snite manuscript.[21] The Kremsmünster manuscript likewise has large illuminations of scenes from the life of Christ, but these function as historiated initials. The layout of the Snite text, in twenty-six long lines with rectangular illuminations typically spanning the equivalent of twelve to fifteen lines, more closely approximates the format of the illustrated *Ways of Prayer of St. Dominic* in the Biblioteca Apostolica Vaticana, MS Rossi 3. It is a manuscript of similar size which, though regarded by Boyle as a product of Southern France, could well depend on an exemplar from Bologna.[22] While the *Ways of Prayer* in Rossi 3 is clearly addressed to the devotional practices of the Dominican novice, the scale and function of its pictures as visual summaries is not dissimilar to the Snite *Meditationes*, though in the Dominican manual the pictures conclude each segment of text whereas they mostly introduce each chapter in the Snite manuscript.

In the field of manuscripts, Bologna's renown rests largely on the lavish legal codices produced for the scholars, clerical and lay, who flocked to the city to study canon and civil law at its prestigious university. A fine example, and one that sheds light on the date and attribution of the Snite manuscript, is provided in an illuminated manuscript, now in the Ambrosiana, of the *Novella*, a commentary on canon law written by the Bolognese scholar Giovanni d'Andrea. Happily, its famous illumination of the personified Virtues and Liberal Arts was signed by the artist, Niccolò da Bologna, and dated 1354.[23] While Niccolò's talents surpass those of the Snite Illuminator, the style of two further illuminations (fig. 8.1) in the Ambrosiana *Novella* provides some clues.[24] These have been attributed to Stefano di Alberto Azzi, a contemporary of Niccolò da Bologna, with an equally lengthy career spanning the whole second half of the fourteenth century.[25] Stefano's father, Alberto di Prendiparte Azzi, was also an illuminator, probably active from at least the fourth through the sixth decades of the century, though no work has yet been attributed to him.[26] I am inclined to think that Alberto's style may have resembled that of the illuminator known as the Master of the Crucifixion D who participated in the decoration of liturgical manuscripts for the Servites in Bologna in the 1330s.[27]

FIG. 8.1. Biblioteca Ambrosiana, B 42 inf., f. 159r. Used by permission of the Biblioteca Ambrosiana.

The style of the Snite illuminations, which appear to be the work of a single artist, constitutes a mid-point between the work attributed to the Master of the Crucifixion D, who was active from the mid-1320s until ca. 1340, and that of Stefano Azzi. Not only does the Snite illuminator show a familiarity with the iconographic motifs of the Master of the Crucifixion D, he also tends toward the blunt, almost rubbery, facial features and direct, stocky figures reminiscent of the earlier miniaturist's work, and similarly favors his saturated, opaque pigments and dark contour lines. Yet, at the same time, it is clear that the Snite artist is aware of the stylistic advances of the most sophisticated Bolognese illuminators active in the late 1330s and the 1340s and epitomized in the work of the Illustratore and the 1346 Master. Consequently, the Snite miniatures aspire to, but do not achieve, the greater suavity and refinement that is realized only later in Stefano's mature work, due partly, no doubt, to Stefano's frequent collaboration with his more gifted contemporary, Niccolò da Bologna. The Snite illuminator, whom I believe to be a slightly older colleague to Stefano, does not indulge in the complicated multiple drapery folds that are more characteristic of Stefano; his figures tend to be stockier and less refined than Stefano's; his draftsmanship is less precise; and his style, as a whole, is simpler and more direct than Stefano's. In short, the Snite illuminations, and others in diverse manuscripts that are strikingly similar in style, would seem to be the work of a miniaturist of an age somewhere between the father, Alberto, and the son, Stefano—perhaps a senior shop assistant who had a hand in the training of Stefano but whose own artistic maturity was achieved sometime in the 1340s.[28] For now, a date of ca. 1350 for the Snite illuminations and the anonymous appellation of the Snite Illuminator are the most prudent proposals. Setting aside these stylistic questions, the present study will focus instead on issues clustering around patronage and iconography that the Snite illuminations pose.

The badly abraded miniature (fig. 8.2) that opens the manuscript compels one to consider both aspects. At first glance, from the basic configuration of the image and from the emphasis on the love between Mother and Son that is so prominent in the text, one assumes that the central group must be a Madonna and Child Enthroned. Closer examination reveals, though, that the seated figure is most probably Christ, and that it is a closed book, not a baby, which he props up in his lap with his left hand

FIG. 8.2. Opening miniature: *Christ Enthroned with Kneeling Patrons* (University of Notre Dame, Snite Museum of Art, Acc. No. 85.25, f. 1r). Used by permission of the Snite Museum of Art.

while making a blessing gesture with his right. While a venerable type, the image of Christ the Redeemer enthroned is not a common independent devotional subject in Trecento art. The theme's inherent majesty is suitable for a more public image: one of the best Trecento examples appears in the central panel of the singular Stefaneschi Altarpiece that was made for Old St. Peter's.[29] In what would originally have been the subsequent miniature representing God the Father enthroned in Heaven,[30] which opens the celestial prelude to the Annunciation, the illuminator employed an elderly patriarchal physiognomy for the Father, but retained the essentials of Christ's pose, including the blessing gesture and the attribute of the book, now opened. These cognate figures of Son and Father and their joint attribute of a book, while common enough motifs connotative of divine authority and wisdom, would have had special meaning for the clerical and lay scholars engaged in the study of law—and thus fixated on justice and book—at the University of Bologna. In fact, the format of the Snite introductory miniature recalls the nucleus of the typical opening illustration of most Bolognese legal manuscripts, which depicts a central enthroned authority, such as Christ, Justinian, or the Pope, flanked by kneeling figures who receive attributes of office or alternatively present the products of their labor, for example, law books.[31]

Unfortunately, the two figures flanking Christ in the Snite miniature, whose poses suggest patron/donor identities, resist any specific identification. Unlike the opening illustration of the Paris *Meditationes*,[32] whose figures are conveniently labeled as the Franciscan author and St. Cecilia, invoked in its opening line as exemplar for his intended reader, the two figures in the Snite illumination are neither saints nor religious. Their lack of haloes and kneeling poses are typical of supplicant patrons and the cut and color of their dress suggest lay rather than religious status. The serious abrasion of the figure at the viewer's right inhibits speculation: the blue garment and mantle drawn up over the head are appropriate to a woman, resembling the costume worn, for example, by a laywoman in devotion with a lay male counterpart before the Madonna and Child in a small Tuscan panel of the second quarter of the fourteenth century now in Ottawa.[33] The dress of the figure kneeling at the left is more telling: his snug red tunic (calf-length if standing), low slung belt, and almost invisible spurs all indicate knightly identity.[34] Were the figure standing and his hood raised, his resemblance to the *cavalieri* on the Bolognese tomb of Taddeo Pepoli or to the knightly saints represented in a lavish illumination of Penance from a *Decretum Gratiani* manuscript, both works of the mid-fourteenth century, would be obvious.[35] The fact that the male figure in the Snite miniature kneels in the favored position at Christ's right hand implies that he was the primary patron, but, recognizing that Christ's gesture of benediction is oriented equally to the woman at His left prompts one to keep in mind the real probability that this devotional book was also read by women in the family. Highly literate lay women were no anomaly in medieval Bologna: there are records of the participation of women in the manuscript trade there[36] and hints that women—for example, the wife and daughters of the great canonist Giovanni d'Andrea—might even be learned in the law.[37]

Though the original owner of the Snite manuscript eludes precise identification, the miniatures of Christ's Incarnation and Infancy do introduce motifs consistent with the interests of a learned male reader hypothesized as the primary client. The *Presentation of the Virgin to the Temple* (fig. 8.3), opening the chapter on the life of the Virgin Mary before the Incarnation, picks up the "bookish" theme introduced in the preceding images. In contrast to the several illustrations for this chapter in the Paris manuscript which show the Virgin Mary mounting the Temple stairs, praying, spinning with her companions, and receiving and donating food (but not reading),[38] the Snite miniature prefers the studious. At the left, the three-year-old Virgin presented by Anna submissively meets the open arms of the High Priest, while in the cell to the right, her subsequent years in the Temple precincts are summarized in the scene of her literary devotions.[39] That this was a conscious choice, intended to allude to her future role prophesied in the Old Testament, is underscored by the marginal instructions to the artist which specify: "show here how the Virgin Mary is offered to the temple . . . and how she is in her cell and studies in her book and [here the line has been partly trimmed], <reads of> the Virgin who will conceive and bear the son of God,"[40] referring to Isaiah 7:14. Of equal interest is the fact that the Snite Illuminator eschewed the usual format for the Presentation scene, which generally requires as its attribute the fifteen steps of the Temple staircase that the precocious child ascends of her own volition.[41] Instead, the Snite artist employed a compositional scheme that recalls an earlier, unusual Riminese work.[42] More striking still is the close relationship of the Snite miniature to an illumination from a mid-fourteenth-century *Decretum Gratiani* miniature which illustrates the vesting of the young novice as she advances to full vows.[43] Such an apt transferral of imagery from a religious milieu to the legal realm and back again testifies to the sophistication of fourteenth-century Bolognese pictorial production and consumption, efficiently meeting the practical needs of illuminators and no doubt satisfying to their literate clientele, ideologically predisposed to appreciate visual manifestations of the congruence of the two spheres.

While the theme of the literary devotions of the Virgin, customary in Annunciation scenes and present too in the Snite miniature of the subject, was certainly not an exclusively male preoccupation,[44] the remaining miniatures of the Infancy cycle do hint at concessions to male concerns. Al-

FIG. 8.3. *Presentation of the 3-year-old Virgin to the Temple* (University of Notre Dame, Snite Museum of Art, Acc. No. 85.25, f. 5v). Used by permission of the Snite Museum of Art.

though the Snite manuscript does not include a representation of the Marriage of the Virgin, an episode which receives but one sentence in the text, in the Visitation miniature (fig. 8.4) the figure of Joseph is introduced in a central role. While the encounter of Mary and Elizabeth receives the dominant stress, framed by the simple architecture of Elizabeth's house, the figure of Joseph, represented in a mature and dignified way, is given almost equal visual weight, silhouetted near the center against the pink and gold

FIG. 8.4. *Visitation* (University of Notre Dame, Snite Museum of Art, Acc. No. 85.25, f. 10v). Used by permission of the Snite Museum of Art.

patterned background.[45] In place of the female attendants frequent in a Visitation, Joseph is followed by a group of elderly men whose gestures and head-shawls indicate them to be disbelieving Jews characterized according to the pejorative medieval stereotype.[46] These incredulous Jewish priests are probably intended as opposites to Zacharias, entering from the far right, his own faith tested by Elizabeth's miraculous pregnancy.

Unlike the Visitation illustration in the Paris *Meditationes*, itself unusual in the embrace of the male in-laws alongside the female cousins,[47] Joseph is shown in the Snite manuscript in distinctively contemporary dress,[48] not conventional "holy persons" garb. Indeed, to the fourteenth-century Italian reader, Joseph's appearance would probably connote professional—someone like a notary, for example[49]—or perhaps mercantile status. The style of his costume, with its long gown, elbow-length capelet, and head-

FIG. 8.5. *Joseph Wishes to Leave Mary* (University of Notre Dame, Snite Museum of Art, Acc. No. 85.25, f. 12r). Used by permission of the Snite Museum of Art.

piece comprising a rolled-up fur-trimmed hood, is typical of the representation of erudite, prosperous, or prominent urban men.[50] At the same time, its sober grey color concedes the virtue of humility that is integral to Joseph's persona.[51]

Having introduced the theme of the dignity of Joseph as a keynote in the early Snite miniatures, there arises, of course, the "picture that proves the rule." In the illumination (fig. 8.5) for the chapter narrating Joseph's anxieties about the cause of Mary's pregnancy, Joseph's humility is given a different inflection. He is shown twice: once in a short garment with the tools of his carpenter's trade as he turns to abandon Mary, and, again, absorbed in meditative sleep where he is visited by the reassuring angel.[52] Both the crouched pose and the cropped dress are markers of humility; short dress is consistently reserved in the manuscript for figures of low social status or villainous occupation, and, although it is consistent with this Franciscan text's emphasis on the poverty of the Holy Family, it is telling that for *this* patron, these motifs seemed appropriate to Joseph in his unfortunate time of doubt. Ambivalence best characterizes the late medieval attitude towards Joseph's manual trade. There was a spiritual interpretation of his carpentry as the work of the artisan perfecting the soul,[53] but, in this miniature, the figure of the expectant Virgin patiently waiting at home embodies the superior vocation. Again, she is shown reading, not spinning or praying as in the parallel scenes in the Paris manuscript.[54] The particular configuration of the pregnant Virgin Mary reading—her swollen belly above the book is accentuated with fine white hatching—was especially developed in Dominican circles, female and male, in the fourteenth century. The middle register of a mid-century altarpiece by Tomaso da Modena, probably made for a Dominican women's convent in Bologna, which represents the Virgin Mary in three aspects, first shows her pregnant and reading, then nursing her Child, and finally knitting the seamless garment.[55] In such theologically attuned circles, the literate *Madonna del Parto* made a fitting emblem of the Logos enfleshed, merging the incarnational and sapiential emphases of their Christology. The theme received special elaboration, for example, in the church of the Dominican friars at Treviso, as exemplified in one of its column frescoes (ca. 1350), which shows Thomas Aquinas presenting his theology for inspection to the conspicuously gravid Virgin Mary.[56]

Once Joseph's doubts are banished, though, he appears in the Nativity scenes enjoying virtually equal billing with the Virgin Mary. At the opening of the chapter on "how Jesus Christ was born in this world," he joins Mary to adore the Child (f. 13v) and, shortly after, watches as she gives the infant his first bath (fig. 8.6), an innovative image that avoids the indecorum that would attend a literal representation of the text immediately below, which describes the Virgin bathing her child with her copious breast milk. Still, the miniature may have been driven by reasons more compelling than mere discretion or even an artistic impulse to experiment with the traditional

FIG. 8.6. *Bathing of the Child* (University of Notre Dame, Snite Museum of Art, Acc. No. 85.25, f. 15r). Used by permission of the Snite Museum of Art.

iconography of the bathing of the Christ Child, which assigned the task to the midwives who attend the Virgin in the apocryphal gospels.[57] Kitzinger, in observing the persistence of the subject of the First Bath in Byzantine iconography, speculated that the imperative must have been theological rather than anecdotal, that is, "to demonstrate the humanity of Christ and the reality of the Incarnation."[58] As the extraordinary Nativity fresco from the Oratory of Mezzaratta shows, in mid-fourteenth-century Bologna the dynamic participation of Joseph in the task was proclaimed, captured there by Vitale da Bologna in the acrobatic gesture with which Joseph pours a jug of water into the tub as the Virgin reaches to test its temperature.[59] More conservative by nature, the Snite artist reserves the actual bathing of the Child for Mary. Yet, by representing Joseph equally in the foreground, on his knees before the duo, he still casts the foster father as the foremost

FIG. 8.7. *Circumcision of Christ* (University of Notre Dame, Snite Museum of Art, Acc. No. 85.25, f. 18r). Used by permission of the Snite Museum of Art.

human witness to God's assumption of human nature, manifested here in Christ's submission to the care required of the normal human infant even though, as Son of God, his perfect purity obviated any need for ablution.

Joseph's participation in the drama of the Incarnation persists through the Infancy illuminations. In the *Circumcision of Christ* (fig. 8.7), he asserts his role as *paterfamilias,* presenting his Son for the priest's ritual act in disregard of the text's assertion that the Child's flesh was cut by his Mother.[60] In fact, Joseph is not even mentioned in the chapter on the Circumcision in the Snite manuscript, which, like the Paris *Meditations,* lingers over the duet of weeping and consolation shared between Mother and Son. How-

FIG. 8.8. *Adoration of the Magi* (University of Notre Dame, Snite Museum of Art, Acc. No. 85.25, f. 20r). Used by permission of the Snite Museum of Art.

ever, his presence is implicit in its opening lines, which note the other signal event of January 1—the naming of Jesus—for this was Joseph's prerogative, reported in scripture (Matthew 1:21, 25), affirmed by theologians and, moreover, consistent with fourteenth-century social custom.[61] And he continues as an engaged, solicitous presence, for example, seated beside Mary, acknowledging the homage of the Magi (fig. 8.8) in an image that finds its three-dimensional equivalent in the painted wood Epiphany group, ca. 1370, in the Bolognese pilgrimage church of S. Stefano.[62]

In all these cases, Joseph is alert and attentive, never the introverted figure that he is, for example, in Giotto's *Nativity* or in the Epiphany fresco from the Arena Chapel. Comparison to the graver, more momentous work of Giotto admittedly highlights the unselfconscious charm of the Snite illuminations, but I think it worth considering that the naïveté that we delight in may in fact be deceptive. The immediacy of the Adoration of the Magi sculpture from S. Stefano, famous for the recreation of the holy sites of Jerusalem within its walls, raises the real possibility that images like the Snite *Epiphany* were apprehended with more reverence and credulity than the twenty-first-century viewer would be inclined to posit. Again, like the Snite St. Joseph, the father in the Epiphany sculpture, there exchanging glances with his Son, is represented as an integral and essential member of the Holy Family, the very model of solicitous, responsible and dignified paternity. I suspect that the scriptural appellation of Joseph as a "just man" (Matthew 1:19), a title which most exercised medieval theologians, was specially resonant in Bologna with her preponderance of jurists; in fact, one of the earliest churches dedicated to St. Joseph was built there.[63] Without compromising the centrality of the Virgin and Child as the crux of the Incarnation, the promotion of St. Joseph to near visual equality in the Snite Infancy miniatures represents a further nuance to the basic stylistic impulse of the text whose wealth of mundane detail, in John Fleming's words, "domesticated the mysterious."[64] The illuminator's attention to Joseph in the Snite *Meditationes* insinuates a sort of masculinization of the domestic, accommodating the piety of the worldly layman, presumably no less eager than his wife to identify with this story in which the humble and intimate are celebrated.[65]

Like the Infancy illuminations, those that illustrate the Passion chapters blend tradition and innovation, and, despite the bluntness of the figure types and condensed character of the scenes, reveal a sensitivity to the emotional engagement exhorted in the text. The Holy Week account opens with a conventional representation of the Entry into Jerusalem—with the inclusion of a book propped in Christ's lap—and then proceeds to an unusual image (fig. 8.9) that illustrates a chapter narrating Christ's meal on Wednesday at the house of Mary Magdalen, an episode interpolated between the Entry and the Last Supper that the author himself acknowledges is without any scriptural warrant. Yet the illuminator provides a scene that clearly trades on visual tradition. He adapts the iconography proper to the anointing of Christ's feet in the house of the Pharisee, an episode lacking

FIG. 8.9. *Meal at the House of the Magdalen* (University of Notre Dame, Snite Museum of Art, Acc. No. 85.25, f. 57v). Used by permission of the Snite Museum of Art.

from the shorter text of the *Meditationes*, by including only Christ's faithful followers, substituting the Virgin Mary for the protesting figure of Simon the Pharisee or Judas.[66] And, while he retains the prostrate Magdalen, performing her emblematic act of penitence and love at Christ's feet, he appends the figure of Martha as cook, standing at the hearth, in juxtaposition to the seated figure of Christ, book in his lap, addressing his attentive disciples.[67] This pastiche, linked in only a tenuous way to the author's description of the desperate pleas of the Virgin Mary and Mary Magdalen that Christ not go to Jerusalem for the Pasch, may suggest that the illuminator had recourse to the pictorial repertoire of a long version of the *MVC*, whose treatise on the active and contemplative lives occasioned an extended Mary and Martha sequence.[68] However, the fact that here Martha turns her back to the hearth and looks attentively toward Christ may indicate an intention to cast her role as hostess in a positive light, showing Martha focused on her guest rather than preoccupied with domestic responsibilities.[69] An appreciation of Martha's hospitality as exemplary for the Christian informs the text devoted to her in Jacobus de Voragine's *Golden Legend*, where the repeated use of the terms "hostess" and "guest" characterize her welcoming disposition toward Christ.[70] For the married female reader of this manuscript, such a St. Martha would provide a heartening model of spiritual service compatible with a laywoman's life.[71]

As the chapters advance to those devoted to the core Passion episodes, the illustrations correspondingly increase in number and in intensity. The illuminator interrupts the account of the Flagellation of Christ in the chapter of the meditations at Prime with a vivid illustration (fig. 8.10), subsequently defaced by a reader in an apparent attempt to wipe the spatters of blood from Christ's body. The text just above and below the miniature is graphic: "the flower of all flesh and of all human nature was covered with welts and bruises and the royal blood flows from all parts of the body. / He is beaten and re-beaten, and the torturers renew their efforts, adding bruises upon bruises and one gash above another."[72] The figure of the distraught Virgin Mary outside the closed door of the chamber effectively heightens the reader's sense of the Mother's torment at the brutalizing of her Son, her agony redoubled by the fact that she can only *hear* but not *see* the torture. The text, which merely describes the Virgin following Christ as he was led to Pilate's residence, does not specify this particular motif. However, it does have a rare precedent in an earlier fourteenth-century Flagellation panel attributed to the Master of Forlì.[73]

Strangely, though, the illumination of *Christ Carrying the Cross on the Way to Calvary* (fig. 8.11) lacks the motif of Christ turning back to exchange glances with his desperate Mother, a favorite theme in Trecento painting usually associated with the *Meditationes* account. By cropping the scene, so to speak, after the persecuting figures of the Jewish priests, the Snite Illuminator only partly heeds the marginal instructions for the picture that specify "a multitude of Jews following and deriding Christ, and

FIG. 8.10. *Flagellation of Christ* (University of Notre Dame, Snite Museum of Art, Acc. No. 85.25, f. 76r). Used by permission of the Snite Museum of Art.

the Mother and St. John, weeping."[74] In this he seems content to revert to earlier Riminese tradition for the abbreviated *via Crucis*, as in a diptych with Passion scenes attributed to the Master of the Choir of S. Agostino, now in Munich.[75] As Anne Derbes has noted in connection with her discussion of the Munich panel, a Bolognese account of 1223 testifies to a local awareness of the anti-Jewish Tale of the Wandering Jew which may account

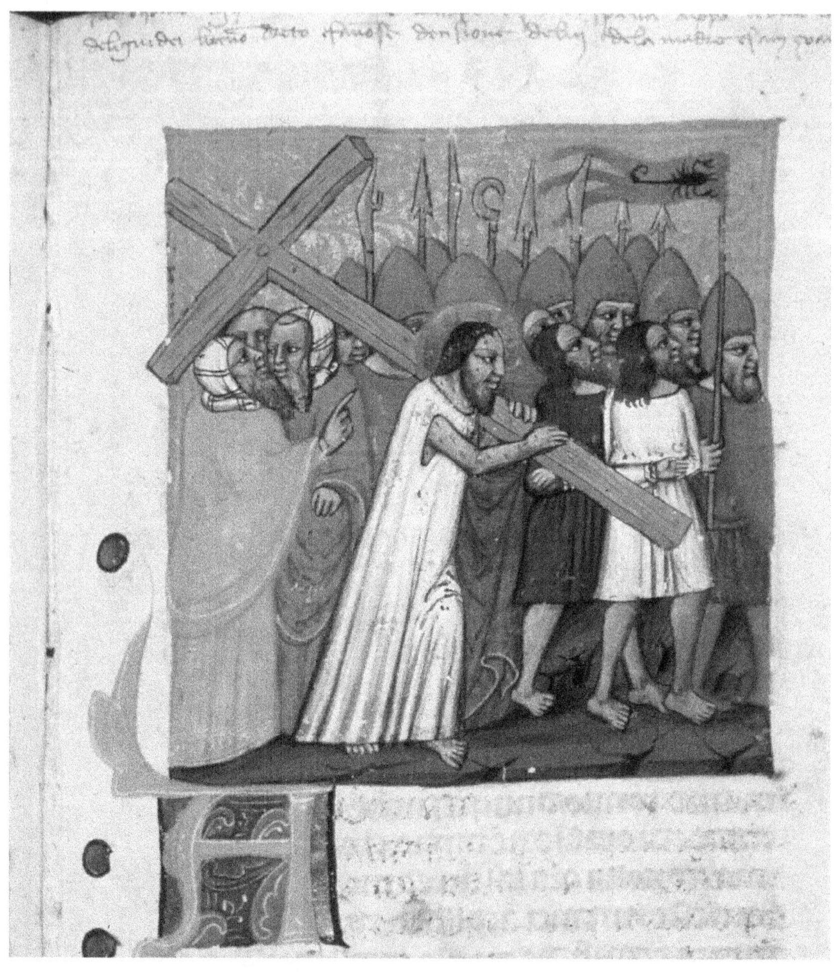

FIG. 8.11. *Way to Calvary* (University of Notre Dame, Snite Museum of Art, Acc. No. 85.25, f. 78r). Used by permission of the Snite Museum of Art.

for the interest in this figural group.[76] It is noteworthy that, through the course of the Passion scenes, the Snite Illuminator takes care to implicate a range of social types as tormentors of Christ, regularly including civic dignitaries, soldiers, and knights among his persecutors.

The artist's inventiveness and his apparent liberty, even in the face of the marginal instructions for several of the Passion images, whose length and specificity suggest that the illustrational tradition for this text was still fluid, are apparent in the sequence of the Passion meditation at midday. On the lower half of the recto of folio 80 (fig. 8.12), at the point where the narrative has Christ finally at his destination at Calvary, the reader is offered a group picture of the Virgin and Holy Women lamenting and St. John, at the right, pivoting away and raising his head and joined hands in supplication. Upon turning the folio, the reader confronts the object of John's anxiety: Christ being nailed to the cross (fig. 8.13). This intermediary figure of the watchful St. John, his pose meaningful only with the reader's action,

Fig. 8.12. *The Virgin, Holy Women, and St. John Lamenting* (University of Notre Dame, Snite Museum of Art, Acc. No. 85.25, f. 80r). Used by permission of the Snite Museum of Art.

FIG. 8.13. *Nailing of Christ to the Cross* (University of Notre Dame, Snite Museum of Art, Acc. No. 85.25, f. 80v). Used by permission of the Snite Museum of Art.

cleverly fuses the pictorial matter of the manuscript with the somatic and intellectual experience of reading a book, where anticipation is prelude to recognition and comprehension.[77]

The iconography of the *Nailing of Christ to the Cross* merits further attention. The text for this chapter first describes at length the affixing of Christ to an upright cross, which he mounts by ascending a ladder. That iconography was universally favored in fourteenth-century Italian art,[78] its popularity probably due to the Franciscan emphasis on Christ's willing acceptance of his sacrifice as a model for evangelical perfection—a notion that was conveyed effectively by Christ's energetic ascent of the ladder.[79] The composer of the marginal instructions just above the Snite miniature in fact seems to have been thinking of the vertical mode for he explicitly mentions "the hammer and . . . others nail the feet, the other on a ladder." However, that same message to the artist closes with the injunction to "make [the picture] in the most piteous way you know and [according] as God gives [you] the grace."[80] In his choice of the prone Cross and Christ, the illuminator apparently exercised his own judgment, presumably after reading further into the text which only briefly mentions the recumbent Crucifixion as an alternative way to envision the event. He may have had recourse to a model-book recording some of the more than three hundred historiated initials, constituting a comprehensive Christological cycle, which appear in a Latin florilegium with lives of the Virgin and Christ, now in the Bodleian Library.[81] Its illumination has been attributed to a group of artists, some Bolognese or trained in Bologna, associated with the decoration of liturgical books for S. Marco, Venice, in the second quarter of the fourteenth century.[82] Recalling earlier Byzantine Psalter illumination, the Bodleian manuscript includes at least three images of the affixing of Christ to the Cross in which the cross hovers ambiguously at an oblique angle. Alternatively, the Snite Illuminator may have been familiar with a recumbent Nailing from a Northern source; one of the early Western examples of such a format appears in an early fourteenth-century English Psalter,[83] and Northern Gothic images were certainly available to Bolognese artists, chiefly in the books of visiting scholars,[84] but even in such media as the *opus anglicanum* of the famous cope from San Domenico.[85] While rare in fourteenth-century Italian art, the Nailing type encountered in the Snite *Meditationes* had wide dissemination in late medieval Books of Hours from Northern workshops, elaborated, for example, in the Hours of Charles the Noble, ca. 1400, whose illumination was shared between a Netherlandish artist, the Egerton Master, and the Master of the Brussels Initials, trained in Bologna before working in Paris.[86]

The Crucifixion accomplished, for the meditation at Compline the Snite Illuminator provides a scene of the Lamentation (Fig. 8.14), a markedly restrained variant of Giotto's famous composition,[87] with the odd detail of the totally enshrouded Christ whose veiled face is practically

FIG. 8.14. *Lamentation* (University of Notre Dame, Snite Museum of Art, Acc. No. 85.25, f. 87r). Used by permission of the Snite Museum of Art.

unprecedented.[88] The diaphanous shroud is a feature of other fourteenth-century Lamentation scenes, such as the Cloisters panel by the Master of the Codex of St. George:[89] I suspect that the translucent swathes of drapery were appreciated not only as an artistic *tour de force* but also for the special sort of attention they draw to the body of Christ—proof of the Incarnation[90]—and, in the case of the Snite illumination, as a means to refer back to the linen bands that had wrapped, in a similar fashion, the vulnerable Infant.

One other aspect of the Snite *Lamentation* deserves notice. While the text describes at length the ministrations of the Magdalen at the feet of her dead Lord, exemplifying the love of the penitent, in the miniature she is nudged forward to the center foreground, her usual place instead occupied by two male figures, one holding Christ's feet and making a gesture of display, the other drawing his hand to his chest in a gesture of lament. The unusual "winged" cap—actually a scholar's bonnet with upturned ear-flaps—of the figure at the far right of the miniature and the placement of him and his companion wearing a beret, at the edge of the scene, could indicate that they are intended as, or at least derived from, figures of Joseph of Arimathea and Nicodemus.[91] As protagonists in the Deposition and burial of Christ, they often appear in Entombment scenes, usually nimbed but frequently with conspicuous headgear and contemporary dress.[92] In Bolognese illumination, similarly dressed figures populate the court rooms, classrooms, churches, and marketplaces so often depicted in the legal manuscripts.[93] The reputations that had accrued around Nicodemus and Joseph of Arimathea, drawn from from scriptural and apocryphal sources—that they were educated and socially prominent men—would justify the illuminator's appropriation of contemporaneous types who met such requirements and, in so doing, underscore their potential as exemplars of devotion for the urban male.[94] The contemporary dress and reverent demeanor of these two male figures at Christ's feet in the Snite *Lamentation* urge the reader to emulation, reminding him of the exalted service to the body of Christ performed even by privileged men like Nicodemus and Joseph of Arimathea.[95]

In accord with the text, the extensive sequence of post-Passion miniatures shifts to a lower key. While the canonical subjects of the *Three Maries at the Tomb* (f. 95v) and the *Noli me tangere* (f. 97v) make an appearance, the illuminator must also illustrate unconventional episodes such as the *Apparition of Christ to James Minor* (fig. 8.15) and then to the repentant Peter (f. 101r). For these he tends to turn to venerable models, replicating the format of *Noli me tangere* for the Christ and Peter group and adapting the composition of an earlier Anointing at Bethany panel,[96] attributed to the Bolognese painter of the second quarter of the fourteenth century known as Pseudo-Jacopino di Francesco, for the meal scene where Christ appears to the grieving James, who had sworn not to eat until he saw his resurrected Lord. The illuminator's adherence to the latter model is striking: it

FIG. 8.15. *Apparition of Christ to James Minor* (University of Notre Dame, Snite Museum of Art, Acc. No. 85.25, f. 100v). Used by permission of the Snite Museum of Art.

extends from his retention of the memorable servant at the right end of the table to the repetition of the older male type (the Pharisee in the Anointing scene) with the addition of a halo for the figure of James the Less, who traditionally was represented as a youthful male akin to Christ in appearance.

The final scenes of the post-Passion chapters, lacking the human touches and poignant drama of the Infancy and Passion pictures (perhaps because of the theological imperative to attest to the truth of Christ's glorified, resurrected body), exploit a basic compositional format consisting of a central figure of Christ flanked by symmetrical groups of apostles or saints.[97] This static formula is used for the final seven miniatures, and, in the case of the *Appearance of Christ to the Disciples in Galilee* (f. 107v), and then *His Appearance to more than Five Hundred Faithful* (f. 108v), with the most minimal variation. The final illumination of the manuscript illustrates Pentecost (f. 117r), an episode similarly resistant to dramatic movement, apart from the descending rays of the Holy Spirit, and thus traditionally cast in a static way.[98] It concludes the pictorial program with a composition identical to the final Apparitions, with the significant substitution of the Virgin Mary, type of the Church, standing in the central position formerly occupied by Christ.

Though the final miniatures seem anticlimactic, examples of the Snite Illuminator at his most routine, a return to the midst of the Passion narrative and the miniature of *Christ before Pilate* (fig. 8.16) provides a focus for my concluding observations. When compared to the restraint of Tuscan painting or to the elegance of French Gothic, the accessibility and immediacy of Bolognese Trecento illumination are striking. Confronted by the liveliness, variety, and predilection for quotidian detail that pervade Bolognese work, especially the multifarious miniatures for the deluxe legal manuscripts, art historians inevitably characterize them in terms of the vernacular, the popular, and the anecdotal—a vocabulary that tends to obscure the elite character and intellectual sophistication of the urban university clientele.[99] At the same time, it tends to trivialize the religious, in both its intellectual and emotional dimensions, as incidental to this community's identity, splitting off in an arguably anachronistic way the "spiritual" from the "mundane."[100] To the contrary, what we moderns take as separate seems, in this environment, to have been thoroughly interwoven. While one cannot be certain of the moment of the occasional defacing evident in the Snite manuscript, nor of the reasons behind it, that the figure of Pilate—the epitome of the corrupt judge dressed in the scarlet robes of the Doctor of Civil Laws—incited a reader's rage, implies the tangle of religious, secular, spiritual, and professional motivations inspiring such a response.[101] Further, that these diverse strands could be mutually constitutive—especially in fourteenth-century Bologna—is apparent, for example, in the *persona* of Giovanni d'Andrea, the preeminent lay canonist whose devotion to St. Jerome found expression not only in books, legal and otherwise, but also in an extensive fresco cycle painted on the exterior of his house.[102] In this milieu, the illumination of legal and religious manuscripts were complementary endeavors, involving not only the meaningful and expedient transferral of compositions from one to the other,[103] but, even more, sharing

FIG. 8.16. *Christ before Pilate* (University of Notre Dame, Snite Museum of Art, Acc. No. 85.25, f. 74v). Used by permission of the Snite Museum of Art.

basic pictorial strategies that appropriated iconographical tradition to instill authority while introducing innovative genre-like detail to elicit the reader's assent to their veracity and continued relevance to his life. In the nuances of its miniatures, the Snite *Meditationes* testifies to the ways in which the illustrations of a devotional text could be adjusted to appeal to the married lay reader enmeshed in a worldly urban setting. Devout and literate, pious and probably powerful, the patron of the Snite manuscript would have found its images a source of consolation and reproach, speaking to the complexities and contradictions of his life.

NOTES

1. Since C. Fischer listed 217 manuscripts in his study, "Die 'Meditationes Vitae Christi': ihre handschriftliche Ueberlieferung und die Verfasserfrage," *Archivum Franciscanum Historicum* 25 (1932): 3–35, 175–209, 305–48, 449–83, scholars such as A. Vaccari, "Le 'Meditazioni della vita di Cristo' in volgare," in his *Scritti di erudizione e di filologia*, vol. 1, *Filologia biblica e patristica* (Rome, 1952), 341–78, have identified others.

2. An extreme example of this approach informs E. S. Varanelli, "Le *Meditationes Vitae Nostri Domini Jesu Christi* nell'arte del Duecento italiano," *Arte medievale*, 2nd ser., 6:2 (1992): 137–48, where she argues for an early date of origin for the text, ca. 1260, largely on the grounds of the direct impact that she perceives it having had upon the leading artists of the late thirteenth century. S. McNamer, "Further Evidence for the Pseudo-Bonaventuran *Meditationes Vitae Christi*," *Franciscan Studies* 50 (1990): 235–61, addresses the issue of the relationship between text and picture from the opposite direction, holding that the author of the *Meditationes Vitae Christi* was inspired by the new style and iconographies of early Trecento art.

3. McNamer, "Further Evidence," provides an historiographical summary.

4. M. Stallings-Taney, ed., *Iohannis de Caulibus: Meditaciones vite Christi olim S. Bonaventuro attributae*, CCCM 153 (Turnhout, 1997).

5. M. Stallings-Taney, "The Pseudo-Bonaventure *Meditaciones vite Christi: Opus Integrum*," *Franciscan Studies* 55 (1998): 253–80, at 258, repeats her acceptance of McNamer's arguments concerning dating but proceeds to indicate 1346 (not 1336) as the *terminus post quem*, an error also present in her introduction to the critical edition (see *Meditaciones vite Christi*, xi).

6. McNamer, "Further Evidence," 236–51.

7. Ibid., 251–58.

8. Stallings-Taney, "*Opus Integrum*," 263–64. In the introduction to their translation, *John of Caulibus: Meditations on the Life of Christ* (Asheville, N.C., 2000), F. X. Taney, Sr., A. Miller, and C. M. Stallings-Taney assert that "though the original language of the *MVC* is Latin, the author thinks in Italian" (xv).

9. S. McNamer, review of *Johannis de Caulibus: Meditaciones Vite Christi*, ed. M. Stallings-Taney, *Journal of Theological Studies*, n.s., 50:1 (1999): 378–85.

10. University of Notre Dame, Snite Museum of Art, Acc. No. 85.25, gift of Ann McNear, in memory of her husband, Everett McNear; my gratitude to Dr. Dean Porter, Director *emeritus* of the Snite Museum, for his encouragement of this research. While in the collection of Everett and Ann McNear of Chicago, the manuscript was twice exhibited at Notre Dame; see *Everett McNear: Painter, Designer, Collector* (exh. cat., Notre Dame, Ind., 1975), no. 97; *Medieval Art, 1060–1550: Dorothy*

*Miner Memorial* (exh. cat., Notre Dame, Ind., 1974), no. 14. One of its folios is reproduced in *Selected Works from the Snite Museum of Art* (Notre Dame, Ind., 1987), 61. These publications refer to the manuscript as *The Life of Christ* or *The Life of Christ and the Life of the Virgin*, and attribute it to the shop of Niccolò da Bologna.

11. Notre Dame, Snite Museum, Acc. No. 85.25, parchment, 121 folios (unnumbered) with two modern paper end leaves at beginning and end and modern binding; 180 x 125 mm (written space 127 x 80 mm); 25 or 26 long lines of text. Collation:$1-2^{6}$, $3-5^{8}$, $6^{7}$, $7-11^{8}$, $12^{6}$, $13-16^{8}$. Catchwords. My thanks to Maureen Boulton for her guidance in the codicological aspects of the manuscript.

12. In the anecdote, Albert beseeches Christ during Mass to tell him what to do to be a good Christian. Christ responds by articulating eight aphorisms in which he juxtaposes the quiet, genuine Christian behavior that is pleasing to God against the extravagant but insincere act of piety. G. Nitz, *Albertus Magnus in der Volkskunst: Die Alberti-Tafeln* (Munich, 1980), reviews the history of this legend and its representation in later Northern art.

13. In the Infancy chapters, for example, there are subtle omissions of some of the repetitious assertions about the virtues of poverty (and the vices of worldliness) that might have made the text more palatable to a prosperous reader. Conversely, in the chapter devoted to Christ's Entry into Jerusalem, at the point where he goes to the temple, a passage is interpolated into the Snite manuscript that describes his devotions in the temple as a model for the reader who should similarly go directly to his oratory to give thanks when he returns home from a journey. This would suggest a reader of means accustomed to travel and with a dwelling that included a private room for prayer; cf. L. B. Alberti, *De re aedificatoria: On the Art of Building in Ten Books*, trans. J. Rykwert, N. Leach, and R. Tavenor (Cambridge, Mass., 1988), bk. 5, 17, who suggests that the first room off the entrance in a villa should be a chapel where "the head of the family on his return home may pray to the gods above for peace and calm for his family."

14. I. Ragusa and R. B. Green, eds., *Meditations on the Life of Christ: An Illustrated Manuscript of the Fourteenth Century, Paris, Bibliothèque Nationale, MS ital. 115*, trans. I. Ragusa (Princeton, N.J., 1961). See also B. Degenhart and A. Schmitt, *Corpus der italienischen Zeichnungen: 1300–1450*, pt. 1, vol. 1 (Berlin, 1968), no. 55; F. Avril et al., *Dix siècles d'enluminure italienne: VIe–XVIe siècles* (exh. cat., Paris, Bibliothèque Nationale, 1984), no. 50.

15. H. Flora, "A Book for Poverty's Daughters: Gender and Devotion in Paris, Bibliothèque Nationale, MS Ital. 115," in *Varieties of Devotion in the Middle Ages*, ed. S. C. Karat-Nunn (Turnhout, 2003), 61–97.

16. See N. R. Ker, *Medieval Manuscripts in British Libraries*, vol. 3 (Oxford, 1983), 612, no. 410; and J. J. G. Alexander and E. Temple, *Illuminated Manuscripts*

*in Oxford College Libraries, the University Archives, and the Taylor Institution* (Oxford, 1985), no. 908. O. Pächt, "Künstlerische Originalität und ikonographische Erneuerung," in *Stil und Überlieferung in der Kunst des Abendlandes,* 3 vols., Akten des 21. Internationalen Kongresses für Kunstgeschichte in Bonn 1964 (Berlin, 1967), 3:262–71, suggested that Corpus 410 might reflect an early illuminated *MVC* manuscript of ca. 1300 whose iconographic innovations were accessible to Giotto. According to McNamer, "Further Evidence," 261n.79, the miniatures of the manuscript have been studied by Pamela Busby in an Oxford, BPhil dissertation, a work not yet consulted by the present writer.

17. Stallings-Taney, *Meditaciones vite Christi,* xi, considers Corpus 410 the most reliable of the four fourteenth-century manuscripts which contain an older, less-altered Latin *MVC* text.

18. A Latin manuscript identified as the *MVC,* illustrated with 27 miniatures, has recently been published in a catalog produced by the manuscript dealer Heribert Tenschert: E. König (ed.), *Leuchtendes Mittelalter, Neue Folge II: dreiunddreissig mittelalterliche Handschriften aus Byzanz, Italien, Frankreich, Deutschland, Flandern und den Niederlanden vom 11. bis zum frühen 16. Jahrhundert* (Rotthalmünster: H. Tenschert, 1998), cat. no. 8. The list of its textual contents suggests that it contains only excerpts from the *MVC,* interspersed with assorted moralizing and religious texts. Although the catalog entry designates it as work produced in Padua after 1305 and illuminated by an artist in the circle of Giotto, the concluding remarks on style point to an artist from the alpine regions of Italy. The Tenschert manuscript illuminations are iconographically dependent on the Arena Chapel frescoes but, stylistically, they do not resemble the early fourteenth-century illuminations attributed to Paduan and Bolognese artists long recognized as drawing upon Giotto's famous cycle. See, e.g., A. Stolte, "Maestro di Gherarduccio kopiert Giotto: Zur Rezeption der Arena Fresken in der oberitalienischen Buchmalerei zu Beginn des 14. Jahrhunderts," *Mitteilungen des Kunsthistorischen Institutes in Florenz* 40 (1996): 2–41.

19. The 48 miniatures are: *Christ Enthroned* (f. 1r); *Presentation of the Three-year old Virgin in the Temple* (f. 5v); *Annunciation* (f. 8r); *Visitation* (f. 10v); *Joseph Wishes to Leave Mary* (f. 12r); *Nativity* (f. 13v); *Bathing of the Child* (f. 15r); *Annunciation to the Shepherds* (f. 16v); *Circumcision* (f. 18r); *Adoration of the Magi* (f. 20r); *Presentation of the Christ Child in the Temple* (f. 23v); *Flight into Egypt* (f. 26r); *Return from Egypt* (f. 33r); *God the Father in Heaven* (f. 37r); *Baptism of Christ* (f. 45v); *Temptation of Christ* (f. 49r); *Entry into Jerusalem* (f. 54v); *Meal at the House of the Magdalen* (f. 57v); *Christ Washing the Feet of the Disciples* (f. 59r); *Last Supper* (f. 59v); *Christ's Sermon to the Disciples* (f. 65r); *Agony in the Garden* (f. 67v); *First Mocking of Christ* (f. 72v); *Christ before Pilate* (f. 74v); *Flagellation of Christ* (f. 76r); *Second Mocking of Christ* (f. 77v); *Way to Calvary* (f. 78r); *The Virgin Mary, Holy Women, and*

*St. John Lamenting* (f. 80r); *Nailing of Christ to the Cross* (f. 80v); *Crucifixion* (f. 85r); *Lamentation* (f. 87r); *The Virgin, Holy Women, and St. John Lamenting as St. Peter Returns* (f. 91v); *Descent into Limbo* (f. 93r); *Christ Appears to the Virgin Mary* (f. 94r); *Three Maries at the Sepulcher* (f. 95v); *Noli me tangere* (f. 97v); *Christ Appears to the Three Maries* (f. 99v); *Christ Appears to Joseph of Arimathea* (f. 100r); *Christ Appears to James Minor* (f. 100v); *Christ Appears to Peter* (f. 101r); *Way to Emmaus* (f. 102v); *Christ Appears to the Disciples on the Day of the Resurrection* (f. 104r); *Doubting Thomas* (f. 106r); *Christ Appears to the Disciples in Galilee* (f. 107v); *Christ Appears to More than Five Hundred Faithful* (f. 108v); *Ascension* (f. 110r); *The Ascendant Christ Praised by the Saints* (f. 112v); *Pentecost* (f. 117r). As the leaves of the manuscript have not been numbered, the foliation used throughout this study is based upon my own calculation. The miniatures of the Snite manuscript are the subject of my doctoral dissertation at Yale University: "The Illustration of the *Meditations on the Life of Christ*: A Study of an Illuminated Fourteenth-Century Italian Manuscript at the University of Notre Dame" (in progress). I am most grateful to my advisor, Professor Creighton Gilbert, for his help.

20. C. Nordenfalk, review of *The Corpus of the Miniatures in the Manuscripts of the Decretum Gratiani*, by A. Melnikas, *Zeitschrift für Kunstgeschichte* 43 (1980): 319.

21. G. Schmidt, "'Andreas me pinsit': Frühe Miniaturen von Nicolò di Giacomo und Andrea de' Bartoli in dem Bologneser Offiziolo der Stiftsbibliothek Kremsmünster," *Wiener Jahrbuch für Kunstgeschichte* 26 (1973): 57–73; H. Fill, *Katalog der Handschriften des Benediktinerstiftes Kremsmünster*, pt. 2, *Zimeliencodices und Spätmittelalterliche Handschriften nach 1325 bis einschliesslich CC 100*, Phil-Hist. Kl. Denkschriften, Bd. 270 (Vienna, 2000), CC Cim. 4, 25–29.

22. L. E. Boyle, "'The Ways of Prayer of St. Dominic': Notes on MS Rossi 3 in the Vatican Library," *Archivum Fratrum Praedicatorum* 64 (1994): 5–17.

23. Milan, Biblioteca Ambrosiana, MS B 42 inf., f. 1r; repro. in O. Capitani, ed., *L'università a Bologna: Personaggi, momenti e luoghi dalle origini al XVI secolo* (Milan, 1987), 124.

24. Folios 159r and 205r, repro. in D. Formaggio and C. Basso, eds., *A Book of Miniatures*, trans. P. Craig (New York, 1962), pls. 17 and 18 respectively (the latter plate is misidentified as f. 204r).

25. The pertinence of these two illuminations to the Snite manuscript and their attribution to Stefano Azzi were kindly suggested to me by Professor Robert Gibbs. On Stefano Azzi, see the discussion, list of attributed works, and bibliography in R. Gibbs, "Recent Developments in the Study of Bolognese and Trecento Illustration," *Burlington Magazine* 126 (1984): 639–40 and n. 28. See also F. Avril, "Azzi, Alberto di Stefano [*sic*]" in *Enciclopedia dell'arte medievale*, vol. 2 (Rome, 1991), 816–18; both in the title and throughout the article, the illuminator is incorrectly

referred to as Alberto di Stefano Azzi when it is clear that Avril is writing about Stefano di Alberto Azzi.

26. In addition to F. Filippini and G. Zucchini, *Miniatori e pittori a Bologna: Documenti dei secoli XIII e XIV* (Florence, 1947), 4 (Alberto), 221–22 (Stefano), further archival evidence is published in A. I. Pini, "Miniatori, pittori e scrittori nelle 'venticinquine' bolognesi del Due e Trecento (Integrazioni ed aggiunte ai regesti documentari di Filippini-Zucchini)," *Il Carrobbio* 7 (1981): 358, 360 (Alberto), 365 (Stefano).

27. M. Medica discusses the style and work of the Master of the Crucifixion D in *Francesco da Rimini e gli esordi del gotico bolognese* (exh. cat., Bologna, Museo Civico Medievale, 1990), 101–5 and nos. 11, 18.

28. Among the illuminated manuscripts in which the Snite Illuminator is present are Munich, Bayerische Staatsbibliothek, MS Clm. 3503, and Venice, Biblioteca Marciana, MS Z. L.449a (formerly CCCLIX.1634). The former is a manuscript of Justinian's *Digestum vetus*; see F. Ebel, A. Fijal, and G. Kocher, *Romisches Rechtsleben im Mittelalter* (Heidelberg,1988), 17, 29, 47, 59, for reproductions of folios attributable to the Snite artist. The Marciana codex is an illuminated manuscript of Ovid's *Metamorphoses*; its illuminations are reproduced without attribution in Ovid, *Metamorfosi*, ed. P. B. Marzolla (Turin, 1979). Gibbs, "Recent Developments," 640n.28, attributes the Marciana *Metamorphoses* illuminations to Stefano Azzi and places them late in his career. E. Mattia, "Due Ovidio illustrati di scuola bolognese," *Miniatura* 3/4 (1990/91): 63–72, also discusses these illuminations but is unaware of Gibbs's attribution and does not suggest her own. While Mattia, like Gibbs, considers them to be works of the later fourteenth century, she notes their balance of archaic and innovative elements and concludes that their creator will most probably be found among those who at mid-century tried to emulate the Illustratore's achievements—a characterization that also suits the Snite Illuminator.

29. On the iconography of the Enthroned Christ of the Stefaneschi altarpiece, see J. Gardner, "The Stefaneschi Altarpiece: A Reconsideration," *Journal of the Warburg and Courtauld Institutes* 37 (1974): 57–103, at 72–79; and B. Kempers and S. de Blaauw, "Jacopo Stefaneschi: Patron and Liturgist," *Mededelingen van het Nederlands Instituut te Rome* 47 (1987): 83–113, at 87–88. Kempers and De Blaauw, 96–102, argue that the Stefaneschi polyptych was commissioned for the second main altar of the basilica, i.e., the one in the canons' choir located in the nave just before the triumphal arch.

30. The folio bearing the miniature of God the Father Enthroned was originally half of the center bifolium of the first quire; at some point it was detached, its cognate was lost, and it was subsequently tipped into the manuscript as the first leaf of the sixth quire, i.e., f. 37.

31. On the opening illustration of Bolognese manuscripts of the *Decretum Gratiani* representing Christ as the source of the law that is distributed to his ecclesiastical and temporal representatives, see A. Melnikas, *The Corpus of the Miniatures in the Manuscripts of Decretum Gratiani* (Rome, 1975), 3:41–53. Given the Order's involvement in the teaching of law and the adjudication of doctrinal controversies, it comes as no surprise that the deliberate adaptation of legal and conciliar iconographies for picture schemes in religious settings around mid-century seems to have been a Dominican specialty. See, e.g., the analyses of J. Gardner, "Andrea di Bonaiuto and the Chapterhouse Frescoes in Santa Maria Novella," *Art History* 2 (1979): 119–25; J. T. Paoletti, "The Strozzi Altarpiece Reconsidered," *Memorie Domenicane*, n.s., 20 (1989): 285–300; and R. Gibbs, *Tomaso da Modena: Painting in Emilia and the March of Treviso, 1340–80* (Cambridge, 1989), 74–76.

32. Ragusa and Green, *Meditations*, ill. 1.

33. M. Boskovits, *The Fourteenth Century: The Painters of the Miniaturist Tendency*, sec. 3, vol. 9, of R. Offner with K. Steinweg, *A Critical and Historical Corpus of Florentine Painting* (Florence, 1984), 234 and pl. 92.

34. Cf. the scene of the Knighting of St. Martin in the Lower Church at Assisi where Martin is vested with the sword belt and spurs; my thanks to Andrea von Hülsen for noting the spurs in the Snite illumination.

35. The tomb is reproduced in R. Grandi, *I Monumenti dei dottori e la scultura a Bologna: 1267–1348* (Bologna, 1982), pl. 134; the miniature, from Biblioteca apostolica vaticana, MS Urb. lat. 161, f. 297, in Melnikas, *Decretum Gratiani*, 3:1082. It bears noting that chivalric dress need not preclude professional activity: among the accoutrements that William Durandus allows to the well-dressed advocate in his late-thirteenth-century work, the *Speculum iudiciale*, are breast-plates, spurs, and buckles. See W. Durantis, *Speculum iudiciale (illustratum et repurgatum a Giovanni Andrea et Baldo degli Ubaldi)* (Aalen, 1975, reprint of Basel, 1574 printed edition), 1: 265 (Lib. I, Partic. IV, 2, 5). I am grateful to Professor Julius Kirshner for bringing Durandus's treatise to my attention.

36. C. Frugoni, "The Imagined Woman" (trans. C. Bottsford), in *A History of Women in the West*, vol. 2, *Silences of the Middle Ages*, ed. C. Klapisch-Zuber (Cambridge, Mass., 1992), 400.

37. The principal testimony for the legal erudition of Giovanni d'Andrea's daughter, Novella, comes from Christine de Pisan, *The Book of the City of Ladies*, trans. E. J. Richards (New York, 1982), 154 (II.36.3). Christine, whose father was educated at the University of Bologna, describes Novella, who shared the same name as one of her father's legal treatises, lecturing from behind a curtain when her father was unable to teach. G. Rossi, "Contributi alla biografia del canonista Giovanni d'Andrea (L'insegnamento di Novella e Bettina, sue figlie, ed i presunti

*responsa* di Milancia, sua moglie)," *Rivista trimestrale di diritto e procedura civile* 11 (1957): 1451–1502, gives the issue serious consideration; S. Kuttner, "Johannes Andreae and his *Novella* on the Decretals of Gregory IX," *The Jurist* 24 (1964): 396, remains skeptical.

38. Ragusa and Green, *Meditations*, ills. 5–9.

39. The representation of successive narrative episodes through the conjunction of distinctive architectural settings as backdrops for separate but related events is ubiquitous in the illuminations of Bolognese legal manuscripts.

40. "Fac qui chomo la vergene maria e offerta al tempio. . .e fac qui chome la vergene maria e in la cella sua e studia in sunno libro [instructions trimmed] vergene sera qui concepa e apartiese lo fijolo de dio," f. 5v.

41. In one of the most striking fourteenth-century examples, Taddeo Gaddi's fresco in the Baroncelli Chapel at Santa Croce, the stairway becomes a visual protagonist in the drama. In the Book of Hours of Maria of Navarra, Venice, Biblioteca Marciana, MS Lat. I. 104, a manuscript illuminated ca. 1340 by a Catalan artist with close Italian ties, the Presentation, again with a prominent staircase, prefaces the fifteen Gradual psalms. See A. Saulnier-Pinsard, "Une nouvelle oeuvre du Maître de San Marcos: Le Livre d'Heures de Marie de Navarre," in *La miniatura italiana tra Gotico e Rinascimento, Atti del II Congresso di Storia della Miniatura Italiana, Cortona, 1982*, ed. E. Sesti (Florence, 1985), vol. 1, pl. 1 (while the plate caption identifies this as f. 259v, the list of illustrations, 40n.6, specifies f. 287v).

42. See the scene in the upper left of a diptych panel attributed to Giovanni da Rimini, in the collection of the Duke of Northumberland, Alnwick Castle, repro. in D. Benati, *Il Trecento Riminese* (Milan, 1995), no. 14; Benati identifies the subject of the scene as the tomb of St. Augustine.

43. Biblioteca apostolica vaticana, MS Vat. lat. 1366, f. 198r, repro. in *Bibliotheca Apostolica Vaticana* (Florence, 1985), pl. 65.

44. For the appeal of images of the literate Virgin Mary to medieval women, see S. G. Bell, "Medieval Women Book Owners: Arbiters of Lay Piety and Ambassadors of Culture," in *Women and Power in the Middle Ages*, ed. M. Erler and M. Kowaleski (Athens, Ga., 1988), 149–87; and P. Sheingorn, " 'The Wise Mother': The Image of St. Anne Teaching the Virgin Mary," *Gesta* 32 (1993): 69–80. The frequent representation of the Virgin reading among the historiated initials in a Missal illuminated by Niccolò da Bologna for the antipope Clement VII suggests its appeal to male clerics; see the list provided by M. Paoli, "Il messale avignonese dell' antipapa Clemente VII con miniature di Niccolò di Giacomo," in *Il codice miniato: Rapporti tra codice, testo e figurazione, Atti del III Congresso di Storia della Miniatura, Cortona 1988*, ed. M. Ceccanti and M. C. Castelli (Florence, 1992), 169n.5.

45. M. Meiss, *French Painting in the Time of Jean de Berry: The Late Fourteenth Century and the Patronage of the Duke* (London, 1967), 213, observes the infrequency of Joseph in representations of the Visitation, noting as exceptions panels by Deodato di Orlando (Berlin, Gemäldegalerie) and Pacino di Bonaguida (Tucson, University of Arizona) and connecting the introduction of Joseph to the impact of the *Meditationes* account. Significantly, Joseph (and Zacharias) appear in the Visitation illustrations of both the Paris *Meditationes* (f. 13v) and the Oxford manuscript (f. 10r).

46. A similarly dressed figure presents the accused woman to Christ in the illumination of Christ and the Woman taken in Adultery in Ambrosiana, MS B 42 inf., f. 205r, repro. in Formaggio and Basso, *Miniatures*, pl. 18.

47. This juxtaposition may have been inspired by an Old Testament type for the Visitation: the embrace of Moses and Aaron, listed by M. R. James, "Pictor in Carmine," *Archaeologia* 94 (1951): 151.

48. This is characteristic of other Trecento Bolognese images, e.g., Infancy scenes in polyptychs attributed to the Pseudo-Jacopino, Nativity panels attributed to Simone dei Crocefissi, and various Infancy illuminations by Niccolò da Bologna.

49. See R. Abbondanza, *Il Notariato a Perugia*, Fonti e Strumenti per la Storia del Notariato Italiano, vol.1 (Rome, 1973), pls. 2, 8.

50. For example, the representation of Dante in a Sienese *Divina Commedia*, ca. 1360, repro. in *Biblioteca Medicea Laurenziana* (Florence, 1986), pl. 84; the men who give alms to Christ in the Paris *Meditations*, repro. in Ragusa and Green, *Meditations*, ill. 94; and the procession of magistrates in Ambrogio Lorenzetti's *Allegory of Good Government*, repro. in E. Borsook, *The Mural Painters of Tuscany*, 2nd ed. (Oxford, 1980), pl. 47.

51. Cf. Gibbs, *Tomaso da Modena*, 126, where he observes that the grey and white woolen habit worn by the "merchant princes" of the Cavalieri Gaudenti (in whose ranks he places the patron of the Ursula cycle at Treviso) was a self-conscious expression of their renunciation of personal ostentation.

52. For the iconography of Joseph's Doubts, see Z. Urbach, "'Dominus possedit me. . .' (Prov. 8, 22): Beitrag zur Ikonographie des Josephszweifels," *Acta Historiae Artium: Academiae Scientiarum Hungaricae* 20 (1974): 199–266.

53. C. Hahn, "'Joseph Will Perfect, Mary Enlighten and Jesus Save Thee': The Holy Family as Marriage Model in the Mérode Triptych," *Art Bulletin* 68 (1986): 54–66. The Franciscans, of course, emphasized Joseph's manual trade as evidence of Christ's poverty; the Dominicans were less interested in the literal meaning of his occupation. In the Snite text, Joseph's trade is mentioned both in the Nativity and the Flight into Egypt chapters, but the emphasis is on how he supported his family, not the lowliness of his occupation.

54. Ragusa and Green, *Meditations*, ills. 22–23.

55. Gibbs, *Tomaso da Modena*, 42–43 and pl. 6a. In his discussion of the panel, Gibbs acknowledges its theological sophistication, yet at the same time, by seeing its source of inspiration in Franciscan writings like the *Meditationes*, explicitly distances it from the discourse of scholastic theologians.

56. Reproduced in M. Lucco, ed., *La pittura nel Veneto: Il Trecento* (Milan, 1992), vol. 1, ill. 246. On the motif in fourteenth-century Bologna, see E. Cassee, "La Madonna del Parto," *Paragone* 29, no. 345 (1978): 94–97.

57. For example, the historiated initial of the Nativity in the Missal of Cardinal Bertrand de Deux, repro. in E. Cassee, *The Missal of Cardinal Bertrand de Deux: A Study in Fourteenth-Century Bolognese Miniature Painting*, trans. M. Hoyle (Florence, 1980), fig. 46, which largely conforms to the traditional iconography where the midwives bathe the child in the foreground.

58. E. Kitzinger, "The Hellenistic Heritage in Byzantine Art," *Dumbarton Oaks Papers* 17 (1963): 104; and see further R. Deshman, "Servants of the Mother of God in Byzantine and Medieval Art," *Word and Image* 5 (1989): 33–70.

59. Reproduced in C. Gnudi, *Vitale da Bologna and Bolognese Painting in the Fourteenth Century*, trans. O. Ragusa (New York, 1964), pls. 27–28. The testing of the water temperature would likewise be more than a genre motif; as Kitzinger, "Hellenistic Heritage," 104, notes with regard to this gesture by the midwives in some Byzantine representations, it underscores the potential vulnerability of the Child's flesh.

60. On f. 19r, ll. 10–13, the Snite text specifies: "Odi ancora ke oggi [i.e., January 1] sparse el suo sangue preciosissimo. E fue la carne sua preciosissima taliata dalla madre sua" ["On the same day as today he shed his most precious blood. And his most precious flesh was cut by his mother"]. In their illustrations for the Circumcision, both the Paris and Oxford manuscripts attend to the text. The former (f. 24v; Ragusa and Green, *Meditations*, ill. 34) illustrates Mary circumcising Jesus; the latter (f. 16v) depicts the circumcision, immediately below the Virgin and Child in the cave of the Nativity, being performed by an un-nimbed female figure who is assisted by two women with Joseph in contemplation at the edge.

61. In his treatment of the Feast of the Circumcision, Jacobus de Voragine, *The Golden Legend*, trans. W. G. Ryan, 2 vols. (Princeton, N.J., 1993), vol. 1, no. 13, observes that "the name of Jesus was imposed upon him by God the eternal, by the angel, and by his putative father, Joseph." C. Klapisch-Zuber, "The Name 'Remade': The Transmission of Given Names in Florence in the Fourteenth and Fifteenth Centuries," in her *Women, Family and Ritual in Renaissance Italy*, trans. L. G. Cochrane (Chicago, 1985), 288–89, describes the Florentine father's primary responsibility for specifying his child's name. It should be noted that the Circumcision fresco from the Mezzaratta cycle, which the Snite miniature closely resembles

in composition, albeit in reverse, shows a male figure dressed in contemporary chivalric costume in the right foreground kneeling in prayer as he gazes upon the central group: Joseph holding Jesus for the operation by the kneeling Mohel. The latter configuration visually distills the theological interpretation of the Circumcision, i.e., the paradox of Christ's triumph in his submission to the Old Law. The Mezzaratta *Circumcision* is reproduced in D. Benati, "Simone di Filippo (o *dei Crocifissi*)" *Enciclopedia dell'arte medievale*, vol. 10 (Rome, 1999), 682.

62. On the S. Stefano sculpture, see M. Ferretti, *Rappresentazione dei Magi: Il gruppo ligneo di S. Stefano e Simone dei Crocefissi* (Bologna, 1981).

63. P. M. Branchesi, "Una chiesa bolognese dedicata a San Giuseppe dal secolo XII," *Cahiers de Joséphologie* 19 (1971): 576–90. When the Church of San Giuseppe in Via Galliera came into possession of the Servite order in the early fourteenth century, the order took steps to promote the cult of St. Joseph and formally proclaimed its devotion to him in 1324, antedating the Franciscans' approbation in 1399. See also A. Battiston, "Le patronage de Saint Joseph en Italie," in *Le patronage de Saint Joseph (Actes du Congrès d'études tenu à l'Oratoire Saint-Joseph, Montréal, 1955)* (Montréal, 1956), 33–60. While C. C. Wilson, *St. Joseph in Italian Renaissance Society and Art* (Philadelphia, 2001), 11, acknowledges the early veneration for St. Joseph in Bologna, she focuses on the cult during the late fifteenth and sixteenth centuries and the Observant Franciscan role in its promotion.

64. J. V. Fleming, *An Introduction to the Franciscan Literature of the Middle Ages* (Chicago, 1977), 248.

65. Devotion to St. Joseph is generally considered a phenomenon that emerged in Northern Europe ca. 1400, and is usually related to the promotional efforts of the Parisian theologian, Jean Gerson, as well as those of the Franciscans. However, the esteem accorded St. Joseph in the Snite illuminations has a precedent in the work of scholastic theologians, above all the gospel commentaries of Albertus Magnus. E. P. Dunne, "Albert the Great's Theology of St. Joseph," *Cahiers de Joséphologie* 7 (1959): 223–62; 8 (1960): 113–130, analyses Albert's teaching, which discerned in Joseph a model of perfection: a chaste husband in a true sacramental marriage and a willing and responsible father to the *bonum prolis*, i.e., Jesus, born into that marriage. Given the concluding passage on St. Albert in the Snite manuscript, it is possible that the patron was familiar with such views. To observe the positive presentation of Joseph in the Snite manuscript, of course, does not deny that he must have been a perplexing figure to the patriarchal culture of late medieval Italy, where paternity and legitimacy were crucial concepts; e.g., David Herlihy, "The Family and Religious Ideologies in Medieval Europe," *Journal of Family History* 12 (1987): 3–17, at 14, notes the rarity of the name "Giuseppe" among Florentines prior to 1500.

66. For the visual tradition of the Anointing at Bethany, which rests on the conflation of various scriptural episodes and identities, see the summary in R. W. Sullivan, "The Anointing in Bethany and Other Affirmations of Christ's Divinity on Duccio's Back Predella," *Art Bulletin* 67 (1985): 36–42.

67. The representation of Mary Magdalen was well developed in Bologna, as elsewhere, by the fourteenth century; ca. 1350, Vitale da Bologna was engaged in a series of frescoes of scenes from her legend for S. Maria dei Servi, of which only fragments remain. While the representation of Martha is less common, it is possible that there was a local interest in her, a remnant of the preaching activity of the charismatic Dominican, Venturino da Bergamo, who, during his sojourn in Bologna ca. 1331–34, promoted her cult. See M. Fanti, *La Confraternità di S. Maria della Morte e la Conforteria dei condannati in Bologna nei secoli XIV e XV,* Quaderni del Centro di Ricerca e di Studio sul Movimento dei Disciplinati, 20 (Perugia, 1978), 19–20.

68. Though the execution of the pictorial program was interrupted before this point, the instructions for the Paris *Meditationes* indicate six illustrations, Ragusa and Green, *Meditations,* 245.

69. In contrast, Giovanni Milano, in his fresco of Christ's Meal at the House of Martha in S. Croce, represents her gesturing almost indignantly toward the hearth as Mary Magdalen sits rapt at Christ's feet.

70. Jacobus de Voragine, *Golden Legend,* vol. 2, no. 105.

71. Cf. L. Jacobus, "Piety and Impropriety in the Arena Chapel," *Renaissance Studies* 12 (1998): 177–205, in which she analyses Giotto's frescoes for the behavioral models that they prescribe for the female patrician viewer and her household.

72. "El fiore d ogna carne e di tuta l umana natura si si rinpiete e foe cuperta di bateture e de lividuri ese tuto quel sangue inperiale di tute le parte del corpo. . . . E batuto e ribatuto e ricomincansi e renovansi li flagellaturi e açunguno luvaduri sopra luvaduri e l una scrafiatura sopra l altra," f. 76r, ll. 3–11.

73. J. Pope-Hennessy, *The Robert Lehman Collection,* vol. 1, *Italian Paintings* (New York, 1987), no. 37.

74. "Como la multitudi[ne] deli giudei li ten*no* dreto e fan*no* se derisione de lui e dela madre e sam goane li teni dret[o] piangen[do]," f. 78r.

75. Reproduced in C. Volpe, *La Pittura Riminese del Trecento* (Milan, 1965), figs. 155, 157.

76. A. Derbes, *Picturing the Passion in Late Medieval Italy* (New York, 1996), 134–36.

77. Bolognese illuminators had long delighted in dynamic marginal figures who interact between text and miniature. In the complex historiated initials with scenes from the life of Christ from the Kremsmünster Hours, Niccolò da Bologna

exploited the conceit of the figure which, by means of its twisting pose or intense gaze, effectively links the successive narrative moments that are separated by the contours of the letter, albeit within the single page. The Snite figure of the vigilant St. John, bridging two independent scenes, has a close analogue in the newly-sighted figure at the right edge of the *Healing of the Blind Man* from Duccio's *Maestà* who, as observed by J. White, *Duccio: Tuscan Art and the Medieval Workshop* (New York, 1979), 122, turns to gaze at the transfigured Christ of the succeeding panel.

78. On the iconography of the Nailing of Christ to the Cross in Italian art, see M. Boskovits, "Un dipinto poco noto e l' iconografia della preparazione alla Crocifissione," in his *Immagini da meditare: Ricerche su dipinti di tema religioso nei secoli XII–XV* (Milan, 1994), 189–231.

79. Derbes, *Picturing the Passion*, 154–57, discusses the way in which Christ's ascent of the cross was linked typologically with Elisha's ascent at Bethel and Jacob's ascent of the heavenly ladder, and both, in turn, were associated with St. Francis.

80. "Como foe crucefisso e [line trimmed] lo martello ei altri li inchiodano li pei laltre in sula schala fac al piue pietoxo modo che say e come dio tene datay la gratia," f. 80v.

81. Oxford, Bodleian Library, MS canon. misc. 476. The manuscript is included within the catalogue compiled in R. A. Katzenstein, "Three Liturgical Manuscripts from San Marco: Art and Patronage in Mid-Trecento Venice" (PhD diss., Harvard University, 1987), 134–37, no. 31. I am most grateful to Adelaide Bennett Hagens for bringing both this manuscript and Katzenstein's study to my attention.

82. Katzenstein, "Three Liturgical Manuscripts," passim.

83. G. Warner, *Queen Mary's Psalter* (London, 1912), pl. 257.

84. For example, J. Oliver, "An Early Parisian Book of Hours Remodeled in Italy," *Journal of the Museum of Fine Arts, Boston* 2 (1990): 5–17, studies a Book of Hours initially produced in Paris ca. 1300 for a female owner but later transported to Italy and renovated by a Bolognese illuminator perhaps ca. 1330. The references to the canonical hours in the rubrics of the Passion meditations in the Snite manuscript might well have prompted its illuminator to turn to a Book of Hours for an appropriate model. Unfortunately, there is no representation of the Nailing of Christ to the Cross in either the Boston manuscript or in the Kremsmünster Hours illuminated by Niccolò.

85. The impact of the cope on Bolognese style is noted in F. Bignozzi Montefusco, *Il Piviale di San Domenico* (Bologna, 1970), 14, 43.

86. See W. D. Wixom, "The Hours of Charles the Noble," *Bulletin of the Cleveland Museum of Art* 52 (1965): 50–91; and C. Sterling, *La peinture médiévale à Paris, 1300–1500*, vol. 1 (Paris, 1987), no. 40.

87. Giotto's fresco had long been emulated by Bolognese illuminators, e.g., in the Choirbooks at Padua, Biblioteca Capitolare, MS A. 15, f. 159, and, in Bologna, S. Maria dei Servi, MS D, f. 60.

88. The way in which the shroud is wound and the extent of the coverage is most nearly approximated in an historiated initial of the Death of Moses which illustrates the opening of the Book of Joshua in the late-thirteenth-century Bassetti Bible, Trento, Biblioteca Comunale, MS 2868, p. 207. The attribution of the Bible has been much debated, with Bolognese illuminators among the contenders; see M. Bernasconi and L. Dal Poz, eds., *Codici miniati della Biblioteca Comunale di Trento* (Florence, 1985), 74–77 and fig. 33. While it is unlikely that the Snite Illuminator had access to this particular image, it is possible that this type of shrouded corpse persisted among the models available to Bolognese illuminators who worked on illustrated Bibles or typological manuscripts.

89. Reproduced in *Painting and Illumination in Early Renaissance Florence: 1300–1450* (exh. cat., New York, 1995), 103.

90. L. Steinberg, *The Sexuality of Christ in Renaissance Art and in Modern Oblivion* (New York, 1983), especially Excursus XX.

91. The loss of the center bifolium of this quire of the manuscript prevents one from turning to a Deposition from the Cross miniature to confirm the identities of Joseph of Arimathea and Nicodemus.

92. For a later fourteenth-century example of the representation of Nicodemus and Joseph of Arimathea as well-dressed but un-nimbed figures, see the Lamentation scene in a Cristoforo da Bologna panel in J. Bentini, ed., *La Pinacoteca Nazionale di Ferrara* (Bologna, 1990), no. 3. On the iconography of the two, see W. Stechow, "Joseph of Arimathea or Nicodemus?," *Studien zur Toskanischen Kunst: Festschrift für Ludwig Heinrich Heydenreich* (Munich, 1964), 289–302, and C. Schleif, "Nicodemus and Sculptors: Self-Reflexivity in Works by Adam Kraft and Tilman Riemenschneider," *Art Bulletin* 75 (1993): 599–626.

93. For example, Cassee, *Missal*, figs. 8, 26, 111.

94. While Schleif, "Nicodemus," focuses on the attraction to Renaissance sculptors of Nicodemus's identity as carver of the *Volto santo*, she also notes, e.g., 604–7, the traditions testifying to the eminence of Nicodemus and Joseph of Arimathea, the former as Pharisee and scriptural scholar, the latter as rich man and council member. By the fifteenth century, patrons assimilate the identity of these figures; cf. F. B. Polleross, *Das sakrale Identifikationsporträt* (Worms, 1988), 227–32.

95. Further, the prominence of the tomb in the Snite illumination and its proximity to these two male figures recall Matthew 27:60, which specifies that Joseph laid Christ's body in his own new tomb. As Dunne, "Albert the Great's Theology of St. Joseph," 122–23, notes, Albert the Great explicitly paralleled the roles

enacted by Joseph of Nazareth and Joseph of Arimathea, the one caring for Jesus at birth, the other at death; the one guarding the secret of the virginal birth with his silence, the other sealing the dead Christ in a pristine tomb.

96. Raleigh, North Carolina Museum of Art, repro. in F. R. Shapley, *Paintings from the Samuel H. Kress Collection: Italian Schools, XIII–XV Century* (London, 1966), fig. 189.

97. A similar inclination to the symmetrical for the post-Passion appearances of Christ is evident in the illuminations on a leaf from a choirbook (Cambridge, Fitzwilliam Museum, MS 194), attributed to Pacino di Bonaguida, repro. in *Painting and Illumination in Early Renaissance Florence*, 69.

98. A notable deviation from the conventional symmetrical composition for Pentecost was created by Niccolò da Bologna for an illuminated manuscript of the works of the canonist Giovanni da Legnano, made in 1376–78 for presentation to the Pope and repro. in Cassee, *Missal*, fig. 78.

99. R. Longhi expounded this view, particularly with regard to the Illustratore, and it has prevailed among scholars ever since. See his *Lavori in Valpadana del Trecento al primo Cinquecento, 1934–1964*, Edizione delle opere complete di Roberto Longhi 6 (Florence, 1973), 24–25 and 159–160. Only recently have motives other than a mere delight in genre-like detail been considered for the profusion of naturalistic settings in Bolognese legal manuscript illuminations; e.g., R. Gibbs, "Landscape as Property: Bolognese Law Manuscripts and the Development of Landscape Painting," *Rivista di Storia della Miniatura* 1–2 (1996–97): 207–16, speculates that such scenes may have been developed in response to the business and property interests of the Bolognese legal elite.

100. This inclination has been reinforced by the dominant art historical focus on stylistic distinctions and attributional problems. While the work of Melnikas outlined the iconographic complexities presented, e.g., by the *Decretum Gratiani* manuscripts, his lead has only recently been taken up, most notably by Susan L'Engle, "The Illumination of Legal Manuscripts in Bologna, 1250–1350: Production and Iconography" (PhD diss., New York University, 2000).

101. From the list of chapter headings at the close of the *Meditations* text in the Snite manuscript and from irregularities evident in the collation, one can deduce that two of the three illuminations now missing from the manuscript because of lost folios very likely had juridical nuances. The Dispute between Mercy and Truth before God the Father would seem to beg for an illustration of a courtroom scene like those that proliferate in the legal manuscripts. And the subject of Christ Among the Doctors in the Temple, disputatious by nature, was in fact appropriated for canon-law manuscripts as a scripturally sanctioned representation of Christ's teaching as the source of ecclesiastical authority; on this see Melnikas,

*Decretum Gratiani*, 1:139–140; 3:1063. The outrage that Pilate's unjust judgment might have provoked in a reader trained in the law should be considered in the light of the discussion of sermons directed to men in authority and in the legal profession in D. L. D'Avray, "Sermons to the Upper Bourgeoisie by a Thirteenth Century Franciscan," in *The Church in Town and Countryside*, ed. D. Baker, Studies in Church History 16 (Oxford, 1979), 187–99.

102. On the intermingling of intellectual, religious, and even domestic concerns in Giovanni d'Andrea's scholarship, see Kuttner, "Johannes Andreae," 395–96, 401–3; on his devotion to St. Jerome, see E. F. Rice, *Saint Jerome in the Renaissance* (Baltimore, 1985), 64–67. The medieval etymology of Jerome's name, "holy law," must have made him attractive to a canon lawyer, and, further, one wonders whether Jerome's particular devotion to the Infant Jesus and the crib at Bethlehem inspired emulation among Bolognese laymen.

103. For example, the composition of the Snite *Christ before Pilate* miniature was adapted by the same illuminator for a civil law manuscript (Munich, Bayerische Staatsbibliothek, Clm. 3503, f. 219v; repro. in F. Ebel, Fijal, and Kocher, *Römisches Rechtsleben*, 47) to illustrate laws restricting a woman's right to assume debt on behalf of others, with the woman standing in the place for Christ; the inspiration for this appropriation might have been the related themes of incapacity before the law.

# index of manuscripts

Manuscripts in private hands are not included in this Index.

Footnote references to manuscripts are cited only when the manuscript in question is not mentioned in the body of the text; references in the body of the text are treated as including the accompanying footnotes.

# general index

The names of modern scholars and editors are not included in this Index. Footnote references are included only when they are independent of any corresponding reference in the main body of the text.

www.ingramcontent.com/pod-product-compliance
Lightning Source LLC
Chambersburg PA
CBHW060238100726
47907CB00003B/690

* 9 7 8 0 2 6 8 0 3 4 9 6 2 *